# *LYRICAL INDIVIDUALISM*

COLUMBIA THEMES IN PHILOSOPHY,
SOCIAL CRITICISM, AND THE ARTS

## COLUMBIA THEMES IN PHILOSOPHY, SOCIAL CRITICISM, AND THE ARTS

*Lydia Goehr and Gregg M. Horowitz, Editors*

Advisory Board
Carolyn Abbate
J. M. Bernstein
Eve Blau
T. J. Clark
John Hyman
Michael Kelly
Paul Kottman
In memoriam: Arthur C. Danto

Columbia Themes in Philosophy, Social Criticism, and the Arts presents monographs, essay collections, and short books on philosophy and aesthetic theory. It aims to publish books that show the ability of the arts to stimulate critical reflection on modern and contemporary social, political, and cultural life. Art is not now, if it ever was, a realm of human activity independent of the complex realities of social organization and change, political authority and antagonism, cultural domination and resistance. The possibilities of critical thought embedded in the arts are most fruitfully expressed when addressed to readers across the various fields of social and humanistic inquiry. The idea of philosophy in the series title ought to be understood, therefore, to embrace forms of discussion that begin where mere academic expertise exhausts itself; where the rules of social, political, and cultural practice are both affirmed and challenged; and where new thinking takes place. The series does not privilege any particular art, nor does it ask for the arts to be mutually isolated. The series encourages writing from the many fields of thoughtful and critical inquiry.

Richard Halpern, *Leibnizing: A Philosopher in Motion*

Arthur C. Danto and Demetrio Paparoni, *Art and Posthistory: Conversations on the End of Aesthetics*

Jason Miller, *The Politics of Perception and the Aesthetics of Social Change*

Emmanuel Alloa, *Looking Through Images: A Phenomenology of Visual Media*

Barbara Carnevali, *Social Appearances: A Philosophy of Display and Prestige*

Monique Roelofs, *Arts of Address: Being Alive to Language and the World*

Maurizio Lazzarato, *Videophilosophy: The Perception of Time in Post-Fordism,* translated by Jay Hetrick

Fred Evans, *Public Art and the Fragility of Democracy: An Essay in Political Aesthetics*

Paolo D'Angelo, *Sprezzatura: Concealing the Effort of Art from Aristotle to Duchamp*

James A. Steintrager, *The Autonomy of Pleasure: Libertines, License, and Sexual Revolution*

*For a complete list of books in the series, please see the Columbia University Press website.*

# LYRICAL INDIVIDUALISM

*Selected Writings on Henri Bergson and Anarchism*

André Colomer

Selection, translation, introduction, and commentary by Oskar De Wolf

With a foreword by Mark Antliff

Columbia University Press

New York

Columbia University Press
*Publishers Since 1893*
New York    Chichester, West Sussex
cup.columbia.edu

Mark Antliff and Oskar De Wolf wish to thank the Department of Art, Art History &
Visual Studies at Duke University for its generous financial support toward the
publication of this collaborative project.

Library of Congress Cataloging-in-Publication Data
Names: Colomer, André, 1886–1931, author. | De Wolf, Oskar, editor, translator. |
    Antliff, Mark, 1957– writer of foreword.
Title: Lyrical individualism : selected writings on Henri Bergson and anarchism / André
    Colomer ; selection, translation, introduction, and commentary by Oskar De Wolf,
    with a foreword by Mark Antlif.
Description: New York : Columbia University Press, 2024. | Series: Columbia themes
    in philosophy, social criticism, and the arts | Includes bibliographical references
    and index.
Identifiers: LCCN 2023049711 (print) | LCCN 2023049712 (ebook) | ISBN 9780231215060
    (hardback) | ISBN 9780231215077 (trade paperback) | ISBN 9780231560603 (ebook)
Subjects: LCSH: Colomer, André, 1886–1931–Translations into English. | Anarchism. |
    Individualism. | Avant-garde (Aesthetics)–France. | Bergson, Henri, 1859-1941–
    Criticism and interpretation. | Anarchism–France–History–20th century. |
    Literature, Experimental–France. | France–Intellectual life–20th century. |
    LCGFT: Poetry. | Essays. | Literary criticism.
Classification: LCC PQ2605.O3537 L97 2024  (print) | LCC PQ2605.O3537 (ebook) |
    DDC 848/.91209–dc23/eng/20231103
LC record available at https://lccn.loc.gov/2023049711
LC ebook record available at https://lccn.loc.gov/2023049712

Cover design: Milenda Nan Ok Lee
Cover images: Portrait of André Colomer, Wikimedia Commons; *L'humanité*,
December 18, 1927, RetroNews (1631-1952).

# Contents

# Foreword: André Colomer's Insurrectionary Micropolitics

MARK ANTLIFF

Despite André Colomer's status as a major activist and theoretical voice who introduced anarchist thought to key figures among the European avant-garde, he remains a neglected figure who is rarely acknowledged in histories of that political movement or of modernism.[1] This is all the more surprising when one considers Colomer's role as one of the first anarchists to synthesize the tenets of anarchist individualism with the philosophy of one of the most celebrated thinkers of the twentieth century, Henri Bergson (1859–1941).[2] Given the resurgence of interest in Bergson across the humanities, Colomer's philosophical and cultural interventions are ripe for a broader reconsideration. Moreover, Colomer was not alone in making Bergson's thought central to a version of anarchist ideology that affected the avant-garde. The controversial French agitator Georges Sorel did likewise in his anarchist syndicalist polemic *Reflections on Violence* (1908), which had a wide readership among European activists and avant-gardists, including the chief exponent of Italian futurism, F. T. Marinetti.[3] In England the radical feminist Dora Marsden similarly drew on Bergson in developing her theory of anarchist egoism, which influenced such major figures as the writers Rebecca West and James Joyce, as well as the vorticists Ezra Pound, Wyndham Lewis, and Henri Gaudier-Brzeska.[4] After World War I that synthesis was further developed by the anarchist art critic Herbert Read, who marshaled Bergson's notion of creative evolution in his interpretation of the biomorphic sculpture of Barbara Hepworth and Henry Moore.[5] Sorel, Marsden, and Read have been the subject of numerous studies profiling their contributions to anarchism and to the history of modernism; by contrast, Colomer has been largely ignored, despite his equally important role in the development and promotion of Bergsonian anarchism at the beginning of the twentieth century. Colomer's chief contribution to this anarchist tradition was in interpreting that ideology from the standpoint of states of mind and interpersonal relations, a correlation facilitated by Bergson's theory of intuition and the central role of emotive feelings of joy within that configuration. Philosopher Alexandre Lefebvre has drawn renewed attention to Bergson's interwar writings on love and joy in his groundbreaking study of the ethics and politics of human rights; Colomer's reflections on joy arguably anticipated issues raised by Lefebvre, and as such Colomer's ideas are worthy of comparative analysis with Bergson's later meditations on these themes in his magnum opus, *The Two Theories of Morality and Religion* (1932).[6]

Colomer was foremost a major theorist of anarchism, and the timeliness of this volume lies precisely in the fact that anarchism as a movement has undergone a major renaissance, particularly following the demise of the Soviet Union in 1991.[7] In academia and beyond, this had led to the establishment of journals (*Anarchist Studies, Anarchist Developments in Cultural Studies*), professional associations and institutes (Institute for Anarchist Studies, Anarchist Studies Network), the creation of new presses (AK Press, PM Press), and the launching of academic book series devoted to the subject (for example, "Contemporary Anarchist Studies," published by Manchester University Press). Within academia, anarchism as a subject area now has the kind of prominence once reserved for Marxism, and academics allied to anarchism such as David Graeber (now deceased, formerly at the London School of Economics), Noam Chomsky (formerly at MIT, now at the University of Arizona), and James C. Scott (Yale University) have gained the status of public intellectuals. Colomer's important interventions in French cultural and political life as a poet, philosopher, orator, publisher, polemicist, and union organizer arguably attest to his own elevated status in the public arena, which accounts for historian Richard Sonn's assessment that he was much more than an influential "anarchist intellectual."[8]

To get a fuller sense of Colomer's relevance one has only to consider his journal *L'action d'art* (1913, 1919), in which he first systematized his theory of anarchism. Published bimonthly in folio size, *L'action d'art* was initially headquartered at 138 Avenue du Maine in Paris's Fourteenth Arrondissement, but in the summer of 1913 the offices moved to 25 rue Tournefort in the heart of the Latin Quarter, a favorite haunt of the cosmopolitan avant-garde. Subscription numbers for the journal are unknown, but its readership extended well beyond Paris. *L'action d'art* had a list of correspondents throughout France and in Brussels (Abel Gerbaud), Rome (Giosi), New York (Lara Pardo), Guadalajara, Mexico (Cirilo Murillo),

Rabat, Morocco (Jean Suzy), Barcelona (B. Gili Roij), and London (Eugène Bévant). Moreover, it was circulated through a network of bookstores and radical study groups in Lyons, Châteauroux, Bordeaux, London, Marseilles, Brussels, Tunis, and Munich.[9] Despite the journal's short life, the Action d'art movement itself proved a success, resulting in the establishment of a bookstore, a theater, and an art gallery. Major avant-gardists affiliated with the journal included Dr. Atl (Gerardo Murillo), who further developed the aesthetic and political implications of the Action d'art project under the auspices of the interwar Mexican muralist movement, and the Paris-based futurist Gino Severini, who embraced Colomer's precepts while participating in the Action d'art collective.[10] Colomer's journal also played a crucial role in the defense of sculptor Jacob Epstein's famous *Tomb of Oscar Wilde*, which had been censored as indecent by Paris's municipal government when it was initially installed in Père Lachaise cemetery in 1912. *L'action d'art* not only reintroduced Wilde's anarchist text *The Soul of Man Under Socialism* (1891) to a Parisian public, but the journal also celebrated Wilde's homosexuality and aestheticism as yet another expression of Colomer's Bergsonian anarchist precepts.[11] Concurrently, Colomer and his colleagues launched a public petition in defense of Epstein's monument that won the support of such literary luminaries as Guillaume Apollinaire, Paul Fort, Max Jacob, Olivier-Hourcade, Louis Mandin, Jean Muller, and Alexandre Mercereau. Prominent cubists and futurists also supported the protest, most notably Alexander Archipenko, Albert Gleizes, Pierre Dumont, Francis Picabia, Tobeen (Félix-Elie Bonnet), and Gino Severini. Even artists and writers from England were recruited to the cause, including art critics Frank Rutter and Horace Holley and artists Wyndham Lewis, William Roberts, Charles Ginner, and Spencer Gore.[12] In sum, Colomer deserves to be recognized as a significant cultural emissary within the anarchist movement, fully comparable to his Paris-based anarchist communist rival, Jean Grave, who had forged similar ties with an older generation of neoimpressionists and symbolists in the 1890s.[13]

While I cannot undertake to address those links here, I will consider André Colomer's philosophical anarchism in greater detail to illuminate why he regarded Bergson's metaphysics and theory of temporal duration as so central to his anarchist project. I will also examine the myriad ways in which Colomer's Bergsonian anarchism addresses paradigms and activist strategies that are germane to the anarchist movement today. This issue seems to me to be a pressing one in part due to our academic tendency to parse our study of Bergson's influence into separate disciplinary categories, whereas modernists and ideologues claiming allegiance to Bergson almost invariably integrated politics into their aesthetics and aesthetics into their politics. Their effort was in emulation of Bergson's own conception of his method as akin to a way of being that could potentially transform society. Key to this transformation both in Bergson's thinking and that of his followers was the development of malleable, flexible forms of representation and organization expressive of the vital order and reflective insight they sought to evoke. Cultivation of our faculty of intuition, a form of empathetic consciousness, enables us to experience the continuous, creative unfolding of temporal duration— in ourselves, in evolutionary processes, and in the universe writ large—as a form of immediate, absolute knowledge. The development of forms of representation capable of evoking this ineffable experience was at the heart of Bergson's method, as manifest in his recourse to perceptual and mnemonic images in his attempts to convey an intuition; his lauding of those artists able to intuitively evoke duration through their art; and his call for scientists and mathematicians to transform their disciplines to better convey *durée* (Bergson cited infinitesimal calculus as exemplary of his philosophical method). Thus Bergson's project was premised not only on an ability to employ intuition to grasp temporal duration but also on developing forms of representation able to awaken that intuitive capacity in others.[14] I would argue that Colomer set about integrating art and politics by folding aesthetic processes into this wholistic vision of societal transformation. By considering aesthetics in terms of creativity and creative self-expression, artistic methods, materiality, activism, and collectivity, Colomer's Action d'art project reframed notions of ideology in terms of states of mind and interpersonal relationships, the very categories that proved so compelling to those ideologues and artists claiming allegiance to Bergson's methodological project.

## BERGSON AND ANARCHISM: THEN AND NOW

Colomer's synthesis brings to mind a more general question: How is it that anarchists were drawn to Bergson's philosophy in the first place? Michael Freeden's morphological definition of ideology allows us to discern why it was that Bergson's method was especially attractive to anarchists, as against Bergson's own alliance of his philosophy with democratic values.[15] Freeden argues that all ideologies are in fact dynamic and made of up an interactive cluster of core precepts around which secondary principles and concepts are fluidly structured.

Anarchy in its etymological origins means "contrary to authority" or "without a ruler," signaling a fundamental opposition to all forms of discursive representation, governmental or otherwise, as the means by which social hierarchies are generated. Immediacy rather than mediation is therefore at the heart of anarchist ideology. Such resistance encompasses a rejection of the centralization of power in the guise of institutions or other forms of organization, whether economic, ethical, or political. By contrast, anarchists call for the creation of nonhierarchical, unmediated relationships and modes of socioeconomic organization that would maximize individual freedom for the self as well as others.[16]

Bergson likewise valued immediacy over mediation, arguing that our intellectual faculties, by virtue of their pragmatic function, cannot adequately represent temporality in its creative unfolding. The intellect fails to grasp our temporal nature as creative individuals as well as evolutionary and temporal processes within the broader universe. To liberate us from such discursive, mediating distortions, Bergson championed empathetic intuition as a means by which artists, philosophers, and scientists could perceive ineffable duration and develop forms of representation more closely adapted to its characteristics. Before World War I Bergson limited his reflections to the fields of philosophy and the sciences, but Bergson's anarchist followers went further by applying his method to a withering critique of religions and of the state, premised on their conception of these institutions as propagating states of mind and interpersonal relations antithetical to those they allied to Bergson's notion of intuition.

In many respects Colomer's activist application of Bergson's theory also anticipated principles that are fundamental to contemporary anarchism. A core precept within this anarchist matrix is the concept of "affinity," wherein a shared worldview combined with empathetic bonds of loyalty, friendship, values, and ethics were to be the basis on which cooperation and a group identity could be nurtured.[17] One of Colomer's chief gambits was to assimilate this anarchist notion of affinity with Bergson's notion of intuition as part of his broader critique of the forms of psychological bondage imposed on individuals by states and oppressive institutions such as religious organizations. Another vital, interrelated principle was that of prefigurative politics, a reference to contemporary anarchists' self-conscious attempts to integrate the movement's tenets into the very means through which they seek to bring about societal change.[18] Prefigurative anarchism constitutes a politics of anticipation or hope, calling for actors to initiate social change through an act of self-transformation in the here and now. This congruence of means with ends had its equal in Colomer's estimation in Bergson's call for the creation of representational forms that were integral to the durational properties they sought to evoke. For Colomer, such prefigurative, direct-action politics had an aesthetic and embodied equivalent in the very processes through which creative self-expression is developed and the aesthetic means through which "art actions" could generate a spirit of intuitive affinity in those who encountered such forms of expression. In sum, the anarchist valorization of immediacy is here merged by Colomer with intuitive insight and creative expression in a radical reimagining of the relation between art and politics.

## READING BERGSON THROUGH MAX STIRNER

As I have shown elsewhere, Colomer forged a unique synthesis of Bergson's ideas with the egoism of the German philosopher Max Stirner, author in 1844 of the polemic, *Der Einzige und sein Eigentum* (The Ego and Its Own), and secondarily with the anarchist aestheticism of Oscar Wilde.[19] Colomer recognized that Stirner, like Bergson, called on individuals to engage in processes of self-liberation, but in Stirner's case in the context of what contemporary anarchist theorists Kathy Ferguson and Saul Newman perceptively refer to as an insurrectionary form of micropolitics, "addressing the power that works on us within our subjectivity."[20] It is in this context that Stirner's theory of radical nominalism condemned Cartesian rationalism, scientific discourse and what he called "fixed ideas" as pernicious abstractions, constructed by vested interests to divert us from an "egoist" focus on the cultivation of our own personalities, free of all societal constraint. These abstractions in Stirner's view posited an artificial division between mind and body to fabricate an ethereal realm of "pure spirit," composed of general ideas, symbols, and concepts divorced from the temporal world of our corporeal being. Stirner identified this nominal or "egoist" self as the "unique one," calling on us to behave solely in response to our embodied interests; but he also argued for the potential existence of a "union of egoists" conjoined in a contingent alliance.[21]

Colomer synthesized Bergson and Stirner by drawing on Bergson's pronouncements in the *Introduction to Metaphysics* (1903) and related writings outlining the philosopher's opposition between intuition and analysis and the role of what Bergson called "fixed" or "abstract ideas" in distorting and obscuring our understanding of our own inner duration. Having begun his *Introduction* by distinguishing between "two profoundly different ways of knowing a thing," Bergson concluded that attainment of absolute knowledge of an object from within can only be achieved by means of "an *intuition*, whilst everything else falls within the province of *analysis*." Intuition is a form of willed "sympathy by which one places oneself within an object in order to coincide with what is unique in it"; analysis, on the other hand, "is the operation which reduces the object to elements already known, that is, elements common to it and other objects."[22] Analysis, in short, ignores an object's particularity, what Bergson refers to as *its uniqueness*, the defining characteristic of duration; further, this comparative method leads to the fabrication of imperfect "symbols" as substitutes for intuitive insight. Bergson identifies our methods of analysis as especially pernicious for their denial of duration, whether in the guise of "the flow of my own conscious life" or the inner life of living beings surrounding us.[23] Recourse to analysis is "the ordinary function of positive science" since it works exclusively with "symbols," but it is also the method used by "even the most concrete of natural sciences, those concerned with life." These natural sciences "confine themselves to the visible forms of living being, their organs and anatomical elements," and in making "comparisons between these forms, they reduce the more complex to the more simplified."[24] *Creative Evolution* considered the role of such thinking with reference to biology, but his earlier books, which are central to Colomer's thinking, specifically focused on human psychology. In *Time and Free Will* Bergson charted this paradigm with reference to the scientific theory of psychophysics, which sought to subject our qualitative sensations, including that of color, to quantitative measurement, thereby denying their durational heterogeneity.[25] In *Matter and Memory* he critiqued the related theory of "associationism " for dissociating the continuous flow and interaction of mnemonic and perceptual images that make up our durational being into a series of discrete "ready-made things, given cut and dry in the course of our mental life," somehow combined by virtue of a "mysterious attraction" like a "psychical atom."[26] In short, analysis and the scientific method it generates translate living duration into symbols devoid of durational properties.

Concepts exact a similar process of abstraction, ignoring what is particular and unique and instead focusing on "abstract, general, or simple ideas." Unlike "images"—which, as forms of representation, at least keep us in the realm of the concrete—concepts are even further divorced from representing "constitutive duration," "the flow of my own conscious life."[27] Following Bergson, we need to think of the image as at the interface between perceptual experience and memory, wherein sensate experiences mnemonically intermingle with our imagination, bringing to mind an unfolding stream of associated images revivified through this durational process. In *Introduction to Metaphysics*, Bergson represents his own intuition of duration solely as a series of images, including "the unrolling of a coil," a "myriad tinted spectrum," or "an infinitely small elastic body," claiming that such diverse images, by virtue of the "convergence of their action" in our imagination, may "direct consciousness to the precise point where there is a certain intuition to be seized." Concepts, by contrast, point consciousness in the opposite direction, away from the willed effort of intuition and towards habitual forms of analysis. When "examined closely," a concept "retains only the part of the object that is common to it and others, and expresses, still more than the image does, a comparison between the object and others which resemble it."[28] While "abstract ideas can render service to analysis, that is, to scientific study of the object in its relation to other objects," they are "incapable of replacing intuition, that is, the metaphysical investigation of what is essential and unique in the object."[29] Bergson calls on us to "invert the habitual direction of the work of thought"—our predilection to think in terms of "fixed concepts"—in favor of intuition, in order to develop forms of representation "capable of following reality in all its sinuosity and of adopting the very movement of the inward life of things."[30]

For Colomer, Bergson's metaphysics amounted to an apologia for Stirner's politicized nominalism. What Stirner called "the unique" coincided with what Bergson described as the durational nature of our "inmost" self, our personality in all its particularity. Following Stirner, Colomer endorsed the idea of a self-devouring subjectivity and added intuition to the equation as the means by which an egoist could tap into inner duration.[31] Colomer also followed Bergson in claiming that conventional science, like abstractions, had a "practical role" with no other purpose "than to serve our action" with regard to our "use of matter."[32] Scientific method therefore was "a marvelous instrument" allowing us to grasp the material world to meet our "external necessities," but it was ill suited to grasp individual duration. Colomer likewise claimed that images, in inciting intuition, are a catalyst for creative forms of action wherein the whole of our personality is given greater scope for self-expression.[33] The effort was also seen by Colomer as an expression of a Nietzschean form of will to power.[34] Drawing on Bergson's metaphorical method, and his description in *Matter and Memory* of our bodies as centers of action among an aggregate of images,[35] Colomer called upon us to act in relation to our own aspirational self-image to achieve greater harmony between the internal world of our imagination and the expressive acts that mark us as creative beings. Colomer created his own image to reiterate the philosopher's claim that the intellect was incapable of inverting habitual thinking to grasp the creative freedom that defined our individualism: "One can compare the life of a human to a circle in which destiny is represented by the circumference. His acts will be the radii. With science he can construct radii that go toward the circumference. That leaves us with the center; and this invisible but moving center, without which no radii could ever be, without which the circumference could not be able to form itself, this free and creating center is being itself, its consciousness, its life."[36]

Having marshaled Bergson and Stirner to banish abstractions, Colomer's next task was to clarify the relation of Bergson's notion of duration to Stirner's idea of the unique and the special status of art and artists within that matrix. Bergson, in describing duration, invariably used musical metaphors, a practice repeated by Colomer. In *Time and Free Will* Bergson compared duration to "the notes of a tune, melting so to speak, into one another" to constitute "a musical phrase" "constantly altered in its totality by the addition of some new note." Our consciousness therefore is composed of a multiplicity of "qualitative" sensations whose unity resembles "that of a phrase in a melody."[37] In *Laughter* Bergson describes the artist as one uniquely able to plumb the depths of duration to grasp "our inner life's unbroken melody" and, with it, "the individuality of things or of beings." The various arts, Bergson argued, sought to evoke qualitative duration through a "rhythmic arrangement of words" in the case of poetry or an original "harmony of forms and colors" in painting to suggest "certain rhythms of life and breath that are closer to man than his inmost feelings."[38] Melodic harmony and rhythmic form were artists' means of creating what Bergson later referred to as "fluid concepts," capable "of adopting the very movement of the inner life of things."[39]

## RADICAL CREATIVITY

In *Creative Evolution* Bergson incorporated a theory of human creativity into the equation, a maneuver that had special import for Colomer, arguing that the universe was composed of durational activity animated by a vital impulse manifest in terms of lesser or greater degrees of freedom. Vibratory molecular matter was lowest on the scale of free activity, since its actions were almost wholly predetermined and reactive: as such, pure matter is perfectly adapted to scientific analysis. Living organisms, on the other hand, possessed varying degrees of freedom ranging from inactive forms of plant life to creatures governed by instinct (an unreflective form of activity) and to humankind. Humankind's actions were not only instinctual and pragmatic (intellectual) but on rare occasions also the product of intuition. Intuition or willed empathy serves to define artistic expression in Bergson's narrative, but intuitive consciousness can also be cultivated through individual effort to address other aspects of human endeavor. Human activity that is not an expression of this free will—whether the product of coercion or habit—fails to forward our own creative development. By contrast, intuition allows us to grasp the creative force or *élan vital* within and without us and gives birth to actions that contribute to its ongoing development. Thus, creative expression is synonymous with self-expression and is the most advanced instance of a life force permeating the cosmos. As Bergson states in *Creative Evolution*, "life, like conscious activity is invention, is unceasing creation," and it is through artistic creation that our personality "shoots, grows and ripens without ceasing."[40] In 1914, Bergson went so far as to refer to the development of our very personalities as a form of artistic expression: "Each personality is a creative force; and there is every appearance that the role of each person is to create, just as if a great Artist had produced as his work other artists."[41]

While Colomer endorsed Bergson's description of duration and his exaltation of humanity's creative capacities, he stopped short of embracing Bergson's vision of a "great Artist" akin to a cosmic *élan vital*, preferring instead to circumscribe this vital—and artistic—impulse within the parameters of Stirner's nominalism. Through an intuitive focus on one's own durational self, Colomer claimed that the egoist could discover his or her uniqueness and in doing so radically transform consciousness by augmenting an individual's creative capacities. This cultivation of the self, amounted to a form of artistic creation, for such intuitive self-consciousness gave birth to sensations of intensity, rhythm, harmony, and a vitalist joie de vivre. Colomer described an artistic sensibility—the most unique and individual of our faculties—as integral to duration itself and thus able to translate these sensations into forms of representation saturated with the same durational qualities. In sum, Colomer (like Wilde before him) collapsed art into life by declaring the self to be a work of art and then asserted that art as a form of representation was integral to our personal development and, as such, an expression of our protean ego, an insurrectionary form of micropolitics.

## RECONFIGURING BERGSON AND WILDE'S JOIE DE VIVRE

Colomer's fundamental maneuver was to claim exceptional status for an artistic sensibility as a faculty uniquely adapted to grasping duration by virtue of its nominalist—*and therefore anarchist*—properties. According to Colomer, it is "precisely because the sentiment of beauty is the least fixed, the least rational, the least settled, the most variable of human sentiments I choose it as the basis of *my* philosophy, as the principle of *my* action." Following Stirner, Colomer dismissed conventionalized moral and ethical criteria for behavior as abstractions, but unlike the former, aesthetic discernment "is of no risk to create a law for us humans, a common law, an immutable law; it can only accord with *my* individual law—that is to say my harmony, the feeling of an accord between my sentiments. It is the rhythm of my life, the synthesis of my being." The "beautiful," we are told, "is the synthesis of the many élans of a personality in search of its harmony," and as such it not only expresses individual "freedom" but the life force itself, what he referred to as an individual's "Joie de Vivre."[42] This notion of joy was also central to Wilde's aestheticized anarchism, as outlined in excerpts of Wilde's *The Soul of Man Under Socialism* (1891) published in *L'action d'art*. According to Wilde, "when man has realized Individualism he will also realize sympathy and exercise it freely and spontaneously." The individualist will sympathize "with the entirety of life," including "life's joy and beauty and energy and health and freedom." Moreover, true individualism "requires unselfishness," since sympathy will guide one's relations with others.[43] In contrast to selfishness, "which always aims at creating around it a uniformity of type," the unselfish individualist "recognizes infinite variety of type as a delightful thing, accepts it, acquiesces to it, enjoys it." "Man," states Wilde, "will have joy in the contemplation of the joyous life of others" for "sympathy with joy intensifies the sum of joy in the world."[44] Wilde's text anticipated Colomer's Bergsonian blueprint for a union of egoists founded on intuitive sympathy and life-affirming joie de vivre. Thus, Oscar Wilde's own self-fashioning as an ardent individualist and aesthete made him exemplary of the rebellious exuberance Colomer and his colleagues wished to cultivate.

Colomer cited Bergson's *Time and Free Will* (1889) as seminal to this theory, as in that text Bergson first analyzed the import of such feelings of joy.[45] Bergson described our experience of joy as instigating "qualitative alterations in the whole of our psychic states," and in the case of "extreme joy," an "astonishment simply at being alive."[46] He further underscored the significance of this qualitative emotion by noting that *aesthetic* pleasure yields a feeling of inner joy by virtue of our empathetic reaction to sensations of grace, rhythm, and harmony that are integral to artistic expression, positing a theory of intersubjectivity that accounted for the profound impact of art on the individuals who experience it.[47] Bergson argued that such joyful pleasure arose through our sympathetic response to a dancer's movements; for Colomer joie de vivre emerged when we experience the actions and thoughts of an anarchist animated by intuition. Colomer claimed that individuals inspired by this life-affirming joy would spontaneously attract like-minded individualists to join them in the formation of a contingent grouping akin to what Stirner described as a union of egoists. What united these ardent individualists was an "intuitive sympathy" and mutual enthusiasm that enabled them to delight in each other's radical difference. Thus, in anticipation of Bergson's later writings of the interwar period, Colomer's "fluid concept" of joy was an open one, that, while indiscriminate in its magnanimity, encompassed attention, responsiveness, and affective attachment to the other.[48]

## BERGSONIAN ILLEGALISM

However, Colomer did not embrace the full implications of such openness, since he sought to circumscribe his notion of vitalist joie de vivre within the confines of his rebellious anarchism. On this basis Colomer declared himself to be opposed to any external force that would seek to suppress or negate this life-affirmative force—including state-sponsored war, capital punishment, and police oppression—while paradoxically claiming that the anarchist-individualist is equally prepared to resort to violence if his or her individual freedom is under threat. Such was the case with the Bonnot gang, whose armed members actively defended their individual and collective "harmony" when faced with a hostile social order, seeking to suppress it.[49] The members of the Bonnot gang were reportedly engaged in a reactive, egoist defense of individualism: it is only because of the repressive economic and social conditions promoted by capitalism and state institutions that

Bonnot and his *compagnons* were forced to "become tragic" by undertaking an armed insurrection against the overwhelming power of the state. It is on that basis that Colomer could declare their revolt to be a form of "beauty."[50]

Colomer also deployed this Bergsonian paradigm to critique the anarchist-communism of Grave and the doyen of that movement, Peter Kropotkin. In a "Bergson to Bonnot" series essay subtitled "Art, Anarchy and the Christian Soul," Colomer mocked Grave and his colleagues for making their anarchism synonymous with Christianity. "Christianity taught us human brotherhood," wrote Colomer; "anarchist-communists of today" reportedly preached a similar line by following "this humanitarian and altruistic ideal, this belief in a universal concord and in an egalitarian fraternity to which the individual must devote himself." Colomer dismisses such universals as "idols that are even more tyrannical than those of divinity or royalty," for "Anarchy needs to be individualist, or it does not exist."[51] Colomer later expanded this stinging rebuke into a Bergsonian critique of communist notions of collectivity and of the communitarian groups Grave and his colleagues wished to generate. Colomer claimed that Kropotkin, Grave, and fellow "communists" called on individuals to subordinate their egos to an abstract conception, whether in the guise of a utopian vision made up of "common interests" or the a priori set of moral principles outlined earlier.[52] Their concept of a union premised on communist ideals thus constituted a preestablished framework, a set of rigid precepts to which individuals must adhere if they are to gain membership in the group. "The idea of communism thus ends up simply taking the place of patriotism," for the individual is condemned "to suffer in the company of people whom [he does] not like just for the good of the cause—for the prosperity of the colony." Such causes or "theories" are "nothing but empty frames," and those who would subordinate themselves to such abstractions are not true anarchists, for they have "never thought about the reasons for their anarchism," namely, that it should facilitate the cultivation of their personality. "Communist colonies" therefore constitute "hybrid assemblies of inharmonious elements," a random gathering of individuals lacking in empathy and thus predisposed for conflict.[53] Form and content—the communist ideal and the individuals who bring about its realization—are therefore bifurcated in the anarchist-communist imagination.

Colomer's polemic brings to mind Bergson's own critique in *Creative Evolution* of the intellect's propensity to fabricate such empty frames in order to foster our pragmatic activity. "The intellectual faculty," states Bergson, focuses solely on "relations" rather than on "things" and as such "possesses naturally only an external and empty knowledge, but it has thereby the advantage of supplying a frame in which an infinity of objects may find room in turn."[54] Unaware of the utilitarian origins of such thinking, we mistakenly identify the intellect as a faculty designed for pure speculation and take its general frames for reality itself. This radical bifurcation of abstract form from material content is something Bergson seeks to overcome by means of intuition, a faculty of willed empathy that enables us not only to grasp inner duration but also to develop pliable forms of representation molded to this durational content. Intuitive knowledge produces representational forms that are integral to the content they wish to represent and, as such, are akin to the vital order of living organisms.

For Colomer, the Bonnot gang had its ideological corollary in Stirner's "union of egoists," characterized as an anarchist band. "The band," in contrast to the empty frame governing the anarchist-communist collective, "is not a fixed form," "it is not an entity," or "a cause," for it cannot exist apart from the individuals who constitute it. "The *bande* is, a priori, nothing. It is formed by the very force of the individualities who compose it. It could transform or dissolve following this same force." Further, the band "cannot encompass a very large collectivity" by virtue of the manner in which it is formed.[55] This is in contrast to the large-scale groupings marshaled by "ideologues, preachers, politicians, and the leaders of crowds" through their manipulative recourse to "imperfect symbols," "idols for the public," such as God, patriotism, justice, democracy, or in the case of anarchist communists, "fixed ideas" defined in terms of a "cause."[56] Colomer's extension of Stirner's critique to include contemporary anarchists anticipated comparable critiques today. For instance, Kathy Ferguson, citing Slavoj Žižek, cautions that "the ideas and values around which anarchists often rally—the People, the Toilers, the Revolution, Justice, Freedom—are susceptible to becoming exactly the sort of fixed idea against which Stirner [and arguably Colomer] railed," by virtue of their function as signifiers that are "too large and amorphous" and that as such "tower over us" as impervious abstractions.[57]

Rather than ask individuals to suppress their unique personalities in the service an abstraction, Colomer defines his collective as a heterogenous grouping that nurtures qualitative difference rather than homogeneity. "To form the *bande*, the individualities who compose it do not look for a common ideal, a common theory, or common conceptions." Instead, this "community of temperaments" arises spontaneously by virtue of an "intuitive sympathy that attracts these the

ones to the other who found each other without even having planned it." "They
have found each other, so to speak, without having looked for one another." More-
over, "members of the *bande* do not resemble one another" but instead are quali-
tatively distinct. What serves to unite them is a sense of "harmony" manifested
as friendship and shared inspiration and enthusiasm, which in turn will nurture
the greatest realization of each individual who composes the band.[58] Thus, dis-
cerning one's own inner harmony can lead intuitively to a sense of harmony with
others, and aesthetics rather than an abstract cause or homogenizing concept, is
the basis for this contingent union. Colomer's vision of an anarchist band closely
resembles contemporary theorist Richard Day's concept of affinity as akin to a
"groundless solidarity," wherein empathetic relations enable us to value all forms
of individual struggle, whether they be defined in terms of "class, race, gender,
sexuality or ability."[59] Such groundless solidarity, states Day, fosters "unity in diver-
sity" as a core precept of anarchist affinity; Colomer arguably anticipated Day by
identifying unity in diversity as a form of qualitative difference, akin to the qual-
itative multiplicity inherent to duration.

Colomer further aestheticized his conception by describing this union of ego-
ists as "a community of blazing souls" that "burn in diversely nuanced colors,"
echoing Bergson's own use of color as a metaphor for duration in such texts as
*Matter and Memory* and *The Introduction to Metaphysics*.[60] To Colomer, intuition is
synonymous with aesthetic discernment and is integral to our creative self-
fashioning. "Intuition is a synthesizing force that is personal to us. It is the indi-
vidual axis of vision that forms a unique being, it is an original force of sensa-
tion, of feeling, of consciousness"; further, "it is only comparable to a musical
symphony whose total value, total meaning, resides in the ensemble, indepen-
dent of each note that it is made up of." Thus "the arts are the child of intuition,"
for a work of art "is nothing other than the free expression of an individuality
that does not recognize other laws except that of its individual harmony." "We
say that a work of art is beautiful not if it obeys whatever common laws defining
a criterion for beauty that might exist but, quite on the contrary, when it mani-
fests most spontaneously and most intensely an original life" and reveals "an indi-
viduality generative of sensations, of thoughts, of new emotions, inexpressible
until then."[61] As an "anarchist of art action," Colomer states that his goal is to
"reveal to the individualist anarchists that they can discover through art, with
their intuition alone, the harmonious unity of their action, their individual
well-being."

## INSURRECTIONAL AESTHETICS: ART AND EMBODIMENT

Colomer's theory of art put a premium on "joie de vivre," a celebration of sensory embodiment as an emotive register of an intuitive state of mind, while exalting all cultural manifestations of novelty, intensity, rhythm, and harmony as fundamentally anarchist by virtue of their durational and life-affirming properties.[62] When Colomer looked to historical precedents for this point of view, Oscar Wilde was his bellwether, but he also lauded Greek poets and writers in the subversive thrall to Dionysus as well as revolutionary Romantics, transgressive advocates of Naturism and free love, and proponents of high lyricism in poetry. "In Athens," wrote Colomer, "the artists and poets were teachers of life, professors of joy. They made Art for Life." In contrast to anarchist communists such as Peter Kropotkin, Jean Grave, and their allies among the neoimpressionists, Colomer did not idolize Gothic cathedrals as expressive of the collective *esprit* of medieval guilds but instead disparaged these edifices as "monuments to celebrate the afterlife," and as such an art "made for Death." Contemporary artists, poets and writers, counseled Colomer, should reject the cult of medievalism and follow the example of Dionysian Athens by exalting, "this joy of *being* under the sun, this drunkenness of sensing, of thinking, of enjoying harmoniously in accordance with nature."[63] Others among the Action d'art collective shared Colomer's views; for instance, in August 1913, Colomer's colleague René Dessambre gave a lecture on "The Pictorial Work of Delacroix" to a group of French poets known as the "Paroxystes," whose leader was the Bergsonian and futurist-oriented poet Nicholas Beauduin.[64] Beauduin's doctrine of paroxysm celebrated the "perpetual dynamism" and "creative violence" of the contemporary age as the vitalist source for his "direct lyricism," which privileged the individual over the collective—an attractive doctrine for Colomer and his allies.[65] In speaking to the group, Dessambre described Delacroix as "the great creator of images, of powerful symphonies, orchestrations of tones" who, through " 'the intensity' of his 'visions of life,' was able to convey his rebellious 'joie-de-vivre.' "[66]

Colomer also praised the most novel artists of the preceding generation, exemplified by the free verse praxis of symbolists close to the anarchist movement such as Stéphane Mallarmé, as well as the dandified self-fashioning of Oscar Wilde, who claimed his own allegiance to anarchism. The symbolists' recourse to vers libre combining poetic images, with rhythmic forms ungoverned by standardized conventions, had long been celebrated by Bergsonists as a literary means for evoking duration.[67] Wilde in turn was especially venerated by Colomer by virtue of his aestheticist self-fashioning and his status as a rebel persecuted by the state for his free sexuality, untethered from state-sanctioned mores. Among his peers, Colomer promoted Gino Severini as the modern heir of Wilde's fin-de-siècle aestheticism.[68] Severini began collaborating with the Action d'art group in the summer of 1913, and in October he wrote to Marinetti of his plans to publish a futurist manifesto in *L'action d'art*. Although the manifesto failed to appear due to Marinetti's opposition, Severini clearly thought its contents compatible with the Colomer's philosophical and political views.[69] In his memoirs, Severini described Colomer's group as advocating an anarchist doctrine of the heterogeneous "Ego" in opposition to "democratic ideas of equality," and in July 1913 he suggested to Marinetti that the futurists should adopt a strategic alliance with Colomer's group and make regular use of the journal as a publishing vehicle.[70] Severini's suggestion went ignored, however, for Colomer's individualist version of aestheticized anarchism proved incompatible with the synthesis of Sorelian anarchism and imperialism Marinetti was then developing in Milan.[71]

Like Wilde, Severini was a self-styled dandy who actively cultivated his reputation as a distinct personality.[72] During the prewar years, Severini endorsed Bergson's interpretation of color as a qualitative metaphor for duration and utilized neoimpressionist techniques to express what he referred to as his "intuitive" sensation of the erotic energy of young female dancers who populated the cabarets and dance halls of Montmartre. Severini viewed the proletarian dancers animating these bohemian establishments as exemplary of Colomer's anarchist vision, and he celebrated their dances as spontaneous forms of actions d'art. Severini—whose status as an accomplished dancer won him free admission to the clubs—repeatedly depicted individual performers and their skilled execution of complex dances, such as the polka or waltz, both referred to in his 1912 painting of two dancers, *Dynamic Hieroglyphic of the Bal Tabarin*. Scholars have noted that many of these popular dances were considered highly erotic and transgressive, and the dance halls themselves were famous locales for sexual liaisons where the spirit of Dionysus reigned supreme.[73] In his memoir Severini recalled that the Tabarin was notorious for its "generous display of scantily clad beauties and a carnivalesque inventiveness."[74] Severini's art and theory was compatible with Colomer's anarchist vision on multiple levels. As we saw, Colomer endorsed a notion of aestheticized self-fashioning as central to his project, and he identified Bergsonian intuition as the principle means for achieving that goal. His conception of a union of egoists was premised on a Bergsonian vision of joie de vivre wherein intuitive sympathy resulted in harmony between individualists who relished their qualitative differences and distinct personalities. Feelings of rhythm, harmony, and exuberance were all indicative of this intuitive state of mind, which found its ideal expression in art actions that were simultaneously acts of rebellion against social conventions. Severini realized these goals in his own individualist self-fashioning as a dandy, his immersion in the hedonistic world of the dance hall, and his intuitive and eroticized response to the female dancers with whom he fell in harmonious step on the dance floor. This shared enthusiasm also accounts for Severini's participation in Colomer's plan to launch an avant-garde theater by contributing stage sets and costume designs to the project. The Action d'art group described the theater as "a field of action for beautiful gestures, realized harmonies" in the service of "lyrical" and "heroic" individualism; presumably, Severini's aesthetic sensibility furthered their aims.[75] Thus Colomer's action d'art movement overturned our conventional notion of fin-de-siècle aestheticism by rejecting the doctrine of "art for art's sake" in favor of "art for life's sake," all the while privileging aesthetics as the primary agent for this anarchist insurrection.[76]

## COLOMER REDUX

As I have demonstrated, André Colomer is an important thinker whose historical significance and legacy has yet to be fully appreciated or examined. His radical interpretation of Bergson bears analytical comparison with that of other significant anarchists of his generation, most notably Dora Marsden and Georges Sorel but also with theorists influential on contemporary anarchism such as the Bergsonian Gilles Deleuze (especially with regard to Colomer's theory of micropolitics and his response to Stirner).[77] The centrality of a Bergsonian interpretation of open, magnanimous joy in Colomer's anarchist vision is arguably a distinguishing feature of his thought, and as such it deserves comparison to Bergson's own usage of that constellation in support of the very democratic "abstractions" (such as republican notions of liberty, equality, and fraternity) that Colomer so vehemently critiqued.[78] Yet another philosophical dimension of

Colomer's anarchism was the impact of Friedrich Nietzsche in his individualist project: this too is worthy of comparative analysis, both from the standpoint of radicals of Colomer's own generation and in light of Nietzsche's influence on the contemporary anarchist movement.[79] Colomer's key role in establishing anarchist networks through his various publications also deserves attention as yet another important manifestation of what Constance Bantman refers to as the anarchist praxis of "relational activism."[80] Likewise, Colomer's deployment of Stirner needs to be contextualized in terms of other instances of insurrectionary micropolitics, especially among anarchists affiliated with the historical avant-garde.[81] Perhaps most important, Colomer's novel interpretation of the anarchist paradigms of affinity and prefiguration deserves to be folded into the history of anarchism and to be reconsidered as to its relevance today. Recognition of André Colomer's myriad achievements is long overdue, and this anthology will enable a new generation of historians and activists not only to reassess his legacy but also to reanimate his *action d'art*.

## NOTES

1.    For instance, Colomer is not mentioned in Peter Marshall's foundational survey of anarchism, *Demanding the Impossible: A History of Anarchism* (New York: Harper Collins, 1992), nor is he profiled in surveys and anthologies specifically devoted to French anarchist individualism and the history of anarchist illegalism. For instance, see Richard Parry, *The Bonnot Gang: The Story of the French Illegalists* (London: Rebel, 1987); *Enemies of Society: An Anthology of Individualist and Egoist Thought* (San Francisco: Ardent, 2011); and *Disruptive Elements: The Extremes of French Anarchism* (San Francisco: Ardent, 2014). In his superb study of the interwar French anarchist movement, David Berry briefly refers to Colomer and his political trajectory, identifying him as a "leading figure" among anarchists affiliated with the interwar Confédération Générale du Travail (CGT). See David Berry, *A History of French Anarchist Movement: 1917–1945* (Westport, CT: Greenwood, 2002).

2.    For studies examining the Bergsonian dimension of Colomer's anarchist theory and his relation to the avant-garde, see Mark Antliff, *Inventing Bergson: Cultural Politics and the Parisian Avant-Garde* (Princeton, NJ: Princeton University Press, 1993), ch. 4; Mark Antliff, "Cubism, Futurism, Anarchism: The 'Aestheticism' of the Action d'art Group, 1906–1920," *Oxford Art Journal* 21, no. 2 (1998): 99–120; Mark Antliff, "Revolutionary Immanence: Bergson Among the Anarchists," in *Bergson and Immanence: Painting, Photography, Film*, ed. John Mullarkey and Charlotte de Mille (Edinburgh: Edinburgh University Press, 2013), 94–111; Mark Antliff, *Sculptors Against the State: Anarchism and the Anglo-European Avant-Garde* (University Park: Pennsylvania State University Press, 2021), ch. 1; and Richard Sonn, *Sex, Violence and the Avant-Garde: Anarchism in Interwar France* (University Park: Pennsylvania State University Press, 2005).

3.  Numerous scholars have analyzed Bergson's profound impact on Sorel; for instance, see John Stanley, *Sociology of Virtue: The Political and Social Theories of Georges Sorel* (Berkeley: University of California Press, 1981), and Richard Vernon, *Commitment and Change: Georges Sorel and the Idea of Revolution* (Toronto: University of Toronto Press, 1978). For analyses of Sorel's influence on the Italian futurists, see Günter Berghaus, *Futurism and Politics: Between Anarchist Rebellion and Fascist Reaction, 1909–1944* (Oxford: Berghahn, 1996); Günter Berghaus, *F. T. Marinetti: Critical Writings* (New York: Farrar, Straus and Giroux, 2006); Ernest Ialongo, *Filippo Tommaso Marinetti: The Artist and His Politics* (Madison, NJ: Fairleigh Dickinson University Press, 2015); and Antliff, *Sculptors Against the State*, ch. 2. On Sorel's impact on modernists in Britain, see Henry Mead, *T. E. Hulme and the Ideological Politics of Early Modernism* (London: Bloomsbury, 2015).

4.  See Bruce Clarke, *Dora Marsden and Early Modernism: Gender, Individualism, Science* (Ann Arbor: University of Michigan Press, 1996); Robert Von Halberg, "Libertarian Imagism," *Modernism/Modernity* (April 1995): 63–79; Antliff, *Sculptors Against the State*, 137–81; and Allan Antliff, "Ezra Pound, Man Ray and Vorticism in America," in *Vorticism: New Perspectives*, ed. Mark Antliff and Scott Klein (Oxford: Oxford University Press, 2013), 139–55.

5.  See Allan Antliff, "Biocentrism and Anarchy: Herbert Read's Modernism," in *Biocentrism and Modernism*, ed. Oliver Botar and Isabel Wünsche (Aldershot, UK: Ashgate, 2011), 160–67; and Matthew Adams, *Kropotkin, Read and the Intellectual History of Anarchism: Between Reason and Romanticism* (New York: Palgrave Macmillan, 2015).

6.  Alexandre Lefebvre, *Human Rights as a Way of Life: On Bergson's Political Philosophy* (Stanford, CA: Stanford University Press, 2013).

7.  For an anthology summarizing many aspects of this resurgence, see Ruth Kinna, ed., *The Bloomsbury Companion to Anarchism* (London: Bloomsbury, 2014).

8.  Sonn, *Sex, Violence, and the Avant-Garde*, 198.

9.  For a list of authorized "correspondents" as well as agents distributing the journal, see "Les correspondants de l'action d'art" and "Nos dépositaires," *L'action d'art*, May 10, 1913.

10. See Antliff, "Cubism, Futurism, Anarchism," 99–120. Rosalio Romero has examined Atl's key role in furthering the Action d'art project in Mexico in her 2019 Duke University doctoral dissertation "Anarchism and Modern Art in Greater Mexico, 1910-1950."

11. Oscar Wilde, "L'individualisme," *L'action d'art*, April 1, 1913, 2; April 15, 1913, 2; May 10, 1913, 3; June 10, 1913, 3. For an analysis of Action d'art's campaign on behalf of Wilde's *Tomb*, see Antliff, *Sculptors Against the State*, 15-18, 25, 37-46.

12. Atl, "Pour la liberté de l'art: Nôtre pétition," *L'action d'art*, April 15, 1913, 1.

13. For a comprehensive study of the close relations between Jean Grave and key artists affiliated with the neoimpressionist and symbolist movements, see Robyn Roslak, *Neo-Impressionism and Anarchism in Fin-de-Siècle France: Painting, Politics and Landscape* (Aldershot, UK: Ashgate, 2007).

14. See Mark Antliff, "Bergson on Art and Creativity," in *Understanding Bergson, Understanding Modernism*, ed. Paul Ardoin, S. E. Gonstarski, and Laci Mattison (London: Bloomsbury, 2013), 299-300.

15. Michael Freeden, *Ideologies and Political Theory: A Conceptual Approach* (Oxford: Clarendon, 1996), and *Ideology: A Very Short Introduction* (Oxford: Oxford University Press, 2003).

On Bergson's politics see John Mullarkey, "Equally Circular: Bergson and the Vague Invention of Politics," and Paulina Ochoa Espejo, "Creative Freedom: Henri Bergson and Democratic Theory," in *Bergson, Politics and Religion*, ed. Alexandre Lefebvre and Stephanie White (Durham, NC: Duke University Press, 2012), 61–74, 159–73; and Philippe Soulez, *Bergson politique* (Paris: Presses Universitaires de France, 1989).

16. See Marshall, *Demanding the Impossible*, 3–11, 679–705.

17. For analyses of the notion of affinity with reference to contemporary anarchism, see Richard Day, *Gramsci Is Dead: Anarchist Currents in the Newest Social Movements* (London: Pluto, 2005), and Uri Gordon, *Anarchy Alive! Anti-Authoritarian Politics from Practices to Theory* (London: Pluto, 2008).

18. See Gordon, *Anarchy Alive!*, and Paul Raekstad and Sofa Saio Gradin, *Prefigurative Politics: Building Tomorrow Today* (Cambridge: Polity, 2020). As Gordon states, "prefigurative politics represents a broadening of the idea of direct action, resulting in a commitment to define and realise anarchist social relations within the activities and collective structures of the revolutionary movement itself" (35).

19. See Antliff, "Revolutionary Immanence," 94–111. When Action d'art announced the creation of a bookstore at its headquarters, Stirner's manifesto, translated as *L'unique et sa propriété* in 1899, was advertised alongside Wilde's *Intentions* (1891) (containing "The Decay of Lying," "Pen, Pencil, and Poison," "The Critic as Artist," and "The Truth of Masks"), and Bergson's three books *Time and Free Will* (1889), *Matter and Memory* (1896), and *Laughter* (1900), under the heading "Philosophy-Aesthetics-Combat." See "Librarie d'Action d'art," *L'action d'art*, July 25, 1913, 4; Stirner and Wilde continue to have a major impact within the anarchist movement; see Saul Newman, ed., *Max Stirner* (New York: Palgrave Macmillan, 2011); and Kristian Williams, *Resisting Everything but Temptation: The Anarchist Philosophy of Oscar Wilde* (Oakland, CA: A. K. Press, 2020).

20. Saul Newman, "Voluntary Servitude Reconsidered: Radical Politics and the Problem of Self-Domination," *Anarchist Developments in Cultural Studies* 1 (2010): 31–49; Kathy Ferguson, "Why Anarchists Need Stirner," in Newman, *Max Stirner*, 167–88.

21. See Antliff, "Revolutionary Immanence," 96–98. The first section of Stirner's *The Ego and Its Own*, titled "Man," focuses on the ideological means through which such abstractions compel individuals to ignore their own self-interest as embodied individuals.

22. Henri Bergson, *Introduction to Metaphysics*, trans. T. E. Hulme, intro. John Mullarkey (New York: Palgrave Macmillan, 2007), 5.

23. Bergson, *Introduction to Metaphysics*, 10.

24. Bergson, *Introduction to Metaphysics*, 6.

25. Bergson, *Time and Free Will* (1889), trans. F. L. Pogson (1910) (New York: Harper & Row, 1960), 60–72. John Mullarkey has cogently analyzed this aspect of Bergson's argument in *Bergson and Philosophy* (Notre Dame, IN: University of Notre Dame Press, 2000), 22–24.

26. Bergson, *Matter and Memory* (1896), trans. N. M. Paul and W. S. Palmer (New York: Humanities, 1978), 214–15.

27. Bergson, *Introduction to Metaphysics*, 10.

28. Bergson, *Introduction to Metaphysics*, 11.

29. Bergson, *Introduction to Metaphysics*, 12.

30. Bergson, *Introduction to Metaphysics*, 40–41.

31. Bergson, "The Perception of Change" (1912), in *The Creative Mind*, trans. Mabelle L. Andison (New York: Philosophical Society, 1946), 173. On the centrality of this idea to Bergson's philosophical method, see Garret Barden, "Method in Philosophy," in *The New Bergson*, ed. John Mullarkey (Manchester: Manchester University Press, 1999), 32–40.

32. André Colomer, "La science et l'intuition," *L'action d'art*, May 10, 1913, 3.

33. Colomer, "L'idéalisme et l'anarchie," *L'anarchie* (1913), 98.

34. Antliff, *Inventing Bergson*, 146–47; André Colomer, "De Bergson à Bonnot: Aux sources de l'héroïsme individualiste 1. Bergson et les 'Jeunes gens d'aujourd'hui,'" *L'action d'art*, March 1, 1913, 1.

35. Bergson, *Matter and Memory*, 1–69.

36. Colomer, "La science et l'intuition," 3.

37. Bergson, *Time and Free Will*, 100, 106, 111.

38. Bergson, *Laughter* (1900), in *Comedy*, ed. Wylie Sypher (Baltimore: Johns Hopkins University Press, 1983), 158–62.

39. Bergson, *Introduction to Metaphysics*, 40.

40. Bergson, *Creative Evolution* (1907), trans. Arthur Mitchel (New York: Henry Holt, 1931), 6, 23.

41. Henri Bergson, "The Problem of Personality," in *Mélanges* (Paris: Presses Universitaires de France, 1972), 1071.

42. Colomer, "Ma liberté c'est ma beauté," *L'action d'art*, June 10, 1913, 1.

43. Oscar Wilde, *The Soul of Man Under Socialism* (1891), in *De Profundis and Other Writings* (London: Penguin Classics, 1986), 48.

44. Wilde, *The Soul of Man Under Socialism*, 50–51.

45. Colomer, "M Bergson et les 'Jeunes gens d'aujourd'hui,'" 1.

46. Bergson, *Time and Free Will*, 10–11.

47. Bergson, *Time and Free Will*, 11–15.

48. For a compelling analysis of Bergson's concepts of love and joy as they relate to his notion of an open society in *The Two Theories of Morality and Religion* (1932), see Lefebvre, *Human Rights as a Way of Life*, 92–97.

49. Colomer, "La bande," *L'action d'art*, November 10, 1913, 2.

50. Colomer, "La bande," 2; "Ma liberté c'est ma beauté," 1.

51. Colomer, "L'art, l'anarchie, et l'âme chrétienne," *L'action d'art*, April 15, 1913, 1–2.

52. Colomer, "Illusions sociales et delusions scientist," *L'action d'art*, August 25, 1913, 2.

53. Colomer, "La bande," 2.

54. Bergson, *Creative Evolution*, 149–50.

55. Colomer, "La bande," 2.

56. Colomer, "Illusions sociales et delusions scientist," 2.

57. Ferguson, "Why Anarchists Need Stirner," 169–70.

58. Colomer, "La bande," 2.

59. Day, *Gramsci Is Dead*, 18.

60. Colomer, "L'individualiste héroïque at l'art quotidienne," *L'action d'art*, December 25, 1913, 1; Bergson, *Matter and Memory*, 268–69; Bergson, *Introduction to Metaphysics*, 221.

61. Colomer, "La science et l'intuition," 3.

62. See references to the Bergsonian and Stirner-inspired import of "joie de vivre" in Colomer, "L'art, l'anarchie, et l'âme chrétienne," 1-2, and "L'illusion individualisée," 1.

63. Colomer, "L'art, l'anarchie, et l'âme chrétienne," 1-2. On the neoimpressionists' and anarchist communists' veneration of the Middle Ages and the guilds that constructed medieval cathedrals, see Roslak, *Neo-Impressionism and Anarchism in Fin-de-Siècle France.*

64. "Les conférences de René Dessambre sur Delacroix," *L'action d'art,* September 10, 1913, 4.

65. On Beauduin's art theory, see Pondrom, *The Road from Paris: French Influences on English Poetry, 1900–1920* (Cambridge: Cambridge University, 1974), 280-81.

66. "Les conférences de René Dessambre sur Delacroix."

67. See Romeo Arbour, *Henri Bergson et le lettres françaises* (Paris: Librairie José Corti, 1955); and references to symbolism and vers libre in Antliff, *Inventing Bergson.*

68. For an analysis of the futurists Severini and Ugo Giannattasio's involvement in the Action d'art project over the summer and fall of 1913, see Antliff, "Cubism, Futurism, Anarchism," 115-17, and *Inventing Bergson,* 164-66.

69. Severini's first publication in *L'action d'art,* "Le futurism pictural," appeared on June 10, 1913; on October 22, 1913, Severini sent Marinetti a draft of a proposed manifesto, asking Marinetti when he should send a copy to *L'action d'art.* See Gino Severini to F. T. Marinetti, October 22, 1913, in Anne Coffin Hanson, *Severini Futurista* (New Haven, CT: Yale University Art Gallery, 1995), 158. At the time Severini was working on two interrelated manifestos, later known as "Les analogies plastiques dans le dynamisme" and "Art du fantastique dans le sacré." Both exist in manuscript form and are published in Severini, *Écrits sur l'art* (Paris: Diagonales, 1987). For a concise history and analysis of Marinetti's objections to the manifestos, see Hanson, *Severini Futurista,* 39-40.

70. Gino Severini, *The Life of a Painter* (Princeton, NJ: Princeton University Press, 1995), 75-76; Severini to F. T. Marinetti, July 9, 1913, in Hanson, *Severini Futurista,* 150-59.

71. Antliff, *Sculptors Against the State,* 78-90.

72. See Zoë Jones, "Gino Severini's Bohemian Paris: Integrating the Italian Artist, 1906-1914," in *Foreign Artists and Communities in Modern Paris, 1870–1914,* ed. Karen Carter and Susan Waller (Burlington, VT: Ashgate, 2015), 239-52.

73. See Jones, "Gino Severini's Bohemian Paris," and Danielle Fonti, *Gino Severini: The Dance* (Milan: Skira, 2001), 11-31.

74. Severini, *The Life of a Painter,* 54.

75. Colomer, "Les poètes joues par les poètes," *L'action d'art,* December 25, 1913, 2. See also Antliff, "Cubism, Futurism, Anarchism," 115-16.

76. Colomer critiqued the concept of "l'art pour l'art" on a number of occasions as a form of psychological retreat from vitalistic embodiment into a condition of self-consuming dilettantism, wherein artists' construct "artificial Paradises" with "alcohol, ether, hash, opium" as the catalysts for their frenzied imaginations. See "L'art, anarchie, et l'âme chrétienne," 1-2.

77. For a comparative analysis of the anarchism of Colomer, Marsden, and Sorel, see Antliff, *Sculptors Against the State,* 183-95. For recent studies examining Deleuze's relation to the notion of anarchism, see Chantelle Gray van Heerden and Aragaorn Eloff, eds., *Deleuze and Anarchism* (Edinburgh: Edinburgh University Press, 2019); and Chantelle Gray, *Anarchism After Deleuze and Guattari: Fabulating Futures* (London: Bloomsbury, 2022).

78.  During World War I Bergson crudely defined the French Republic as the incremental, spontaneous manifestation of an organic, "vital order" while declaring Germany to be an artificially fabricated geopolitical entity founded on an antivital "mechanization of spirit." He deployed such thinking to justify the Allied cause, thereby restricting his notion of vital openness and magnanimity to the confines of democratic nation-states. It was only during the interwar period that Bergson revised his vision of democracy to transcend geopolitical configurations and encompass universalizing notions of openness such as that of human rights. On Bergson's wartime polemics, see Soulez, *Bergson politique*. On Bergson's later universalizing interpretation of the concept of an open society from the standpoint of democracy, see Mullarkey, "Equally Circular," Philippe Soulez, "Bergson as Philosopher of War and Theorist of the Political," and Paulina Ochoa Espejo, "Creative Freedom," in *Bergson, Politics, Religion*, ed. Alexandre Lefebvre and Melanie White (Durham, NC: Duke University Press, 2012), 61–74, 99–125, and 159–73, respectively. On the role of love and joy in this context, see Lefebvre, *Human Rights as a Way of Life*, 90–95.

79.  For an overview of Nietzsche's influence on anarchists of Colomer's generation in Paris, see Christopher Forth, *Zarathustra in Paris: The Nietzsche Vogue in France, 1891–1918* (DeKalb: Northern Illinois University Press, 2001). For contemporary interpretations, see John Moore, ed., *I am not a man, I am dynamite!: Friedrich Nietzsche and the Anarchist Tradition* (London: Pluto, 2004); Louis Call, *Postmodern Anarchism* (Lanham, MD: Lexington, 2002); and Shahin, *Nietzsche and Anarchy: Psychology for Free Spirits, Ontology for Social War* (Oakland, CA: PM Press, 2022).

80.  Constance Bantman, "Jean Grave and French Anarchism: A Relational Approach," *International Review of Social History* 62, no. 3 (2017): 451–77.

81.  See Kathy Ferguson's concise summation of this influence in "Why Anarchists Need Stirner," 177–81.

## Introduction: Who Is André Colomer?

OSKAR DE WOLF

In 1931, André Colomer died at only forty-five years of age, finally succumbing to cancer after years of suffering the perils of the brutal disease. He found his last rest in Moscow, the bustling capital of the Bolshevik regime, years removed from his greatest successes as the most prominent anarchist affiliated with the Parisian avant-garde. He was poor and had been abandoned by most of his friends. The Soviet Union became the last stop in an incredibly hectic life, and what a surprising one it would have been only ten years before, when Colomer was writing aggressive hit pieces against the Bolsheviks, their self-proclaimed "transitory period" in power, their leaders, their representatives in France, and the entire communist movement as such.[1]

In the late 1910s and early 1920s Colomer was the most recognizable figure in the French anarchist movement. He had written for all the major anarchist journals of the day, was widely recognized as anarchism's most eloquent speaker, and fielded some of the most revolutionary and original ideas in a city that was, in that era, certainly not lacking in creative minds. A poet as well as a political figure, Colomer managed to eloquently express these ideas in writing and developed a refined, idiosyncratic style with a particular ability to sneer with a trademark sudden explosiveness. And of course, like any self-respecting anarchist, Colomer deployed his pen, and he did so in all directions.

All these factors, combined with his remarkable work ethic, meant that Colomer, in his prime, spoke and published multiple times a week while participating in anarchist circles of all kinds. That way the Languedoc native, born in Cerbère on the coastal border of France and Spain in 1886, quickly made a name for himself in the capital. The list of his associates and enemies reads like a who's who of the Parisian political and artistic scene: he was a close ally of the cubists and futurists when those avant-garde movements were just emerging; was an avid defender of the Bonnot gang, the self-styled "illegalists" whose spree of armed robberies rocked prewar Europe; discovered and was the first to publish the celebrated crime novelist and poet Léo Malet; publicly debated the doyen of surrealism, André Breton; and was the subject of a sustained smear campaign by Léon Daudet, one of the leaders of the notorious right-wing group Action Française. In the 1910s and 1920s one would have struggled to find a single politically active Parisian who did not know the name of Colomer, a fact that was all the more relevant because of the major controversies in which the poet was involved.

Despite this résumé, despite the obvious quality of his work, despite his relevance in his day and age, despite the controversies that made him a star in the Parisian firmament, Colomer's legacy seems to be frozen in the cold winter day that saw him breathe his last breath into the Russian air, already rendered irrelevant in his mid-forties.

Why?

Well, there seems to be an obvious reason for Colomer's descent into obscurity, and it is the same reason why Colomer ended up in Russia in the first place. It is the answer to the question that serves as a title to this introduction. It relates in essence to Colomer's unique brand of individualism.

Colomer's friend and fellow anarchist Manuel Devaldès, in his *Anthologie des écrivains réfractaires de langue française* (1927), claimed that Colomer embraced an individualist creed early in life when, at the age of twelve, he discovered the work of Emile Zola amid the Dreyfus affair (1894–1906).[2] In Colomer, the individualist school of thought found a fiery and able defender. As soon as he began writing around the turn of the twentieth century, individualism became one of his main topics of interest, and the philosophy of the "I" became even more important to him when Colomer discovered the work of Max Stirner soon after. No philosopher before Stirner was as intellectually iconoclastic. Stirner's main work, *The Ego and Its Own* (1844), was an open declaration of war against the oppressive forces of religion, the state, and morality. In response, Stirner forged a notion of free individualism, so free that Stirner's egoist rejected conventional notions of love and friendship in developing his radical vision of egoism.[3] Colomer devoured Stirner's cold, radical, and pitiless ideas, but being foremost a French poet with a lyrical orientation, he found the logic of the German Stirner's argument and method to be somewhat sterile. This lacuna was filled by the work of yet another of Colomer's great influences, the metaphysician of intuition, Henri Bergson.

Bergson's major philosophical treatises *Time and Free Will* (1889) and *Matter and Memory* (1896) outlined an innovative philosophy of perception that redefined time as a creative agent in our lives and in the world and promoted intuition as the philosophical method at the heart of scientific modes of discovery as well as all other forms of human creativity. Colomer's unique synthesis of Stirner's radical individualism and Bergsonian intuition led him to forge a new form of artistic individualism, which he christened *action d'art*, anarchist art action.[4]

Colomer's novel integration of radicalism with artistic expression led him to write the following about one of his greatest idols, the bandit and poet François Villon (c. 1431–c. 1463): "His life and his work are one same monument; knowing one means that you must necessarily know the other; because his work was but the chant of his life, and his life but an illustration of his work."[5]

Indeed, the same can be said for Villon's pupil, André Colomer, nearly five hundred years younger. In its real-life implications, Colomer's notion of aestheticized anarchism demands that individuals utilize intuition to plumb the depths of their unique personality, of their dreams and feelings, in order to grasp their own creative potential. This idealized focus on the cultivation of the self is at the core of the individual's worldview, and in developing that sense of selfhood Colomer invites us to create a harmony between our psychological and social being, our inner emotions and our outwardly directed, social forms of self-expression. In making us all the agents of our own liberation, of our own "heroic individualism," Colomer calls on us to reject all moral and ethical conventions and to order our lives in response to the beauty of our inner harmony rather than act in response to the discordant ugliness of external forces, such as those promulgated by capitalism, church, and state. Our aspiration to achieve beauty and harmony in our own lives is itself an anarchist art action that has the potential to awaken such impulses in others, though, of course, Colomer granted every individual their own harmony, their own conception of beauty, and their own ideal. Thus Colomer's version of radical individualism is premised on an understanding of community and a notion of anarchist prefiguration, that is the power of the creative, revolutionary act as both the end sought and the means to achieve an unfolding process of societal transformation.

But just as Villon paid the price for living his renegade life when he was hanged in his early thirties, Colomer's obscurity following his untimely death can be seen as a consequence of how he truly lived his individualized ideal and the actions of his art. Colomer lived his life the way he wanted it, he stood up for his ideas, no matter how unpopular they were with the worldly powers of his time or even among his comrades, and he was ready to endure whichever consequences his acts brought about. This becomes clear when one leaves the realm of theory and the winter of 1931 to track Colomer's biography and see how his individualism, his greatest philosophical contribution, developed and shaped his life.

Colomer's parents moved to Paris in 1892 when he was six years old, and he came of age in Montmartre, a neighborhood full of radical minds of all stripes.[6] In the early twentieth century Montmartre was home to some of the greatest artists of the belle époque as well as a domicile for some of its most radical political thinkers. This was, so to speak, the time of both Pablo Picasso and Albert Libertad, the founder of the influential *Anarchie* (1905–1914), and avant-garde artists of that era—including Picasso—actively forged links with anarchists and radical socialists.[7] Beginning in the 1880s, artists and anarchists in Spain, France, and Belgium established journals identifying avant-garde praxis as a form of political activism, and this synthesis would occupy Colomer for much of his life. An example of this is the work of Belgian art nouveau architect Henry Van De Velde, who was a close associate of the French anarchist Charles-Albert. A generation older than Colomer, Charles-Albert founded the publishing house that would publish *Le libertaire*, starting in 1861, a journal that Colomer would be recruited to edit in 1921. So when, as early as 1898, Van de Velde was pondering how to define the relation of his anarchism and his art, it was Charles-Albert who published his conclusion: "We have chosen beauty to lift society toward better things. Beauty is not the olive branch, it's the Gladius [sword]!"[8]

This phrase and the attitude implied match the temperament of a young André Colomer, who actively entered the avant-garde scene of Montmartre, and Paris at large, about ten years later. As mentioned, Colomer had been politicized by the Dreyfus affair early on in life, and he subsequently deserted his military service in 1906 by joining the perennially ongoing vintners' revolts in southern France.[9] The experience of these revolts, his already solidly entrenched anarchist tendencies, and his relation those tendencies to his aestheticist ideals perfectly matched the synthesis of radicalism in art and politics that typified this era. From his very first publications, his idealism is clearly visible, just as the influence of both Bergson and the German individualists is already palpable in his aesthetic philosophy of the time. A poignant example is his assessment of the sculptor Célestin Manalt, written in his first publication of note, the journal *La foire aux chimères* (1907–1908), in early 1908: "Célestin Manalt has sculpted acts of suffering and revolt in stone, acts that earmark once more the beauty of human consciousness and individual will, as well the liberating force of the arts which, and only which, can create the human who is truly worthy of living."

In the following years Colomer's idealism, anarchism, and aestheticism would further mature and lead to a more and more crystallized position: his anarchism of the action of the arts. To express his ideals Colomer founded a corresponding journal in 1913, *L'action d'art.* In his publications for that journal Colomer transformed the embryonic thesis first articulated in his critical assessment of Célestin Manalt into a fully developed philosophical theory of anarchism that dramatically parted ways with the anarchist theories of his contemporaries. His conception of aesthetics expanded beyond the creation of works of art to encompass a notion of the self as a work of art, premised on a radical interpretation of Bergson's concept of intuition.

The worthiness of Colomer's innovative philosophy was truly tested soon after, in late 1913, when he took a bold stance with regard to one of the controversial affairs that rocked prewar France: the case of the so-called "tragic bandits," who embarked on a crime spree using automobiles, a novelty at the time. The bandits, also known as the Bonnot Gang after their leader, Jean Bonnot, were a self-declared group of anarchist illegalists whose actions reinforced the pariah status of anarchism in the public imagination. They left an equally large impression on Colomer, who, interpreting them from his Bergsonian standpoint, took the anarchist bandits as an example of his notion of "heroic individualism." He defended them against any and all critics, but especially against those anarchists who distanced themselves from the aggressive modus operandi employed by the bandits. In response to those anarchists who denounced the Bonnot gang's actions as detrimental to the collective cause, Colomer replied that their notion of a social or common good was in itself fundamentally anti-individualist and anti-anarchist: "Can we truly ask of an individualist that gives no other end to his acts than his own happiness to only accomplish acts that are likely to augment the common good?"[10]

Indeed, Colomer saw a true materialized will to live in the bandits, one that could perhaps best be summarized, in terms of Colomer's theoretical influences, as a Nietzschean will to intensify a Bergsonian intuition. As such, he interpreted their deeds as the acts of genuinely free individuals, as the oeuvres of artists that turned their life into their art and wanted to make it beautiful, according to their definition of beauty. That is what made the acts heroic: on Colomer's account, they were the acts expressive of the personal ideals of the bandits, their personal heroism. He wrote:

> In order to live intensely and to experience the strongest joys of our being, in order to live a life that is not only our life, but our highest life, it is suitable to not fiddle around with details, but to remember what the best of us is, the best of *our own* ideal, of this living synthesis of our being! The individual ideal is like an image of my own perfection, of my happiness, a marvelous image of what I would want to be and of what I could be, by thinking about it and by acting according to it. And, from that moment on, what do the social consequences of his acts matter to a man. He *is*, that is all. He tries to be even *more*, even *better*. He tends to his beauty, to his harmony.[11]

The bandits embodied Colomer's vision of anarchism in practice, his example for a lived action of the arts, and a realization of the ideal he had been formulated since 1908. Colomer arguably realized a comparable synthesis of aesthetic and social revolt when the youth of France were called up for active military service following the outbreak of World War I in August 1914. Fighting in the French army was obviously not an option for Colomer. Trickery or self-injury to avoid the battlefield wasn't either, for as Colomer wrote in 1919, reflecting on the war: "I did not want to lie, nor did I want to beg—because it is more beautiful to speak one's soul the way that it is and to affirm one's life the way that one wants it."[12] Further wanting to be "neither a voluntary victim nor an involuntary murderer in the ranks of a social troop,"[13] Colomer deserted once again, this time fleeing to Italy in 1914. There he was forced to halt in Genoa because his wife, Madeleine, was pregnant and would give birth to his daughter Tristane while they sought refuge in Italy.[14] For a while, the poet-deserter managed to earn his keep by giving public lectures. However, when Italy entered the war on the side of the Allies in 1915, Colomer was forced to flee again. Having failed in his attempts to reach neutral Switzerland, the Italian authorities arrested him and brought him back to Genoa, where Colomer was jailed in particularly harsh conditions. He became a subject of abuses by the authorities and went on a hunger strike. Following his release he managed to evade deportation to France by hiding with leftist comrades in Genoa, but he was eventually caught and forcibly sent to Perpignan—the place where he once witnessed the revolts of the winegrowers—and was thrown into prison. Colomer languished in a jail cell until the last day of the war, when he was suddenly judged to have been "reformed" and was released back into the society he so despised.[15]

Having obtained his freedom, Colomer promptly resuscitated his revolutionary journal *L'action d'art* in 1919. Although he once again brought together a group of activists and artists in the name of the same animating precepts that were the hallmark of the first series of the journal ("Light, reckless and passionate, it is with joy that we will slash open the scoundrels"),[16] the project proved to be as ephemeral as its first iteration in 1913. As a result, Colomer grew disillusioned with Bergson, Nietzsche, and the unique philosophical synthesis that defined his thought before the war. It is possible that the experience of the war had something to do with it, as some scholars have suggested, though Colomer's own account of the war does not necessarily lead to that conclusion.[17] Having always been critical of Bergson's own personal politics and of his class allegiances,[18] it is however incontestable that in the immediate aftermath of the war Colomer became increasingly critical of Bergson's core concept of intuition, which had been central to Colomer's anarchist doctrine. The most explicit example for this is the article "Mr. Bergson, Master of Thought of the Third Republic." In it Colomer claims that Bergson "denied the free, critical role that intelligence can play for the individual who wants to remove all the weight that, by way of social education, suffocates the harmonious life of his soul"[19]. Later, in his series "Matter, Mind, and Me," he further reflected on his former irrationalism: "even I . . . have hesitated for a long time before renouncing to accord an intrinsic value to certain ideas. I was, back then, an idealist to the detriment of my life: I gave freedom to ideas instead of giving it to myself."[20]

After the war Colomer indeed comes off as a much less idealistic figure, less of a poet and more and more of a political activist. It would go too far to say, however, that Colomer's idealism entirely disappeared. In fact, he even still refers to Bergson in key passages of his philosophical writings[21] and he definitely held on to a more practical reading of intuitionism. It would be more precise to say that during the 1920s, Colomer inserted Bergson into the context of the political struggles of the interwar period, reinterpreting his Bergsonian idealism in light of the pragmatic political realities of the era. This change in orientation is aptly captured in the following line from his article "The Belly and the Mind," in which Colomer explains that because a physically suffering person is unable to freely think, it is necessary to also fight for an individual's physiological well-being so that they might realize their full potential as individuals: "By struggling for the conquest of the bread, the worker simultaneously fights for the conquest of the book, for the conquest of his thoughts, of his reflections, of his consciousness, for the conquest of his personality."[22]

The core of Colomerian idealism thus remained unchanged, but now Colomer was able to marry his individualism with practical manifestations that were more fruitful than, for instance, the illegalism of Bonnot. This allowed him to gradually open up towards other types of anarchism. Most evident in this development is Colomer's adoption of anarchist-syndicalism, which was to become his main focus after World War I. Colomer coined the novel term "individual syndicalization" and saw the syndicates as a way to best organize a society in which every individual would eventually be free to truly live to their own ideal. They would conquer the bread, so to speak, so that the individual could then fight for the book. This led him to formulate the following credo, which became a widely adopted principle among his fellow radicals: "In the revolution, the syndicates are the body and the anarchy is the soul."[23] It is also a doctrine that further illustrates the compromise that the postwar Colomer achieved between his idealist soul and the practical struggle he engaged in: a true union of idealism and activism.

Colomer had already struck this balance in the founding of the Syndicat des Auteurs Dramatiques (Union of Dramatic Authors) in 1919, for which he would eventually take on the role of president.[24] Despite taking on this new administrative function, Colomer also continued to play a fundamental role in the sphere of anarchist publishing. By 1922 he was the editorial chief of both *Le libertaire* (1921–1925) and *Revue anarchiste* (1922–1925) and thus presided over two of the main organs of anarchism during a period when the movement was undergoing a dramatic reorganization after the disruption of the war. One of his greatest achievements in this field was that he managed to turn *Le libertaire* from a weekly into a well-circulating daily paper.[25] While he was not always the most efficient organizer or planner, he was the visionary behind the journals, whose conceptions took center stage, and whose writings further popularized anarchism among the broader public.[26] Given his having been a principal figure in the anarchist sphere since at least 1913, when he founded the action of the arts movement, it is safe to say that Colomer's star shone the brightest during this era of his life. This was also the moment when his failing health—the by-product of his harsh life or perhaps a first sign of his cancer—would first start to compromise his seemingly protean energy.

In addition to his declining health, two other factors came to compromise Colomer's status as revered figure within the anarchist movement: the controversy sparked by his editorial intervention in a notorious court case, and the gradual shift over this same period in his political positioning. The court case in question entered public consciousness under the name "Daudet affair" (1923–1930). It centered around the death of Philippe Daudet, the son of Léon Daudet, a famous royalist and writer for the nationalist publication *Action française*. This was the same Daudet who was a noted enemy of revolutionaries anywhere but was foremost a noted personal enemy of Colomer. Unlike his reactionary father, however, the young Philippe, who at the time was fourteen years old, sympathized with the anarchists. For reasons unknown the rebellious teenager ended up fleeing his parental house in November 1923 with the goal of taking a boat to Canada. Shortly afterward his body was found, and the case was officially ruled a suicide. This sparked a great national debate in which Daudet polemically wrote against the anarchists, claiming that they were responsible for his son's death and thus refuting the official police reports. *Le libertaire* in turn ran an article portraying Philippe as an anarchist hero and blaming his father and the nationalist movement for his death. A final twist came when Daudet and Colomer both came to believe that the alleged murderer, an anarchist librarian by the name of Pierre Le Flaouter, was actually a police informant. Thus, in a truly unlikely turn of events, both Daudet and Colomer blamed the government and the police for the death of Philippe Daudet, and Colomer used his eloquence in court to support the cause of Léon Daudet. The affair and the ensuing conspiracy theories were daily fodder in the press, and the controversy lasted for many months. The circumstances surrounding Philippe Daudet's death remain unresolved up to the present day.

The unlikely alliance of Colomer and Daudet, albeit short-lived and contextual, raised many eyebrows among the anarchists. The journalist Pierre Le Meillour likened Colomer's alliance "with Daudet against the police" to a union "with cholera against the plague."[27] Colomer's positive portrayal within the mainstream papers was equally criticized, the charge against him being a personal weakness for the limelight. It was such infighting that led Colomer to leave *Le libertaire* in 1925 in order to found a own journal of his own, *L'insurgé* (1925–1927).

Concurrently, the openness Colomer showed toward various types of anarchism during the interwar period slowly extended into an even wider embrace of positions from across the revolutionary side of the political spectrum. With the foundation of *L'insurgé*, Colomer pushed this ecumenical disposition even further than he had in the quite dogmatic *Le libertaire*. In October of 1925, he printed a short article on the first page of *L'insurgé* that serves as a great example of this strategic and theoretical turn. Entitled "Our Road Under the Stars," the article argues for a united front of "all enemies of the state" to cooperate against the established powers first, instead of infighting. The article is also proof that Colomer was still motivated in this by his everlasting idealism. The very first line in the article already makes this explicit: "At the *Insurgé*, we know our way: we are guided by the stars in our idealist sky."[28] Further, Colomer also reiterates his anarchist convictions, stating that they remained the logical conclusion of his individualism.

While thus claiming to remain faithful to his anarchist individualist and idealist convictions, Colomer now argued for tactical alliances that proved to be very controversial among radical individualists and anarchists alike. For one, he supported the communist trade union Confédération Générale du Travail Unitaire (CGTU) and argued that it should serve as an organ to unite all revolutionary political camps. He also supported the CGTU's Action Committee and stated that he would "always be ready to unconditionally support [their] movement of general strikes." In the Club des Insurgés, a forum for debates run by Colomer and the *Insurgé* group, Colomer came to defend the communists with increasing frequency. Additionally, he published André Breton's surrealist manifesto "Revolution First and Always!" (1924) that further evidenced his new pragmatic approach of infusing an anti-authoritarian interpretation into the discourse of the fragmented groups that made up the radical left. Colomer's change of heart with respect to the communists unleashed a barrage of criticism among anarchists and especially in the journal *Le libertaire*, where the critiques devolved into personal attacks. Nonetheless, the journal still ran a wide call for donations when Colomer's health reached a new low point in 1927 and he could no longer afford his medical expenses.[29]

Despite all of this he remained an active speaker and writer, and he held firm to his olive branch to the communists. Colomer's public openness to communism eventually resulted in a visit to Russia in late 1927 to celebrate the tenth anniversary of the revolution. An ailing but deeply impressed Colomer was shown around factories, schools, and railway stations, marveled at the monumental architecture of Moscow and Leningrad, and saw theatrical productions and films. He evidently found it all to be inspiring and perhaps even heroic.

Following his return from Russia, Colomer's gradual rapprochement with communism came more and more to look like a full-blown conversion. After his further public endorsements of the Soviet Union, the anarchist backlash against him reached its peak. On March 9, 1928, shots were fired in an auditorium where Colomer debated the anarchist Nicolas Lazarévitch, who himself had been arrested by the Bolsheviks and expelled from the Soviet Union. Soon after this event Colomer finally left the anarchist camp and press. Although his health was quickly worsening, he now affiliated himself with the premier communist publication, *L'humanité*. Beginning in January 1928 Colomer was now mentioned as "our comrade Colomer" in its pages. In August of the same year, large commercials for a rally entitled "Contre la guerre! Pour la défense de l'U.R.S.S.!" (Against the War: For the Defense of the USSR), to be held in the Cirque de Paris, profiled Colomer as the principal speaker representing the organization Amis de l'URSS (Friends of the USSR). Colomer's newfound allegiance to communism culminated in his arrest during a communist-syndicalist rally in 1929, which in turn resulted in a few months in prison. Shortly after being released he left Paris for the last time and moved to the Soviet Union, where he died less than two years later. ·

This brings us back to where we started: Colomer's death in the winter of 1931. By that time his own periodicals had long since disappeared. His work was also no longer printed by his former comrades, the anarchists: the dramatic conversion of one of their most vocal representatives to the communist cause was viewed as an unspeakable betrayal, and his former allies now became his sworn enemies.[30] At the same time his post-anarchist writings were viewed with great skepticism by his new comrades, the communists. This decline also affected his literary reputation, since his poetry had long ago taken a back seat to his polemic writing. Thus, anarchists and communists alike quickly forgot Colomer's intellectual contribution to the anarchist movement, and the cataclysm of World War II only hastened his descent into relative obscurity.

However, it is clear from Colomer's work as well as from his life that his true legacy lies not with his late adoption of communism but with his spectacular contributions to anarchism, both in theory and in practice. Specifically, it should lie in his most important contribution, the individualism that shaped his thought and his life. This was also the opinion of the prominent, anonymously writing anarchist Ganz-Allein, who wrote in his necrology of Colomer; "He was, with effusive and lyrical plenitude, what he called 'visionary,' that is to say: himself, that is to say, 'Colomer,' that is to say, a lyrical individualist."[31] He lived his life the way that he wanted.

It is therefore appropriate that any reintroduction of Colomer to a contemporary audience should focus on his unique conception of individualism, which proved to be so inspiring to his peers. The present collection accomplishes just that by providing the reader with a comprehensive overview of Colomer's thought from the prewar era, when he edited the key avant-garde journals *La foire aux chimères* and *L'action d'art*, to his postwar polemics for *Le libertaire* and *L'insurgé*. Colomer's sustained engagement with the writings of Stirner, Bergson, and Nietzsche in many ways mark him as a precursor to the contemporary anarchist movement and as such as a voice once again worthy of our consideration. Colomer endured personal hardship, exile, imprisonment, public persecution, and controversy, but throughout the vast majority of his short life he remained true to his special brand of individualism and to a lyrical spirit that shaped his art and politics.


## OUTLOOK

As stated earlier, the aim of this publication—the first republishing of Colomer's oeuvre since his death in 1931—is to make all of these aspects of Colomer's oeuvre accessible to a wider audience, both inside and outside of academia.

Outside of academia, his extensive writing on the realpolitik of his day, as well as his subtly changing relationship to the powers of his era, can prove to be just as insightful as they are stimulating. Here is a man who, pacifistically, negotiated his way through his turbulent life and the perilous times of interwar left-wing actionism, all while extensively documenting his ever evolving thought while not shying away from any debate or controversy. Then he lived through World War I and documented the behavior of an individualist anarchist in those most trying of times. Through it all, he crafted a unique attitude that he himself called refractory: a way of life in the margins of society, somewhat parallel to it, yet free and maximally independent from it. This is as relevant as ever.

In academia, the multifaceted writings of Colomer are ripe for consideration within many of the diverse fields that he weighed in on, not only as historical documents but also as fully mature standpoints that serve as an interesting blend of the philosophical landscape of the interwar period, all while providing heaps of original thought as well. Thus, Colomer can be read in the context of not only anarchist and political theory but also wider philosophical fields, such as ethics and population ethics, civil rights, and, poignantly, epistemology and metaphysics through his brilliant reception of Bergson. Colomer's reading of Stirner and Nietzsche is similarly intriguing, since he manages to accommodate the nihilistic schools of thought emerging in Germany in the quite different French context, and even the historical French canon. But even outside of philosophy, scholars might be interested in Colomer's views regarding theater studies, art criticism, performance art, and literature studies, just to name a few. After all, Colomer considered himself a poet first and extensively wrote on contemporary theater and literature, as well as on some of the great authors of the past that he thought relevant to his time and/or aesthetic ideal (Villon, Corbière, Balzac, and Stendhal, to name just a few).

Reading and critically receiving Colomer will thus be worthwhile in a number of fields. Scholars will find productive arguments in the work of André Colomer.

## NOTES

1.  In this context, especially note Colomer's introduction to the book *Repression of Anarchism in Soviet Russia*, written by exiled Russian anarchists and translated into French by the famous exiled anarchist Volin (1882–1945). See Colomer, "Introduction," in *Répression de l'anarchisme en Russie soviétique*, ed. Groupe des Anarchistes Russes Exilés en Allemagne (Paris: Éditions de la Librairie Sociale, 1923), 3–4.

2.  See Manuel Devaldès, "André Colomer," in *Anthologie des écrivains refractaires de langue française*, ed. Manuel Devaldès (Paris: Édition de la Revue Littéraire de Primaires Les Humbles, 1927), 26.

3.  See Max Stirner, *The Ego and His Own* (1844), trans. S. T. Byinton (New York: Benjamin R. Tucker, 1907), 388–91.

4.  For very explicit examples of this synthesis, see André Colomer, "De Bergson à Bonnot: Aux sources de l'héroïsme individualiste 1. Bergson et les 'Jeunes gens d'aujourd'hui,'" *L'action d'art*, March 1, 1913, 1–2; or André Colomer, "La matière, L'esprit, et moi 3," *L'insurgé* 12 (1925), 3. For a thorough scholarly view on this marriage of Stirnerian individualism and Bergsonian intuition in Colomer, see Mark Antliff, "Revolutionary Immanence: Bergson Among the Anarchists," in *Bergson and the Art of Immanence*, ed. J. Ó Maoilearca and C. De Mille (Edinburgh: Edinburgh University Press, 2013).

5.  André Colomer, "Les poètes réfractaires 3: François Villon," *L'action d'art* 9 (1913), 1–3.

6.  See Devaldès, "André Colomer," 26.

7.  For more on Picasso's involvement in the Parisian anarchist scenes, see Patricia Leighton, *The Liberation of Painting: Modernism and Anarchism in Avant-Guerre Paris* (Chicago: University of Chicago Press, 2013).

8.    Henry Van de Velde, "Une prédication d'art," *La société nouvelle* 11 (1895): 733-44.

9.    The revolts of the Languedoc winegrowers were a nearly fifty-year-long series of tensions that escalated in the summer of 1907. Several governmental regulations and the sale of counterfeit wines had caused an increasingly desperate crisis of overproduction in the region, that would regularly escalate into open violence. See G. Martin, *Understanding Social Movements* (Milton Park, UK: Routledge, 2015), 49, and A. Smith, ed., *Terror and Terroir: The Winegrowers of the Languedoc and Modern France* (Manchester: Manchester University Press, 2016). In 1906, when Colomer witnessed one of these rebellions, all the factors that finally caused the deadly 1907 outbreak would already have been present. The sense of revolt that he saw in the "peasants" in Southern France must have truly inspired Colomer, as these revolts served as a recurring motive in his early writing. See also the *France nouvelle* of July 11, 1957, where a few local workers were asked to recapitulate the revolt fifty years after the facts.

10.   André Colomer, "L'idéalisme et l'anarchie," *L'Anarchie* 416 (1913), 1.

11.   Colomer, "L'idéalisme et l'anarchie," 1.

12.   André Colomer, "L'individualisme héroique et la guerre: En individualiste," *L'action d'art* 2 (1919), 3.

13.   Colomer, "L'individualisme héroique et la guerre," 3.

14.   Tragically, the infant Tristane, born shortly after Colomer's arrest while attempting to reach Switzerland, did not survive the war. See André Colomer, "Et *L'action d'art* renaît . . . ," *L'action d'Art* 1 (1919), 1.

15.   Guillaume Davaranche, "Colomer, André," in *Les anarchistes: Dictionnaire biographique du mouvement libertaire francophone,* ed. Marianne Enckell et al. (Paris: Les Editions de l'Atelier, 2015), 217.

16.   See Colomer, "Et *L'action d'art* renaît," 1.

17.   See Richard D. Sonn, *Sex, Violence, and the Avant-Garde: Anarchism in Interwar France* (University Park: Pennsylvania State University Press, 2010), 200.

18.   See, for instance, Colomer, "Bergson et les 'Jeunes gens d'aujourd'hui.' "

19.   André Colomer, "M. Bergson, Maître-à-penser de la 3ᵉ république," *La revue anarchiste* 13 (1922).

20.   André Colomer, "La matière, l'esprit, et moi 2," *L'insurgé* 11 (1925), 3-4.

21.   See Colomer, "La matière, l'esprit, et moi 2," 3-4.

22.   André Colomer, "La bedaine et l'esprit," *Le libertaire* 4, no. 163 (1922), 1.

23.   André Colomer, "Pour l'individu, avec le prolétariat," *Le libertaire* 4, no. 173 (1922), 1.

24.   See Davaranche, "Colomer, André," 217.

25.   See Sonn, *Sex, Violence, and the Avant-Garde*, 200.

26.   See Davaranche, "Colomer, André," 216.

27.   See Sonn, *Sex, Violence, and the Avant-Garde*, 201.

28.   André Colomer, "Notre chemin sous les étoiles," *L'insurgé* 22 (1925), 1.

29.   See, for instance, *Le libertaire* of November 3, 1927, 2.

30.   See Sonn, *Sex, Violence, and the Avant-Garde*, 198.

31.   See the appendix, "André Colomer: Apostle of the 'Action of the Arts,' or the Illusion of Lyrical Individualism."

## Acknowledgments

First and foremost, this book is dedicated to André Colomer.

I discovered his oeuvre by pure coincidence while working on my master's thesis during the lockdown spring of 2020. The translation project began, just a few days later, with the humble goal of sharing some of his ideas, which had thoroughly electrified me, with my friends. Soon after, I realized that many more people may be interested in Colomer and that the time was perhaps ripe to help awaken Colomer's ideas from a near century-long slumber.

Having nothing but time over the ensuing year, this anthology began taking shape. I need to thank the many archives and databases that made the research possible – chief among them the very helpful CIRA in Lausanne and Marseilles.

At this point, however, I still had no concrete plan for the project. The goal was an abstract notion of "paying Colomer back" for the inspiration I received from him and the wish to allow a larger audience to access and enjoy his work. How exactly, that I would figure out later.

Once I had a substantial amount of translated material ready, I reached out to Charlotte De Mille. Our ensuing correspondence changed everything: it let me figure it out. It was Charlotte's enthusiasm that made me believe I was doing something important, and it was Charlotte who pointed me the right way – with her advice and by introducing me to the right people. Charlotte has a big part to play in the fact that this book exists today.

One of the great people Charlotte put me in contact with was Dr. Lydia Goehr. Thanks to Lydia, my project was proposed, and eventually accepted, to be published as a part of the Columbia Themes in Philosophy, Social Criticism, and the Arts series. And, thanks to Lydia, I got to work with the unbelievable team at the Columbia University Press, without whom this book would never have been as elegant and thorough as it turned out to be. Specifically, I want to thank Gregg Horowitz, Wendy Lochner, Lowell Frye, and Susan Pensak for their priceless and tireless guidance through the many phases of this project.

A small personal note that I've thus far not shared with anyone at the CUP: in 1998, my father was a visiting student at Columbia University, working toward his PhD on Marcel Duchamp. A toddler then, it was on Columbia's campus that I learned to walk. To now publish my first real book here feels quite poetic.

Speaking of, a word of thanks is due to my family. To my parents, Cornelia Tietz and Hans De Wolf, and their two so different ways to see the world, the perfect synthesis of which I am. It would do no justice to express my thanks in just a few words. They know.

I also want to mention my brother, Eddy—who may be the closest living embodiment of Colomer's heroism—and my grandmother Cécile, the most unconditional supporter I will ever have.

As the book started taking shape, I relied on a number of my friends for proofreading. I specifically owe recognition to Ciara Kristensen and the irreplaceable Jon "Wholesome" Er. Also a part of this project (and many others) is my loyal brother Giorgio Millesimi, the most sensitive reader I know—not only of words.

As to the editing process, I further owe thanks to the book's anonymous early readers, who provided some very valuable pointers.

Finally, I need to express my gratitude to Mark Antliff. Working with Mark was nothing less than transformative for me: the generosity with which he took me under his wing and shared his experience was truly humbling. I can't wait to pay the trust he instilled in me forward to the next generation. His contributions to this project are immeasurable and go much further than his splendid and important foreword. Seldom have I seen so much wisdom, humility, and friendship in one individual. *Tu est une grande personne.*

And so, thanks to all the people mentioned here and many more, Colomer will be published once again. May individualists everywhere be lyrical.

## Note on the Selections

As expressed in the introduction, the scope of the present publication is limited to André Colomer's philosophical oeuvre, and specifically to his contributions in the field of individualist anarchism. To establish this selection of texts I have analyzed his publications throughout all eras of his life and determined the ones relevant to this current anthology. My intention is to offer a complete overview of Colomer's lyrical individualism: its development, all of its nuances, and its ties to Colomer's larger political and aesthetic points of view.

Colomer's work extends a bit further than that, however. For instance, he maintained several columns, of which the two most long-lived discussed weekly developments in syndicalism and a current view of the Parisian theatrical scene, respectively. A number of political articles concerning daily events also survive, though most of them, while interesting, have lost their relevance now that the facts in question lie many decades in the past. Nonetheless, a few of these columns, notably those in which Colomer departs on longer reflections into his own philosophical views, have been chosen for this collection.

Most of the notes are my own. The rare notes that Colomer did make can be found in the endnotes alongside my own, but with the signature "—A. C."

I have also included two eulogies about Colomer, both published in the year of his death. They provide good insight into his character and individualism in practice. These can be found at the very end of the volume. I have also included a dictionary of relevant words and an index of names.

## Note on the Translation

While translating the work of André Colomer, I have sought always to stay close to the original and to convey the same flair that enlivens his French. The language is refined yet coarse, poetic yet clearly marked by the anarchist and workerist slang of the era, full of wordplay and wit yet accessible and unpretentious. I gave my translation the same character and kept the original imagery as much as possible. While I made the obvious choice of substituting popular proverbs with their English equivalents, I have decided to keep some longer-winded descriptions and the syntax and word order more or less in place. The same goes for expressions: You will find the occasional *Hélas!*, *Voilà!*, or *Eh bien!* in the translation. This is done in the hope that they provide access to the exhilarating nature of Colomer's articles from an authentically revolutionary and historically thrilling era.

As to the translation of some more complex philosophical terms and concepts, I have carefully weighed each and followed conventional translations used in academic publishing to yield a faithful account of Colomer's argument. The logical structures and setups he employs are unchanged and kept identical to the original; they are also reproduced here in the same layout for additional clarity.

When it comes to slang or proverbs from the rich language of the early twentieth century that have died out in modern French, I have generally followed the advice from Alain Rey's *Le Robert: Dictionnaire historique*.

# LYRICAL INDIVIDUALISM

# PART I

# An Anarchist Poet (1907–1911)

*LA FOIRE AUX CHIMÈRES* 1 (DECEMBER 1907)

*1. Us!*

—Poets . . . Again? What an epithet! Very well then, poets; but "poets" alone. . . .
That does not suffice.[1]

We need a superb neologism that ends with the traditional "ists." Didn't the symbolists, naturalists, integralists, unanimists all also follow the school of the "ists"?

—*Eh bien!* No. You will be spared the horror of such a baroque term; we won't give you the pleasure of such a scandal! The biggest scandal would be to make us read and to make us listen.

—But who are you then, anyway?

—We are "Us," and that is all! Just some people who commit to this enormous paradox of loving life and saying so. Just some who don't scream from the top of the towers.[2] Some who will speak truthfully and sound loudly.

Wanderers who have passed through the streets and the fields, through the suburbs of the factories, and through the rocks of the highest mountains.

Madmen who have this nonsensical illusion to believe in the beauty of their vision of the world.

Monsters who pretend that beauty and happiness are not found elsewhere but in life and who engage in this fantastic dream of throwing thousands of golden chimeras into the modern sky in order, in one single burst of their illuminating wings, to remove the unhealthy fog from over it.

—Chimeras—how so?

—Oh! It won't be those mystical Chimeras, singers of superhuman ideals. Ours will sprout from our amorous imaginations of living.

As peaks of snowy illuminations, they will leap upon the high chimneys of the Faubourgs, then descend as sources of sprouting clarity, running along the dry rocks and vast quarries, down to the busy banks of the rivers in the large cities.

Their eyes filled with light, their hearts beating to the world's fever, and feeling the blood of mankind singing in their veins, their large, warm wings will chase the bad chimeras away. The chimeras of neurosis with their green eyes, the chimeras of madness with their red eyes, the chimeras with poor eyes filled with decadence, and the chimeras of cowardice with no eyes at all.

—And what will the eyes of the good chimeras be like?

—They will be large eyes full of clarity, illuminating eyes that embrace the tendencies of mankind, inspiring their joyful desires, stoking up their good hatreds and fermenting, in the bustling large cities, the thirst of living, like a generous wine in enormous carafes.


## 2. The "Visionaries"

One could, if need be, call us the "Visionaries," because we have awareness of the creative force of artistic vision. To have vision is to originally express the harmony of the world with our own individual harmony. To have vision is certainly more than to see. It is to see as one *wants* to see, with one's full education of senses and of thought.

True artists are visionaries. Visionaries believe in the beauty of their visions. They want their visions to penetrate into the awareness of others.

*They are egoists.*

But their egoism blossoms superbly in things and in individuals.

In things, because they avidly search for occasions to enrich their visions in the invigorating sources of reality. In individuals, because they force themselves to indefinitely amplify their influences. By fighting for their visions, they harmonize them marvelously with the visions of other visionaries; the vivacious beauty of their work is not endangered by this, because nothing inharmonious can have durable links with the harmonious. All that we take in from other visions becomes truly our work from the moment where we have the awareness of its harmonious integration into our vision.

*The Visionaries are "aristocrats."*[3]

The visionaries are interested in any kind of human activity; because the desire that lets them live is the desire to live in harmony and to realize the harmony that they love within them, around them too.

*The Visionaries are creators.*

The visionaries who we are have had the vision of the disappointing chaos of universal movements, of the disabilities of the so-called astral masses, of the tremendous, incoherent force of formless, unimaginable energies. The visionaries know very well that our world is solely a product of our visions. They have no illusions of the "eternal extension" of our ability to see.

*The Visionaries are aware.*

But the "Visionaries" know even better that nothing is as good for man as to *see* and to *see one humanely*.

They have experienced the sublime trance of wanting to be "the golden spark of natural light."[4]

They have understood the sincerity of superhuman follies and the hallucination of a Rimbaud who wanted to re-create himself outside of daily visions.

They have experienced the infinitely impersonal of the movement of the worlds, the drunkenness of not being. Nonetheless, there was a time when other thrills of madness had embraced them through their ancestors. They remember, through Baudelaire and Rollinat, another infinite, one where happiness slumbers.

They have known the irritating drunkenness of living within the intimate fermentation of our flesh, to feel oneself only by the friction of the skin, by the exasperation of the senses, by the yeast of daily existence, by all the little deaths that slowly consume us; to be a bad fever that sings itself, the fever of a buried man that lives at the bottom of his thrilling flesh.

Between these two infinities—dreadful chasms of reason—the Visionaries do not choose.

They do no longer feel these hallucinations clasping them with their fiery claws. Through memory, they see and they understand—and realize, in their vision, the synthesis of these two hallucinations.

*The Visionaries are synthesists.*

Held by the flesh. Ah! That we are. We proudly proclaim ourselves to be fleshly! In the flesh, we feel our link to everything that swarms about in nature, to everything that grows, to everything that dies, too; but what is death to us? Assimilation, again, assimilation to everything that ferments here, there, by the infinite.

Flesh, of course, we claim to be flesh. For it is howling in pain which sparked revolutions. For it is runaway swoons of pleasure that evoked in beings the genius of the best harmonious visions?

The flesh, matter of movement, the unrestrained fabricator of the world's incidents, the flesh that was carefully modeled by the prestigious fingers of reality that moves to create reality in its own right.

The flesh and its wonderful attractions and subtle affinities, giving life back to itself, perpetuating itself in screams of joyousness.

What fool would dare to insult it now! The flesh, we are made of, and joyously we want to proclaim and celebrate it!

*The Visionaries are of flesh.*

And thus we build the bridge, with a single arch, obviously, over the two abysses of madness.

We are also of infinite movement, we travel loudly in the big All, but in the flesh, we conserve our astral reality.

For us, the time of the metaphysics that seek to impose the same homogenous visions on all forms of energy is over. Over are also the incoherencies of the hallucinated ones who search the "homeland of shadows and vortices." Why would we want to live like "the fly, drunken off the pissotière and in love with borage,"[5] when the fly—itself!—is not interested to intoxicate itself with *our ideas?*

Therein lies our reason. It is only for us. We remember—confused but with certainty—the ancestral fights that forged it, the gasping efforts of the flesh that illuminated it; we have vision of the entire tragedy of its birth.

Our reason is there; let's follow it!

*The Visionaries are rationalists.*

Oh! Our reason, fruit of our revolting and conquering flesh; the Visionaries will be its Argonauts who dare to do everything.

We are the real artists, the creators of latent harmonies, we believe in the worth of our own visions because we know that they could only sprout out of fruitful contact between our amorous senses and vibrating matter.

We see, we see . . . But mankind will also see, because we will make sprout, upon their closed eyes, illuminations of life so sudden and so fiery that they will open their eyes, wide open, and see a transformed world.

*We truly are Visionaries.*[6]

## LIBERTARIAN AESTHETICS: CÉLESTIN MANALT, SCULPTOR OF THE PROLETARIAT

*LA FOIRE AUX CHIMÈRES* 2 (JANUARY–FEBRUARY 1908)

*I*

It was in "the land of the Gueux." In Perpignan. In 1905. In the middle of the revolt of the sons of the vineyards.[7] Through the streets, which were littered in red signposts, the impacts of drums echoed, and sudden rumors rolled through the crowds. Patrols of soldiers hammered over the high pavements. United outside in the bright July sun, the small town acclaimed the heroism of its peasants.

We, that is I and my friend Pellegrin, walked through crowds where eyes full of hatred shimmered under heavy masks, all surprised by the abrupt awakening of the countryside, of this invasion of old women dragging along their muddy, bratty children; solid little lads with determined expressions who carried their gourds and their little barrels on their shoulders.[8]

We passed by the square of the Augustins, one of those deformed little *placettes* of the provinces that are all equally cranny. All around some stopped chariots stood peasants who loudly debated in that Catalan language of whistling sounds, full of graphic swearwords. On the doorsteps stood the wives and daughters of the workers, in short dresses, with their yellow and red aprons on, and encouraged them with their brilliant smiles and their large dark eyes.

—"My friend," reprised Pellegrin, "this is rare and beautiful. These are the simple and ignorant; they can barely make themselves understood by the laborers of the north, by the revolted in the factories of Paris; and all the while, look, in full suffering, in minds that have slumbered for centuries, an admirable awakening of the large instinct of life that pushes men to revolt has manifested itself.

"Such are these crowds. *Eh bien!* I will introduce you to an artist who originated within them, who suffered all of their misery, who ennobled himself, like the crowds did, by no longer wanting to endure it—and who wants to become, by way of the force of his willing visions, the one who will enable the great acts that will free these people."

—"*Bonjour*, Manalt. Is Célestin home?" In the gray storefront of an old grocery store on the square we found a small man in the middle of a circle of listeners, all fire and nerves, shaking his tensed fists and passionately wobbling his uncovered gray head. If he hears us at all he barely hears us; all the while, in the zeal of his discourse, between two words that growl like a thunderstorm, he responded: Yes, Yes! . . . Ah! . . . My brother . . . Célestin—upstairs . . . always . . ."

We climb the stairs . . .—These are interiors that seem to inhale the passions and suffering of the ones who inhabit them. Every time that I would later hear of Célestin Manalt, I would remember this translucent ascend over the wooden staircase in that old house. With each and every overcome step, the impacts of the voices of the debates on the streets extinguished a bit more; before long it was a silent darkness that was only interrupted on every landing, where, through the open doors, appeared a glance of the wood fires from unlit kitchens where soup was being cooked, or the crying of infants being wiped, the monotonous complaining of an old woman, an entire muffled misery that one deciphered by mounting higher.

And all the way upstairs, on the last landing, we were at Célestin Manalt's.

A room of a worker from the provinces. An old bed, a few chairs, gray walls. But immediately, from the moment I entered the room and before I even saw the artist hidden behind an easel, I saw that greatness intertwined with this poor simplicity, that an interior heroism had transfigured the banality of this setting. In a shadowy corner, a plasterwork figurine stared with uniquely willing eyes; on the walls, in deep relief, fists contracted themselves, members tensed up. An entire latent symphony of outlined acts seemed to temper in the half-light of the room.

—"Manalt, I bring a friend who will understand you," exclaimed Pellegrin. "Show him your work."

Interrupting his drawing, the sculptor simply shook my hand; and I saw, as I expected, his honest artisan face in which dreamed the eyes of an artist.

—"I will show you my work, because you want it," he replied . . .

And it was a revelation of an entire oeuvre of sculpture that bloomed spontaneously out of the suffering of a people. The sculpture of a proletarian.

In the beginning, he showed me his early work. I examined it . . . Célestin Manalt anxiously followed my gaze, fearing to suffer once more the ridicule of yet another dilettante. —It was naive, coarse, and sometimes clumsy; but the will of an era, the liberation of an individual synthesized in his oeuvre.

I admired it for a while . . . and then I laid my eyes upon the artist, and I saw, within this face that was torn from suffering, such simple pride, such spiritual gravity, that I suddenly daydreamed, just by seeing him, about the poor unknown artisans of the Middle Ages who piously erected the great cathedrals.

## II

A work of art is not a copy of present-day life, because art is life altogether, past life as much as the life that is in power, life like the artist needs to create, within himself through the harmonies of his thinking, and in the minds of others through the visions summoned by his work, the way he needs to *want* and impose it with the conviction of his genius. It is in this way that art truly is an active force of creation. The artist of the genius kind uses, in his daily sensations, the ones he lived, the aspects that he shares with the people of his time, to reveal to them a new synthesis of sensations or ideas, an original vision. This is how one can explain the complete incomprehension of the masses towards the great precursors among the artists: Wagner and Debussy in music, Renoir, Raphael, Claude Monet [, Cézanne, and Picasso][9] in painting; Verlaine and Rimbaud in poetry; Rodin in sculpture, they all have been, in their beginnings, logically and necessarily over-looked. They have fortunately *surprised* the taste of the audience. They have sparked movements of outrage that have shaken up human consciousness. But this astonishment itself provoked a transformation of the common vision. With the tenacity of their will to see originally, with the force of their individuality, they have managed to convince the minds of the people, to then give them a magical illusion that makes real and normal what at first sight appeared fictitious.

But that artistic illusion, that vision does not engrave itself deep into the imag-ination of mankind and does not come to *life* if it is superficial, rigid. The con-sciousness of mankind has an eternal, infinite tendency to grow. It has a thirst for space; it has a hunger for action. The work of art that is truly creating is the work that gives it the richest sensations, the most breathtaking joy, the most irre-sistible desire to live and to create.

To meet this will of mankind, the artist also needs to surpass this will. He needs to accomplish a double miracle.

The first is a *miracle of sensitivity and enthusiasm*. The artist needs to have expe-rienced the everyday life of the people, needs to have suffered from their dreary hardships, and needs to have yearned for their chimeric hopes. He needs to know his personal ancestry, his own temperament, and needs to choose his own sphere of observation. He needs to be conscious of the immense influence of our natural impressions; he needs to know the emotionality of his contemporaries, the aspirations of his time, the daily novel of humanity, and the infinite complexity of the tangled web of human thought before he can muse about transforming human thought. He can't forget that we are from nature, that our memories and our indispensable needs tie us to matter; he needs to know humanity, its pain and its hope, its present *disharmony* and its desire for harmony; he needs to be human before he can even think about creating something human.

Only then can the artist muse about realizing the other miracle: the *miracle of will and of creation* from which a strong work will bloom.

The work of art is the least relative of our modern conceptions of "being." Metaphysical theories conceive existence as an absolute, like a standstill of motion, like a beauty with unmovable lines,[10] like a pure good, free from any blending. Modern life, with its demands and its struggles, has taught us that "being," on the contrary, consists of a plethora of accounts captured by a unique consciousness through a force of individualization. For the contemporary mind, *nothing* is absolute or isolated: anything can only exist more than any other thing if it generates more connections. The truly creating artist is the one who manages to give his work the most touching and most extensive force of evoking, so that, in the mind of men, it creates infinitely radiating concentric waves, like a stone thrown into the water.

*Enthusiastic sensibility and creating will*, these are the two perpetual miracles of the arts.

Through this study, we want to show how one can find, in the very conditions of art, the opportunity for an art for a new era; inspiring itself through the real and the renewing, with a material thought and the formidable drive of the artistic enthusiasm of medieval mysticism.

The work of the sculptor and artisan Célestin Manalt will perfectly serve us to distinguish the foundational tendencies of a libertarian aesthetic.

## III

What is the nature of Célestin Manalt's inspiration? What is his artistic temperament? From what sources did he draw the ideas that he realizes in his works?

Manalt is a laborer of art. He is a proletarian, a true modern. He did not endure the artificial sway of the bourgeois half-educations. His brand-new soul has excellently ripened the good seeds of reality. He has not come across this obsession with antiquity that inundates our squares and our museums with dead allegories that lost their sense; far from the écoles and the amphitheaters, he has simply lived the painful life of a worker, but he kept his eyes wide open to the spectacles of everyday life.

In all eras, art is an expression of the fight of human consciousness against the forces that want to impose themselves upon it as destiny. The periods of art are like acts of an immense tragedy: the tragedy of the mind, conquering its liberty.

All the art of antiquity is necessarily and admirably filled with trances of man under the domination of the gods, with the torments of the gods under the complete control of destiny. For the imagination of the Greeks and the Latins, the statues of Zeus, Venus, the Vulcans, Mercury were no simple allegories, no cold allusions. They expressed realities that strongly lived in the consciousness of the people; they corresponded to passions, to suffering, to wills; they provoked true emotions, by shaking up the beliefs of men, by evoking visions of an entire world of illusions through which the people illustrated their invariable belief in a world of harmonies.

The times of staunch cathedrals followed, when the artists of medieval times ingeniously accomplished the feat of giving form to the impetus of Christian souls toward a sky of beauty, and to the terrible nightmares where their faith fought against the temptations of the flesh. And it was again a living art, drawn from the fertile sources of the real. The naves rise supremely toward the sky, but they are heavy of sins, charged with bewildering of terrestrial suffering. The gargoyles grimace with their tortured faces and, leaning down toward the dark earth, seem to still maintain the harmonious impulses of the towers toward the blue sky. The mind of the bad, the daemonic temptations have replaced the "fatum," the "anangke."[11] The soul of the people is tormented again by an anonymous and imposing force, it fights, and the art of the Middle Ages expresses the superhuman effort of an entire crowd of avid consciousnesses to rip itself from the burning grip of the clasps of hell.

But these are the modern times. The gods have deserted the skies. The eternal imagination of mankind no longer transports its dreams for the better into the faraway clouds. Full of pride, it is molding itself a future of harmony where every human would be a God. Science reveals to us the universal bustling, the dynamicity of the natural; it convinces us of the unique beauty of life, by unveiling to us our role in the evolution of beings. By returning us to nature, it gives us the will to be the most intense and influential of all natural powers. The individual, by learning that he is but a hotbed of action, feels the desire to let this hotbed immortally shine and shiver within him.

The modern human has the will to utilize his powers, to reap all the fruits that life can ripen, to conquer his terrestrial happiness, since he knows very well that he can receive none of the others.[12] But death and its powers, also thrown from the heavens, pursue him on earth. There still are consciousnesses that haven't sensed the beauty of individual will: they are imprisoned in the bastions of prejudice and metaphysical ideas. As forces of ignorance and ugliness, they oppose the past of domination to the future of liberty. These are the new Gods of the present time: Society, the State, Authority, the Law; this is the new destiny that guides them: capital. But the will of the people managed to overthrow the powers of the sky; it will surely overthrow the ones on earth, too. It hardened during the fight against the gods, it is strong today from having suffered so much, and it only needs a good impetus of enthusiasm and love to break the old idols of the people, to clear the artificial obstacles and to no longer know anything but the great and good fight for Life. Not a fight against men, but against the sole natural necessities of water, air, and earth.

Célestin Manalt's work is an illustration of this modern era, shaped by the evolution of human consciousness. His art wants to express the sentiments of a generation of work and revolt that frees itself, painstakingly but full of pride, from the grip of false social necessities.

Because Célestin Manalt is truly the laborer of his work. His sculptures are sober and simple like he is, almost rugged. But their entire power is in this simplicity; they are but an act; however, this act is tied to so many memories of suffering and fighting, to so many human aspirations, that it seems to illuminate, in a single strike, the entire life of a people, the entire future of a generation.

Célestin Manalt has lived the lackluster and burdensome life of the intelligent proletarian. Before knowing the pain of the isolated artist, he has undergone the pitiful torments of the worker at length, steadily constrained to tedious daily tasks. He spent thirty years painfully toiling away to gain his bread.

And yet he felt, within himself, the tumultuous wills of creation and harmony. Despite the hardships of his work he spent every evening reading beautiful pages that illuminated his enthusiasm: Zola, Mirabeau, Philippe. . . . Further, he knew the enchantments of music and, on his own, during the coldest nights, patiently convinced as he was, taught himself to play the violin and improvised tunes that would make him forget the pains of the next morning. But the morning would always return, worse than ever, after the dreams of the night. Thus, he learned to hate what repulsed him; he *wanted* the art where he expressed his revolt against the anonymous forces that affected him. He wanted to be a sculptor. He understood that nothing was as hard and evoking as figures made in stone. He remembered the ignited artisans of the Middle Ages, who, secretly laborious and enthusiastic as he was, sculpted their horror of hell and their desire for heaven into stone.

His time come, he now wants to be the great worker of the good hatreds and the conscious dreams of the modern times, the one who erects unforgettable statues sketching the acts of suffering and revolt of the oppressed.

## IV

Three great works epitomize Célestin Manalt's artistic temperament.

Behold the *Méprisé*.[13] Wildly planted on his fine, still standing legs, a child from the Faubourgs, with a nervous body, uplifts his pale face in which eyes of suffering gleam under a willful forehead. In his prominent jaw, he clamps his teeth; all the while, in an admirable movement of hindered defense and repressed hate, his bony little fists, on the ends of his childlike arms, seem to tremble in muted anger. The left arm crosses his chest, and this aggressive motion takes in his collarbone and pushes his shoulder forward. The right arm, jammed against his flank, is the act that restraints the anger and gives a silent majesty to the ripening hatred.

Manalt didn't find the inspiration for his *Méprise* among the models of the academy. It was in the streets; at the gates of the factories where work is being refused, in the processions of strikes, in despair, in the sleazy promiscuity of the attics of the Faubourgs, in the daily misery where the soul of the children of the people astonishingly ripens if it doesn't grow bleak. A stubborn forehead, an outthrust jaw, and the clenched fists, what do you presage us, little scorned one? . . . Will you be the assassin who leaps from a dark corner of a grim road, blinded by his suffering, onto a random, unknown passer-by? Will you be the one who disregards crushes and whom anger intoxicates? We don't know it, we don't know; your forehead is quite hard, your fists are quite clenched! And meanwhile your eyes, full of bitterness, seem to see further than your own anger; your small eyes are wrinkled so bizarrely on your contracted cheeks! Maybe they remember having seen other scorned ones; maybe they dream of an entire world of scorned ones scorning what scorned them, all straightening their backs and lifting their fists—and taking, one beautiful day, what is kept from them. Maybe they dream of all of that, of justice and of beauty! We don't know, we do not know . . .

Behold the *Prostituée*. It is also a figure from the streets; a heroine of this tragedy of life that the artisan-sculptor wants to evoke. But here the pain is not muted. It is poor suffering that cries out its pain, in all naivety.

A woman, half-naked, disheveled, fallen onto her knees, crushed on the floor, desperately stretching toward the sky, like a flag that calls to the revolt, an immense arm on whose end a fist trembles, full of menace.

*Le méprisé* and *La prostituée* are two works that characterize the truly human, truly modern temperament of Célestin Manalt. They are moving realizations of a consciousness that was developed in the dumps of our contemporary society, on the daily sufferance of this fight for life; they express a new period of combat between man and the anonymous forces of oppression; they continue the great tradition of art that glorifies the will of the individual, clearing away the mighty empire of evil idols of the past.

A divinity, more fearsome than the Greek "anangké" or the mystic Satan troubles this new art. It is a God who does not content Himself with reigning over the mind of people but who also rules over their flesh, over their stomach. He does not decide the destiny of the future world, but destiny in everyday life. He does not impose damnation upon the dead but upon the living; he does not bind his faithful with the horrors of hell or with qualms of conscience but with grueling toils, perspirations of physical effort, fear of impending blows, animalization of people, hunger, and the horror of life.

Célestin Manalt has sculpted acts of suffering and revolt in stone, acts that earmark once more the beauty of human consciousness and individual will, as well the liberating force of the arts which, and only which, can create the human who is truly worthy of living.

Would that be what the visionary artist believes the future paradise to be, one in which mankind, freed from evil genies, can peacefully taste absolute happiness? No. His mind is filled with a human, natural philosophy that perpetually reminds him of the strong attachment of man to the earth. He knows that our entire being owes its development to the fruits of this earth, that our bodies are a product of its making, and that our mind itself owes its capacities of reason and logic to its incessant contacts with its natural needs. Like the stoics of antiquity, we do not distinguish the things that depend on us from the things that do not. But we have expanded the empire of our will. We do, today, no longer need any necessities apart from the material necessities that physical life gives us and that can cause our death. These need not revolt us. Nevertheless, mankind needs to take note of them; if we free ourselves from the false necessities of divinity and society, it is to reserve all resources to its demands, all forces of our bodies to the serene conquest of the true necessities of this nature that we only manage to beat by clutching its infinite richness, comprehending it, and by becoming part of it once more.

This sane natural philosophy finds its expression in Célestin Manalt's third main work: *Man and Earth*.

Imagine, in a deep trench of the earth, something like a formidable plant. A man who has both the resigned and proud attitudes of a peasant at work. His head lowered, he hustles, like an ox tied to a plough; in the effort, his rump juts out, his neck swells up and his shoulder blades protrude. On the left, he is taken, encased by the nourishing earth; there his body forms but a frightening block with her, and the bottom sinks into it like the root of a tree. To the right, with a push of his arm, thrown forward, and his leg, stretched backward, all his muscles tensed up in vigorous effort, he superbly frees himself. But it is in vain; he can force all he wants, he is taken, he belongs to the earth. His eyes, fixated onto the floor in a grave and voluntary expression, show that he understands. In reality, he needs no other reason to live than to become the most harmonious of the products of the earth. He will no longer attempt to muster up a future life in the world of the gods. He will no longer have the stupid pride to live above the invigorating passions, to scorn the act and to contemplate, indifferently, the joys and the sufferings. But he will want to, with the zeal of the most beautiful tree of the world, feel the push of all of his best lifeblood, draw all the elements of his terrestrial happiness in with all his natural powers, infinitely hear the powerful roots that tie him to matter, so that the leaves from his gigantic branches can simmer at the caresses of the winds and the golden heat of the sun. Man will then, out of his thought and his art, make the glistening flowers of this harmonious vegetation.

## LIBERTARIAN AESTHETICS: DOWN WITH DEATH!

*LA FOIRE AUX CHIMÈRES* 3 (MARCH–APRIL 1908)

*I. The Unnerved*

In modern amphitheaters, under the decomposing day that falls over their tarnished glass panes, I have seen young people avidly listen to the recitals of old men, of which the speech alone seemed to extend an inextricable weight of grief onto their hearts.[14] But I wanted to listen; and, I convinced myself that these children wallowed in the moldiness of their thoughts, that they gave all the energy of their existence to the lamentable recitals of these moribund elders in adoration of the dead things of antiquity. —And thus my eyes already thought they could see, through their soft and pale flesh, their skeletons delineate in these slumping bodies, while the atmosphere of the rooms suddenly dissolved the bland and mordant odors that are concentrated in mortuaries or tombs.

I have visited small chapels where the aesthetes with plated hair, pale and jewel filled hands and phosphorescent, fevered eyes fluster themselves. In them, I have seen the horror of flesh that feels itself shudder, very skillfully, in artificial days. I have tasted the annoyance of the senses, swooning to the frictions of haunting music. The poor, fully naked and pink love of the naive legends was transformed into a lecherous being, asexual, monstrous, and catlike, of which the magical and infernal nostrils emptied brains. And we heard strange speeches, confused harmonies, and stuttered words; —music of madness grating the nerves of young men and reverberating in echoes of hysteria in the minds of women; —a wind of incomprehension breathing fumes of opium and ether over the nascent generations; mixing the smell of flesh and the odor of incense.... The God Neurosis let his worshippers sing.[15]

Meanwhile the tiles of the small chambers trembled to the audible rumblings of a large autobus; outside the screams of Paris spouted like rockets to the sun. But the windows were closed, and the curtains were well sealed. To the flickering of candles or braziers, in attractive alcoves, it seemed to be the wake before one, or more, painful agonies. Oh, yes! We did die slowly but surely of a voluntary death, in this hunt for the sensations of which our youth made its own quarry, where the refinement of enjoyment would bring onto estranged flesh, the unforgettable friction of death.

It was a cruel rage to deny oneself the beauty of life, a feverish thirst of sickening passions, a morbid and criminal fantasy of becoming the artist of one's own suffering. The poets and the musicians found epileptic rhythms and aphrodisiac music to describe the exquisite joy of feeling the frail limbs of young girls crack on one's torso, divine marriages in the bottoms of coffins, and the "unique" beauty of a kiss from Ephebe.

I saw poor little bakers and charming little girls curl up to these unnerving rhymes, I saw them leave their baskets and their boxes in the street and climb, with beating hearts, on all fours, as if they were ascending to paradise, the stairways that led to the "little chapels." I saw handsome guys, with eyes full of the sky, and beautiful girls, trembling in their kidneys, following the calling that the Sirènes-Gouges and the Faune-Ephebes screamed out from the bottom of their red alcoves. I have seen flesh that was luminous of joy and eyes glimmering of a sunny desire to live, I have seen them avidly close the door of life, of the streets, and the fields. And, outside on the pavement, lifting their noses, their mouths distorted in passion, crying and screaming children whom their mothers had forced to come here waited in front of the closed facades, their desire to taste this happiness devouring them.

But after a morning of sleet, once in early March, a blast of wind and sun beat open the shutters, shattered the windows and busted the curtains, and, under the great, calm day, while the last gusts of opium and ether were scattered, I saw this lamentable spectacle: white as dead faces in which the illusionless eyes were on the verge of extinguishing, poor flesh on which the sun found no more friction, —bodies with broken nerves like violins of which the cords had been cracked. Thus I finished the work started by the gust of wind; with strikes of my fists I opened up the casement windows, and, tilted towards the street, toward the high chimneys of the Faubourgs, toward the roofs of the joyous city, I screamed from the top of my lungs:

"*A bas les morts!*"[16]


## II. The Cooled Down

It was July 1, 1907. I disembarked on the Quai d'Orsay, coming home from the Basque provinces. For months, I had lived the beautiful illusions that radiated in the *méridionaux*, in the southern hearts. I had experienced the monstrous beauty of calm marches of mystery through bustling cities. From high up on the ramparts that elevate over the southern city gates, I had seen, in an impetus of dust all along the white street, the heavy chariots upon which the conquerors stacked their bread. Then I had heard the brutal cadence of the walk of the infantrymen, the impatient stamping of the marching squadrons, the cries of rage and the shots of guns, then the howling of pain. . . . I had seen gritty faces pass by, in which the eyes, burning like a fever, seemed to contain the sun, —the mugs of elder women of which the old, wooden traits, that had long been frozen in place, suddenly animated again in sneers of hate, —and the heads of children, of which the wrinkly foreheads and tensed-up jaws gave away a scary and painful maturity. I had seen the monstrous muzzles of armed men who enjoyed themselves in their murdering gallops and horribly chuckled while cleaning the blood off their sabers in the hair of their mounts.[17]

Finally, on a beautiful, star-filled evening, in the middle of the hurrahs and the chants that erupted like around a children's dance, I saw the palace of the master go up in flames, in a gigantic fire of joy, of which the flames appeared to brush the sky.[18]

I still had a blazing heart from the memories of these epic moments, and here I was, finding my smiling Paris again, just as I left her, with her buzzing streets under a sky of blond smoke.

It was a Sunday. On the Seine, the *bateaux-mouches* passed like rockets of joy, carrying their precious cargo of blonde hair and bright corsets toward Meudon and Suresnes. On the shores, among the shoppers and the cranes, some kids frolicked around in the water, raising their soaking underpants over their pink tights; and some young artists, sitting on stacked timber with their canvasses between their legs, balanced, in some sparkling tones of youth, some fugitive sketches of landscapes and bridges.

I followed the river all along the quays. Paris slowly seized my being, rolled my mind at the discretion of its distractions, and dispersed my thoughts to the four winds of its streets. With my nose in the book boxes, I snooped around for a while; then, in sentimental contemplation, I was surprised to suddenly find myself face to face, between the basket of a baker and the box of a dressmaker, with a child who "had lost his mother."[19] A little confused, I managed to escape, to find myself once more, just about a minute later, on the Place Saint Michel, surrounded by a group of ambulant con artists. With their mocking voices they psalmodied me a complaint, and a family of laborers on their promenade, a couple of grocers in their blouses and with gigolettes in their hair, consciously took over the refrain of the song that ended in these stupid rhymes:

> *Parisians, my friends, we must cry over*
> *The fate of the poor winegrower . . .*

It struck me like a violent gust of memories, and with a shrug of my shoulders I left. I took up the path to Montmartre where I hoped to find my precious friend Anarchist Pan and his big heart, throbbing with life and a spirit of superb convictions. On the corner of the Châtelet, I fell into the arms of Mr. Nirvana.

Mr. Nirvana is a big, red-headed guy, with pink cheeks and blue eyes. It is rare to see him in moving masses, and when he mingles with them, on celebratory days or in the nights of riots, his rosy cheeks keep their perfectly rose color and his blue eyes their impeccable blue, but the edges of his strong lips move into a contemptuous smile of arrogant irony. Under his round skull and his short-shaved hair much more considerable things happen than the accidents that torment most people.[20] Mr. Nirvana's spirit is a remarkable reflection of the chaotic immensity of the world. He is one of the rare geniuses who was born, by I don't know what sacrilege of the poor love of our contemporaries, with the vocation of a God who does not believe in the existence of His work and who enjoys the spectacle of His own dissolution.

Mr. Nirvana displays a certain curiosity toward me. Without a doubt I amuse him with my disorderly acts of someone who loves life, because every time he meets me, I see the edges of his strong lips imperceptibly move in the composure of his face, for his immutable smile.

For that reason I know that on that day I had to have the effect on him that a new year's doll has in the eyes of a four-year-old child. There I arrived, during the heat of midday, overly excited by natural enthusiasm, looking for a heart in which I could discharge my surplus of imagination. . . . And I met him! The springs of the toy were wound up: Mr. Nirvana would be amused.

—"My friend," he began, "you are coming without a doubt from having tasted the exquisite joys of the superior irony of the spectacle of a riot in the land of the Tartarins. Last year you arrived here from Béziers, during the same time of year, and you entertained me, if you remember, with the recital of the performance of the little God who was called Castelbon de Beauchostes.[21] This year, it must be said, the character has changed; Marcelin Albert is the name of the big little God, but it is still mere performance; instead of happening in the arena, they happen in the street, that is the only difference, isn't it—?"[22]

I would no longer contain my outrage. —"Mr. Nirvana, you have a heart of stone," I screamed. "You aren't worthy of a life that is this beautiful in its impulsive effervescence; you think you can see everything, but you see nothing.". . .

The sneer of eternal irony dug itself deeper into the corners of his lips. Mr. Nirvana let me ramble along all I wanted. Without warning me, he made me walk back the way I came. We turned our back to the attractive animation of the boulevards and to the sunny joys of the landscapes of the Seine. We were at the foot of the Panthéon.

—"Have you ever ascended the tower?" he brusquely asked.

—"My faith, no!" I responded, dumbstruck by the unexpected banality of the question.

"*Eh bien!* We will climb up to its top."

Mr. Nirvana scaled the steps of the peristyle, blindly leading me past the sunlit frescos of the Puvis de Chavannes and dragging me to the cold humidity of the never-ending staircase of the tower. He walked up to them, with an even step, resolutely, almost solemnly. For a moment he halted under the daylight that passed through an opening, and I was seized with emotion by the strange expression in his eyes, which were even more implacably blue than usual. He ascended, in silence, in a dry, mechanical movement of his strong legs, and suddenly, on top of the tower, under the impeccable sky of midday, he stood before me with the rigid attitude of an inflexible statue of fatality.

But the statue spoke.

—"Let's contemplate," he said, "the stupid incoherence of this poor humanity. It wants to stir us up with the spectacle of its revolutions, and it builds towers from which we can no longer hear the murmuring of men.

"Ah, you are, dear friend, a lover of Paris and her songs? . . . Behold the city; we only ascended a few meters into the air, and it is already, in our eyes, but a confused mass of stones. See the river where you go to cradle your nostalgia, you and your Basques! It is a puddle of dirty water between black sidewalks. —Ah! Truly, there is the cathedral, of which the bell towers look, sometimes, like the eyes of the people or like prayers crossing the sky. . . . Don't they look now as if they were thrown from the top of this tower, and that they lamentably crashed onto earth? —Ah! And there are the monstrous palaces of the kings, the Louvre, the Tuileries; the triumphant arches of the emperors, the monuments of democracy; but look from up here how flat they are, how small and short they are. . . . Finally, behold the Faubourgs where your revolutions break off, where what you call the modern power grumbles. You can blink with your eyes, but there they are: There are Montmartre, Montrouge, Belleville, Ménilmontant, Pantin. . . . Are you looking for your great chimneys of the factories, the cathedrals of labor, as you call them? Everything is whipped out from here, everything disappears in the same way, we are on top of the tower, and we can only see stone, lots of little piles of little stones scattered on the floor.

"Ah! Are you trying to listen to the songs of Paris? What foolishness! . . . There are no more songs; the stones are mute, and we are no longer in the land of illusions. We have barely ascended a few meters into the air, and we already feel the natural indifference of the elements that pass and that evolve, without knowing the decay of joy and of pain"—

But for a while already I had let him speak without paying attention.

I had gained interest in a nest of swallows that hung in a cornice of the tower. Our arrival had frightened a little world that now tottered and squeaked with all the power in their little wings and their little beaks.

—"Mr. Nirvana," I said to him quietly, "I do not want to insinuate that you are deaf; but if you aren't blind, lift your eyes over your head. You are not yet high enough in the air, to my liking. We no longer hear the songs of mankind, that is right, but we already start hearing the ones of little beings who perhaps do not know about the decay of joy and of pain, but who certainly feel, just as well as we can, if not more, the spoils of joy and the torments of pain. It is, in all simplicity, this noisy bird nest, suspending from a stone on top of the tower that will offer you a response in my place. Listen to the squeaks of these tiny creatures that ask for a beakful of food, the alarming cries of the mother who defends them, the joyful flapping of the wings of those who fly off. All these natural noises, all these baffled murmurs show you the simple beauty of life, the joy of the act, the youth of these beings who are drunk on their works. They also have their illusions; they believe in their songs, and, like the people down there in their piles of stone, it is in their nests that they keep their reasons to sing.

"Higher up than your tower, you will still find beings that will teach you the joy of life. I have clambered up the high tops of the Pyrenees where the heaps of arid rocks made me think of chaos; from the summits of those naked tops, I have contemplated the high sea of the mounts that hoist their formidable, mute waves toward the Azure Coast in the impeccable sky. More than you, I have thus mused about the vanity of the human existences that hurry around at the bottom of the valleys, between two folds of the earth's crust, under the perpetual menace of the slightest cosmic movement. But I have seen butterflies fly about the precipices, and they still amaze me with the drapery of their wings; I have seen troops of wild Chamois bouncing around from top to top in the abysses, dismissive of the emptiness and the immensity; and I have found under my feet, stretched out on their rocks, some lizards that blissfully took their great baths of sun.

"And thus I have remembered that living beings stick to the environments in which they have created their strongest reasons to live; that the consciousness of mankind and the instinct of the animal are most of all products of the conditions of their existence; that they were, before anything else, forces of life that rendered only those accidents of nature to be true and beautiful that most perfectly harmonize with the useful play of their actions. I have seen that beauty and truth are only sentiments that mankind uses to express its joy of collecting bouquets of memories of landscapes in nature, bouquets of phenomena and discoveries that, since their childhood, have alimented their will and illuminated their heart to give them the force to live."

—"Illusionary beauty!" screamed Mr. Nirvana. "The truth of a moment, thrown out of the window for the poor, narrow imagination of beings that believe in the importance of their ephemeral task in a world that is itself but a fragment of the infinite."

—"Animals, surely, have neither metaphysics nor morals of any kind, Mr. Nirvana; they do not search further than their own joy, they do not know any other task than the one of living as comfortably as possible. But they know how to accomplish this task. They perfectly understand the necessity of living according to their own nature, of putting their act in accordance with the needs of their organism, of believing in the beauty of the things that permit them to be born and to persist. You are right, Mr. Nirvana, when you compare our riots, our revolutions, our great societal efforts to the obscure hurrying of a colony of ants under a patch of earth, or to the imperceptible evolutions of microbes in the air; in the chaotic immensity of the worlds, they are certainly each as insignificant as the next one; but if we think that mankind, like the ants and like the microbes, finds its only reasons to live in these movements, and that they all are, in hurrying as they do, looking for bread and light, on the conquest of life, *eh bien!* Don't you find that these imperceptible movements take a moving grandeur in our eyes, then? They might be futile illusions for the salt of whatever superior philosophy that contemplates the vanished worlds; but surely, if one has rejoiced and suffered among the men on earth, if one has given a bit of one's own heart to life, one can affirm without any doubt that these illusions that radiate strong enough to illuminate the entire existence of a living being and give it the will to create are generally superior to your sterile ones."

—"*Hélas!* my poor friend," exclaimed Mr. Nirvana with a prophetic voice, "a day will come when everything that you will have created will collapse; the earth will crumble in an accident of dissolution of worlds; the work of mankind will lamentably melt away, and life itself will extinguish off the surface of our globe."

—"Certainly you are quite the modern thinker," I responded, "and you will be shocked if your ideas were ever to be considered obsolete. *Eh bien*, pity yourself. I think that your philosophy hails entirely from two very old cults, which already torment the mind of poor, old metaphysicians for centuries. You are the unconscious admirer of these two scholastic deities that have the name of the 'universal idea' and the 'idea of the eternal'; your mind has developed under the magic of the mystical hymns that all philosophers sing in their honor. For a long time now, you have lived in the deceiving illusion of an absolute ideal that would impose itself upon the infallible reason of men. You are born, Mr. Nirvana, with the vocation of a sage of antiquity. But life sometimes holds strange contradictions. It has wanted you to be born two hundred years too late. It made you know about modern sciences; it has revealed the history of geological upheavals to you, the evolution of the species, the transformations of the societies, the diversity and the contradictions of religious beliefs and of metaphysical doctrines, the utilitarian tendencies of the human spirit. But you kept the cult of the universal and the eternal in your heart, the love of the absolute that your forefathers had bequeathed to you. Still exalted to the memory of an ideal and intangible reason that you have learned to respect in the holy books of metaphysics, you have never wanted to believe in our poor human reason, that simply flows out of the spirit of men under the irresistible push of their natural needs and of accidental circumstances; you have scorned it as a 'capacity' that the scholars could analyze like a chemical product of which they can discover multiple transformations.

"We are more modern than you, Mr. Nirvana. If at all, then the metaphysical ideas have barely skimmed our action-loving spirit. We love life exactly because it changes; because it takes elusive forms, because it permits our spirit to indefinitely modify itself.

"We are proud to consider our reason as a product of the conditions of life, like a savory fruit of nature that draws its life sap from the same wealth of air and of ground that aliments the great trees in the forests and the lush vegetables in the fields. We know good and well that it is no superior essence; every one of us feels it live within them. It is no static and unchanging either; every time we think, it changes its form. Depending on the wood that the lost travelers in the mountains light up at night, the flames of their fires color the moonless landscapes differently. But they know to profit from the glimmer to orient them and to find the right route, as long as the fires burn.

"It is flames like that which life lights up in each one of our consciousnesses. They do not all burn in the same way; some enlighten the right better than the left, some light best ahead and others behind. It is never perfect clarity, but what do we care! That only makes the route more picturesque. We walk a little adventurously; and groups of travelers, in which we mutually aid each other with our glow, get founded. There are some who have a more brilliant clarity. They leave alone and dare to venture into unknown trails, in virgin forests full of shadows, from where they sometimes return to guide their companions.

"Ah! I know so well that one starless night gushes of wind will come to blow out the flames that illuminate the travelers on the great obscure route; I know well the shadows will take over the illusionary landscapes from the carriers of the torches. But, again, what do we care! Let's walk ahead. That does not stop us from seeing in the night!

"The glimmers of hope that shine in the hearts of the people have not yet been extinguished. They are neither universal nor eternal, Mr. Nirvana, but they have an otherwise precious quality: they manage to give to mankind its love for life. Our minds no longer torture themselves trying to find a morality that should elevate the ideal of its absolute foundations into the sky. We do not see the need of our ways of life having to be universally recognized for them to be true. We no longer ask ourselves whether they could be conserved in all their purity for all of eternity. We no longer want to establish perfect 'ethics' nor 'demonstrations of correct morals'; we want to make mankind happy. It suffices, to believe in the value of a revolution or of a social reorganization, that it will content the generations of our era. We are modern and utilitarian. We merely joke about whether our works crumble or collapse in a thousand years, as long as their construction has succeeded in making us happy, us and those whom we love.

"You, Mr. Nirvana, call the reason of mankind a transient illusion. *Eh bien*, I concede to that definition. The illusion that we love and that we strive to enlarge to make it triumph belongs to an era. Other men will come who will create different ones, different beings and different worlds will arise, and each bringing their new illusions with them; those will be *forces of life* that will be consumed in the immense movement of worlds.

"Meanwhile, we can anticipate a day in which all lights in the universe will be extinguished, where the *forces of life* will no longer find nourishment on the dried up heavenly bodies, where life, despite its transformations and its adaptations, can no longer illuminate enriching experiences. But then we won't be anymore; the human will has no reason to be preoccupied with an era in which all reasons to live would have disappeared.

"In reality, Mr. Nirvana, your heart is not yet ripe for those times. Your heart still possesses fruitful illusions that make you believe in life. If you had the courage to scorn mankind and to blasphemize the little houses that have seen your childhood, it is only because you have the certitude to find them again once you descend from this tower.

"On one moonless evening in the mountains, I have experienced the horror of immense nothingness. The sun had plunged the mountaintops into deep red during long hours of sundown; I had seen the valleys engulfed into deep chasms of silent shadows, and then everything was buried in the night. And there, I thought of you and your fellow kin, Mr. Nirvana, those of which the mind wallows on tower tops, who stand tall amidst the cities to mock its little houses; and I asked myself whether you had ever ascended to tops of faraway mountains where one quickly feels the inextricable, instinctive, bestial anguish of solitude invading and overwhelming one.

"But look. The swallows are coming home. . . . They have flown over the city and the fields all day. Their little birdy soul unconsciously filled itself with the chants of nature; and they return all simmering of life, all drunken of clarity. The swallows are coming home. . . . Around their nests, tonight, they will express their joy of life in joyous songs that their offspring will learn. Some of them, the riskier ones, have been further away in their fantastic voyages, and those, coming back panting and by feverishly batting their wings, will sing even louder and longer tonight, to delight their companions.

"Mankind, Mr. Nirvana, is a bit like these swallows. They need to exhilarate in light and sing, loudly, the joy of life in their houses. Some also fly higher and go further in mysterious voyages to unknown regions. But they always need to come home to their little houses, like the swallows to their nests, fully out of breath, heart beating, but the soul loaded with a plentiful harvest of new illusions that they will distribute among mankind.

"Stay, if you prefer, on top of your tower, Mr. Nirvana.

"I will redescend to be among the people.

"Like the voyaging swallows, my soul is full of new songs. I come from the land of vast illusions, and I bring these to the pasture of hearts that lack them. On the modern wings of steam I return, simmering with memories of the noble, avidly happy struggles of the Basques. I have heard, there in the land of the sun, unique calls to revolt, hymns that celebrated the right to live. I want my songs to be fully inspired by them tonight, and that they might bring the hate of shameful miseries we endure to the hearts of the Faubourgs, along with a desire for natural joy and the will to create a harmonious existence gushing out of the clear dream of our fruitful minds."

### NOTES

1. This article was the opening of *La foire aux chimères* and, as the title suggests, it served to set the tone of the newly formed radical journal. That Colomer was chosen to write it proves the esteem that was had for the then twenty-one-year-old poet and that his aesthetic individualism was a core tenet to him from the very start of his literary life.

2. The phrase "From the top of the towers" is a reference to a poem with the same title by Colomer which appeared side by side with this manifesto in the first issue of *La foire aux chimères* in December 1907. The poem describes a view of Paris from a fictional tower that rises five hundred meters over the city, a height at which the author may be far from the daily misery of his hometown, but describes it looking lifeless, its many stones appearing as a graveyard, while he further laments that he can't hear her songs anymore. A few months later, Colomer would employ a strikingly similar image in his article "A bas les morts!" (Libertarian Aesthetics: Down with Death, in this anthology). There the image is presented in more detail by way of a dialogue between Colomer and a certain Mr. Nirvana. From the top of the Panthéon Mr. Nirvana praises the distance and vantage point he has overlooking the city, while Colomer focuses on the many small details that the height alienates them from and eventually decides to descend from the tower as quickly as possible.

3. See the theory of aristocracy in Lacaze Duthiers: the human ideal of art. —A. C.

4. Rimbaud, *A Season in Hell*. —A. C.

5. A *pissotière* is an early twentieth-century public open-air toilet. The entire quote is from Arthur Rimbaud's *A Season in Hell.*

6. For more see Gérard de Lacaze Duthiers, *L'ideal humain de l'art*, originally published in 1896. In it Lacaze Duthiers outlines an individualist concept in which the "artistocrat" shapes his life like an artwork . This idea is, of course, quite close to Colomer's early work: in fact, both Lacaze Duthiers and Colomer are seen as cofounders of the aristocracy movement. See Joseph Peterson, "Gérard de Lacaze-Duthiers, Charles Duthiers, Charles Péguy, and Edward Carpenter: An Examination of Neo-Romantic Radicalism Before the Great War," MA thesis, Clemson University, 2010, 8.

7. Here Colomer refers to the revolt of the Languedoc winegrowers, a nearly fifty-year-long series of tensions that exploded in the summer of 1907. A number of regulations had caused an increasingly desperate crisis of overproduction in the region that would regularly escalate into open violence. See Greg Martin, *Understanding Social Movements* (Milton Park, UK: Routledge, 2015), 49, and Andrew W. M. Smith, *Terror and Terroir: The Winegrowers of the Languedoc and Modern France* (Manchester: Manchester University Press, 2016). In 1905, when Colomer witnessed one of these flareups, all the factors that finally caused the deadly 1907 outbreak would already have been present. The sense of revolt that he saw in the "peasants" in southern France must have truly inspired Colomer, inasmuch as these revolts were a recurring motive in his early writing. See also the *France nouvelle* of July 11, 1957, where a few local workerists were asked to recapitulate the revolt fifty years after the fact.

8. In the context of this article, this idiosyncratic passage can be read as a metaphor for the generational suffering of the people (the old women) and the young, newly awakened refractionary spirit (the bratty children).

9. Cézanne and Picasso did not appear in the 1908 original publication of this article but were added to the list in the 1922 reprint.

10. This is a nearly direct quote from the poem "La beauté" in *Les fleurs du mal*, likely a reference to Baudelairian conceptions of beauty. See Baudelaire, *Les fleurs du mal* (Paris: Librairie Générale Française, 1999 [1857]), 66.

11. *Fatum* is Latin for destiny, fate, or lot. *Anangke* is the Greek personification of inevitability, compulsion, or necessity.

12. Specifically, the Modern who knows he is a modern. —A. C.

13. A literal translation would yield something like "scorned one," or despised one.

14. The "young people" are a play on Agathon's "Young People of Today." Agathon was the pseudonym of two nationalist writers, Alfred de Tarde and Henri Massis. Published in 1913, *Young People of Today*, a famous nationalist pamphlet that sparked hate against the Germans, was their most notorious work. For Colomer the text and its authors are the personification of the revival of traditionalist, militarist, and nationalist views in French prewar society. As such he often refers to Agathon and his "young people," directly and indirectly, to stigmatize reactionary positions. In this specific passage, the imagery is not lost on anybody: Colomer cynically describes young people listening to old, dying ideas. For the full pamphlet, see Henri Massis and Alfred de Tarde (Agathon), *Les jeunes gens d'aujourd'hui: Le gout de l'action, la foi patriotique, une renaissance catholique, le réalisme politique*, 11th ed. (Paris: Librairie Plon, 1919).

15. In contrast to the grim nationalist ideas aimed at in the imagery of the last paragraph, Colomer here takes on a critique of the Parisian art scene. Caught in cloistered scenes and quixotic ideas such as *art for art's sake* ("aesthetes"), a position Colomer despised, he portrays the artists of the capital as ill, sentimental, toothless, and melodramatic.

16. This final scream epitomizes the moral of the entirety of intermixed metaphors and allegories that Colomer employs in this idiosyncratic section to serve as an interlude before the following part of the Libertarian Aesthetics series, ironically titled "the cooled down" after the rage of its introductory pages. "Down with death!" to Colomer is a slogan not only against the old ideas of *Young People of Today* but also the aestheticists whom he attacks in the second paragraph (the "art for art's sake" generation of artists) and the various people locked away behind the thick curtains (moral/social obligations, drug use, and so on) of the allegorical house that imprisons them, away from the "real world." Poignantly, it is that real world of bustling Paris that Colomer attempts to show these people by ripping open a window—an act of the action of the arts, in which he is helped by nature (in the form of a gust of wind).

17. Again, the reference is to the Languedoc winegrower uprisings. Now, two years later, Colomer is describing the 1907 revolts. There Colomer would have witnessed the final escalation of the crisis, when Georges Clemenceau decided to send in the army to suppress the revolt. However, the Seventeenth Regiment of the French army mutinied, which led to the uprising persisting for many months throughout the summer of 1907 before dying out amid reforms in the fall of the same year. See Martin, *Understanding Social Movements*; Smith, *Terror and Terroir*; François Pic and Jean Sagnes, "La crise de 1907 en Languedoc et en Roussillon: Bilan historiographique et essai de bibliographie," *Annales du Midi* 101, no. 187 (1989): 289–320; and *France nouvelle*, July 11, 1957.

18. This is likely a reference to the burning of the city hall and police headquarters of Beziers during the peak of the 1907 uprising.

19. The reference is to a well-known trick to scam or rob people in early twentieth-century France.

20. Colomer often includes an image of their skull shapes when he describes people. This is likely due to the then-popular pseudoscience of phrenology, which attempted, by measuring the bumps on the skull of a person, to predict their mental and character traits.

21. Fernand Castelbon de Beauchostes was one of the ringleaders of the 1907 Languedoc revolts. He was a winegrower as well as theater director and pianist.

22. Marcelin Albert was a café owner and winegrower who was seen as the leader of the 1907 revolt. In the prime of the uprising he was known as the best orator among the winegrowers and even referred to as "messiah," "prophet," and "redeemer" in, for instance, *Le soir* of August 7, 1907, and *L'union libérale* of June 28, 1907. Chased down by the police, he fled to Paris, where he had an eventful meeting with Georges Clemenceau in which he agreed to try to calm the protests. This immediately turned public opinion among those revolting against him, and after sitting out a jail sentence he fled to Algeria, where he lived in obscurity. Mr. Nirvana's dismissive attitude here may owe to the fact that minor uprisings happened every summer in southern France and did not bring about any apparent changes.

# PART II

# The Action of the Arts (1912–1914)

## ANARCHIST OF THE ACTION OF THE ARTS

*L'ACTION D'ART* 1 (FEBRUARY 1913)

"I am an *Anarchist of the Action of the Arts*." For me and a few of my friends, this is clear and explicit in the same way that, for most people, "two and two are four." And yet there has been nothing but confusion about it, nothing but false interpretations of this formulation. This has been going on ever since the day when we, Paul Dermée and I, first employed it!—*Anarchists* . . . and some people think to assimilate us into the *Jeunes Gardes* of Mr. Hervé or into the "militants" of the CGT or into the Knights of the Grand Soir,[1] into the insurrectionaries and the revolutionaries. . . . A pitiful mistake! —*Action of the Arts* . . . and there will be many who will remember the ones who prostituted this phrase to "scream" about the arts, under the pretext of the arts—"Art" being but a start to something, a nobility whose title they took in order to acquire a status, a presentation that gave some figure in the world—the first syllable of *Ar(t)-rivism*.[2]

What is an Anarchist of the Action of the Arts? I will not pretend to define it here in a few lines. In *L'action d'art*, the journal—following my cries of revolt, of hate, or of enthusiasm as provoked by the struggles of my life—and in the *L'action d'art*, the review—in a series of more meditated articles where I will assemble my ideas—I will try, in the day by day of my evolution, to explain the term. Today I would be satisfied if I only showed to the few whom I love, among the anarchists on one side and among the artists on the other, all that they would have to gain, for their own life, for their individual happiness, for the intensity of their being, by coming closer to one another and by aligning two points of view that have been distinguished from and opposed to one another for too long—anarchy and the arts, the revolt and beauty.

But, some will say, that has already happened. Twenty years ago there already were writings of poets, of artists who defended the anarchy. And from then on many intellectuals were sympathetic toward the revolting and often came to their help in their writings. . . . I do not deny that. It is true that in 1894 many writers defended anarchist ideas. There was Laurent Tailhade, there were Adolphe Retté, Paterne Berrichon, Emile Gautier, Hamon, Loise Michel, Elisée Reclus, Henri Heéon, Paul Adam, etc. . . . But let's not fool ourselves. Some of them were dilettantes, acrobats of the verb, like Tailhade and Retté—and they saw in anarchy but a "subject," a brilliant subject for the rhetoric, that they abandoned after they had drawn a few volumes from it. The others were socials—insurrectionists, democrats, revolutionaries; between them, the most remarkable was Kropotkin, a theoretician of Communism.

As exploiters of original or humanist sociological ideas, they were, the ones as well as the others, far from realizing or even preceding our Anarchism of the Action of the Arts. Those of the first kind were not sincere enough, nor were they alive enough. Their art was a game without consequences . . . Art for Art's sake. The second kind did not care about individualism, and obsessed with universal ideas of happiness and fraternity they collapsed into socialism or syndicalism. Why thus be surprised by the disgust for action coming from the most beautiful minds of the era? Action was only presented to them as a form of collective and fatal class struggle. The individual, in the anarchism of Kropotkin, of Jean Grave, of Sebastian Faure, and of Yvetot, only counted in function of its usefulness for mankind or the proletariat. The fate of humanity, the fate of the proletariat, that was all that mattered for the Anarchists. How could the artist or the poet be able to gain interest for such a cause? By looking for the triumph of a societal organization based on corporatism or on communism, would they have not convinced themselves to death as much as they would have by respecting the current bourgeois society?

We have thus only known, until now, a communist anarchism, that is to say the very negation of the anarchist spirit.

Anarchism, however, has a perfect etymological meaning. It signifies the negation of any authority, *of whatever kind that may be.* Quite some time ago, an isolated and in his time almost unknown thinker, Max Stirner, showed that there cannot be an anarchy without individualism—and that the only cause of a being must be its own cause, which he calls his "Unique," that is to say his individual life. And, nonetheless, for almost ten years, some free and courageous minds have committed to developing this individual point of view—one that negates every authority, from wherever it may hail, from the slaves or the masters, from the tyrants or the crowds. Libertad founded in 1904 a bold little journal: *L'anarchie*, which is now solely known, for a few months now, from police communications that are slavishly reproduced by the "mainstream press." When Libertad died, André Lorulot, then Le Rétif (Kibalchich), Rirette Maîtrejean, Armand, and Robert Lanoff continued despite persecution and arrestations to regularly publish this organ of the individualist anarchist movement.

As individualist anarchists, the "friends of *L'anarchie*" have, in a series of articles, perfectly moved on from any social solidarity to affirm the only reality, the only ideal of the revolting: "to live one's life," affirm one's being, one's individuality, by all means, "outside of the herd."

They have shown the vanity of social movements, the gross carelessness of the masses; they have further very well assumed the only attitude that is possible for the anarchist: to desolidarize from all that governs, provokes, or suffers from a societal order. Finally, they have denounced the different modes of economical organization (collectivism, communism, or syndicalism) as new forms of authoritarianism. And they have said to the individual: "Your cause, your progress, your salvation are within your very self. Cultivate yourself, develop yourself. Act in accordance with your own reason; and if one hinders your evolution, then fear nothing to affirm the logic of your life, defend your being. Count only on yourself to liberate yourself. As an individualist, revolt within yourself."

I approve of this teaching; it is the only one that can sometimes delve in beautiful energy and create fruitful activity. But I see even more in it. . . . I mostly see the magnificent seeds of a new heroism. If the "exploits" of the "tragic bandits"[3] have served the journalists of the "mainstream press" and the "militants" of the revolutionary press to condemn what they call the "insane" and "imbecile" individualist theories—then for me, quite the opposite is true.[4] These staunch struggles in which young men risk everything to stay refractories, in which they furiously affront societal masses to live their individualist lives no matter the cost and would go until death to sacrifice nothing of their being, these tragic events in which heroes are made—are the best justification of anarchist individualism.[5]

That is, however, not how the "friends of *L'anarchie*" understood the "bandits." They only wanted to see victims of social determinism in them, and, if they defended their acts, they did it too often with an unfair comparison to those of the men whom society honors and glorifies.

I insist on this difference in perspective. It already serves to characterize the anarchist of the action of the arts.

The only ones whom I value among the Anarchists of today—the "friends of *L'anarchie*"—have a sense of action that is analogous to mine. They have, most of all, and this is what I like most about them, a hate for resignations, ardor, and the will to live. But they are too proud of scientific theories; they have the vice of limiting their being with exclusively materialist conceptions. They render themselves, in a way, to be slaves to the physical and physiological laws from which they don't think it possible to exempt personalities. And thus, by conceiving the development of their being only according to a fatal determinism, I ask myself how they can even remain individualists.[6]

The sciences, occupying themselves only with the objective and the general, possess universal laws, common laws that can add nothing to the happiness of an individual life. Born from practical experience, they have no other end but to serve our action. Wanting to surrender our entire being to them, to reduce our consciousness and our will to its determinism, would be to render the individual into the slave of an instrument.

To the individualist anarchist, I would say: "In order to be yourself intensively, do not only search to learn everything from the world, search primarily to feel ably, to personally feel, to discover your temperament, your tendencies, your intimate tastes, your original force—search for all of that to guide your action, search it passionately within yourself—all of that is what the poets call "your soul," it is what a contemporary philosopher calls *intuition*,[7] it is what distinguishes you from other humans, what creates for you this unique and marvelous event: your life! And I would add: "To realize the personal harmony of your life, once that you will have gained consciousness of all your intuitive richness, you will mock logical truths to prefer your fantasy over them; you will be much more preoccupied with being beautiful than with being wise, and you will find in the arts no longer just a sort of game, a pastime for man or a rattle for the Gods, but an ideal and individual form of life. And, from that moment on, you would want to live your life in beauty."

There are not many artists who can understand my current attitude—and most writers, without a doubt, would scorn these lines screaming: "But that is not literature!" Ah! Certainly not, that is indeed not literature. I do not pretend to create "a masterpiece" here. I express myself, that is all—but at least I say what I think, freely, and without being worried about the opinion of clans or groups, and without hearing the "benevolent" voice of the "dear confrere" who charitably warned me: "you will drown, be careful. . . . These ideas are too violent for a man of letters." —Gentlemen, I am not a man of letters, and when I talk of "artists" I understand myself . . . I mean to say by "artist" those who put the high and harmonious expression of their individuality above everything, the ones who prefer to create their oeuvre sincerely, according to their intuition, according to their ideal, and to affront the ridicule or the indifference of the public rather than prostituting themselves for glory!

To those artists I say: To want to live according to your temperament, that is to say to integrally create the works of your art, means to also be condemned to the worst tortures. Society is the reign of the mediocre, spawned from ugliness; it maintains itself only by accumulating ugliness upon more ugliness. It constrains you, you the creators of harmony, to the most deadening tasks, the most horribly everyday ones, just in order to nourish your bodies. It sells you a piece of bread for the price of your entire soul, and if you refuse this scandalous deal it lets you die like dogs . . . like Gérard de Nerval, Tristan Corbière, and Paul Verlaine. In every civilized and administrated society a man who has some soul and who wants to manifest it freely is fatally condemned to be violated, hurt, tortured, crushed. One of our elders, the beautiful poet Stuart Merrill, said this recently: "There is decidedly no place for poets in a policed society!" —But do not beat yourself up over it, that is where your entire greatness lies. Do not resign; you could not do it without ugly suffering. Revolt within yourself!

Artists, thinkers, poets, imitate your brethren of the individualist movements, the refractories of action. In the face of the coalition of masters and slaves, in the face of the solidarity without conscience and without harmony formed by the classes or the races, be a few *Ones* who intend to stay beautiful, a few *Ones* who have recognized each other's good: their soul, and who do not intend to die of shame or misery because of that reason. . . . It is better yet to die while struggling, with your chest out, the soul up high, and the heart beating of pride—to die for *oneself*, heroically, like Valet, Garnier, and Bonnot.

## AT THE SOURCES OF HEROIC INDIVIDUALISM 1:
## MR. BERGSON AND THE "YOUNG PEOPLE OF TODAY"

*L' ACTION D'ART* 2 (MARCH 1913)

Old ideas are like old women; when their decay starts to pronounce itself a little too much, they feel the need to do themselves up, to refresh their youth. Remember; at the height of biologic scientism, maybe fifty years ago, when the triumph of Darwinism showed the stupidity of theological creationism, there immediately was no lack of stern defenders of Catholicism who strived to "fix" the foundations of religion. The goal at hand was to find a renewed foundation that would not look too much in discord with the probable truth; and so subtle, pious minds affirmed that the paradise on earth, Adam and Eve, were but symbols—and that God, by creating matter, didn't forget to attribute to this paradise, evidently, the gift of evolution.

Certain "young people of today" similarly want to convince us of a nationalist feeling, of an awakening taste for discipline, and of an irresistible push of Christian spirituality.[8]

To that end they have had the advantage of possessing intelligence, enough style, and quite a lot of money. From that point on they had the opportunity of finding editors, of having extensive connections, and of founding biweekly newspapers with a considerable circulation. They "touched" the public and have convinced it that they all were the youth of this era. The public, a client for everything, naturally walked . . . as a crowd. The parliamentarians were first affected by that, and then converted . . . and that is how M. Poincaré was voted to be president of the republic.

—But tell me, these "young people of today," are they then politicians? —Oh! Not at all. . . . They have however brilliantly supported this arduous thesis that they could have entitled: *From Bergson to Mr. Poincaré* . . .

Nonetheless, I am not being ironic here. I do not want to doubt the sincerity of Agathon and his friends; I only wanted to—from the start of this series, which I will call "From Bergson to Bonnot"—show how demanding it is for the ones who want to think about their own direction to find, between the men who realized themselves as acts, symbols of their will; I also wanted to affirm the value that I attribute onto the solidarity that is created between theoretical and practical people. A house is as much the work of the architect as it is of the workers who build it—and the role of the one is not inferior to the role of the other. To each their task according to their temperament—that is all. And in that houses all the dignity of our role as writers, we don't consider our thought as an abstraction without importance—and we are aware that each and every one of our sentences has all the value of an act, because it can suggest an act. We are no cowards who hide behind a sacred verb.

With this I do not at all criticize Mr. Bergson. This thinker is not more responsible of Bonnot than he is of Mr. Poincaré—and I think that he will be as surprised of hearing me speak of banditism in relation to *Time and Free Will* as he had to have been *intimately* by seeing the "young people of today" draw a need to respect for the "high" functions of the leader of the state from "intuitionism." Nevertheless, since Mr. Bergson is a member of the establishment now, he will perhaps be less flattered to have an "anarchist" as a "disciple" who plays the mean trick on him to utilize his ideas to justify "facts that have been qualified as crimes" than the "young people of today," who have a bright future and respect for the social order.[9] For . . . reasons of the university, Mr. Le Dantec denied the "bandits"— and in what terms! Mr. Bergson would not have more tenderness for us—and would probably prefer to offer his gracious collaboration to the *Études*, the official magazine of the Company of Jesus, than to our refractory journal—Oh my companions of *L'action d'art*!

But what does it matter! As I do not recognize a master (in the scholastic sense of the word), I do not feel constrained to follow until the end the one whom I enjoyed walking my first steps with. Mr. Bergson might now acquiesce to Catholicism, he can, late in life, approve of his traditionalist disciples, he could condemn, attack, even have my ideas persecuted, that will not stop me from saying that his early work, *Time and Free Will* and *Memoires*, are the savage sources of my heroic individualism. In a forthcoming study I will commit myself to explaining in great detail how a stream of feelings and thoughts has conducted me from Bergsonian intuitionism to a conception of anarchist banditism. Today I will content myself with untying the web that the young reactionaries have purposefully tangled up. The most beautiful, the most alive, the most creating ideas of Bergson are not more at home with the Catholics and the nationalists than the tenets of Nietzsche were suitable for the hard arrivistes and the bourgeois authoritarians. The former, like the latter, wanted to counter their decay with the blooming flowers of a young thought. They only appear more lamentable for trying.

Bergson has distinguished *intuition* from intelligence. In an era in which we knew no other psychology but the one of English-school associationists, where we reduced human will to an absolute mechanism, where the realm of sensation was submitted under measures, under calculations, under practical experiences, where individual freedom was dismissed, where we drove to establish a science of the mind using the same methods as for the sciences of the body—he screamed out: "Stop it here! That is dangerous! . . . " and he wonderfully convinced us that every being carried an original world within itself—its *intuition*—and that this individual world had no law but the one of its own life, of its course, of its amplitude, of its intensity, of its harmony. And we have seen from him that freedom does not consist, as the metaphysicians thought, in the possibility to act absolutely without any motive, as per miracle, but to act with *one's own* motives, to act with the approval of all of *one's* intuitive being, the act in *harmony with oneself*—this being not at all equivalent to the scientists "conscious determinism" by the way, because they have to keep all determinants in mind, including the ones that reside outside the being, whereas intuitionist liberty is truly an individual liberty because it affirms itself in a *sentiment of approval* that can only be perceived by the individual itself—in harmonious wholeness over the course of *his* being.

This is the essence of Bergsonianism. After the terrible crisis of analysis and of positivism that we had only just overcome, his ideas were like the hatching of fresh flowers in a desert. The young men eagerly refreshed themselves in its dew.

Thus science, all-powerful in the domain of the practical, could no longer attempt to legislate over our thoughts and acts. Thus the individual found himself to be the master of a gift that is both unique and multifaceted: his *intuition*. Thus, thanks to it, he could make of his action, it seemed, a work of freedom, follow the course of his personality without obstacles; model his life in the image of *his* dream. Bergsonian intuitionism thus seemed to rejoin, with more fantasy, with more elegance and more imagination, the individualism of Stirner. The *intuition* would be the sister of the *unique*, a younger sister, a more gracious and more passionate one, with indescribable dreaminess in its eyes.

But very cautious gentlemen watched over the virtue of this child. They placed her under guardianship and, so she would not wander off onto troublesome paths, they traced out good routes for her, full of rest. For one, they taught her to fear individualism, by only letting her become aware of the most skeptical, the most off-putting or the most desiccated of its sons: the individualists of the mind. They showed her Taine, in his speculative solitude, going so far as to glorify his inaptitude to live—Barrès, disgusted of contemplating his "I" and giving the church his mummified heart as a sad present—Anatole France playing some ideas like they were on a chessboard . . . and all of their disciples, all in their ivory tower, or their pretentious "when it comes to me," or the ironic "who knows?" of the intellectuals from twenty years ago. And thus, by anti-intellectualism, they separated intuition from individualism. From that moment on they found it easy to slowly conduct it, without it noticing, to the same moralist or social conclusions in which reason, dialectics, and positive spirit once culminated. Oh! It was not smart; they contented themselves to pose what the positivists researched by an analysis of the relative into a synthetic absolute. Instead of saying: "Order, discipline, social solidarity, patriotic duties are imposed by sociologic laws and because we find reasons for them in the conditions of life in our arrangement into groups"—they say: "They impose themselves because each one of us finds within themselves their necessity," they made of intuition an internal necessity, a sort of moral policeman, guardian of its honest principles. They made of it a "synonym for *good sense*."

That is how, thanks to a few sleights of hand worthy of the best students of Mr. de Loyola,[10] the most libertarian, the most innovative of all philosophical conceptions was transfigured, castrated, nullified. But that was not enough for the "young people of today" who seem to me to be, so to say, "the young wardens of the past." The anti-intellectualism did not stem only from Bergsonian theories. The youth of the start of this century was still strongly impressed by Nietzsche's lessons on energy and heroism. We no longer knew how to be sorry; we no longer wanted to tender up; we loved the struggle. Certainly the author of *Thus Spoke Zarathustra* was as little susceptible to incite in men the love of their country as Mr. Bergson is to take them to the "good sense"; but our notorious "young people of today" are not dragged down by such exactness. They affirm, categorically, that there could be no other courage than the one of the soldier, no other struggle than the one of the citizen, and no other energy than the one gushing from the "unanimous heart of the nation."

Nietzsche joining Bergson to raise a patriotic Marianne and a holy relic onto the pavise shield—voilà a delightful incoherence, one that does not merit, in all seriousness, another critique but that of the caricature, if only some of the charlatans would indulge in and understand this paradox. *Hélas!* I fear that there are sincere minds; very alive hearts that let themselves get taken by it. They were weary of overly logical systematizations, weary of sociological analysis, weary also of Tolstoyism, and of pity, and of the universal good, and of humanitarian whining. An entire generation of youth was eager for action, for an intense life, for heroism. There could have really been a renaissance of energy; everyone felt the piaffing of the horses that were shaking with enthusiasm for a great burst to expend oneself, to burn oneself up, to affirm oneself.

But what to do? Embark on which route? Socialism, syndicalism drowned in questions of economical organization barely offered to nourish this craving for heroism; Anarchism lost itself in vain discussions about a future and unattainable paradise. The activity of the youth had awaited a struggle for so long . . . that it threw itself into the first one that came—blindly—in order not to shadowbox around in emptiness. They engaged in sport . . . for the fatherland![11]

A few of them, meanwhile, did not let themselves get tempted more by this neo-nationalism then by syndicalism—a few of them, who were touched by the individualist teaching of Max Stirner, and who weren't duped by the most charming words of the old entities. But those, as we will see, turned to the most dried-out scientism for fear of the intuition that was so well reappropriated by the reactionaries of today.

Our task will be to show all the liberty, all the internal harmony that the individual can find in intuition, and how, thanks to it, he can satisfy his desire for autonomy and his thirst for heroic actions.

## AT THE SOURCES OF HEROIC INDIVIDUALISM 2: ART, ANARCHY, AND THE CHRISTIAN SOUL

*L'ACTION D'ART* 5 (APRIL 1913)

The action of the man who does not agree to follow the normal course of the environment in which he operates is always perilous. The individual who seeks to affirm himself through differences rather than through assimilations needs contempt for ironies, sectarian opinions, and needs belief in himself, in his enthusiasm. Most of all, he needs disdain for agreed-upon terms and the courage to look for "his own," even among the ones who seem to be our worst distractors. What I find important in another man are not his doctrines, his theories, but his temperament, his life, his aspirations, all of which reveal an eagerly blooming individuality.

As an anarchist of the action of the arts, I have found for myself two paths where I can realize myself, in the search of "mine"; following one, I want to reveal to the individualist anarchists that they can discover, through the arts, with their intuition alone, the harmonious unity of their action, their individual well-being; following the other, I want to inspire in the artists the taste for action, the love for life.

However, we know how many anarchists have mocked the arts and poetry—and what some of them consider as a dangerous lie, like a treacherous illusion, or as an amusement without a benefit.

We also do not ignore either that the artists, even great and sincere artists, more often than not have averted the action in despair or in worry, in fear of losing the most original, the purest of their personality within it.

Both are right in respect to certain conceptions of the arts and of anarchy. But they erred, I believe, in the conceptions themselves. By "art" the anarchists heard absolute artifice, the negation of life, the resignation to practical ugliness so as to refuge oneself in an imaginary paradise. That or a dilettante *passe-temps*, a caprice of the "rich," a game with colors, of words, of notes, "*l'art pour l'art*" outside of life.

By "'anarchy" the artists and writers understood a sort of inorganic democracy, a violent collectivism, a blind fraternalism, or a struggle of classes in which every intellectual consideration had no place.

This type of art and this manner of anarchism are indeed incompatible. But one and the other are neither art nor anarchy. They are caricatures of it, their respective social deformations.

I don't think that it is more worthy of an artist to resign, to suffer the ugliness of his time, to refuse himself to life, than it is worthy of an anarchist to prostitute himself to social struggles, under the pretext of humanity—to sacrifice his being to a cause that is not the one of his temperament, under the pretext of a humanist brotherhood.

Before anything, one needs to convince oneself of this. There is only one important good: my good. There is only one worthy cause: my cause. Stirner has perfectly shown us that there is absolutely nothing that can be of importance to us besides that which he calls: the *Unique*, that is to say our *individual life*.

"*My life*." Muse over this word, deep as an abyss in which there is only death—and you will have the intense desire of making of this passage through consciousness, which is your individual life, a celebration of sensations, of thoughts, of pleasures, the most intense and the most harmonious of celebrations—because you know that it will not be repeated.

The joy of life . . . the Greeks of antiquity conceived it in all its greatness, and they made of it a God, the most beloved of them all, Dionysus. Poets and artists wouldn't take any other glory but to exalt this joy *of being* under the sun, this drunkenness of sensing, of thinking, of enjoying harmoniously in accordance with nature. They also were, all while being creators of images, men of action of which the poems, the music, the paintings all found echoes in the conscience of their contemporaries. In Athens the artists and poets were teachers of life, professors of joy. They made Art for Life.

With Christianity art was made for Death. Obscurely, anonymously, the great workmen-sculptors of the cathedrals edified monuments to celebrate the afterlife. In them, they dreadfully caricaturized the joys of life that Catholicism had transformed into "sins." The artists of the Catholic Middle Ages sacrificed their individual lives to their work, a work they dedicated to the God they feared, the God in face of which they found themselves trembling come the hour of their death.

From there we can understand their horror of the joys of life, their hatred for action, the crushing of their liberty to sense, to enjoy, to imagine.

It might seem stupid to us, but at least it was in logical unison with their belief.

Social ideas have the particularity that they leave, even after their death and in the minds that consider themselves furthest removed from them, permanent traces of their passage, habits of thinking, of acting, of sensing; they assemble within mankind a mechanism that functions even long after they have died.

This is the case for Christianity.

Under the influence of Catholic ideas of renouncing life, of fear of sin, the artists who sang the Christian paradise lost interest in action and condemned themselves to despise the human joys.

Now, what happened when religious sentiments started to disappear? Did the artists become the teachers of the joy of life again that they were during the time of Paganism? Not in the slightest. A habit was taken on: the one of despising life. Thus, as they no longer believed in the Paradise of the Evangelium, they threw themselves on what we have called the artificial Paradises—and, from there on, there was no sincere poet who, disgusted by his century, didn't find a solution: the one of searching consolation in alcohol, ether, hash, opium—or in art that would only be a game—outside of life . . .[12]

As to the others, the clowns and the cabaret players, they flattered the public, the crowds, or the sovereigns and became the ones whom Han Ryner formerly skewered as "prostitutes."

This unconscious and detrimental influence of Christianism I do not find only in the manifestations of art but also in some forms of anarchy.

Christianity taught us human brotherhood: altruism. It had said: "Love your neighbor as you love yourself." It was the ultimate teaching of anti-individualism.

It had preached blind self-denial, charity, absolute dedication.

What else do we find with the anarchist-communists of today, if not this humanitarian and altruistic ideal, this belief in a universal accord and in an egalitarian fraternity to which the individual must dedicate himself?

For those individuals who reject all tradition, all prejudice, all formulas, to listen only to the voice of his eagerness to live, altruism does not exist. Ideas of humanity and fraternity are entities, idols that are even more tyrannical than those of divinity or royalty, because they have the hypocrisy of making themselves up to be anarchist. Anarchy, however, has a precise meaning. It stands for the negation of all authority, whatever it may be. Anarchy needs to be individualist, or it does not exist. The individual who aspires to uphold his entire individual liberty is constrained to struggling, to not taking the common good into account, because the common good is an abstraction empty of any sense; it is nothing else than what people previously called God. The common Good is an anonymous and blind force that can only bring about evil and individual pain.

The individual who realizes that there is nothing beyond his life cannot have the consideration of a universal fraternity. Being good for all humans is to be evil for oneself, because, as Christianity has shown us, wanting the good for everyone is equivalent to resigning oneself to the suffering of all.

Anarchists, it is thus necessary that every one of us has the exclusive will to be oneself, to realize oneself individually.

And I think that the arts can wonderfully help us with that.

## AT THE SOURCES OF HEROIC INDIVIDUALISM 3: SCIENCE AND INTUITION—THEIR ROLE IN INDIVIDUALISM

*L'ACTION D'ART* 6 (MAY 1913)

Don't think that I want to dismiss the blessings that science has bestowed upon the individual. But science has her role, a precise role, let her have it, and let's also recognize what the arts can bring to our well-being.

Science has a practical role. Born from experience, she has no other end than to serve our actions. She is, in the hands of the individual, a wonderful tool. She allows us to use matter, to assimilate objects in order to serve the ends of our being. She forms herself incrementally, always as we need to create her. She is our oeuvre, she is made for us and by us, and she is fully relative to our exterior necessities.

Science can do a lot for our material well-being. But you also know how she can do as much to our misfortune. She is like a knife that can serve as well to cut the bread that nourishes us as it can to slice our own throat. Science is a double-edged sword. For the individual it is important that she is held at the right side; it is important to know how to use her to realize one's well-being. It is necessary that the individual integrates her into its personality, that it assimilates her into its own life. And for that the individual needs to know the sense of its life; and to know its direction it is necessary that it comprehends where it started.

One could compare the life of a human to a circle in which destiny is represented by the circumference. His acts will be its radii. With science he can construct radii that go toward the circumference. That leaves us with the center; and this invisible but moving center, without which no radius could ever be, without which the circumference would not be able to form itself, this free and creating center is being itself, its consciousness, its life.

That is what Bergson called *intuition*.

Intuition is to be distinguished from reason. While reason provides us, with analysis and logic, the means to discern the external world and to cope with the complexity of objective facts, intuition is a synthesizing force that is personal to us. It is the individual axis of vision that forms a unique being, it is an original force of sensation, of feeling, of consciousness—it is with what my life, my thought, my imagination are distinguished from the ones of a different being. It defines the quality of my being. It is disgusted by analysis because it is a force of synthesis. It is only comparable to a musical symphony whose total value, total meaning, resides in the ensemble, independent of every note that it is made up of; it is a whole of which the parts are inseparable because each one of these pieces only has value in rapport to the whole.

The arts are the child of intuition. Indeed, what is a work of art? It is nothing other than the free expression of an individuality that does not recognize any other laws except that of its individual harmony. We say that a work of art is beautiful not if it obeys whatever common laws defining a criterion for beauty that might exist but, quite on the contrary, when it manifests most spontaneously and most intensely an original life. And when it reveals, with a minimum of practical means, an individuality generative of sensations, of thoughts, of new emotions, inexpressible until then. The works of the great artists have been in the world of psychology what the great discoveries have been in the physical world.

But, while science, to make us discover the physical world, makes us research a succession of universally linked facts, the arts, to reveal our personality, invite us on the contrary to desolidarize us of collective thought, of collective sense, of universal sentimentality so as to realize an individual harmony. In the realm of the external world, the objective world, the sciences operate by analysis; in the domain of my consciousness, the subjective world, the arts realize themselves through synthesis.

But how can the limits of these domains be determined? I don't think that the two domains have fixed borders. The happiness of his being, that is the only thing of importance to a living being, it is by that criterion that every being will accord more or less importance to the arts or the sciences, to their intuition or their reason.

As a fundamental individualist I cannot affirm that what constitutes my happiness can realize that of another individual. All that I can say is: "*Voilà*, this is how I understand the happiness of my life."

Individualist anarchists are, for the most part, scientists.[13] That is to say, they're absolute materialists, they extend the limits of the world indefinitely by analysis. They dismiss the world of synthesis, the unity of the soul, the world of intuition.

The artists strongly affirm the life of the soul, they recognize the world of intuition, but they narrowly restrict it, they confine it in a fully theoretical activity, in an activity of luxury, so to speak. They turn their soul into a very little thing which they consider to be incredibly precious and which they cultivate far from life, at the top of their ivory tower.

For the anarchist of the *action d'art* that I am, these two conceptions of life do not suffice to realize my happiness. The former dismisses the most living part of me, the one that differentiates me from other beings, by which I am, by which I qualify myself, by which I color and dye the hours of my life. Scientism removes the prism from my vision, the reason for being of my individuality.

The second conception, the one of the artists, conserves the prism of vision very well, but only to utilize it in darkness. The artists who remove themselves from the action, who despise life to "cultivate their I" and make "their works" make me think of a crazed fool who lets himself be served on a flowery tablecloth, on a table filled with cutlery encrusted with diamonds and gold, royal plates that are empty of any dishes.

They vow an unmitigated cult to their "I," and they stupidly renounce the very nourishment of that I; they let it starve on wrong substances.

The anarchist of the action of the arts does not look down upon the objective matter any more than he does the subjective consciousness. He loves his I, certainly, but he wants that this I is truly alive, living a healthy life, an intense and harmonious one; and that is why he accords to it, as a field of experiences, everything that life offers him, all phenomena of nature, all accidents, all of the external world.

But to be guided in this external world, to not drown amid the universal contingencies and to not be duped by one's own will of extending one's being, it is also necessary that individuality, in every counting minute that determines its action, feels truly in accord with itself, that it knows its direction.

From a religious point of view, nothing was easier for a man who wanted to decide to act. There was virtue and sin; the allowed and the forbidden by divine forces; what procured for an eternity in paradise and what precipitated hell.

This is also true from a social point of view, with the difference that here society has replaced God. "It's good" becomes equivalent to "it is according to the orders of society; "it's bad" is synonymous with "it's against the orders of society." An action called moral is an action that maintains a social equilibrium; an immoral action is any action that tends to disjoint this equilibrium.

It is not of importance whether this equilibrium works to the benefit or the detriment of the individual; it is not of importance if the social order is based upon disorder and individual disharmonies; the Societal God orders it, and one has to submit to it.

The individualist revolts against these fundamentally identical social or religious conceptions; he cannot consent to his crushing to maintain an idol.

And meanwhile, he needs to act, he needs to drive in a direction, he needs to decide in favor of this or that action. How can he do that without a directing idea?

The scientific anarchists have told us: "Nothing is good nor bad; there are facts, that is all; every being acts according to the determinism that makes it commit these or those acts. Nothing can be said about these acts, apart from that they are determined actions." But on this account everything would need to be accepted; the worst betrayals, the worst tyrannies, the least honest opportunisms should not generate any outrage; they are acts that are as determined as the acts of revolt. And meanwhile, the same scientific individualists do not hesitate to be outraged at treachery, to condemn authoritarian tyranny.

To be honest, I believe that there is confusion around the word "determinism." There is a big difference when it is said that a certain phenomenon of physics was materialized following determinism and when, while talking about a living being, it is said about it that it acted according to *its* determinism. In the second case, there is the word *its*, and this possessive pronoun is of importance. It signifies that the being follows a determinism that is its own, according to *its personality*. While the ones who act according to determinism tout court, the ones who are a part of social determinism just as facts are in the physical determinism, these ones are the unconscious, shipwrecks who hat are buffeted without a personal will; they are slaves who undergo everything without reacting, or masters who profit off everything without much more consciousness.

But to be a personality, an individualist, it is necessary to surpass this social determinism, it is necessary to become aware of one's center, to cease the rhythm of one's life, it is necessary to act following *one's* determinism. And this subjective determinism, this psychic determinism, has nothing comparable with physical determinism; while this latter one consists of a universal sequence in space, the determinism of a consciousness resides in a personal harmony captured in time—it's the intuition.

For the individual who wants to act, this initially means for him to understand his harmony, to know in what conditions his individuality feels a sentiment of accord between all its parts. It then means that he realizes his synthesis, consequently that he recognizes his beauty, that he makes of his life a work of art.

And when it comes to the moment for him to decide over an act, instead of asking if it is good or bad, if it is real or false, he will simply ask himself: is it beautiful? Is it ugly? Which will return to him asking himself: Would I be, by accomplishing this action, in accord with the harmony that realizes my being? And thus he will decide, and thus he will be able to choose, *without judging,* without appealing to a universal criterion, to an abstract criterion, or to a social criterion. Without ever leaving himself, by appealing only to the inherent rhythm of his life, freely he will take a direction, *his* direction, as an individualist.

## AT THE SOURCES OF HEROIC INDIVIDUALISM 4: MY FREEDOM IS MY BEAUTY

*L'ACTION D'ART* 7 (JUNE 1913)

The manufacturers of universal happiness, the humanist moralists or sociologists of whichever caliber can rarely find their account in my writing. We are, they and me, ill-arranged to see eye to eye.

Nonetheless, some of them, fearful, driven by a logic of discussion to "bring back to reason" the "most lost of the ewes," don't tire of arguing.

This is what they say to me:

"Since the beautiful is, on your account, a sentiment that varies from individual to individual, how do you want to make the beautiful into a criterion for human acts?"

Careful, gentlemen, don't accuse me so quickly of such a crime as to want to endow this "poor humanity" with yet another balance with which to precisely weigh its acts! I am not *that* cruel . . .

In reality, a question like that shows an absolute incomprehension of my ideas. It is not my intent to fixate a common law, to establish a rule for life, to found a moral, to set a table of values. It is, on the contrary, a question of rendering all of that impossible. What I want to make possible is my individual life, my fantasy, my "Unique."[14]

Flowing out of the sources of intuition, my life cannot determine its riverbed. It is its own stream that will create its riverbed.

I don't want to be subject to any moral law, my own not more than that of anybody else. In order to be that, I will try by my actions first to distance myself as intensely as possible from all other humans, then to contribute to an increasingly large distancing of the individualities who surround me. I thus commit myself to destroy, in the entire worlds of action and thought, the universal, the collective, the amorphous, the common, the sources of misery—so that the individual, the distanced, can flourish.

And precisely because the sentiment of beauty is the least fixed, the least rational, the least settled, the most variable of human sentiments I choose it as the basis of *my* philosophy, as the principle of *my* action. The beautiful is of no risk to create a law for us humans, a common law, an immutable law; it can only accord with *my* individual law—that is to say my harmony, the feeling of an accord between my sentiments. It is the rhythm of my life, the synthesis of my being—and by that I don't mean of my social life or of my abstract being as a part of humanity—but of my individual life, of my refractory life; of my intimate being, my intuitive being, my being that is eager to sense, to enjoy, to consume itself, to flourish—and struggling until death in order to affirm itself. The beautiful is the synthesis of the many élans of a personality in search of its harmony. "My liberty is my beauty."

Some will surely be appalled: "By preaching such a philosophy, you will eventually unchain even more human struggling." Eh! What does it matter, when the struggles are beautiful! It is not the fighting that is bad, it is to fight without individual reasons; it is, contrariwise, good and beautiful to fight for oneself, for one's conception of life, to defend one's being and to affirm it. Just as war is vile because it pushes beings, grouped into herds, unconsciously toward death, so is the individualist revolt beautiful.

I do not hate war out of compassion for mankind or from fear of the flowing of blood, but I hate it out of love for individual liberty, I hate it for its unconsciousness, I hate it because it lives of sacrifices and of devotion, because it is, for a living being, the ultimate negation of its joy of life.

Whereas the struggle for oneself, the revolt, as merciless, as painful as it may be, and even if it might lead to death, I admire it because it is one big scream, shouted out by the individual who wants to be and who aspires to his liberty like a plant does the sun.

Thus, in the face of all religion and of all morality that always seek to overcome the problem of human liberty and happiness through further assimilation, for us, on the contrary, it is by the differentiation that one can, on the discovery of *one's* harmony, attempt to reach *one's* liberation.

To sociological sciences, we have opposed the aesthetic conscience—the intuition of individual beauty. To humanist collectivism, we oppose *heroic individualism*.

## AT THE SOURCES OF HEROIC INDIVIDUALISM 5:
## SOCIAL ILLUSIONS AND SCIENTIFIC DISILLUSION

*L'ACTION D'ART* 11 (AUGUST 1913)

Mankind feuds, discusses, fights most often over words of which they do not know the meaning, of which they do not even search to know the value. Ideologists, preachers, politicians, and leaders of crowds have always, during all times and in all settings, known how to exploit this promptness of men to unite or to throw themselves onto each other without knowing one another, blindly, and full of prejudice. The charlatans of the verbs never saw real images of life in the words; instead they merely used them as imperfect symbols. They only made them out to be idols for the public—good flags, one by one, and following the circumstances, to be planted in manure or to be deployed in the four winds of "propaganda."

Today the ones we call "theoreticians or "militants" do not preoccupy themselves anymore—*Hélas!*—of the living sense of their phrases. They daydream too much of the effect that they produce on their public. Too often, this type of narrow social opinionating is the only consideration that they want to achieve, in order to best conduct social opinion toward the ends they deem the best.

This doesn't surprise me at all, coming from the communists. And aren't they like that, in their role, they of whom the ideal is very social, they who dream of a transformed mass, of a uniformed mass, and who believe in the beauty of a future society composed out of individuals with common interests? To whoever is more concerned with the common good than with the individual good, it is logical to linger around in the choice of his means and to have few scruples, to distort one's conscience when needed, in order to conquer the energy—for the needs of the cause.

But that an individualist would also utilize words, eloquence, the ease of his style—not to wholly affirm himself, not to arouse consciousness and individual energies, not even to separate personalities—but to form groups, masses, with a common will and common ideas, to create an "anarchist" opinion, an "anarchist" mind state, an "anarchist" crowd; just like the orators and educators of the bourgeoisie who work to maintain, with their morals and their action, a "sane public opinion," I will never tolerate them. And if I revolt against such enterprises, it is because I find them to be not at all *anarchist*; it is because such proceedings are of an indirect authoritarianism that is worse than the open tyranny of the masters. Anarchism is no political opinion, let's not forget that. "Anarchist" has a very clear etymological meaning, I repeat it. It is composed of an *an*, which means *without*, and an *arché*, which means commandment. *Without commands, without constraints.* And how could an individual who constructs a morality for *other* humans be considered *without commands, without constraints,* and how could individuals who follow the moral laws of *other* humans? Not only societal laws oppress and impede personal blooming. Moral laws may be less brutal, but that does not make them less dangerous for the consciousness. We submit to them without any protest because they do not violently sanction; but the day we consent to them, we immediately consent to individual sacrifices that are a lot worse than the sentences of the law, because they neuter the only original good of our life: individual sensitivity, personal intuition, the sense of our unique. Morality assimilates us into a crowd of other beings; morality turns an individual into a cell of a social organism; it provokes reflexes in a being, actions, attitudes that will make him into a being who is determined in relation to his environment by the simple fact that he will have acquiesced to this social determinism. By teaching an individual, especially when he is young, in which circumstances he has to act in what fashion, he will end up no longer knowing how to, by no longer *being able* to act differently, because he will see no other way of acting.

I believe in the force of personal illusion. She can be a benefit or a danger for the individual depending on whether this illusionary force is used by a being in the direction of his largest and most harmonious expansion, or in the sense of social restrictions. Psychological activities do not obey the same rhythm as physical or psychological life does. A consciousness is organized by synthesis. She finds her own rhythm, in her own life, the very conditions of her creating force. A consciousness that would not believe in its existence could not be. A consciousness that would not want to be strong could not be strong. A consciousness that would not endeavor to find its harmony could never be harmonious. Take this example: Why have females stayed, to this day, terrible idols, cruel little devouring beasts, or toys without an own will in the hands of a male? Because, for centuries, in all ages, we have not stopped, with words, with acts, with writings, to convince the woman that her only role is amorous, that her only function is the one of the amusing doll, able to charm the leisure of a man or to distract, with her catlike play, the strongest of wills. Take literature: dramas, plays—How do they present women . . . the woman? She is never a creator of energy, a personality of decent value. We only give her value in relation to passion, desire, or the fantasy of a male. She is never anything but a heroine of love—and of what love! Or what kinds of loves! Mostly the most egoistic, the lowest, the shabbiest, the cruelest.

Now, as a result of always being considered along those lines, seen along those lines, the woman could not but stay like the idea that was had of her. Take a small girl who, through her reading, learns from books; she sees there what she should be, what is imposed on her to be; as a youthful girl, then, from the attitudes of the young men, she understands what she has to be or stay in order to please, in order to be loved. She has socially become what society has socially given her the illusion she was.

This is but one example, amid so many others. The same thing is true for everyone. The force of illusion is a creator in the psychological domain. But if social illusion is the creator of social ugliness, then social illusion may perhaps just as well be a creator of individual beauty, a creator of harmonious consciousness.

In my view the first individualists of *anarchy* were wrong in saying that individualist anarchy was a philosophy that believed in nothing. This invites confusion. I believe in nothing that is external to me, that much is obvious; I love nothing of what is social and societal. But, if I want to live, and live with force and élan, don't I have to believe in my life, don't I have to believe in my force, in my beauty, in my ideal?

I abhor every illusion that hails from my environment; I am in revolt against an ideal that is imposed upon me by others, by a master or by a crowd, or by a group. And as much I am persuaded that my belief in me, the individual illusion that I created for myself, my personal enthusiasm, my idealism are all necessary for me to integrally flower. If you persuade a man that he is but a coward, that he lacks courage, disillusion him of his powers, and he will flee in moments of danger. By reproaching kids that they are vicious, parents manage to make them just that.

*Eh bien*, in an analogous fashion, by convincing themselves that nothing exists outside of material facts, facts that are ruled by an universal determinism, and that solely the external reality is of importance and that individual liberty is but a ploy, the scientists have finished by rendering themselves into playballs of events and circumstances. By negating the ideal, they have finished by having nothing left at all and by acting emptily, in a disorderly fashion, incoherently following the coincidences of a universally material life, without any harmony. They have engaged in action for the sake of action quite similarly to how some artists make art for art's sake. They lacked conviction, illusion, enthusiasm, ideals.

But some of the scientists had temperament, character, and they were often times beautiful in their actions because they abstracted their doctrines in them, they abstracted their positivist theories to give free flow to their intuitive force of being—and those scientists, I am certain, even though the word "idealism" would have shocked them because they associated it with the old religious idealism or humanitarian idealism, those scientists very often felt in them the desire to surpass themselves, to be most intensely and most harmoniously in accord with their own tendencies; they had a belief in their power, in their life, because they struggled to affirm them, because they would have risked their death for their *being*. On the ruins of their social illusions bloomed, without them even noticing, the rare flowers of individualized illusion.

## AT THE SOURCES OF HEROIC INDIVIDUALISM 6: INDIVIDUALIZED ILLUSION

*L'ACTION D'ART* 12 (AUGUST 1913)

What is the individualized illusion?

Take a moment to abstract yourself from everything that societal life has taught you, of everything that it imposes upon you; imagine a moment without any links to society, untouched by any sort of morality, all customs, and all prejudices. You will then be able to feel in you a muffled, irresistible push of all your senses, of all your wills, solely to *be* with the strongest intensity and the most harmony; you will feel something of a drive, analogous to the one of the sap that rises in the trees to let the leafiest branches reach the light at the top of the forest.

Of this great pushing of life, you have received consciousness. Each one of you knows that all these sensations, all these ideas, all these tendencies, only have their value in their rapport to the individual who has the consciousness of being.

It would be absurd to want to isolate a single psychological fact. From the moment on where one would separate it from the consciousness that feels it, it would by definition cease to be psychological. Take any emotion: from the moment where one would pretend to analyze it, when one would extract an element from it, the emotion would no longer be. Psychological life finds its conditions in synthesis. It cannot be submitted to the laws of analysis; it is like a symphony in which each part has no value except in relation to the ensemble.

Having seen where idealism drove the communists, and attaching, from then on, no longer just a religious or metaphysical sense of taking from the individual the will to realizing itself during its life to the word "idealism"—the individual anarchists fought until now against every idealist tendency and attached themselves to an absolute scientistic utilitarianism.

Because they had seen mankind conceive the ideal only in a social form, they figured that every idealism was a pest to the individual. They didn't imagine an ideal that could be different from the common thought of a cult, of a society, of a group. When condemning idealism, they only thought about its social forms. They forgot that the individual does not only live physiologically, that his life is not settled in a corporal activity in relation to matter; every one of us feels in themselves an entire cluster of aspirations, tendencies, wills, ideas, images, dreams; an entire cluster of love or of hate, of hope, of revolts; all of those constitute the psychological life of a being, his "soul," as the poets would phrase it. *Eh bien*, if we want to harmonize this simmering ensemble of thoughts, sentiments, and wills to live our life, to truly be an individuality, to push our action in the most intense and harmonious way, it is necessary that everyone seeks the rhythm of life that suits him best and, once he has found this rhythm, it suits us to give it the largest possible magnitude, not only to be and to be oneself but to be oneself in beauty! That is what I call idealism. It is a tendency that pushes me to not be content with the real, that is to say with the past or the present that is about to be the past. It is an élan of my being to realize itself fully and most highly. The individual ideal is a force of life that sharpens my will of action and renders me increasingly powerful by giving the courage to realize myself.

The individual who has gained awareness of this unique force that is within him, of this psychological wealth that he carries in his being, cannot see another reason to be.

What will be important to him, much more than the fate of the universe, the development of the races and the lots of the nations, will be his joy of life. How could he then be worried about a real and a false? The problem for him will no longer consist in asking himself if he is on the right or the wrong road, and if the route leads somewhere among mankind; the only question for him will be to know whether he follows his way, the only problem for him will be the one of his individual happiness. In order to solve it he will need a belief in himself, the individualized illusion.

For who never wants to be somebody socially and realize works in the domain of humanity—for who never wants to be a politician, a moralist or a businessman, surely this illusion will be a bad counselor.

But for the being of which the only end is individual blooming; for the individualist who has seized the great reality of his soul, and who wants to search nothing further than his proper life to live, this illusion is a marvelously strong hatching power. If I believe myself to be strong, I will have confidence, and I will be strong in any circumstance. If I believe myself free I will reject all constraints, I will revolt against all domination, I will at least feel myself in a voluntary struggle against all that wants to oppress me, and this very conscience of my refractionary sentiments, inspiring my force of resistance, will permit me not to fear to go, perhaps, as far as death, just to conserve my joy of sensing, even alone against all men, even physically crushed by society, at least unwavering in my individualist attitude. If I believe in myself I will not fear the death that other men can give me. I will prefer to die with the conscience of having abandoned nothing of myself, of having prostituted nothing of my soul; dying with the joy of possessing my wholeness in all my harmony of sensations and of thoughts.

My sense of individualism is thus laid down. It is for me a reason for living; it is the end of my action, the incessant goal of my life, that cannot disappoint me because I carry it within myself—and that solely on my will, which is only tied to the enrichment and the integrity of my conscience, my destiny will depend.

## AT THE SOURCES OF HEROIC INDIVIDUALISM 7: LET US BE NEW MEN

*L'ACTION D'ART* 13 (SEPTEMBER 1913)

Being new men by staying "oneself" heroically.

That is what is important.

Knowing the ideal of one's personality and, once one has seized it, fearing nothing to affirm it.

But, for that, it is necessary first and foremost to *be* individually.

The individualist anarchist, whether he comes from the ranks of the bourgeoisie or the proletariat, needs to renew himself in order to no longer be a social man, to no longer be a man of a class; he cannot keep anything from the wool of his sheep; he has to have, from that moment on, an antisocial attitude in life, an individualist attitude, *his* attitude—and, no matter where, in no matter which circumstance, he will stay himself, he will act only following the rhythm of his personality, without minding public opinion. And by way of seeing some beings going this way with confidence in life, with this decision to stay themselves and to attain their harmony, their happiness, their beauty, may it cost whatever it cost, in the face of these individuals with new gestures and a strong will—perhaps the men of the herd will, one day, have shame of their ugliness and fear of their mediocrity.

We find ourselves today in an era that is terribly social and where we are constrained to accomplish deeds that do not always convene to our temperaments.

Some endure social work, in factories or offices. Others engage in illegalisms; they steal, they burglarize. Coincidence has better served yet others who are able to do nothing, living off of the money they inherited.

But in any scenario, let's not be the men in economic environments where we painfully subsist. Let's be weary of every social sense, whichever it may be, and of every professional sense.

It is not more fitting for an anarchist who does illegalisms to be only a burglar, to take up that mentality, and to keep those habits, to adopt the customs and the language of the *apaches* than it is for the one who works in a factory to be but a laborer and to assimilate into the workman mentality.[15] We need to be *new men*. If I am forced to work in a factory, whether it is for me or as means to an end, I may not let my entire activity be absorbed by this function. May the people who surround me in the workshop or in the office feel that I am not of their race, of their class—that I am a *déclassé*, an anarchist, a *new man*.

If I find myself forced, to assure my subsistence, to struggle or to trick, to steal, to burglarize or to kill, that this be but an accident for me, a means. That this does not absorb my entire will and that I do not assimilate myself with the vulgar social criminals; that, in my attitude, one can feel individuality.

Let's be new men. That every one of us repels the old, used skin of the social man to clothe oneself in a stronger, more beautiful one, with, on the forehead, the new flower of one's personal ideal.

From here on it will become clear how much my individualism differs from the one of certain recent theoreticians of anarchy who, however, also use the term.

What do they pretend? To use individual force to reach social ends. To assure common happiness, to solve the social question through individual means. Their pretended individualism can be reduced to this: a social revolution is possible if every individual personally wants to contribute to it; if every man consents to take an individual part in the action. But the capital point for them was above all the social issue, the common goal. Without a doubt we could agree, in practice, on certain matters that regard the attitude of the individual in its daily struggle—but what differences from the moment when this struggle goes further than customary acts and could compromise, through the grandeur of its affirmation, the balance of our social environment. Then these pretending individualists scream out: "Stop there! . . . The individual exaggerates. He loses sight of the human goal. He hits his head against a wall. His action remains pointless. He does not know where he is going."[16] As if the individualist could even bother to go anywhere! The only way he can follow is the one of his personality.

As long as a being is in accord with his temperament and acts in harmony with his conscience, how could he be worried about the social consequences of his acts? One is not an individualist out of tactics and to better serve a cause. One is an individualist by one's essence, for the only reason that one is a being and that there is nothing for a being that is greater than its own sensations, greater than its own will, greater than its own vision of the world and of its joy to sense itself believe in all of its strength and all of its personal harmony.

Meanwhile, I very well know that I am not perfect; I know that my human condition ties me by heredity to my flesh and the coincidences of my education, to all sorts of contingencies that are sources of ugliness. In fact, I feel in me, in certain hours, lingering needs that remind me of my form as an animal; I feel, in certain moments, pushes of beastliness that seem to chain me to my biological kind. Every individual can find within him enough similarities to the brute to imagine that "living one's life" consists in unleashing within him the most animalistic passions. But if one realizes that all of that is not what characterizes an individual, if one comprehends that this cruelly physical life does indeed not distinguish between one being and another—if one sees that the sole preoccupations of the stomach conduct to a bestial stampede where one loses all sense of personality, where the individual soul dies of thirst, one would want to dominate the physiological reality, one would want to give one's being an individual rhythm, one would want to affirm oneself in all one's beauty; one would like to be *heroically.*

## AT THE SOURCES OF HEROIC INDIVIDUALISM 8:
## WHAT IS OUR HEROISM?

*L'ACTION D'ART* 15 (OCTOBER 1913)

Individualism is completed, harmonized, intensified by the sentiment of heroism.

By talking of our tendencies, by criticizing or discussing each other, we have established great confusion about this "heroism" that we have asserted to qualify our individualism. We need to specify it to well dispel any errors.

By heroism I do not understand this sort of fury in action that happens in unconsciousness and by a sort of psychological drunkenness. I do not understand the desire to be considered a great man, immortalized as a living legend amid the adoration of the crowds, to any more heroic, either.

For that I love consciousness too much, the harmony and mastering of the self. I despise the stupidity of the crowds too much, and I care too little about the opinions of others to desire to be a figure of "social hero" among them.

Individualist heroism is the polar opposite of that.

You know all the force that I attribute to the illusion in the psychological domain; I tried to show how much she was necessary for the individual to be something else than a brute wallowing in his pleasures like a pig in its filth. For the individual to differentiate himself and to conceive of himself through illusion, it is necessary, first and foremost, that he believe in himself. It is necessary that he imagine himself in all his beauty; it is necessary that he see himself not as society constrained him to stay but as his consciousness, his individual ideal, makes him dream to be.

Every individual who, despising social life, despising brutal life, wants to affirm his personality, not only in how it is but especially in what he wants it to be; every individual who has the sentiment of being better, of being more, carries within himself the image of a hero. The heroism that I conceive is primarily an internal sentiment: the sentiment of intenseness and of harmony in individuality.

But as I have said, as an effect of believing oneself to be strong and beautiful, as an effect of believing oneself to be better and more harmonious, one necessarily ends up becoming oneself. The illusion is the sensed thought; it is a sort of psychological autocreation. It transforms the very consciousness that conceived it.

By musing of the hero that one carries within oneself, it is very likely that one becomes very naturally heroic.

Be then "heroic," from now on, every individual who, having become conscious of the greatest interest and the greatest happiness of his being, is ready to sacrifice all social conventions and daily pettinesses and tiny material satisfactions and small joys of life–to attain the ideal that he set out for himself–to grant himself the great joy of realizing himself the way he dreamed himself, the way he wanted himself. Be heroic every being that tends toward the most complete blossoming of its personal life, every being that, having made itself a clear and harmonious idea of its destiny, will go to the bottom of that idea and will not be concerned with any consequence, sociological or physiological, no external outcome (albeit death!) to experience this one joy of every conscious being: to let all flowers of its life bloom, and to passionately feel all the sap that created it rising up within it.

Does this mean that the attitude of the heroic individualist will be the one of the misanthrope, taking refuge at the top of an ivory tower? Will the idea and the sentiment that guide him lead him to the idleness of solitude? That would be to misjudge his temperament remarkably.

How could the one who feels all passions of living boil in him–and as powerfully that he cannot oblige himself to contain them, to be a social entity–how could that exceptionally alive being not search for sympathies around him? How could he stay impassive?

If he feels the entire original force of his growth, if he knows himself to be a unique flower, he can love to surround himself only with other original forces, other unique flowers, in order to taste the joy of life being understood by a different being, the joy of understanding a different being, the ineffable joy of feeling loved and of loving. He will look for "his own," that is to say the ones with whom he could find an increase of his joy, an exhilaration of his being, a larger expansion of his personality. He will search out the ones with whom he can sense, think, act in harmony.

This does not mean, not in the slightest, that he will look for another just like him, or that he will try to remake in his image the activities and consciousnesses he will encounter. No, the heroic individualist will look for the company of personalities that are different from his–personalities of which he will love the proud integrity, the rare unity–personalities that will all be like rare flowers that will bring their note to the symphony of the ensemble of personalities. And thus, a *bande* will be founded.

## AT THE SOURCES OF HEROIC INDIVIDUALISM 9: THE *BANDE*

*L'ACTION D'ART* 15 (OCTOBER 1913)

In order to be intensively and to be able to, in harmony, affirm his growth, the heroic individualist has searched *his own*. And if he has found them, these brethren of the hearth that his unique love will infinitely call for, the "*bande*" will be born.

And that they won't come to tell us, as Mr. le Dantec has purported by talking of the "tragic bandits," that this is nothing but a new, more restrained society.[17] By its essence, its nature, by the very fact of its composition, by the conditions of its birth, the *bande* absolutely differs from society. Society imposes itself onto people from the moment of their birth; they are forced to accept it with all its traditions, all its laws, following the coincidental arbitraries of religion and of the nation. In society the individual is taken up into an organism of which he isn't the originator. In society the individual is the slave of an anonymous group: he is constrained to be in solidarity with all those whom the contingencies of time and space have made his community of faith or his fellow countrymen. In society the individual has not chosen following his spirit, nor following his heart. He is but an unconscious cell of an organism without any harmony. The *bande*, on the contrary, has only been created by the conscious will of the individuals who formed it. It is conditioned to the happiness of its members and can be maintained, persist, and last only by virtue of its harmony. How could one compare the imprisonment of birth that society imposes on its subjects to the free choice that forms a *bande*? In one, the beings are assembled by the often monstrous coincidences of birth in one place or another, and in one class or another. In the other, individuals have freely associated, united by a community of tendencies.

But it is also necessary to distinguish what I call the *bande* from what the communists call *colonies*.

The communist *colonies* are certainly fairer than the societal spheres because at least there the individuals incorporate themselves by their own digressions. But they do not seem more likely to bring about harmony. The individual cannot find his happiness there any more than in society.

This is due to the form or their constitution. How are the entities that we call the *milieux libres* actually founded? A comrade or a group of "comrades," united through common projects, through seemingly common ideas, indiscriminately call for all comrades who would like to cooperate in their work, for all who, pretending to be anarchist, would want to try a communist experience. However, what does this result in? Men with the most diverse temperaments, the most opposing tendencies, even being most antipathetic toward each other, associate to live together, to share all hours of their existence, and most of the time they do not even know each other yet. Fatally, rifts and conflicts will occur between them. That would not be much of a problem if they just separated there. But no. As victims of the social illusion of a cause to uphold, duped by an altruist ideal, they oblige themselves to not break this new social contract. Behold them now, looking just like the patriots who are at each other's throats in midst of this country that ties them together. The idea of communism thus ends up simply taking the place of patriotism. Beings condemn themselves to suffer in the companionship of people whom they do not like, just for the good of the cause—for the prospering of the colony. That should not be surprising: they associated themselves with a theoretical community. However, theories are nothing but empty frames; they can contain the most beautiful paintings, but also the most different ones or just the most horrendous smearing. How many individuals label themselves anarchists who have never thought about the reasons for their anarchism, who have especially never thought about what they could personally be. If they do, then communist colonies, hybrid assemblies of inharmonious elements, are doomed, either to disintegrate, or to provoke as many constraints as societal environments.

The *bande*, on the contrary, has no fixed form. It does not exist without individuals; it is nothing without their happiness. It is not an entity, or a cause, or a project; it is not a subject to a theory. It doesn't propose a solution to the economical question.[18] The individuals who form it find in it only an opportunity to be individually better.

The *bande* is, a priori, nothing. It is formed by the very force of the individualities who compose it. It could transform or dissolve following this same force.

To form the *bande*, the individualities who compose it do not look for a common ideal, a common theory, or common conceptions. It suffices to have a community of temperaments, an intuitive sympathy that attracts the ones to the others who found each other without even having planned it. They have found each other, so to say, without having looked for one another.

The members of the *bande* do not resemble one another. They can have very different conceptions, what does it matter! They understand each other, they form a harmony; they are capable of loving one another, to inspire together. For that they do not need to eat off the same plate or to sleep in the same chambers. It suffices that they find each other in the hours of actions, in the hours of spiritual pleasures, in the hours of labor or in the hours of struggle.

The *bande* cannot encompass a very large collectivity. The individuals who form it must be weary of the mania of expansion. Why want to be a hundred or a thousand? It is all the better if that is possible harmoniously, but if it consists only of three or four, the oeuvre of the *bande* will not be less interesting. It is not necessary to look for anything else in a *bande* but the greatest harmony between its elements.

There will therefore certainly be a multitude of *bandes*, some larger, some more curtailed, all according to the needs and temperaments of the different individuals who will group up. The more rationalist ones will unite for a more scientific existence, the more mystical ones will have a more spiritual oeuvre, the more artistic will give their *bande* a more aesthetic sense—but all of these *bandes* will have no other fundament than the happiness and the greatest realization of each individual.

The *bande* is not necessarily tragic.[19] It exists at the periphery of society. Every individual who composes it has to act like the world only consisted of him and the ones he loves: *the bande*. This will primarily involve being and self-realization in harmony with oneself and with the ones whom one has chosen as companions. The *bande* is thus constituted only to create life; it does not have as an initial goal sowing death around it.

However, it will also fear nothing to ensure its most natural, most harmonious blossoming. If its societal environment is ugly enough to fear its hatching of beauty, then too bad for the men of society! We don't know them, and we don't want to get to know them. We avoid contacting them, but we will not permit them to affect our oeuvre.

In the hour where the oeuvre is in danger, when the *bande* feels harassed from all sides, when the individuals who form it feel that the hits from societal men aim to murder their united hearts—then, and only then, the chased-down *bande* will see itself forced to become tragic. To defend their troubled harmony, to affirm their will of individual flourishing, they will know to fight. And in what way then would the death inflicted to them matter to them: they will leave nothing behind: the heroic individualist who has formed his *bande* recognizes the existence of nothing, except for himself and his own.

## AT THE SOURCES OF HEROIC INDIVIDUALISM 10:
## HEROIC INDIVIDUALISM AND DAILY ACTIONS

*L'ACTION D'ART* 17 (DECEMBER 1913)

In my previous studies I have painted a picture of my conception of the individual; I tried to discern the rhythm of his personal life, the spiritual forces that could help him live, and the individual ideal that could drive him to act.

I have first shown the roots of every intensely unique life to be in the intuition, and I have found in it this sense of personality, this love for the joy of life following the rhythm of its temperament that turns the being who has become conscious of it into an indomitable psychic force. Then I have shown how science can help us to live. I have said that affirming the spiritual strength of a being does not entail the negation of scientific research.

I have tried to discern only what needs to be separated. I have shown that science, hailing from practical life, from physical action, cannot impose on us a law of individual happiness.

On one hand we have our personal activity, our psychological life, our sensation of living, our rhythm of life. On the other there is physical life, the external world, the practical phenomena. These two worlds stand in a very complex relation to one another, two worlds of which the facts very often get mixed up and get juxtaposed—to create, one by one, either scientific mistakes—when subjectivism intrudes onto the territory of objective facts—or individual suffering, when we let the laws of the external world, of the physical world, attain the psychological life of a being.

It is as absurd, as dangerous, as criminal to castrate a physiological or physical activity by wanting to assimilate all facts of the world into absolute spiritualism as it is to mutilate, to compress, to unify the psychological activities of the individual consciousness, by wanting to order and legislate according to a conception that is universally, uniquely, and uniformly scientistic.

When I say: "There is but one truth, but one affirmation, but one goal: my individual life," I do not negate science with that—on the contrary, I permit it to act more freely, by not letting psychic or metaphysical considerations interfere with its research. Science can thus pursue its work in the domain of objective facts. But I simultaneously move the problem of my happiness; by freeing myself from every collective law, I affirm the universally objective, the analysis of practical life, in order to be able to better distinguish the uniqueness of my personal life, of my intuition, of my individual force of being. The more I will be a scientist for the exterior world, for the objective, for the material, the more I will be an intuitionist for the life of my being, for my subjective, for the spiritual. By having a clear view of the exterior world the way it is I will be all the more able, through the contrast, to discover myself and to know how my happiness, which depends only on what I want to be, can be realized even among the most contrarian elements, in the most opposing and hostile environments. By discovering what hurts me in my surroundings, by discovering what shocks me and what wants to destroy me—I will discover at the same time who I am, if I have the strength for that. Eventually I will be able to discriminate between two orders of facts; I will distinguish what I feel and what I want from what is around me—and to live my life, I will end up by discovering *my* methods to live. Thus, through the distinction between the objective and the subjective, I will know that for the external world, that is to say for all that stands in the way of the development of my intuitive being, of my individuality, I will be happy to serve myself of analysis to destroy it, I will be happy to be a scientist, brutally or skillfully, whatever the circumstance calls for, for everything that is not mine—for everything that slows down my blossoming, for all that is opposed to my will of my sympathy. I will be a scientist in the domain of science (and I understand societal facts to be a part of this domain as much as physical or chemical facts are). In contrast, I will be an intuitionist for all that is mine, for all that I feel to be with me, for me; for all that adds to my joy of life, to my free harmony, to my heroic interests, to my individualized illusion, to my beauty. I will be an intuitionist in the world of intuition. That is to say that there I will not act according to an inflexible logic but according to the harmonious curve that I will have chosen. There I will be preoccupied first and foremost with finding an accord, a harmony; I will search for beauty and the greatness of my soul.

I will now illustrate examples for these ideas, in order to discern how the one whom I call a heroic individualist can act in his daily life, according to these two motives of action, in parallel against his enemies and for his own. And thus I hope to show to so many boisterous revolutionaries, and to some logicians who claim to be individualists, that our aesthetic attitude does not lead us to deny the action—but on the contrary, that it can, in this way, incite us to enthusiastic, fruitful struggles for the individual—with truly anarchist attitudes.

In these articles on the "Heroic Individualist" I have described my ideal of an individual life that is satisfying in the search for the most harmonious creation, the most intense realization of the personality. Ultimately I have said how I conceive of the blossoming of the individualist, outside of a collective humanity, outside of every nation, of every race, of every traditional society, outside of every social hierarchy, an individualist finding his own through sympathy, living in a *bande* with the brethren of his intuitive temperament, the brethren of his heart, for the highest joy of his own life.

That is an ideal. How can an individualist, in the practical daily action, realize himself while staying, heroically, fully in accord with this ideal?

## AT THE SOURCES OF HEROIC INDIVIDUALISM 11: HEROIC INDIVIDUALISM AND DAILY ACTIONS 2

*L'ACTION D'ART* 18 (DECEMBER 1913)

Of all the arguments that are brought forward against us, the most frequently heard can be formulated as such: "Your integral individualism is not practicable, because by taking abstraction of your societal environment and negating all that exists, it does not grant you the rational territory of partaking in the struggle for life. Your individualism turns you into illusory beings who arbitrarily disclaim a society with which you will have to deal with in order to act." That is the most incredible misapprehension that one can have of our account. We suffer too much from the ambient ugliness around us not to be able to perceive its existence; we are too hurt, tortured, enclosed by societal men as that we could entertain any doubts of their horrendous powers; authority shocks us, constrains us, hinders us sufficiently so that we know its laws well. We do not deny the existence of societal life any more than we do the existence of physical life. But both of them have no part in my happiness. Society cannot, and not any more than nature, have my individual harmony and personal good in its consideration. My happiness depends only on my own character; it is within me, it will only be according to my own will, according to my unique sense of joy, following the ideal that I created in order to intensively live my life.

In his encounters with nature, man uses the phenomena following his interests, following the best rhythm of his life. He endeavors to generate the physical facts that he recognizes as useful around him, that is to say the facts that are in harmony with his existence, with his growth and development, with his happiness. He also endeavors to prevent the materialization of physical phenomena the apparition of which trouble the course of his life and break up the equilibrium of his happiness. All of the sciences have no other goal than to accomplish these two endeavors, to permit mankind to use the phenomena of nature to its greatest comfort, to its largest enjoyment. From the physical and chemical sciences that enable mankind to extract from material elements the parts that are most profitable to its well-being to medicine that allows it to discover the conditions for harmony or imbalance of its bodies, all of science has no other end: to discern the best utilization of material phenomena that our experience presents to us, to eliminate pain and to promote well-being.

However, I know no sensation of pain or of well-being outside of the consciousness of an individual. Human pain, or the happiness of humanity, these are myths, absolutely analogous to the one of divine justice, to the one of a Supreme Being. Only the individual can be conscious of its well-being, of its pain. The sciences are instruments for the individual. They can have no other ambition than to satisfy the individual. Only the individuals feel, only the individual suffers, only the individual rejoices. Outside of the individual, there is no other reality. The individual is the supreme end. It is the only goal of life. A science that does not serve the happiness of the individual, a science that tends to enslave it to whatever else, to make him serve for other ends, to neglect the individual end, would be analogous to theology; it would be but a science of death. The science of life is an instrument of individual happiness.

In the physical domain I thus serve myself of science to differentiate the phenomena that are susceptible to cause me pain, and from the ones that can lead to my harmony and joy. I don't think we have to change methods when it comes to the societal environment.

Some will raise against that the community of the species, human fraternity, social solidarity, etc. . . . But we have spoken of that subject enough, in many discussions and preceding articles, so we don't need to come back to it here. Let it be enough to repeat that the only living reality, the only sensed reality, the only experienced one, resides in individual intuition. There can be no other end for a being but the very affirmation of this being; it can be realized only in its own force and its own harmony. Consequently, I have shown that a being can only find solidarity or fraternity with its own, which is to say with those who truly are the brethren of its sensation, of its will, and of its work: the ones who want to be in accord with it, the ones for whom it found enough sympathy to be able to confide its soul to them, its entire widely opened soul. A heroic individualist can have no other community but that one: the community of intuitive sympathies. It is a community of blazing souls, each with its own personal ideal, flames that burn in diversely nuanced colors but that unite to mutually enlighten, and creating in this union a vast, harmonious glow in the night of monsters, the night of nightmares of the societal world.

But let's return to this nightmare. It is haunting enough, and haunting on a daily basis, that we have to be bound to occupy ourselves with it. Too often the monsters that inhabit it come to blow, with their monstrously deformed mugs, against the flames that we nurture with the blood of our heart, with the passionate sap of our life; then we must, out of pure love for the flames, so that they do not get blown out by the stinking breath of social realities, struggle against the ambient monstrosities, and we must know all their dangers. We need to be ready to use trickery or violence, depending on the circumstance, to defend ourselves against the attacks from our societal environment. For the defense of one's individual harmony, for the defense of one's joy of life, for the defense of one's idealized I, the heroic individualist must not despise being armed in this battle for his beauty as surely, as scientifically as his enemies are to defend their nation, their society, their ugliness. It suits the heroic individualist to ignore none of the conditions, none of the circumstances of societal life in order to be able to act against it better and more effectively for the defense of his happiness. *Against it*, I have said—and I insist on that, because that is where his attitude distinguishes itself from the one of the opportunist or the one of the conqueror, or the one of the authoritarian Nietzschean. The opportunist and the conqueror accept societal life as much as the pacifist bourgeois does, and all of them act in concord with society; they affirm themselves only with societal forces, and they aim only at societal powers. They acquiesce to the laws from which they want to profit. They accept the rhythm of societal life; they want to be societal powers. They can only find joy in the most social recognition of their powers. They want to impose upon men, upon all men, their will to power. They become inebriated by their societal success. They find enjoyment, contentment in human glory, only in societal triumph, in success.

The heroic individualist who has found his good in his own individually sensed life, he who places his ideal in his own beauty, his own happiness in his own personal harmony, his triumph in the integral affirmation of his I, his success and his expansion in the discovery of his own, in the sympathetic formation of his *bande*, this individualist who finds his heroism in the most absolute renunciation of societal prejudice, of mediocre pleasures of societal life, of all societal considerations, to affirm himself the way he is, the way he wants to be, the way that he likes being individually; this individualist of new heroism can want only the destruction of the societal environment; he can affirm only himself by destroying, brutally or patiently but with an equally iron will, the constructions of a societal world. Individual harmony can blossom only on the ruins of societal harmony. All creations who want to assure a common good contain within themselves a principle of authority over individual life. They have to create a new dogma; to be collectively imposed, they are forced to make abstractions of the consciousness and of the sensibility of the individual; they edify themselves in the approval of everyone, against the forced acquiescence of some; they construct upon individual suffering, because an individual getting crushed matters little to them considering that they are—themselves—the societal oeuvre.

This is true, but the inversion of the previous is just as much. There cannot be an individual oeuvre without the destruction of the societal. A life that is personal, harmonious, and fruitful in noble joy can only hatch in a struggle to affirm it; it can only unite with other lives that are as beautiful, it can find its sisters in harmony and creation and with them, the great music of intuitive actions, only is the condition of being able to desolidarize of universal ugliness. This includes not being weary of the destruction of the social and being ruthlessly hard for all that compromises individual happiness, and for all that tries, through efforts of domination or of servitude, to consolidate, to support, to fortify societal edifices.


## REFRACTORY POETS 1: THE BOHÈME AND ITS CLOWNS

*L'ACTION D'ART* 8 (JULY 1913)

While the course of my reflections during my study "At the Sources of Heroic Individualism" will take me, after shedding light on my tendencies, to affirming my attitude and describing my action, I believe it would be good to concurrently illustrate, with the example of some heroic lives, a philosophy that I do not want to leave up to any speculation.

In order to better find myself and to be able to look for *my own* more heroically and without fault, in order to be able to harmoniously discern the circumstances of my banditism among the living—and to only unite in a *bande* with people who are worthy of me and worthy of themselves—I will dwell upon evoking some rare figures from the dead who were *my own* in the past, and whose revolutionary blooming warmed up the often hardened flower buds of my own youth.

First I want to portray a few to whom this name very well suits: *The refractionary poets*.

This is obviously not about the contour-poets of the revolts or the bards of the *grands soirs*. I do not confuse poetry for eloquence—and I am more and more mistrusting of this low romanticism where the snoring of the words weighs the subtle rhythm of their sense to sleep; that, if a thunder of oratory periods doesn't eternally cover the chant of the soul.

I am also not concerned with watering over the fate of "poets of misery" or to delight over the eccentricities of the Bohème.

Misery is ugly; it is a flaw that a poet cannot boast about. He who resigns to the filthiness of poverty can hardly have this proud flame that must burn in the heart of every poet. As to the Bohème, it is a fake attitude which young bourgeois, apprentice notaries, budding lawyers and even magistrates indulge in, as a way for them to divert themselves during their studies by mimicking artists, and by committing a few farces at the Quartier Latin, protected by the watchful eye of the police and by future stipends that are very carefully reserved for them by their families, with a good number of recommendations that these "rascals" will very well know how to use when the time is right. And if the Bohème is not, again, this parade that so many opportunists use to impress or silence the public, and to give themselves the allures of the beggar or the "wolf"—for a cheap price—then we also had, albeit some time ago, the Bohème of Jean Richepin and his picturesque embarrassments—his scandals, wanted exaggerations, false hardships, artificial skin—his disguise as a beggar, which he was able to quickly get rid of once its effect was materialized, to appropriate, at the right moment, an academic dress and the tailcoat of the "Annales."[20] But he at least, while he barely had a conscience, had talent, and it was a pity.

Since then Jean Richepin generated disciples, and a great number of fools wanted, on his coattails, go from the lowest to the highest points of societal hierarchy. We witnessed a *cabaretier* doubly using his teachings to boast about the quality of his *aramon*[21] and the quality of his poetry . . . and forgetting it all, like a good devil would, to enter into the Academie Française—where he very well fit in, by the way, besides Mr. Raymond Poincaré, academic and president of the republic by the combined power of a people of drunkards.19

We witnessed a young butcher drop meat for poetry, which he started trading in the most repugnant way, by bluffing, blackmailing, and snitching. This evil buffoon once had even the sincerest of us fooled about his intentions. We knew he had little talent; we discovered no genius in him, but we thought him to be, with his verbal ardor, capable of biting the butts of the masters and slaves of the letters. A brief illusion! We quickly realized that he didn't carry the teeth of a wolf but the tongue of a dog. From the moment on when he was nothing but a poet of misery, he became a miserable poet, surely now also aspiring to the Academy . . . to the Academy of moral sciences, where his place is perfectly found next to Mr. Lépine.[22]

A well-known truism in the literary and artistic scenes is to affirm: "The life of the Bohême is limited in time. It is good to have lived it, but one has to get out of it." What, then, do the good gentlemen of the Gensdelettres understand by "the life of the Bohême?"[23] A certain irregularity within daily life, a loosening of mores, the life of the café, some noctambulism, an apparent nonchalance about the next day, and the desire to impress the bourgeois. I insist on this last point because the rest can be abbreviated by it: "to impress the bourgeois." The Bohème poses before the bourgeois, it looks to surprise it. It does not desolidarize from it; quite on the contrary, it wants to attract its attention. It only works to scandalize it in order to create a spectacle for itself. And as soon as the sufficiently diverted bourgeois will have judged the spectacle, and if the bohemian artist has talent, he will seize the first opportunity to become the great comedian applauded by the public, the favorite poet, or painter, or musician of his time. Callously he will go from boul'-Mich or Montmartre to the Academy. If there is no grand address for him, he will none the less leave and become a fashionable clown or a civil servant.

The story of the old Chat Noir Cabaret perfectly illustrates my notion. All bohemian life of twenty years ago can be characterized by it. In this hostel in Montmartre, where Rodolphe Salis invited the Parisians, the bourgeois, to dazzle in the audacities and eccentricities of the "talented" among his poet and artist friends, there was an erotic poet by the name of Maurice Donnay who today is in the Académie Française as a substantial dramatic author. There was the revolutionary chansonnier Maurice Boukay, today known as Mister Couyba, senator, former minister of commerce. But there were also myriad young bohemians who we can find today as deputies at the offices of the ministry of the interior and of agriculture, or as police commissioners, or as Montmartrian chansonniers in the music halls, on the condition that they concoct a few patriotic stanzas to honor the law of the three years or the arrival of his majesty Alphons XIII.[24]

Behold there the products of the life of the Bohême, truly sad products as they are. "The life of the Bohême is limited in time." Surely, and the ones who lead it know that very well before they engage in it. They play a role, their role as prostitutes to societal life. They are the same as those girls who, wanting to launch themselves in courteous circles, are forced to in order to make an initial name for themselves, go make a fool of themselves at Chahut balls. Some manage to meet rich men to maintain them, who make them posh and triumphant courtesans; others, who are less crafty, go on to populate the brothels. I will halt the analogy here; it seems obvious enough.

The Bohême, from more than one angle, resembles a prostitute. Like her, it is ready for any task to gain some money. Like her, it avidly aspires for some societal attention. One, like the other, when they manage to take up a societal status, will become the most obscurely, the most stupidly fierce of bourgeois, and if they stay on the gutters, one like the other will crack with a heart full of rage of not being able to be "*like the others*."

The refractory poet, a complete opposite to that, takes pride in not being like the others. He has, before anything else, love for his personality, and his great joy is to feel like a unique being.

## REFRACTORY POETS 2: TO LIVE ONE'S DREAM

*L'ACTION D'ART* 9 (JULY 1913)

My conception of the arts is known. In many a discussion and my preceding articles, I have devoted myself to describing it. I have shown that the arts are not that amusement without any importance, not this distraction for neurotics, not this dilatant game coming, so to say, over the market from the other acts of life, and not "*l'art pour l'art*"—but also not, and even less so, some adjuvant to the good functioning of society, a sort of accompaniment to the tragedy of humanity, or social art. Instead, it is a blossoming of an individuality that is avid to improve, the drive of a personality toward its most harmonious realization, the affirmation of a being, of a soul that wants itself in all its personal force, in all its personal beauty, in its most perfect individual cohesion. The true artist is the one who, having discovered within himself his own tendencies, having learned the élan of his heart, of his temperament, of his intuition, wants to realize the most perfect accord among them, the largest and most intense symphony. If he writes, if he sings, if he paints, if he sculpts, that is not to realize works for which his nation or society or humanity can reward him; it is to realize himself, it is because he senses within himself a great need to scream out his soul, to push the clamor of his being toward the sun, like a tree in the forest pushes its branches full of leaves toward the highest of the lights.

For the artist, the way I conceive him, "living his life" is not enough. He wants to "live his dream"—or, more exactly, for this artist "living his life" is synonymous with "living his dream."

I do not want to say by this that he only wants to live in his dream, which would correspond to not acting.

Quite the opposite. He wants to make his dream a reality. He wants to model his action after his ideal. He wants to sculpt his life after the image of his dream.

Let's then define this word "dream." It could lead to confusion. I do not at all understand by it some saraband of vague images like the ones we see in our dreams at night. I understand by "the dream" that which is opposed, for the consciousness of a being, to the brutal reality of the external world. Around me, societal life is ugly; the circumstances of my life are mediocre, oppressive; I myself am forced to undergo this ugliness; society makes me ugly. These are exterior necessities; these are determined facts, exact facts, and true facts. But am I forced to consent to them? Is there nothing else within me? Is there not my temperament in revolt, my consciousness that uplifts itself, *my mind* that, uniting all its tendencies, all its personal wills, all its images, evokes in me the vision of what I should be, of what I would want to be, of what my acts could be? This vision of my individual ideal, this image of my harmony, of my perfection, of my happiness, that is what I call my dream.

"Living my life" without taking my dream into account would consist of living like the bourgeois and like the slaves: that is to say to accept the facts as they are, to adapt to the circumstances, to resign. To be intensely myself, to affirm and realize myself, I need to carry an ideal within me, my ideal; I need to want to "live my dream."

The refractory poets are the ones who have intensely and ultimately wanted to live their dream. In their souls, glowing melting pots of the most magnanimous hopes, the most sumptuous images, the most delicate sensations, the most grandiose ideas, their dreams found an irresistible blossoming: they imagined a harmonious personality, a free and ideal one; they wonderfully sensed within themselves all the rare beauty of an individual life, and they ended up by not conceiving any other goals in their life than to affirm the harmony of their being! How now could any honors, any societal considerations, any glory amidst their contemporaries have any importance to them? Or all further rattles for which the showoffs and know-it-alls of the letters and the arts, all the charlatans of the pen tear each other apart?

The only goal of their life was to affirm themselves through their personality. The only joy of their being was to give up nothing of what they wanted to be; to stay true to themselves, to flourish in all their originality only for the joy of flourishing under the sun.

But societal life exists—ugly, dirty, inharmonious, with all its economic necessities, with all its tyrannies, all its slaveries, and its blind aim to level everything out, to ruthlessly equalize everything.

For whoever refuses to subdue its laws, society is terrible. Against everything abnormal, it is cruel. It doesn't suffer when we deviate from the great route that it traces. But if it is already obscenely murderous for the ones who, without wanting to, inadvertently, leave its frame, it is all the more ferocious for the ones who, of their own free will, despise it in order to commit themselves to a life of dreams. Society is the realm of the mediocre. Grown out of ugliness, it maintains itself only by accumulating further ugliness upon more ugliness. Woe to the one who does not surrender to this law of ugliness; woe to the one who is only concerned with keeping a harmonious conscience, a free individuality; woe to those who listen only to the voice of their dream.

In every civilized and administered society, a man who has a soul and who wants to freely manifest it is fatally condemned to be violated, hurt, tortured unto death. Every poet who is truly a poet, every artist who is truly a creator, is considered by society as a dangerous monster. It has every interest to enchain him, to crush him, or to slaughter him. In this it does its job well. However, there are some poets who, having understood this situation, managed to desolidarize from the community of mankind, to live in the margins of society, illegally, as refractories.

## REFRACTORY POETS 3: FRANÇOIS VILLON

*L'ACTION D'ART* 9 (JULY 1913)

It is to discover oneself, to sense oneself intensively, to better love oneself that the heroic individualist can search in the past for the ones who were with their era, despite their era, against their era, personalities that were both strong and harmonious.

For me the history of a people only has objective value; it doesn't affect me; I take note of it with the same indifferent impartiality as I do the history of terrains. My heart is not more impassioned by descriptions of sociology as it is by the ones of geology.

They are facts—nothing more, collisions of matter that prove nothing for my own development, that help in nothing toward my personal blossoming.

It is in the history of individuals that I am looking to educate myself. There I can find profit by searching for my cause. I do thus not speak of "individuals" who were only events created by social phenomena. What do I care about the lives of "brave soldiers," of "great leaders" for the royalty or the revolution, of the "heroes" of the empire or the republic? These weren't true individuals; they existed only societally, as units to serve the interest of causes that were external to their own being, forces that were randomly generated by societal currents; they had no more existence than the atoms that work toward some chemistry; they were nothing but societal tools. Their history does not interest us.

But I rejoice in discovering the life of those who in the past were individual forces.

To know their thoughts and their actions is a fertile ground to nourish the sap that rises through my branches.

The memory of their personalities is the sun that warms and illuminates me in order to help me to better reach my treetops.

The ones whom I call the refractory poets are the select few among them, of whom the past is more alive than the present of so many pitiful men. To narrate their past life can incite us to better live our own lives.

•••

Behold first the most beautiful, the highest of them all—the oldest, too: Maître François Villon, the bandit-poet of the Middle Ages. His life and his work are one and the same monument; who knows one is forced to be interested in the other, because his work was but the chant of his life and his life but an illustration of his work.

What imbeciles would want to differentiate between the life and the works of a poet, and what hypocrites would pretend, by circumstance, to excuse the "darkness" of the life with the "naivety" of the work? In reality, official critics, pawns of the universities, you are here: forced by admiring the work of the poet to glorify the life of a bandit—and you try to get out of that by a few subtle distinctions, but you will never succeed. A man like Villon is to be taken in his entirety, life and work, crimes and rhymes, leaving you unable to choose between them at your convenience.

With the poet, the bandit has forced open the narrow doors of your admiration to invade the small house of your conscience, and there you are, appalled by all that he has shattered of your petty moral conventions, but you have to undergo it, because he is a genius—and if you experience some shame, that is but normal!

That is the story of François Villon. He was born in 1431—"of small and poor origins,"[25] as he put it. After some years at school, where he was an undisciplined student, he entered university in 1450. Back then the university was in major disorder and the scholars, rebels against the police and the church, were like the revolutionaries of that era. This had been the case since 1444: after a few violent troubles, some scholars had been imprisoned, bloody riots ensued, and from then

on there was a ten-year-long, incessant struggle between rebels and public offi-
cials. Taking refuge on the hills of Sainte-Geneviève, the scholars went out only
to pillage stores, to commit assassinations, to ambush the lookouts, and to grap-
ple with the soldiers.[26]

For these environments of revolt, Villon and his friends had about the same
attitude that the "anarchist bandits" have for our revolutionary environments today.

Initially they took part in the movement and were the most convinced of the
rioters. Then they grew weary of these communal actions and launched themselves
onto the path of individual revolt, to do what we would today call "illegalism."[27]

In 1452 Villon linked up with Colin de Cayeux and Régnier de Montigny. Like
their poet companion, these two young men had come to banditism by way of
the revolt. They weren't some of those professional "wrongdoers" to whom theft
and crime were societal functions that were as absorbing as work and a good repu-
tation are for the "honest people." They were just as little like the vulgar highway
robbers who haunted the roads of that era as the "anarchist bandits" today are
dissimilar to the *apaches*. By committing their misdeeds they followed no tradi-
tions and no customs; they didn't obey the morals of the criminals. They were no
"sociological cases," no "products of their environment."

François Villon and his companions formed a *bande*, an association of a few
who were, before anything else, animated by a refractory spirit.

If they were criminals, that was only due to a consequence of their will to be
"individually," of their thirst to live outside of societal environments—on the mar-
gins. If they came to banditism, they weren't pushed toward it by their societal
constitution, by their ascendance and by the determinism of their conditions; they
went toward it without fear of the ensuing adventures, unbothered by external
consequences but prepared to sacrifice nothing of their lives, heroically having
decided to do everything in order to let their joy of life glow, like a fantastic fire
of Saint-Jean illuminating the night of the people and around which, until the
morning, they want to dance until they lose all breath.

Refractories before everything else, Villon and his companions became ban-
dits only through the force of their personal temperament. Their crimes were but
acts provoked by their initially defensive, then aggressive attitude toward every-
thing that intervened in the blooming of their being. They arrived at banditism
by way of the revolt.

Colin de Cayeux and Régnier de Montigny were both of "good origins," as Vil-
lon phrased it, that is to say that they could have been, had they followed family

traditions, good presidents of the parliament or decorated pontiffs; but they were, like Villon, undisciplined students, more "courageous" than all others and very avid of liberty.

Their first conviction was for having punched, one night, two sergeants on lookout during a fight. "Rebellion against agents," we would call that in our age of courtesy. Consult the files of the "bandits" of today; at the dawn of their exploits you will often find an analogous "peccadillo." This will stay, surely, a trivial mistake without consequence for the "good," for the "prudent man" and for the "citizen." But consider a being who was pushed into the world as a surly herb in a cleanly raked lawn; consider it, with all its force, all its enthusiasm, all its youth and all pride and love for itself.... For such an individual it will no longer be a "peccadillo" but an event, a catastrophe; it will be its first step outside of the law, and from then on nothing will be able to stop it on its dizzying course on the conquest of its life—until the moment of its death.

Meanwhile, the troubles at the university continued to inspire terrible riots. Soldiers and scholars doggedly fought over the hill of Sainte-Geneviève. The battles were heated. But they didn't excite François Villon and his friends much anymore. They were too individualist to care about these revolutionary battles. They preferred fighting for themselves and conquering, individually or among "companions," the joy of life, instead of stupidly risking death, blindly within a crowd.

On June 5, 1455, a row took place between Villon and the preacher Philippe Sermoise. Threatened, Villon defended himself and killed the clergyman. The crime was very grave; in that era the murder of a member of the clergy was considered doubly punishable. Villon managed to flee. But chased down, he was soon arrested and condemned to death by hanging. Meanwhile, after an appeal, the punishment was reduced to banishment.

Near the end of the month of June 1455, Villon thus left Paris, banished by the courts. He left behind the good lodge of Saint-Benoit, the relations with his dear uncle Mr. Guillaume de Villon, and the talks at the Hotel de Jouy.

He entered in a life of vagrancy, almost without any money, unable to work any craft. He went into vagabonding, heroically.

But he had friends. And if he abandoned the "leader of the houses" Casin Cholet and the "sewerage operator" Jehan le Loup, who only had little experience of a life outside of Paris, he returned to see Régnier de Montigny and Colin de Cayeux, who didn't hesitate to teach him the ways of living illegally on the large routes of the kingdom.

## REFRACTORY POETS 4: FRANÇOIS VILLON (CONTINUATION)

*L'action d'art* 12 (September 1913)

Banished, the poet François Villon, more refractory than ever against all societal constraints, will become, to assure his life, a tragic bandit.[28]

From the moment he left Paris, he had become part of a large association of wrongdoers who were then known under the name of Coquilles. The companions of the Coquille (or the Coquillards) committed illegalisms in the area around Dijon, on the large streets. A first investigation was opened against them by the procurer of Dijon in 1455. The Coquillards stayed elusive for a long time. But traitors, like flies, are of all times. The companions of the Coquille were betrayed, sold out, by one of them, a man named Perrenent le Fournier. On December 18, 1455, three Coquillards were burned alive on a pyre on Morimont Square in Dijon for counterfeiting. There were also Coquillards being tortured in Lyon, Grenoble, and Amiens.

But now that the Coquille was disorganized, Villon no longer wanted to join an already established gang. Instead he wanted to organize, with some of his friends, people he had loved for a long time and more than brothers, a small gang of intimates, *his bande*. To live his individual revolt, he thus associated with Colin de Cayeux, Guy Tabarie, Petit-Jehan, Petit Thibaut, and dom Nicolas.

Their first coup was sensational. It caused as much of a stir in those days as the assassination of the Rue Ordener did in ours.[29]

Villon and his friends stole six hundred golden écus (a fabulous amount back then) from the Grand College in Navarre. It was then the most considerable theft that was ever registered.

But that was not enough for the new gang. Villon wanted to immediately try a new attack. He left for Angers, to learn about the "estate of another old monk that should be worth another 500 or 600 écus."

Living as such, the small Parisian gang had to one day, as he put it, "prepare all its forces to rob a man that waited for nothing else so that he had a good case to beat someone up."[30] And, of course, this occurred in Angers.

The gang thus discovered and chased, Villon has to leave Paris once more, but he has a hundred écus with him, and now he knows all the ways of living on the routes. He knows, if need be, how to compose a "farce or moral" to play in any city to gain some money.

From December 14, 1447, until May 1456, the poor master of the arts vagabonded all across France, always on the run, always living of the coincidences of the routes.

In October 1461 we find him again in chains, on a diet of water and bread, in the oubliettes of the prison of Meung-sur-Loir, where he was detained by the bishop of Orleans for an aggravated theft in Montpipeau.

Ah! The prison of "Mehung," as they called it, what a bitter memory did it leave with him! He underwent there, as he said, the worst miseries of his life. And the bishop of Orleans, what curses Villon had for him!

Finally, though, in his accession to the throne, Louis XI, more generous than Mr. Poincaré, liberated all prisoners in his kingdom. And it was as such that Villon could return to his adventures, to his free life and his poems, to die—we do not exactly know how—some say that he was hanged.

## REFRACTORY POETS 5: FRANÇOIS VILLON (END)

*L'ACTION D'ART* 13 (SEPTEMBER 1913)

The work that Villon has left us consists of what he called his *Small Testament* and his *Big Testament*. He wrote both in the most tragic moments of his existence, in hours where, condemned to death, he let his entire life of magnificent struggles pass him by. He remembers all his companions who had already been hanged and those still alive who were his real friends and to whom he leaves some good advice for the future. He remembers his old mother who always stayed affectionate toward him, despite his being hunted like a stupid fawn. Then he sings his revolted soul. Listen to this verse of his big testament where his entire wrath bounces against the suffering of his stomach:

> Povre je suis, dès ma jeunesse
> De povre et de petite extrace.
> Mon père n'eut oncq grant richesse
> Ne son ayeul, nommé Erace.
> Povreté tous nous suyt et trace

Sur les tombeaulx de nos ancêtres,
Les âmes desquels Dieu embrasse
On n'y voit couronnes ne sceptres.[31]

En povreté me guermentant,
Souventes foys me dit le cueur:
"Homme ne te doulouse tant
Et ne demaine tel douleur,
Se tu n'as tant qu'eust Jacques Cueur.
Mieux vault vivre, soubz gros bureaux
Povre, qu'avoir esté seigneur
Et pourrir soubz riches tombeaux!"

. . . .

Il est bien vrai que j'ay aymé
Et aymeroye voulentiers:
Mais triste coeur, ventre affamé
Qui n'est rassasié au tiers,
Me oste des amoureux sentiers.
Au fort, quelqu'un s'en recompense,
Qui est rempli sur les chantiers,
Car la danse vient de la panse.[32]

And the poet, remembering his misery, his torments, does nevertheless not lose the taste for life. He finds in the idea of death a strange stimulus on his avid search for sensations:

Je cognoys que, povres et riches,
Sages et fols, prebstres et laiz
Nobles, vilains, larges et chiches,
Petits et grans, et beaulx et laidz,
Dames à rebrassez colletz,
De quelconque condicion,
Portant attours et bourreletz,
Mort saisit sans exception.[33]

He philosophically awaits death. But before dying he at least wants to cry out his hate and his love for the ones who were, in this world, the occasions for his suffering or his joy.

And he muses first about the youth who accompanied him in his adventurous struggles, about those whom he loves for their beautiful, enthusiastic drive, and whom he fears might too early and too madly follow in his heroic footsteps. François Villon, condemned to death and anxiously waiting for the agony of torture, engages in reflections that are strangely analogous to the ones of a Raymond Callemin or a Soudy on the eve of their executions.[34]

> Beaux enfans, vous perdez la plus
> Belle rose de vos chapeaux,
> Mes clercs apprenans comme gluz
> Si vous allez a Montpippeau
> Ou à Ruel, gardez a peau:
> Car, pour s'esbattre en ces deux lieux,
> Cuydant que vaulsist le rappeau
> La perdit Colin de Cayeulx.
> Ce n'est pas ung jeu de trois mailles,
> Où va corps et peut-estre l'âme.[35]

But these regrets are the ones of the prisoner, of the vanquished; they were no longer in the heart of the poet-bandit, once he, pardoned, found the fever to live his earlier heroic audacity again, unencumbered.

"Evade death, be stronger or smarter than it," that is the sense of his "beautiful lesson." There is no need to search for any other moral within it.

> A vous parle, compaings de galles,
> Qui estes de tous bon accords:
> Gardez-vous tous de ce mau hasles,
> Qui noircit gens quands ils sont morts.[36]

He thus wishes a beautiful and good life to all those who were his *bande*. But to all of those who betrayed or judged him, to the flies, the people of justice, to the false companions, he unleashes his hate or his irony.

He knows how much of the gossiping and defamation did him injustice; he is aware of the fault of talking too much, and he has his revenge on it by composing this ballad:

> En reagal, en arsenic rocher,
> En orpigment, en salpestre et chaulx vive;
> En plomb boillant, pour mieulx les esmorcher;
> En suif et poix, destrampez de lessive
> Faicte d'estrons et de pissat de Juifve;
> En lavaille de jambes à meseaulx;
> En raclure de piedz et vieulx houseaulx;
> En sang d'aspic et drogues venimeuses;
> En fiels de loups, de regnards et blereaux,
> Soient frittes ces langues envieuses!

> En cervelle de chat qui hayt pescher,
> Noir, et si vieil mastin, qu'il n'ait dent et gencive;
> D'ung vieil mastin, qui vault bien aussi cher,
> Tout enragé, en sa bave et salive;
> Detrenchée menu à bons ciseaulx;
> En eau où ratz plongent groings et museaulx,
> Raines, crapauds et bestes dangereuses,
> Serpens, lezards et telz nobles oyseaulx,
> Soient frittes ces langues envieuses!

> En sublimé, dangereux à toucher,
> Et au nombril d'une couleuvre vive;
> En sang qu'on veoit ès pallectes secher,
> Chez ces barbiers, quand pleine lune arrive,
> Dont l'ung est noir, l'autre plus vert que cive;
> En chancre et ticz, et en ces ords cuveaulx
> Où nourrices essangent leur drappeaulx;
> En petits baings de filles amoureuses
> (Qui ne m'etend n'a suivy les bordeaulx),
> Soient frittes ces langues envieuses!

ENVOI

Prince, passez tout ces friands morceaulx,
S'estamine n'avez, sacs ou bluteaux,
Parmy le fonds d'une brayes breneuses.
Mais, paravant, en estrons de pourceaulx,
Soient frittes ces langues envieuses![37]

What virulence and what verve in this ballad, and how one feels in it, with earthliness and fantasy, a will that is ready to do everything to affirm its life!

And finally, on another note, the *Sated truths*, where Villon, in a good mood, addresses the ones he ransacked, robbed, by tricks as much as by force, in order to not starve the refractory that he wanted to stay.

## LES REPEUES DE VILLON ET DE SES COMPAGNONS

"Qui n'a or, ny argent, ny gaige,
Comment peut-il faire grant chere?
Il fault qu'il vive d'avantaige:
La façon en est coustumière.
Sçaurions-nous trouver la maniere
De tromper quelqu'ung pour repaistre?[38]
.  .  .  .
Qui le fera sera bon maistre!"

Ainsi parloyent les compaignons
Du bon maistre François Villon,
Qui n'avoient vailant deux ongnons,
Tentes, tapis, ne pavillon.
Il leur dit: "Ne nous soucions,
Car, aujourd'huy, sans nul deffault,
Pain, vin et viande à grant foyson
Aurez, avec du rost tout chault."

La maniere d'avoir du poisson

Adoncques il leur demanda
Quelles viandes vouloyent macher:
L'ung de bon poisson souhaita,
L'autre demande de la chair.
Maistre François, ce bon archer,
Leur dist: "Ne vous en souciez;
Il vous faut voz pourpointz lascher,
Car nous aurons viandes assez."

Lors partit de ses compaignons,
Et vint à la Poyssonnerie,
Et les laissa, dela les pontz,
Quasy plains de merencolie.
Il marchanda, à chere lye,
Ung pannier tout plain de poysson,
Et sembloit, je vous certiffie,
Qu'il fust homme de grant façon.

Maistre François fut diligent
D'achapter, non pas de payer,
Et dist qu'il bailleroit l'argent
Tout comptant au porte-panier.
Ils partent, sans plus plaidoyer,
Et passerent par Nostre-Dame,
Là où il vit le Penancier,
Qui confessoit homme ou bien femme.

Quand il le vit, à peu de plait,
Il luy dist: "Monsieur, je vous prie
Que vous despeschez, s'il vous plaist,
Mon nepveu, car je vous affie
Qu'il est en telle resverie:
Vers Dieu il est fort negligent;
Il en est tel melencolie
Qu'il ne parle rien que d'argent.

—Vrayement, ce dit le Penancier,
Tres-voulentiers on le fera."
Maistre François print le pannier,
Et dist: "Mon amy, venez ça;
Vela qui vous despechera,
Incontient qu'il aura faict."
Adonc maistre François s'en va,
Atout le panier, en effect.

Quand le Penancier eut parfaict
De confesser la creature,
Gaigne-denier, par dict parfaict,
Accourut vers luy bonne alleure,
Disant: "Monsieur, je vous asseure,
S'il vous plaisoit prendre loysir
De me despescher à ceste heure,
Vous me feriez ung grant plaisir.

—Je le vueil bien, en verité,
Dist le Penancier, par ma foy!
Or, dictes Benedicite,
Et puis je vous confesseray,
Et en aprés vous absouldray,
Ainsy comme je doy le faire;
Puis pénitence vous bauldray,
Qui vous sera bien nécessaire.

—Quel confesser? Dist le povre homme:
Fus-je pas à Pasques absoulz?
Que bon gré sainct Pierre de Romme!
Je demande cinquante soulz.
Qu'esse-cy? A qui sommes-nous?
Ma maistresse est bien arrinée!
A coup, à coup, despeschez-vous:
Payez mon panier de marée.

—Ha! Mon amy, ce n'est pas jeu,
Dist le Penancier, seurement:
Il vous fault bien penser à Dieu
Et le supplier humblement.
—Que bon gré en ait mon serment!
Dist cet homme, sans contredit,
Despeschez-moy legierement,
Ainsi que ce segneur a dit."

Adonc le Penancier vit bien
Qu'il y eut quelque tromperie;
Quand il entendit le moyen,
Il congneut bien la joncherie.
Le povre homme, je vous affie,
Ne prisa pas bien la façon,
Car il n'eut, je vous certifie,
Or ne argent de son poysson.

Maistre François, par son blason,
Trouva la façon et maniere
D'avoir marée à grant foyson,
Pour gaudir et faire grant chere.
C'estoit le mere nourricière
De ceulx qui n'avoyent point d'argent;
A tromper devant et derriere
Estoit ung homme diligent.

La maniere d'avoir des trippes pour disner

Qu fist-il? A bien peu de plet,
S'advisa de grant joncherie:
Il fist laver le cul bien net
A ung gallant, je vous affie,
Disant: "Il convient qu'on espie:
Quans seray devant la trippiere.
Monstre ton cul, par raillerie,
Puis aprés nous ferons grant chiere"

Le compaignon ne faillit pas,
Foy que doy sainct Remy de Reims!
A Petit-Pont vint par compas,
Son cul descouvrit jusque aux rains.
Quant maistre François vit ce train,
Dieu scet s'il fit piteuses lippes,
Car il tenoit entre ses mains
Du foye, du polmon et des trippes.

Comme s'il fust plein de despit
Et courroucé amerement.
Il haulsa la main ung petit,
Et le frappa bien rudement.
Des trippes, par le fondement;
Puis, sans faire plus long caquet,
Les voulut, tout incontinent,
Remettre dedans le baquet.

La trippiere fut courroucée
Et ne les voulut pas reprendre.
Maistre François, demourée,
Sen alla, sans compte luy rendre.
Par ainsi, vous povez entendre
Qu'ilz eurent truppes et poysson.
Mais, aprés, il fault du pain tendre,
Pour ce disner de grant façon.

La maniere d'avoir du pain

Il s'en vint chez un boulengier
Affin de mieulx fournir son train,
Contrefaisant de l'escuyer
Ou maistre d'hostel, pour certain,
Et commanda que, tout soubdain,
Cy pris, cy mis, en chappellast

Cinq ou six douzaines de pain,
Et que bien tost on se hastast.

Quant la moytié fut chappellé,
En une hotte le fist mettre;
Comme s'il fust de prés hasté,
il pria et requist au maistre
Qu'aucun se voulsist entremettre
D'apporter, après luy courant,
Le pain chappellé en son estre,
Tandis qu'on fist le demourant.

Le varlet le mist sur son col,
Aprés maistre François le porte,
Et arriva, soit dur ou mol,
Emprés une grant vielle porte,
Le varlet deschargea sa botte,
Et fut renvoyé tout courant,
Hastivement, tenant sa hotte,
Pour requérir le demourant,

Maistre François, sans contredit,
N'attendit pas la revenue:
It eut du pain, par son edit,
Pour fournir sa franche repeue.
Le boulengier, sans attendue,
Revint, mais ne retrouva point
Son maistre d'hostel; il tressue,
Qu'on l'avait trompé en ce point.

La maniere d'avoir du vin

Après qu'il fut fourny de vivres,
Il faut bien avoir la memoire
Que, s'ilz vouloyent ce jour estre yvres,

Il falloir qu'ilz eussent à boire.
Maistre François debvez le croire,
Emprunta deux grans brocs de boys,
Disant qu'il estoit necessaire
D'avoir du vin, par ambagoys.

L'ung fist emplir de belle eaue clere,
Et vint à la Pomme de Pin,
Atout ses deux brocs, sans rencherc.
Demandant d'ilz avoient bon vin,
Et qu'on luy emplist du plus fin,
Mais qu'il fust blanc et amoureux.
On luy emplist, pour faire fin,
D'ung tres-bon vin blanc de Baigneux.

Maistre François print les deux brocs,
L'un emprés l'autre les bouta;
Incontinent, par bons propos,
Sans se haster, il demanda
Au varlet: "Quel vin est-ce là?"
Il luy dist: "Vin blanc de Baigneux.
—Ostez cela, ostez cela,
Car, par ma foy, point je n'en veulx.

Qu'esse-cy? Etes-vous bejaulne?
Vuydez-moy mon broc vistement.
Je demande du vin de Beaulne,
Qui soit bon, et non aultrement."
Et, en parlant, subtillement,
Le broc qui estoit d'eaue plain
Contre l'aultre legierement
Luy changea, à pur et à plain.

Par ce point, ilz eurent du vin,
Par fine force de tromper;

Sans aller parler au devin,
ilz repeurent, per ou non per.
Mais le beau jeu fut au soupper,
Car maistre François, à brief mot,
Leur dist: "Je me vueil occuper
Que mangerons ennuyt du rost."

La maniere d'avoir du rost

Il fut appointé qu'il yroit
Devant l'estal d'ung rostisseur,
Et de la chair marchanderoit,
Contrefaisant du gaudisseur,
Et, pour trouver moyen meilleur,
Faignant que point on ne se joue,
Il viendroit ung entrepreneur
Qui luy bailleroit sur la joue.

Il vint à la rotisserie,
En marchandant de la viande;
L'autre vint, de chere marrie:
"Qu'est-ce aue ce paillart demande?"
Luy baillant une buffe grande,
En lui disant mainte reproche.
Quand il vit qu'il eust ceste offrande,
Empoigna du rost pleine broche.

Celuy qui bailla le soufflet
Fuyt bien tost et à motz exprés.
Maistre François, sans plus de plet,
Atout son rost, courut aprés.
Ainsi, sans faire long procés,
Ils repeurent, de cueur devot,
Et eurent, par leur grant excés,
Pain, vin, chair, et poisson, et rost.

That is, I think, a little treaty on illegalism that is fairly complete for the era. And do not deceive yourself now with the prudence of those pedagogues who carefully try to distinguish the life from the oeuvre and to only admire—today, centuries after the death of the author—only certain poems by which, they say, Villon redeemed, thanks to his perfect form, the misdeeds of his existence? . . . *Hélas!* If François Villon had lived in our days, I do not think that he even would have had the leisure of writing these beautiful works. They would not let him have the time. Quickly chasing him down, they would make his body jump with shots from a machine gun, or, if they could stop him and condemn him to death, there would be no Louis XI to pardon him in a gift of happy ascension. In our days, a François Villon could persist for only a month or two.

Also, our modern refractory poets do not have the possibility to be as highly heroic as François Villon. Some, however, are very dignified by the measure of our era.

## REFRACTORY POETS 6: TRISTAN CORBIÈRE

*L'ACTION D'ART* 13 (SEPTEMBER 1913)

Society is a giggling ghoul that pleases itself with farce after having had the drama play. During their life it starves, murders, shreds, or chokes, or it lets burn, jump, shoot, decapitate, or die like dogs the highest, most alive, most animated, most thoughtful, or most sensible of the flowering individualities—as if by miracle—at its rotten chest. But after their death, in a grotesque act of revenge, it dedicates statues to them and makes its most authorized representatives crown their stone heads with golden laurels.

About a monument erected to the glory of Jules Vallès, Laurent Tailhade—and nobody else—has said all that had to be said. As an author of the "refractories," a burner of idols, a despiser of everything ceremonial, Jules Vallès would have been outraged that anyone would impose on his mask of ardor and feverish mobility a frozen resemblance in the conventional coldness of a consecrated stone. Now, the newspapers teach us that we have just erected a monument to the effigy of the poet Tristan Corbière, and that the inauguration was presided over by the minister of agriculture.

Tristan Corbière would not have shaken off outrage over it. But I imagine that he would have exploded in laughter—in his most bitterly sardonic laughter—and that he would have found it utterly natural to take part in the ceremony and walk up, during the most pathetic moment of the official elegies—in the middle of the dithyrambs, in the middle of the *Marseillaise*—to piss all over his own monument.

That would have been Tristan Corbière's response to the very literate discourse, let's admit that, it was a very delicate one, yes, surely, but hypocritically bold of Mr. Clémentel. And didn't he foresee all the vanity of this verbiage, he who said: "And that one day the sincere man may say of you—nasty! Ah, splendid! . . . Or may he say nothing. It's shorter."

But they did say things. They have said much too much on Corbière. Suddenly, after a silence of many years, the critics and journalists have fallen onto his personality like crows on a corpse—and their scrounging beaks, ripping at each other for grotesque memories, have yet not managed to discover the unique soul of the poet of the *Amours jaunes*.

Some only wanted to see a great Breton in him, a sailor, the lyricist of the "grand tasse salée"—others indulged only in his absurdity and have painted us a picture of a sort of bohemian, embittered by his suffering and consoling himself of his physical disgrace by ironizing all beauty, by splattering his sarcasm onto all happiness and every ideal. Both these views are grotesquely wrong.

If we truly want to understand Tristan Corbière, we cannot focus on the picturesque incidents of his biography any more than we can just settle on a few drives of great lyricism that we can find in certain parts of his work. It is only appropriate to read him like we listen to a friend alternately cry, sing, talk about his joy or his bitterness—to read him like we receive, confided to us, the secrets of an old confidante. And there is no book, I assure you, that is so honest, so intuitively hatched, more spontaneously spurt than these *Amours jaunes* where Tristan Corbière feared not, to express it more liberally, to break with, to shatter, to disarticulate the form of the verse in order to create a truly new rhythm (a precursor of what we would later call the free verse)—a rhythm that followed the flux and the reflux of his sensations—the very rhythm of his life—a rhythm hectic like his being, at the crossroads of all fevers.

Tristan Corbière truly is a poet. All of his personality, with all its anguishes and all of its drives, can be found marvelously alive in his works. I have just called him a poet, but do not think of the occupation when we speak of Corbière being a poet. For too long we have made of the poet some kind of a sentimental whiner, with no force and of no danger—an inoffensive and naive dreamer in the moonlight or a manufacturer of hymns to the glory of the powers of the day. Of course, there were and are many—*Hélas!*—that fit this mold. But Tristan Corbière was not one of them. He was—alone—against his time, against his society, against all constraints that oppressed his proud soul—against every suffering that pinched him: a perpetual rebel, a cynical individualist, and if he sang it was not to complain but to scourge with hits from the whip of his irony all the foolishness and ugliness of the world. He was a refractory poet.

I have called "refractory poets" the few who, feeling a proud soul and a harmonious imagination within them, did not consent to prostitute their natural gifts to societal life. All of those who, having become conscious of their personality, embarked to live individually according to their own sentiments, to their personal passions, to their original dreams, and to intensely affirm themselves under the sun—albeit by risking their existence. The refractory poets were the ones who did not submit themselves to the exhortations of cowardice and ugliness of the eras that they lived in, the ones who wanted to utter their cry whatever it may cost and who managed to die heroically while singing their song.

To each their life according to their temperament. François Villon, being more tumultuous, had been furious in his treatment of people. Tristan Corbière was not gentler in his behavior toward them, but he simply used his irony.

Of course, the life of Tristan Corbière was thus not as fiery as the one of the poet-bandit. But it was not less the one of a refractory.

While alive he was almost unknown. He died on March 1, 1875, in the thirtieth year of his life, without the glory which he, by the way, despised. It was by accident that, ten years after his life, his completely forgotten book was rediscovered in a box on the quais: *Les amours jaunes*. People began to speak of him again in the young literary papers. We have few details on his life, but we know that he never wanted to bend and that he had profound, bitter hate for the honors of the world, abhorrence for the laws, for all laws, disgust of social conventions—and we have his oeuvre full of irony for the lowly daily life of the men who know only to eat, to sleep, and to languish in their bestial servitude.

"He brought to civil society," writes Mr. Le Goffic in his foreword, "the predestined name of the Corbière. A 'Corbière' in maritime language is the edging on the side of the ship upon which the surveillance of the officers of the customs is exercised, and which is utilized by smugglers and in the search for shipwrecks." A predestined name! The life of Tristan Corbière must in effect also have been one as battered by the winds, as desolate, as hazardous and harsh, as proudly tragic as the landscape of the Corbière.

## REFRACTORY POETS 7: TRISTAN CORBIÈRE

*L'ACTION D'ART* 15 (OCTOBER 1913)

Born on July 18, 1845, in the suburbs of Morlaix, in Coatcongar, Tristan Corbière stayed in the surroundings of Roscoff, in the Corbière of Léon, until 1872. These were rugged and wild lands, without any culture, "the lands of castaways and burners of seaweed, lands that crisp under the wind of the sea." There Tristan Corbière lived the first years of his childhood and youth, truly in accord with this landscape that was both primitive and distressed.

Instead of going to school he preferred to run through the dunes, barefoot through the salty water. In order to skip classes he did not hesitate to administer himself drugs that would make him look ill. Later, as a young man, he could not accustom himself to family life. The Corbière family owned an old house from the sixteenth century there in Roscoff, next to the Italian church of the Notre-Dame de Croaz-Batz, where it came to spend the summer months. Tristan Corbière always stayed there, even in winter, alone with his dog, a very muddy Barbet that he had given his own name, Tristan. He slept in the living room, where he had put his rowboat to serve as a bed. But when his family arrived, instead of bending to the regularity of a bourgeois existence, Tristan fled to live with some fisherman, where he would accommodate himself perfectly well in a hammock. And when that day came, he went, still dressed as a sailor, with the *suroît*,[39] the big hood and the large boots, alone or with the seamen, through the worst of weathers, to accomplish wonders of insane imprudence on his cutter, *Le négrier*. Twenty times he almost sank in the terrible channels of the Leonarde coast. He loved the sea with a strange passion. He loved it without literature, outside of any lyrical convention. We could say that, by singing of it, he revolted against the terrestrial bourgeois poet; against the "great romantic" Victor Hugo, who lived the sea only as a beautiful subject for a poem. And Tristan Corbière found that disgraceful, he who, as a lover of the sea, only spoke of it out of passion.

## LA FIN

"Oh! Combien de marins, combien de capitaines
Qui sont partis joyeux pour des courses lointaines.
Dans ce morne horizon se sont évanouis! . . .[40]

. . . .

Combien de patrons morts avec leurs équipages!
L'Océan de leur vie a pris toutes les pages.
Et d'un soufle, il a tout dispersé sur les flots.
Nul ne saura leur fin dans l'abíme plongée . . .

. . . .

Nul ne saura leurs noms, pas même l'humble pierre,
Dans l'étroit cimetière où l'écho nous répond,
Pas même la chanson plaintive et monotone
D'un aveugle qui chante à l'angle d'un vieux pont."

(Victor Hugo—Océano Nox)

Eh bien tous ces marins—matelots, capitaines,
Dans leur grand Océan a jamais engloutis,
Partis insoiuvieux pour leurs courses lointaines,
Sont morts—absolument comme ils étaient partis.

Allons! c'est leur métier, ils sont morts dans leurs bottes!
Leur boujaron au coeur, tout vifs dans leurs capotes . . .
—Morts . . . Merci: la Camarde a pas le pied marin;
Qu'elle couche avec vous: c'est votre bonne femme.
—Eux, allons donc: Entiers! Enlevés par la lame!
    Ou perdus dans un grain . . .

Un grain . . . est-ce la mort, ça? La basse voilure
Battant à travers l'eau!—ça se dit encombrer . . .

Un coup de mer plombé, puis la haute mature
Fouettant les flots ras—et ça se dit sombrer.

—Sombrer.—Sondez ce mots. Votre mort est bien pâle
Et pas grand'chose à bord, sous la lourde rafale...
Et pas grand'chose devant le grand sourire amer
Du matelot qui lutte.—Allons donc de la place!
Vieux fantôme éventé, la Mort change de face: La Mer!

Noyés?—eh allons donc! les noyés sont d'eau douce.

—Coulés! corps et biens! Et, jusqu'au petit mousse,
Le défi dans le yeux, dans les dents le juron,
A l'écume crachant une chique ralée,
Buvant sans hauts-de-coeur la grand'tasse salée...
—Comme ils ont bu leur boujaron

. . . .

—Pas de fond de six pieds, ni rats de cimetière:
Eux, ils vont aux requins! L'âme d'un matelot,
Au lieu de suinter dans vos pommes de terre,
  Respire a chaque flot

—Voyez l'horizon se soulever la houle;
On dirait le ventre amoureux
D'une fille de joie en rut, a moitié saoûle...
Ils sont la!—La houle a du creux.—

—Ecoutez, écoutez la tourmente qui beugle!...
C'est leur anniversaite.—Il revient bien souvent -
O poète, gardez pour vous vos chants d'aveugle;
—Eux: le De profundis que vous corne le vent.

... Qu'ils roulent infinis dans les espaces vierges!...
Qu'ils roulent verts et nus,

Sans clous et sans sapin, sans couvercle, sans cierges! . . .
—Laissez-les donc rouler, terriens parvenus!

(aboard ship, February 11)

Behold the difference. Victor Hugo, a national poet, a social poet, merely worries about the sad fate of the sailors and laments that he won't see their graves whenever he speaks of the sea. Meanwhile Tristan Corbière, the refractory poet, loves the sea for its unrestrained fury and the men of the sea for their carelessness regarding social destiny, for their intensely wild and vagabond life. Listen to the following poem about the sailors and compare it to the sentimental twaddle of a Théodore Botrel or the simple rhetoric of a Richepin.[41] Here, with Corbière, it is a raw, a vivid impression; one without posing and without regard for fashion, in a beaten language, in gusts of wind, a language that seems to be agitated by the rolling and pitching of waves.

## MATELOTS

Vos marins de quinquets à l'Opéra . . . Comique,
Sous un frac en bleu-ciel jurent "Mille sabords!"
Et, sur les boulevards, le survivant chronique
Du Vengeur vend l'onguent à tuer les rats morts.
Le Jûn'homme infligé d'un bras—meme en voyage—
Infortuné, chantant par suite de naufrage;
La femme en bain de mer qui tord ses bras au flot;
Et l'amiral *** —ce n'est pas matelot![42]

—Matelots—quelle brusque et nerveuse saillie
Fait cette race à part sur la race faillie!
Comme ils vous mettent tous, terriens, au même sac.
—Un curé dans ton lit, un' fille dans mon hamac.

. . . .

—On ne les connaît pas, ces gens à rudes noeuds.
Ils ont le mal de mer sur vos planchers à boeufs;

A terre—oiseaux palmés—ils sont ternes et veules.
Ils sont mal culottés comme leurs brûle-gueules.
Quand le roulis leur manque . . . ils se sentent rouler:
—A terre on a beau boire, on ne peut désoûler!

—On ne les connaît pas—Eux: que leur fait la terre? . . .
Une relâche, avec l'hôpital militaire,
Des filles, la prison, des horions, du vin . . .
Le reste: Eh bien, après?—Est-ce que c'est marin?
—Eux, ils sont matelots—A travers les tortures,
Les luttes, les dangers, les larges aventures,
Leur face à coups de hache a pris un tic nerveux
D'insouciant dédain pour ce qui n'est pas Eux . . .
C'st qu'ils se sentent bien, ces chiens! Ce sont de mâles!

—Eux: l'Océan!—et vous: les plates-bandes sales
Vous êtes des terriens, en un mot, des troupiers:
—De la terre de pipe et de la sueur de pieds! -
Eux sont les vieu-de-cale et les frères-la-côte,
Gens au coeur sur la main, et toujours la main haute;
Des natures en barre!—Et capables de tout . . .
—Faites-en donc autant! . . . Ils sont de mauvaus goût
—Peut-être . . . Ils ont chez vous des amours tolérées
Par un Grippe-Jésus accueillant leurs entrées . . .

—Eh! Faut-il pas du coeur au ventre quelque part,
Pour entrer en plein jour là—bagne-lupanar,
Qu'ils nomment le Cap-Horn, fans leur langue hâlée
—Le cap Horn, noir séjour de tempête gelée -
Et se coller en vrac, sans crampe d'estomac,
De la chair à chiquer—comme un noeud de tabac!

Jetant leur solde avec leur trop-plein de tendresse,
A tout vent, ils vont là comme ils vont à la messe . . .
Ces anges mal léchés, ces durs enfants perdus!
—Leur tête a du requin et du petit Jésus.

Ils aiment à tout crin. Ils aiment plaie et bosse,
La Bonne-Vierge avec le gendarme qu'on rosse;
Ils dont des voeux à tout … Mais leur voeu caressé
A toujours l'habit bleu d'un Jésus-Christ[43] rossé.

—Allez: ce franc cynique a sa grâce native …
Comme il vous toise un chef, à sa façon naïve!
Comme il connait son maitre: Un d'un seul bloc de bois!
—Un mauvais chien toujours qu'un bon enfant parfois!

—Allez: à bord, chez eux, ils ont leur poésie!
Ces brutes ont des chants ivres d'âme saisie
Improvisés aux quarts sur le gaillard d'avant …
—Ils ne s'en doutent pas, eux, poème vivant.

. . . .

Matelots!—Ce n'est pas vous, jeuenes mateluches,
Pour qui les femmes ont toujours des coqueluches …
Oh! les vieux avaient de plus fiers appétits!
En haussant les épaules ils vous trouvent petits.
A treize ans ils mangeaient de l'Anglais, les corsaires!
Vous, vous n'êtes que des pelletas militaires …
Allez, on n'en fait plus de ces purs, premier brin!
Tout s'en va … tout! La mer … elle n'est plus marin
De leur teps, elle était plus salée et sauvage.
Mais, à présent, rien n'a plus de pucelage …
La mer … La mer n'est plus qu'une fille à soldats!

—Vous, matelors, rêvez en faisant vos cent pas
Comme dans les grand quarts … Paisible rêverie
De carcasse qui geint, de mât craque qui crie …
—Aux pompes! … —Non.. fini! Les beaux jours ont passés!
—Adieu mon beau navire aux trois mâts pavoisés;

. . . .

Tel qu'une vieille coque au sec dégréée;
Où vient encore parfois clapoter la marée,
Ame de mer en peine est le vieux matelot
Attendant, échoué...—quoi: la mort?
     —Non, le flot.

It is this privateer of all fears, of which the soul was like a rock sculpted by strikes of the waves of the sea, who decided, on one beautiful day, to make his way to Paris. Up to that point, of life, he only knew his own and that of the sea. He had grown, a proud plant battered by the marine winds, willing to ignore all civilized men and their conventions. Now there he was, arriving in the city of all corruptions and all refinements, the city of mechanisms and high chimneys, the city of crowds and of masters. Certainly, he suffered—but without weeping; the men of Paris were not worthy the gift of his tears. He responded to their insults with jeers; in quick wit he swished the Parisians with a liveliness analogous to the one they so love—but employed in reverse, to whip at their stupidity—they who are so handy at "joking" about their genius.

## PARIS

Bâtard de Créole et Breton,
Il vint aussi là—fourmillère,
azar où rien n'est en pierre,
Où le soleil manque de ton.[44]

—Courage! On fait queue...Un planton
Vous pousse à la chaîne—derrière! -
...Incendie éteint, sans lumière;
Des seaux passent, vides ou non.—

Là, sa pauvre Muse pucelle,
Fit le trottoir en demoiselle,
Ils disaient: Qu'est-ce qu'elle vend?

—Rien.—Elle restait là, stupide,
N'etendant pas soner le vide
Et regardant passer le vent.

———————◆—————

Là: vivre à coups de fouets!—passer
En fiacre, en correctionelle;
Repasser à la ritournelle,
Se dépasser, et trépasser!...

—Non, petit, il faut commencer
Par être grand—simple ficelle;
Pauvre: remuer l'or à la pelle:
Obscur: un nom à tout casser!...

Le coller chez les mastroquets,
Et l'apprendre à des perroquets
Qui le chantent ou qui le sifflent...

—Musique!—C'est le paradis
Des mahomets ou des houris,
Des dieux souteneurs qui se giflent!

———————◆—————

C'est la bohême, enfant: renie
Ta lande et ton clocher à jour,
Les mornes de ta colonie
Et les bamboulas au tambour.

Chanson usée et bien finie
La jeunesse... Eh, c'est bon un jour!...
Tiens:—c'est toujours neuf—calomnie
Les pauvres amours... et l'amour.

Evohé! Ta coupe est remplie!
Jette le vin, garde la lie
Comme ça.—Nul n'a vu le tour

Et qu'un jour le monsieur candid
De toi dise—Infect! Ah splendide! -
. . . Ou ne dise rien.—C'es plus court.

＊

Evohé fouaille la veine
Evohé! Misère: éblouir!
En fille de joie, à la peine
Tombe avec ce mot-là:—Jouir!

Rôde en la coulisse malsaine
Où vont les fruits mal secs moisir,
Moisir pour un quart d'heure en scène . . .
—Voir les lanches, et puis mourir!

Va: Treteaux, lupanars, églises
Cour des miracles, cour d'assises:
—Quart d'heures d'immortalité!

Tu parais! C'est l'apothéose!!! . . .
Et l'on jette quelque chose:
—Fleur en papier, ou saleté.—

Proud soul and deformed body, noble and grotesque—filled with both love and spite—it took him a while to find the woman to understand him . . . and this sonnet has to have been written after some disillusionment suffered by the poet on the lookout for a true companion . . . one measuring up to his heart.

## BELLE FORTUNE ET FORTUNE

Moi je fais mon trottoir, quand la nature est belle,
Pour la passante qui, d'un petit air vainqueur,
Voudra bien crocheter, du bout de son ombrelle,
Un clin de ma prunelle ou la peau de mon coeur . . .[45]

Et je me crois content—pas trop!—Mais il faut vivre:
Poiur promener un peu da faim, le gueux s'énivre . . .

Un beau jour—quel métier!—je faisais, comme ça
Ma croissière.—Métier! . . . Enfin, Elle passa
—Elle qui?—La Passante! Elle, avec une ombrelle!
Vrai valet de bourreau, je la frôlai . . .—Mais elle

Me regarda tout bas, souriant en dessous.
Et . . . me tendit sa main et . . .

m'a donné deux sous.

Nonetheless, he ended up meeting her, the one he could love. She was beautiful, young, elegant, and honest. She managed to penetrate the painful secrets of the poet. But it was too late. Happiness necessitates a learning process that Corbière never completed. He was what one could call tender but compressed. Having to squeeze his heart to stop his élans, having to tie down the sentiments that he could otherwise not appease, the poet no longer knew how to love with the joyous candidness of his sunny twenty-year-old self. The revolt had become his normal state. He could no longer be at ease, even under the caresses of the softest hands. And thus, this is all that he could answer her with.

## À UNE CAMARADE

Que me veux-tu donc, femme trois fois fille? . . .
Moi qui te coryais un si bon enfant!

—De l'amour? . . . —Allons: Cherche, apporte, pille!
M'aimer aussi, toi! . . . moi qui t'aimais tant![46]

Oh! je t'aimais come . . . und lézard qui pèle
Aime le rayon qui suit son someil . . .
L'amour entre nous vient battre de l'aile:
—Eh! qu'il s'ôte de devant mon soleil!

Mon amour, à moi, n'aime pas qu'on l'aime;
Mendiant, il a peur d'être écouté . . .
C'est un lazzarone enfin, un bohême,
Déjeunant de jeûne et de liberté.

—Curiosité, bibelot, bricolle? . . .
C'est possible: Il est rare—et c'est son bien.
Mais un bibelot cassé se recolle;
Et lui, décollé, ne vaudra plus rien! . . .

Va, n'enfonçons pas la porte entr'ouverte
Sur un paradis déjà trop rendu!
Et gardons à la pomme, jadis verte,
Sa peau, sous son fard de fruit défendu.

Qu nous sommes-nous donc fait l'un à l'autre? . . .
—Rien . . .—Peur-être alors que c'est pour cela;
Quel a commencé?—Pas moi, bon apôtre!
Après, quel dire: C'est donc tout—voilà!

—Tout les deux, sans doute . . .—Et toi, sois bien sûre
Que c'est encor moi le plus attrapé:
Car si, par erreur, ou par aventure,
Tu ne me trompais . . . je serais trompé!

Appelons cela: l'amitié calmée,
Puisque l'amour veut mettre son holà.
N'y croyons pas trop, chère mal-aimée . . .
—C'est toujours trop vrai ces mensonges-là!—

Nour pourrons, au moins, ne pas nous maudire,
Si ça t'est égal, le quart d'heure après.
Si nous en mourons—ce sera de rire . . .
Moi qui l'aimais tant ton rire si frais!

A refractory against any law, Tristan Cobière feared the sway of a woman, he feared sentimental chains, he could not imagine becoming the toy of small charming fingers any more than the toy of solid clenched fists. He could not imagine languishing to the rhythm of a tender adventure. He had chosen, with his body of pure ugliness and his soul of pure pride, the prideful yet painful, cruel but apparently intense destiny of the pariah.

Tristan Corbière truly was a pariah. Mr. Le Goffic said: "his personal disgrace and his solitude had developed and almost pushed to paroxysm the anarchist instincts that slumbered within him like in the bottom of all Celtic people." But he was a proud pariah—and, happy to remain one, he enjoyed singing all the joys of this individual revolt out to us.

PARIA

Qu'ils se payent des républiques
Hommes libres!—carcan au cou—
Qu'ils peuplent leurs nids domestiques! . . .
—Moi je suis le maigre coucou.[47]

—Moi, —coeur ennuque, dératé
De ce qui mouille et ce qui vibre . . .
Que me chante leur liberté,
A moi: toujours seul, toujours libre,

—Ma Patrie . . . elle est par le monde;
Et puisque la planète est ronde,
Je ne crains pas d'en voir le bout . . .
Ma patrie est où je la plante:
Terre ou mer, elle est sous la plante
De mes pieds—quand je suis debout

## IDEALISM AND ANARCHY

*L'ANARCHIE* 416 (APRIL 1913)

In a fairly well-documented article of the large literary review *Le mercure de France*, Mr. Pierre Germain has opened a "lawsuit against anarchism" in regard to the "bandits." This author, completely recognizing that individualist anarchism and its illegalist consequences are the most interesting manifestations of the contemporary anarchist movement, persists in criticizing the acts and the tendencies of their representatives by observing them from a stubbornly social point of view. By that very fact his critique has, in our eyes, no value; his objections are valid only in the societal environment and to those who desire to maintain or evolve it.

When a bourgeois writer or "intellectual" (which is essentially the same) neglects to enter in the individualist mentality in order to understand (if not to admire) the acts of economical refractories, that seems to be the most normal thing in the world. But when an anarchist or, as is true in this case, even an individualist anarchist employs the same system of criticism, that seems very surprising to me.

I could also not be shocked to see the "citizen Sené" shed,[48] in the *Réveil anarchiste ouvrier*, streams of tears over the fate of these "miserable victims" of the "pathological cases" of anarchism, and streams of anathemas over the "nefarious theoreticians" of individualism. I have no idea what an anarchist-workerist could even be. A workerist is a man of a class, the defender of a social force, a soldier of the proletariat; An anarchist, if it happens by sad necessity that he is constrained (or forced) to work in a factory, could not boast about that any more than he could boast about having tuberculosis; the anarchist cannot know a cause other than his own, no other reason to act apart for the harmonious development of his "being" or the defense of this "being" against the infringements of his societal environment. The "citizen Sené," workerist and insurrectional humanitarian, is not in disaccord with his class, with his party, when looking at it from a social point of view; but he is mistaken to call himself an anarchist.

I am no longer surprised when I see an individualist anarchist like André Lorulot on one hand defend the "anarchist bandits" by comparing them to the "social bandits," and, on the other hand, argue as a reason to discourage such acts and in a manner of "who does it help?" the negative result of their acts, the death of some of them, the imprisonment of others, the absence of social consequences...[49]

"Where does it all lead?" That could be the conclusion of his latest article.

But can we truly ask of an individualist who gives no other end to his acts than his own happiness to only accomplish acts that are likely to augment the common good? Can we even ask him to act according to the conception that every one of us has of his own happiness?

The truth is that there are serious confusions in this kind of moralism. There had been the same, by the way, in the theory of illegalism. It is as impossible to create a system of life for illegalism as it is for moralism. A man can be an illegal and not any more interesting to me than another man who lives a normal life. An *apache* does not attract my sympathy any more than a "bourgeois," and there are certain peaceful thinkers whom I admire as much as I do certain "bandits."

Everything depends on what an individual *is*.

We in the individualist anarchistic environments have thus far made the mistake of too frequently assuming an exclusively materialist, objective, and scientific point of view—and to consider idealism as a pitfall in which anarchist wills fatally get lost, fall, and break. But I think that it is quite more likely to be scientific realism that conducts to the disaggregation of the refractory spirit.

By considering only the acts of an individual externally, by seeing them only as *facts*, by searching for their consequences and their ties, by integrating them into a universal determinism or by analyzing them as physical phenomena, we skin these acts of all individual value, we judge them according to a collective criterion that necessarily excludes all considerations of happiness for the particular being.

However, what is the source of individual activity? The pursuit of happiness. A moral science that only brings me impotence of being myself and pain of feeling disaggregated by paralyzing my own tendencies, restraining my activity and smothering my joy of life, is as loathsome as a religious dogma.

We are seriously mistaken to turn the sciences into an all-powerful divine force. They are a perfect instrument in the hand of the people, why would one want to reverse the roles? Practically created by mankind, hailing from their experiences to *serve* their happiness, they shouldn't govern this happiness, because happiness has no other law than the one of the rhythms of every individual life. A being who is not obstructed by religious prejudices, social prejudices, or scientific prejudices, a grown man who could remain like a child,[50] sincere with himself and with nature, would feel an impulse to realize himself in his entirety, an incessant desire to unite all his tendencies, all his sentiments, all his thoughts, to form the synthesis of all his aspirations in order to better *be*, in order to *be* more harmoniously, happier, and this drive would dominate each act of his life. That is what I call the ideal.

We have the bad habit of discussing words of which we have not precisely defined the sense. All great philosophical quarrels arose from misunderstandings about terms.[51] More often than not, religious or social powers have also exploited such ambiguities to their profit. The church, and then the state, both having a great interest in monopolizing the most noble conceptions or sentiments in order to elevate their roles, never hesitated to do so. That is how it went with the ideal, too.

First, the ecclesiastical education systems taught the people to associate the concept of the ideal with God. For many long centuries no ideals were conceived outside of religion. Today the secular education systems act in the exact same way, with the difference that the fatherland has replaced God.

These teachings have completed the ends that they suggested. There is no man today who would conceive of an ideal without thinking about a superior force for which the individuals would have to sacrifice themselves. Witness our communists, ready to die for "the Cause" with a sentiment of humility that is completely analogous to the one of the Christian devoting himself to his God or the "good soldier" spilling his blood for his fatherland.

Finally, even the individualist anarchists, in their way, fell victim to such prejudice. By withdrawing themselves from every idealism and by losing themselves in the most depressing of realisms, they remind me of those children to whom the parents repeat that candy rots and stains the teeth so that they would not be tempted to ask them for it too often.

The individual ideal distinguishes itself from a social ideal in as far that, since it originates from the life of the being itself and is not imposed upon it by its environment, it tends to the enrichment of the individual, to its fulfillment, to its triumph, while every social ideal enflames a being only to better consume it for its own ends, which are exterior to the individual. The individual ideal is nothing else but the creative force of a being; it is the individual dreaming to be stronger, more beautiful, and more harmonious; it is a dream of liberty.

It is thus important that the individualist discovers his ideal, and when I say "individualist," I don't mean a fixed type of man defined by a doctrine, like the "Christian" in *Catechism* and the "militant" that the *Bataille syndicaliste* designates. I want to tell every mindful individual to rejoice, to live, to act, to *be* individually and without constraints.

To discover one's ideal one needs to strongly sense one's aspirations, seize one's character, know one's joys and their possibilities. Every one of our personalities possesses something like a particular rhythm. For some it is violent, passionate, combative; for others it can be full of fantasy; for yet others it might well be a large and serene harmony. It is necessary to discover this rhythm of our personal life; that is the essential part. But next it is important not to forget it.

In order to live intensely and to experience the strongest joys of our being, in order to live a life that is not only our life, but our highest life, it is suitable not to scatter around with details but to remember what the best of us is, of *our own* ideal, of this living synthesis of our being!

The individual ideal is like an image of my own perfection, of my happiness, a marvelous image of what I would want to be and of what I could be, by thinking about it and by acting according to it.

And from that moment on, what do the social consequences of his acts matter to a man? He *is*, that is all. He tries to be even *more*, even *better*. He tends to his beauty, to his harmony.

If he discovered in himself the character of a fighter—eh! What would physical suffering then matter to him, if he fights with ardor for his refractory ideal? Of what importance would fatal material issues and the incomprehension of the other beings be, if he senses himself to be in accord with himself? What could death do to him if he dies while heroically struggling, he who has found in the struggle his life's reason to be, his ideal?

When it comes to the more contemplative or more thoughtful individualist who found her ideal in the rhythm of pure thought, she would not be any less admirable, despite being less vivid. But I strongly doubt—*Hélas!*—that such a consciousness could flourish in peace and without being forced, to defend her integrity, to commit some acts of violence!

The important thing is to follow *one's* ideal, to want *oneself* intensively in all of one's force and in all of one's beauty. That is the end. As to the means, they are whatever the complex circumstances of our actions and our exterior life do not manage to withhold from us. And, by the way, let that be all that we want, we would not care!

Above the theories, above practicalities and methods of all sorts, the individualist anarchist must place this excellent tenet: *Be yourself.*


## LET'S BE NEW MEN!

*L'ANARCHIE* 420 (MAY 1913)

The people quarrel, debate, fight, most often, for words of which they don't know the meaning, of which they do not even care to know the value. Ideologues, preachers, politicians, and the leaders of crowds in all eras and in all environments have always managed to exploit this promptness of men to throw themselves onto each other to defend terms, entities, words that were, so to speak, grabbed out of thin air, words that were like flags under which they sacrificed their lives—blindly.

Idealism . . . Anarchy . . . those are two words of which the fortunes were associated or opposed, two words that orators and their troops used for the most diverse ends, for the most unforeseeable goals.

For example, if twenty years ago you would have interviewed one of those random mediocre consciousnesses that form the public, and if you had asked this atom of public opinion: "What is an anarchist?" . . . it would have not hesitated to reply to you: "a utopist, a chimerian, a fool, an idealist!" And at the same time, a peaceful thinker could not call himself idealistic without having been gratified with the title of anarchist.

Today things are quite different. Idealism is well respected. These men of the *bonne presse* have turned it into a national item and when they want to insult one of us, they find nothing better but to exclaim: "Beings deprived of ideals! Gross destructors! Brutes!" and other gentleness of the same caliber.[52]

That proves the incoherence of public opinion. But that barely interests us. Stupidity is a key characteristic of the social herds!

It will be more profitable for us to remark the fate that the refractory minds, the anarchists reserved for idealism.

In the so-called heroic era, from 1886 to 1900, the anarchists proclaimed themselves to be idealists; they welcomed the most beautiful minds of that time among them, and it was with faith, with enthusiasm, in a sort of passionate delirium that the men of action committed their assassinations. For more than ten years that was an extraordinary fever of consuming oneself without thinking, of acting without too much reasoning, with the broken heart as the only drive. The anarchists of back then lived for their ideal; they sometimes even died to defend or affirm it.

The drive was beautiful, certainly, but it was inspired by consciences that were too cloudy, by ideas that were too vague to not lose themselves in regrettable confusions. On the one hand some literates, some artists had superficial admirations for anarchism, where they saw only an opportunity for beautiful acts. Dilettantish, they were impassioned by certain assassinations in a similar way as some Spanish women are by the running with the bulls. It amused them for a while, and they wallowed just long enough in it so that they could extract some picturesque chronicles and some scandalous books from it. On the other hand, the social struggle gave way to syndicalism, provided the opportunity for a few tumultuous strikes, for certain conflicts between the working class and the patronage, and for a combative role where an avid activity of revolt could dispense itself.

And because the anarchists had drives only for themselves, because their points of view, their attitudes had not been precisely shaped yet, and because it was, for these men of action, primarily important to act ... they threw themselves, for the most part, into the syndicalist struggle blindly and without asking themselves too much why they engaged in it.

You all know what came out of that. It is not with impunity that the most hardened characters, the proudest and most refractory souls incorporate themselves in social groupings. Now, the syndicate, an economical grouping based on a community of societal *functions*, uniting beings of very diverse temperaments and aspirations for a struggle of classes against classes, is a type of a social grouping. Every man who is a part of it is constrained to act only socially if he is to exercise an action—that is to say he is to act for the good of this society, of this grouping, of his class. He is no longer an individual; he is constrained to being a member of this group, of this class, to oblige his own will, his own action, his individual life to the general interest of the society of which he is a part.

The anarchists entered in large numbers into the syndicates; they infused it undoubtedly with their sense of revolt and their combative spirit; they contributed to making syndicalism revolutionary; they became "good militants." But they had become subservient to a class; they had submitted themselves to the authority of a social group; they had cut down their personality to accord themselves with a crowd; they tamed their drives of individual revolt in the hope of a societal revolution.

In this conclusion the nature of the idealism that animated the anarchists of twenty years ago became visible. They only conceived an ideal in the future and the universal. The ideal was for them synonymous with common happiness, with a found-again paradise, with a perfect humanity, a marvelous earth where men would be brethren. The ideal was the cause, the common cause to which one had to devote oneself.

I have attempted to prove, elsewhere, how such conceptions are rooted in the Christian idea.[53] In effect, I do not see a difference between believing in God and believing in a perfect humanity. Restraining one's own life, smothering one's own aspirations, stopping one's drives, one's originality, one's force to find God in the sky of the perfect humanity in a future that one will never live is exactly the same. It is to build one's happiness on one's own death.

---

Individualist anarchists understood this. They precisely showed that an anarchist could have no other cause but his own. They drew teachings from Max Stirner's individualist writings that were greatly profitable for each individual who consents neither to prostitute nor to sacrifice itself, not for the triumph of the working class or for the prosperity of the bourgeois class. They affirmed with reason that the anarchist cannot be a part of one any more than he can be of the other, that he needs to desolidarize from every class, from every crowd, from every mass, from every social spirit, to own himself, to discover himself, to be himself, to live his life.

But having seen where idealism had driven the communists and attaching from that point on only a religious or metaphysical sense to the word that was marked by it removing from an individual the appetite for realizing oneself during one's life—the individualist anarchists started fighting every idealist tendency and collapsed into an absolute scientific utilitarianism.

Because to that point they had seen idealism's being conceived only in a social form, they figured that all idealism was harmful to the individual. They did not imagine the ideal as being different than the common thought of a cult, a society, or a group. By condemning idealism they only thought of its societal forms. They forgot that the individual does not live only physiologically, that his life is not limited to a corporal activity in relation with matter; every one of us internally feels a cluster of aspirations, of tendencies, of will, of ideas, of images, of dreams; an entire hotbed of love and hate, of hope, of revolt; all of that constitutes the psychological life of a being, his "soul" as the poets like to say. *Eh bien*, if we want to harmonize this entire business of thoughts, of sentiments and of wills to live *our* life, to truly be an individuality, to push our action most intensely and most harmoniously, it is necessary for every one of us to look for the rhythm of life that fits them the best and, once this rhythm is found, it is best to give it the biggest possible amplitude, in order to not only be and to be oneself, but to be oneself in all beauty! That is what I call idealism. It is a tendency that pushes me to not settle for the real, that is to say for the past or the present that is about to be the past. It is a drive of my being to realize itself entirely and as highly as possible. The individual ideal is a force of life that sharpens my will of action and renders me steadily more powerful through having the courage of realizing myself.

On my account, the friends of *L'anarchie* were wrong in saying that the individualist anarchist is one who believes in nothing. That can lead to confusion. I believe in nothing that is external to me, so much is clear; I love nothing of all that is social. But if I want to live, keep the strength to, and have the drive to, don't I have to believe in my life, don't I have to believe in my power, in my beauty, in my ideal?

As much as I expel every illusion that reaches me from my environment; as much as I revolt against an ideal that is imposed upon me by others, by a master or by a crowd or by a group, I am persuaded that my belief in me, the individual illusion that I created for myself, personal enthusiasm, and idealism are necessary for me to blossom integrally. Persuade a man that he is but a coward, that he lacks courage, disillusion him as to his strength, and he will flee when danger comes. Repeat, as it happens—*Hélas*—as it happens way too often, and for centuries! . . . Repeat to a woman that she is incapable to act on her own, that she is a doll, only good to serve for love, and that she will become . . . this will-deprived being whom you know today. By reproaching their children that they are mean, parents will shape them in that way.

*Eh bien*, in analogous fashion, if one convinces oneself that nothing exists outside of material facts, facts that are governed by a universal determinism, and that this external reality is the only important one and that individual freedom is but a lure, the scientists have ended up turning themselves into toys of events and circumstances. By denying the ideal they have ended up by not having one anymore and by acting emptily, in a disorganized and incoherent way, following the coincidences of a uniquely material life, and without harmony. They have committed actions for the sake of actions, much as some artists make art for art's sake. They lack convictions, illusions, enthusiasm, and ideals.

But some of them had temperament, character, and those were often beautiful in action because there, they made abstractions of their doctrines, of their positivist theories, to let free flow to their impulses—and those people, I am convinced, even though the word "idealism" would have shocked them because they only knew the old religious idealism, those often felt the desire to surpass themselves within them, the desire to be most harmoniously and most intensely in accord with their own tendencies. They had faith in their strength and in their life because they struggled to affirm them, because they risked their life to be. They were idealists without knowing it.

◄►

To be new men by staying heroically oneself.

That is what is important.

Knowing the ideal of one's personality and, once that one has seized it, fearing nothing to affirm it.

But for that it is before anything else necessary to *be* individually.

The individualist anarchist, whether he comes from the ranks of the bourgeoisie or the proletariat, must shed his skin to no longer be a social man, to no longer be a man of a class; he must keep nothing of the sheepskin; he must from that moment on adopt an antisocial attitude in life, an individualist attitude, *his* attitude. No matter where, in no matter what circumstance, he will stay himself, he will act only by following the rhythm of his personality, without being worried about public opinion—and as a result of seeing some beings going through their life so assuredly, with this decision to stay themselves and to attain their harmony, their happiness, their beauty, may it cost whatever it costs; by being confronted with these individuals with new acts and a strong will, the men of the social herds might one day be ashamed of their ugliness and learn to detest their mediocrity.

We are actually currently living in a terribly social era where we are constrained to accomplish needs that do not always convene to our temperaments.

Some endure societal work in factories or offices. Others engage in illegalism; they steal or burglarize. Fortune has served some others better, and they can do nothing, living off the money they inherited.

But in any scenario let's not be men of the economical environments in which we painfully exist. Let's be mindful of the social spirit whatever it may be, of every professional spirit.

It is not fitting for an anarchist who lives from illegalisms to be only a burglar, to take on that mentality, to keep those habits, to adopt the code words and the slang of the *apaches* just like it is not fitting for one working in a factory to be only a worker and assimilate in the laborer's mentality. We must be *new men*. If I am forced to work in a factory then let that be only a means, let my entire activity not be absorbed by this function. Let the people who surround me in the factory or in the office know that I am not of their race, not of their class—that I am a *classless*, an anarchist, a *new man*.

If I find myself forced, to assure my subsistence, to tricking or hustling, to stealing, to burglarizing or to killing, let that be, to me, only an accident, a means.

Let it not absorb my entire will, and most of all, let me not assimilate myself to the society of the burglars; let there be in my acts a tangible attitude of individuality.

Let's be new men. That each one of us pushes himself out of the old, used-up social skin, to stand up stronger, more beautiful, with, on the front, the new flower of one's personal ideal.


## ANTIMILITARISM AND ANTIPATRIOTISM

*L'ANARCHIE* 426 (JUNE 1913)

The governments of France, concerned with the increase of the power of their state and the consolidation of the defenses of their fatherland, pushed by the intoxication of nationalism that misleads most young intellectuals up to the point of dementia, suffering from the popular stupidity of always following the ones who bark the loudest, have decided to maintain those among their slaves who should be freed in a just few months "under the flags," and to elongate, from now on, the military service of every "French citizen" by a year.

Now, you know what happened. In some regiments a few soldiers mutinied. A wind of revolt blew through the barracks. The slaves wanted to raise their voices. Some even risked lifting their arms to the height of their hearts. It was a scandal, and a quickly repressed one, by the way. The colonels made solemn apparitions accompanied by "impressive" speeches. The rebels were made to march in front of commemorative monuments . . . then they were administered some well-garnished paternal reprimands of months in prison and terms in the disciplinary companies. And from that moment on it was "silence in the ranks."

The gentlemen of socialism made it a case. Our good syndicalists were seized with emotion by it, and the communists snapped into place. There was thus—o, my Sunday joys!—an "imposing demonstration" at the Pré of St-Gervais where a crowd of thirty thousand or three hundred thousand people (one zero more or less) piled up to sweat in common, to the sound of the "Internationale," to the harmonious cries of "Hou! Hou! The three years."

Those are the facts—as exactly reported as the contradictory accounts that we have allow us—since we follow, simultaneously, *Le temps* and *L'humanité*.[54]

What might the individualist anarchist think of it? How can he respond to the indignations of opposite directions but equal inflammation that the socialists or antimilitarist revolutionaries and the patriots of all nuances give us?

Hostile to every social order, the individualist anarchist can of course only enjoy the spectacle of the disorder that comes to trouble the good functioning of the machine-state. The cogs start to bend . . . All the better! The motor of patriotism no longer snores with its usual enthusiasm . . . Perfect! It is ugliness that starts to disintegrate . . . A comforting spectacle. But it can be only a spectacle for us.

How could it be anything else? Would I ever involve myself with this heterogeneous, piecemeal crowd of pacifist republicans, freemason opportunists, liberal Jews, charitable Christians, unified socialists, revolutionary syndicalists, and communist anarchists? . . .

All crowds equally disgust me. Prompt to run riot to the sound of fanfares, whether they play the "Marseillaise" or "Revolution," the crowd follows a flag, whether it is red or tricolored or black, with the same blinding rage, with the same unconsciousness, in an inferno that is as quickly extinguished as it is lit on fire.

As it occurred, what was the cry that gathered thousands of people, that one afternoon at the Pré of St-Gervais, under a beautiful sky of blue flames? "*Sous au militarisme!*"

What is *militarism*? The desire that comes logically to men who believe in their fatherland and want to maintain it, to assure that it is best defended, and that it is maximally expanded. Who wants the end must want the means. . . . Whoever thus loves the French fatherland and places his national ideal above the individual ideal acts logically in his conviction to demand the increase of the armament and the consolidation of the army.

*Every patriot necessarily has to be a militarist.*

The government of Mr. Poincaré, originating in traditional neonationalism, is logical in its principles when it seeks the most military servitude for the "French citizen." The statists of all nuances, royalists, republicans, progressists, radicals, are true to their program by supporting the law of three years and by declaring themselves militarists.

What to think then of the socialists and their antimilitarism? Behold Mr. Jaurès, for instance, who does not stop speaking emotionally about France, Mr. Jaurès who protests for his patriotism, who affirms his faithfulness to the nation, Mr. Jaurès, the organizer of the Armée Nouvelle. Behold Mr. Gustave Hervé who no longer wants to be stateless, and of whom the heart beats of emotion in memory of the lost Alsace, Mr. Hervé who dreams in diplomatic combinations that could result in a bigger France. Behold your antimilitarists!

But they must be crazy. . . . What wouldn't they demand for the realization of their patriotic wishes, the great necessary armaments, the return to the seven years of service, the mass execution of antipatriotic anarchists; what don't they throw before their social herds to drive them, to the sound of the "Internationale" (or whatever other songs they have to make them look differently), while they are all in a vibrant and sonorous mass, to the barracks, not to destroy them but to populate them with good soldiers ready to support the cause of their fatherland?

But no . . . they are *antimilitarists* and *patriots*! A bizarre illogism. What could it matter! Aren't these gentlemen also demagogues? And that is the last word of the story. They want to have their herds, strengthen the size of their troops, domestic goats and cabbage to drink the mild of the ones and not eat the leaves of the other for their daily soup.

As to the syndicalists, revolutionaries, libertarians, or workerists of all categories, good militants for the cause of labor, what to think of their attitude in this occurrence?

Socially speaking, *their* antimilitarism is logical. The working class is struggling with the class of the bourgeois. The army, an instrument of the bourgeoisie that is currently in power, contains sons of the proletariat in its ranks. These have accepted to go serve, because they don't want to desolidarize from the societal environment. As members of this or that syndicate they feel that they are a part of the societal force, like a member of this or that administration (constable, customs officer, or cop) feels himself to be a fraction of public power. The sons of the working class dream of the triumph of *their* class. They do not want to disintegrate the societal edifice; they hope when their turn comes to occupy it.

For that they go to the barracks in the hope of spreading workerist propaganda and to conquer the army of their revolution. That can sometimes not be chimerical. History shows us a myriad of examples of such societal transformations pushed through thanks to the complicity of the troops.

That explains the enthusiasm of the revolutionaries during the last military mutinies. They can foresee a coming day on which, in the very heart of the same bourgeois republican army, a young, workerist revolutionary army is constituted.

Let's suppose the revolting armed troops were more numerous and more determined than they really were; let's imagine them pushing their action with vigor, seizing weapons, powder, and ammunition, triumphing over the troops with whom the government opposed them, then seizing Paris and starting to modify society following the very conceptions of the CGT. What would happen? Necessarily, the neighboring states would grow worried. The triple alliance would mobilize its troops and invade the French lands in order to reestablish the order that was menaced by this revolution. From then on the revolutionaries would be constrained to discipline their troops and to engage them against the enemy, at the borders, to defend their menaced *common ideal* in order to save their revolutions, their endangered *new fatherland*.

But, they would reply, on the other side of the borders an analogous movement could happen with the proletarians. Evidently. But it could also not happen. In life not everything is perfectly triggered for a perfect apotheosis, as it is in the theater. In any case, nothing of date could make us believe that similar events would have the chance to occur at the same time in the other states of Europe.

Thus, the revolutionaries do not cheat the government when they defend themselves against the accusation of antipatriotism. Their action, though antimilitarist, is in reality not hostile to bourgeois militarism. It does not exclude all militarism, because it does not loathe the use of collective forces to triumph through the armed forces. It leads to patriotism because in the defense of the common ideal it would unite men in arms under the same flag in order to affirm a new social order, the revolutionary fatherland.

But then there are anarchists. We need to carefully distinguish here.

It seems to me that we have been abusing the word "anarchist" a lot for quite a while and that we manage to confound under this one label, in a baroque companionship, many beings with well-opposed tendencies and attitudes.

Exactly this question of antimilitarism and antipatriotism will serve us to establish a few useful distinctions.

The primary reproach that I make to the Communist Federation of Anarchists (FCA) is that they cared too much about growing their ranks at any cost.[55] They wanted the quantity, and it is fatal that they did not get the quality. It is true that with that they obeyed the needs of all collective organizations. They needed units and not individuals. And it is for that reason that we find, strangely assembled under one same banner, some number of communist disciples of Kropotkin, some disgruntled defectors from individualism who left in disgust at some so-called individualists, and a crowd of revolutionary syndicalists, workerists, insurrectionaries, socializers—and everything else that one would want . . . given that they were promised the "paradise of the proletarians" and a *grand soir* of turmoil under the notes of the "Internationale" . . .

It is possible that some of our comrades of this FCA still kept the sharp, bright vision of the anarchist attitude within them. But they prefer to keep its rays to themselves. In that they are certainly like those perfectly nonbelieving thinkers who assert that "there must be a religion . . . for the people." "We need to act," they said. "We need to create a movement; we need to follow the appropriate necessities; we cannot repel obscured good wills; we need to hit the popular soul with arguments that touch it without scarring it." And with that they let the crowd invade them, then mute them so well that they ended up singing the chorus with them, having nothing left in their mouth but the sonorous and hollow phrases in which they did not believe, but to which they exhilarated, in order to find in their agitation some illusion of true activity.

For an example of this, take awareness of the articles, the posters, the leaflets of the FCA campaign against militarism in the light of current events. Do you find in them a language that is very different from the one wielded by the socialists or syndicalists on the same subject? Can one spot in them an anarchist . . . or even communist point of view on the question? Not in the slightest. I cannot find a precise negation of the idol of the fatherland in them. I don't see any minds that are disconnected from all moral links with the "nation" express themselves in them. I don't even hear the cry for an anarchist revolt being screamed in them, either.

All we hear is: "But consider, we must not frighten these good people. . . . Isn't it enough to reasonably talk to them?" Because here we are, with anarchists campaigning for the "law of two years," then associating with "all the left" in fraternal meetings where the socialist deputies recommend "using the reserves" and "organizing in the militias." And there they sit—anarchists!—outraged that the "*army is not preoccupied with safeguarding the national honor,* but only to put soldiers in the service of the capital" (sic)—or affirming with gravity that "an army that massacres *the children of a nation* is an army of hit men that *dishonors the country* where it resides . . . an army that blemishes its weapons . . . an unworthy army" (sic).

Such language deeply saddens me. It is full of implications that force me to sense minds that are entangled in prejudices of class and of race, hearts that are still ready to beat to the thrusts of patriotism and bodies that are still ready to sacrifice themselves on the day when it is no longer about "shooting the poor workers by order of the bosses" or about "sullying one's weapons with French blood" but about running to the border to get one's skin perforated for the defense of the "national heritage."

I have provided precise quotes. They are extracts from a treatise entitled "The Bourgeois Are Afraid," which was released just a few days ago, on the occasion of a meeting by a group of the FCA.

These are supposed to be the unique ways of anarchists affirming themselves. Do you feel in all of this the expression of a soul that is freed of all moral authority, a nonsubmissive will? No, not at all. But instead I do find, in the demagogic vocabulary, in the politically charged langue worn by traditional tares, the social hydra, the public opinion, lying in ambush in the corners of every word.

*Hélas!* It is not only in the FCA that we can find such confusions. I know more than one among those who claim to be individualists of whom the judgment is no longer clear or harmonious.

There are of course the ignorant, the weak, those who only know how to be illusioned by words and who exhilarate in the individualist terminology in the same way as they previously dabbled in socialist or republican vocabulary. These do not know themselves—and the life, the action often find them without a personal attitude, in acts that are completely in disaccord with their words, ready to follow, according to the political circumstances, one or the other social impulsion. At least those are pardonable. . . . They do not know; they do not pretend to "know," they don't have the audacity to teach, to attempt to rule over individualist anarchism.

Finally, I arrive at those who, taking the responsibility to write in *L'anarchie, journal individualiste*, consciously support in it, at the occasion of political or economic events, social opinions, we can maybe even say socialist opinions, and notwithstanding continue to pretend to be individualist anarchists. That appears to me to be less excusable and completely as illogical as the incoherence of the imbeciles of which I spoke earlier.

I remember an address that Mauricius made at the first meeting that he gave in the UP for his "School of Orators" about four months ago.[56] He spoke about the armaments, of the international political situation; he engaged in brilliant diplomatic considerations; he indulged in explaining the reasons for the Balkan War and the interplaying alliances. Then, after some presenting of more thoughts on the European equilibrium, he rose against the "reaction" and started to preach that "unity is strength!" or that "peace leads to justice." It was the first time that I heard this orator speak. I must admit that it left me a bit confused.

How, I asked myself, is he an individualist, an anarchist writer? Was I in the right room, did I enter the right door . . . or did I have the imprudence of risking myself into a meeting of a "committee of conferences for international peace" or into some electoral foundation with the gentlemen of the radical dissidents? . . . *Hélas!* No, I was well and truly at the UP, and it was Mauricius. . . . He spoke . . . and the voters of Mr. Buisson or of Mr. Thalamas would have heard their account.

⬥

Oh you all, who are complacent to peddle in the political sea, parliamentarians of the Bourbon palace, of the Wagram room or of the "*fêtes en camaraderie,*" all you whom the social question "preoccupies," commit to antimilitarism, that is your role. It suits you. Commit to it like you once did with anticlericalism. The mine is a good one to explore, take out of it what you can, it's your case . . .

But, as to me, my heroic individualism, my anarchism of the action of the art incites me to different thoughts, to different acts, and recommends a very different attitude—my attitude—whatever the clamors of the herd and the men-aces of the masters may be.

I will not pity myself or wallow in the faith of the victims. Those who go vol-untarily to bend their spine under the militarist yoke, whether it is for three years, two years, six months—or twenty-eight days—they know perfectly, if they are more than mere cretins, of all that the state can impose, must impose on their bodies and their souls. Who enters the ranks, if he doesn't solidarize with the heart of the army, must individually take the responsibility of *his* struggle, of *his* revolt, of *his* suffering. He will have wanted them.

I will not be outraged by the militarist consequences of patriotism. But as an individualist I will refuse to serve the fatherland, the social idol.

I will not be shocked by the horrors that the army will create, and I will not be startled by the rottenness within the barracks. But as an anarchist of the action of the arts, the love for my individual beauty and the desire to stay harmonious will prohibit me from doing vile acts, acts of ugliness and of incoherence, among the brute disciplinarians and in their filth, between the dirty walls and the mores of these nonaesthetic constructs.

I love myself too much to be able to love the fatherland. I respect myself too much in my personality to ever be able to respect a national order. I intensely sense my beauty of *my* life flourish within me; how could I ever overcome it to see so much ugliness in my surroundings? I know that there is enough heroism for me in my individual struggle without having the need to ask the war to cre-ate "heroes."

I don't want to die for the fatherland. To die for oneself is more beautiful.

NOTES

1.    The Jeune Garde was a radical socialist militia that was active in Paris between 1911 and 1912 and was often associated with one of its leaders, the activist Gustave Hervé. See Alain Colignon, "Les jeunes gardes socialistes, ou la quête du Graal révolutionnaire 1930–1935," *Cahiers d'histoire du temps* 8 (2001): 181–224. They were socialists, syndicalists, and libertarians who practiced violent political action, notably against the police and the Camelots du Roi, the members of the nationalist movement Action Française who sold a publication by the same name. The Confédération Générale du Travail (CGT) was a radical trade union. Founded in 1895 as a union, the CGT came to be mostly dominated by anarcho-syndicalist views in the early twentieth century and changed its political ori-entation multiple times over the years. Today, the party has no official links to

communism and operates as a trade union with more moderate views. Finally, *Grand Soir* means "revolution" in anarchist slang. Knights of the Grand Soir are thus the (opportunist) revolutionaries that "appear" whenever a revolution (or simply a riot) breaks out.

2. *Arrivisme* is French for opportunism or front-running. The wordplay here is obvious.

3. When speaking of the "tragic bandits," let it be clear that I intend to single out, except for Bonnot, Garnier, and Valet, only *unknown strangers*. As to the anarchists who currently stand before the assize courts—in them I see only comrades who fell victim to their ideas and against whom not a single serious proof was brought forward with which the law could persecute them as having taken part in the act of the bandits. —A. C.

4. This is the first time Colomer endorses the Bonnot gang in a major publication. From here on out, the so-called *tragic bandits* will be a major theme in his work.

5. I will explain myself in a series of articles and conferences to develop my personal ideas on the "anarchist bandits." —A. C.

6. This key section illustrates the split between Colomer and *L'anarchie* beautifully. While Colomer continues to compliment the journal, in which he will still publish a few articles, the interpretation of the "Tragic Bandits" will give rise to frustration on both sides.

7. The contemporary philosopher referred to here is Henri Bergson. That is clear from the context, especially when compared to the series "At the Sources of Heroic Individualism" herein.

8. This is a reference to Agathon, the pseudonym of two nationalist writers, Alfred de Tarde and Henri Massis.

9. Colomer here ironically quotes the official police records used in connection with the Bonnot gang.

10. Ignatius of Loyola (1491–1556), later sainted, was a founder of the Jesuit order. The Jesuits had a reputation for sophism and fallacious arguments, which is likely what Colomer refers to here.

11. This is a reference to the cult of the physical body that became popular in France before World War I, analogous to the developments in Germany. See also "Sports for the Fatherland" herein.

12. This is a reference to Charles Baudelaire's *Les paradis artificiels*. The quote, however, is taken from the prose appearing in Baudelaire's *Paris Spleen*, "Enivrez-vous." See Baudelaire, *Le spleen de Paris* (Stuttgart: Philipp Reclam, 2008 [1869]), 174.

13. This is a reference to Peter Kropotkin and his scientific anarchism. By attacking Kropotkin here Colomer once more distinguishes his type of anarchism from scientism, which he was eager to do in writing and in practice. See Mark Antliff, "Revolutionary Immanence: Bergson Among the Anarchists," in *Bergson and the Art of Immanence*, ed. J. Ó Maoilearca and C. De Mille (Edinburgh: Edinburgh University Press, 2013), 94.

14. The word choice here is clearly inspired by Stirner's *Ego and Its Own*.

15. *Apache* is a slang term for notoriously criminal Parisian street gangs in the 1910s. They were a easily recognizable group who were distinguished and identified themselves by their many symbolic tattoos and peculiar way of speaking. Though criminals or illegalists and living together outside of society, they were not individualists on Colomer's account but merely practiced another form of collectivism.

16.    This can be read as a shot against the writers in *L'anarchie* who displayed this attitude in their interpretation of the Bonnot gang.

17.    See Felix Le Dantec, *L'égoïsme seule base de toute société: Étude des déformations résultant de la vie en commun* (Paris: Hachette, 1911). In it Le Dantec, a biologist, offered a sociological theory according to which a group dynamic like the one surrounding Bonnot's bandits would already shape personalities in the same ways as a society does.

18.    Later, in his syndicalist phase, this is exactly how Colomer projects the role of the syndicate: it provides an individualist anarchist solution to economic concerns.

19.    Here, Colomer differentiates his *bande* from Bonnot a bit. Given the contemporary relevance of the tragic bandits, especially in anarchist circles, many readers would have closely or even congruently associated Colomer's *bande* with "La bande à Bonnot." This is thus Colomer's attempt to widen his *bande* as a philosophical concept so that it can stand as on its own as well as an endorsement of the tragic bandits.

20.    A great friend of Arthur Rimbaud's and one of the famous seven people to receive a first edition of *Une saison en enfer*, Richepin lived to be recognized in the mainstream of French society. Colomer reproaches him for the acceptance of this recognition and for how quickly Richepin traded in his nomadic lifestyle for opulent banquets and well-paid lectures.

21.    *Aramon* is a type of red wine.

22.    This refers to Louis Lépine, a feared police prefect and nationalist politician.

23.    Literally: men of the letters, slang for academic types coined by Honoré de Balzac.

24.    A controversial law introduced in France in 1913, lengthening the mandatory military service to three years in order to prepare for the looming war against Germany. For more on Colomer's view of this law, see "Antimilitarism & Antipatriotism" in this part of the anthology.

25.    This is translated directly from the medieval French.

26.    The riots that Colomer describes here were sparked by the decision made by King Charles VII to place the Sorbonne in Paris under the jurisdiction of the city parliament. Before then the university had the liberty to fully govern itself. This was called *libertas academica*, a derivation from the privilege of *libertas ecclesia*. See Sophie Brouquet, "Les grèves d'étudiants au Quartier Latin au temps de François Villon," *Les cahiers de Framespa* 32 (October 1, 2019), http://journals.openedition.org/framespa/6561, 6.

27.    Available sources from the time period do not really support this conclusion of Villon's distancing himself from the Parisian revolts. After all, it seems that in 1455 he still was one of the main organizers among the student protestors. Colomer might have had access to information we do not, or he might have taken some poetic liberty here. See Brouquet, "Les grèves d'étudiants."

28.    Here Colmer uses the term "tragic bandit," hitherto reserved for the Bonnot gang, more generally. This is interesting, because he thus draws a direct comparison between the illegalist anarchists and the widely revered Villon. The move further integrates Bonnot and his companions into the wider context of anarchist thought and makes their story out to be more than just an isolated event.

29.    This was perhaps the most famous crime committed by the tragic bandits. In what was the first ever robbery to use a car as an integral part of the operation. Bonnot,

Callemin, Garnier, and perhaps an unidentified fourth bandit stole bags of money from the Société Générale bank. See Brendan Kemmet, "La bande à Bonnot frappe rue Ordener," *Le Parisien*, July 17, 2001.

30.    This is translated directly from the medieval French.

31.    The first thing a reader will notice in Villon's poetry is the language he employs. As a son of the fifteenth century, his poetry has a distinct late medieval character, which is most obvious in his spelling—it is very different from modern French, and somewhat inconsistent throughout his own work. Some current editions of Villon "clean up" his French to make it more legible to the modern audience. Colomer, however does not; instead, he quotes Villon in the original medieval French. Take, for instance, the very first word in this fragment from Villon's *Big Testament*: "Povre," meaning "poor." Modern French would have "*Pauvre*," an adaptation made in some editions, but not in this article. This is noticeable, because some passages in Villon are much further from modern French than this example and can prove to be challenging even to a highly educated French public today. Yet Colomer sticks to the original. Presumably his target reader, the average worker in the 1910s, was still able to decipher the works of the medieval poet.

32.    Further to the content, the first two stanzas selected here by Colomer describe Villon's upbringing and family history, focusing on the poverty they all had to endure (*Povre je suis, dès ma jeunesse—De povre et de petite extrace*). Powerfully, he notes of the souls God favors (*Les âmes desquels Dieu embrasse*) that they could never see the crowns or scepters, reflecting the crude reality of a unprivileged fifteenth-century family, living far removed from the "God-given" realities lived by the courtly powers. Just as his language is very typical by his century, so is the content of this passage very typical for Villon. Playing into the poetic themes of the late Middle Ages, Villon often takes a diametrical view of the courtly ideals and challenges the common values of his time by contrasting them with the lowest levels of his society, all while celebrating, say, the life of a vagabond or beggar. In this specific poem, the second stanza is an attempt at just that: Trying to make the most of his situation, his heart tells him that it is better to live poor than to have been a master (*seigneur*) only to rot away in a rich grave (*Mieux ault vivre, soubz gros bureaux—Povre, qu'avoir esté seigneur—et pourrir soubz riches tombeaux!*)

    But despite this attempt by his heart to palliate his societal situation, the third stanza shows that Villon is not immune to what Colomer calls "the suffering of the stomach": while he admits that he has loved and will love (life) in the future, his heart is saddened (*triste coeur*) and his stomach is starved (*ventre affamé*). And life is difficult because, as Villon poignantly emphasizes with a poignant inside rhyme, dancing comes from the belly (*la danse vient de la panse*). This, of course, would have been a very attractive outlook for Colomer: despite idealizing the freedom and aesthetic beauty of a poor vagabonding life, Villon notes that this life is hard simply because it is hard to be blissful when hungry.

33.    The master knows, Villon claims in this brief stanza, that rich or poor, wise or foolish, whether one is of nobility or a clergyman or a villain, whether one is beautiful, ugly, short or tall, all will die, because death seizes each of us without exception.

34.    Callemin and Soudy were two of the more famous tragic bandits. More about their eecutions, or rather about Colomer's perception of them, can be read in "The Novel of the Tragic Bandits" herein.

35. In this touching passage, entitled "Beautiful Lesson," Villon warns the youth that may life a life like his from the consequences of this choice. He tells them that if they were to "wander" to Montpippeau or Ruel, famous prisons of the time, they would lose "the most beautiful rose in their hats," presumably their lives. As he further emphasizes in the last two lines of the "lesson:" this life, these places where the body and maybe even the soul will go (*où va corps et peut-estre l'âme*), are not a cheap game (*ung jeu de trois mailles*) and should not be taken lightly. Of course, Colomer reads this warning a bit thinner, as is clear in his comments on the passage in this article.

36. In what reads as a bit of a last word, Villon here addresses his companions at the gallows, telling them to beware "the evil that blackens people after their death" (*ce mau hasles, qui noircit gens quans ils sont morts*).

37. For what makes quite the humorous passage, Villon describes various liquids, elements, situations and/or scenarios in which, literally, "spiteful tongues may be fried" (*Soient frittes ces langues envieuses!*)—this referring to people spitefully talking about him and his *bande*. A few of these include (putting them in) boiling lead to better destroy them (*plomb boillant, pour mieulx les esmorcher*), frying them in the gall of wolves, foxes, and badgers (*En fiels de loups, de regnards et blereaux*), or simply cutting them up with very good scissors (*detrenchée menu à bons ciseaulx*).

38. This lengthy poem, the title of which translates to something like "the fullness (as in, saturated after eating) of Villon and his companions," serves as something of a playful guide to a vagabonding lifestyle for those who, as the author notes in the first lines, have "neither gold nor money or salary" (*Qui n'a or, ny argent, ny gaige*). In the opening, "master" (*maistre*) Villon's companions complain that they don't even have two onions, tents, carpets, or a pavilion (*Qui n'avoient vailant deux ongnons, tentes, tapis, ne pavillon*). Villon calms them down, promising that by the end of the day they will have bread, wine, and meat in abundance (*pain, vin et viande à grant foyson*).

   The discourse then begins with a description of how to procure fish (*la maniere d'avoir du poisson*). Villon simply walks into a fishmonger's, taking a basket of fish before making his way to a priest and playing him against the fishmonger, claiming that the latter is his nephew who is cheap, money-obsessed, and very negligent when it comes to his religious duties (*vers Dieu il est fort negligent*)—all while convinced the fishmonger that that the priest will pay for his fish. Thus fooling them both, he makes off with the basket of fish, while the two men eventually figure out that they had been duped.

   After thus having acquired fish, Villon and one of his companions venture on to procure liver, lung, and tripe for their dinner. In order to do so, François Villon orders one of his friends to post up in front of the *trippière*, the woman selling the organs, and lowering his pants, thereby exposing his bottom to her. Villon, acting shocked toward this great show of disrespect, strongly slaps him (*le frappa bien rudement*) across the buttocks with the offal that he just so happens to hold in his hand. He then nonchalantly moves to put the meat back onto the store shelves (*voulut, tout incontinent, (les) remettre . . . dans le baquet*), but understandably the *trippière* refuses to take back the merchandise that had just slapped the bottom of Villon's friend, whereupon Villon walks out of the store with the now unwanted groceries.

Speaking as a true Frenchman, Villon then notes that soft bread (*du pain tendre*) is indispensable if one is to have a great dinner. To get it and add to the feast he has in mind, Villon thus goes to a baker. Feigning that he is a hotelier (*maistre d'hostel*) in great haste, he orders five or ten dozen loaves. Once half of this order is filled, Villon and a servant make off with the first half of bread, reaching a great old door. Here, Villon sends off the servant to get the second half of the order, but instead of awaiting his return he simply leaves with the first half of the bread, already enough to feed his friends. Shortly after, the baker's servant returns to the spot only to notice that he had been fooled and the pretend hotelier had disappeared.

Next, again proving his Frenchness, Villon states that it is of unequivocal necessity (*qu'il estoit necessaire—D'avoir du vin, par ambagoys*) to have a good wine to accompany his meal, because if he and his friends really wanted to be drunk that day they would need something to drink (*s'ilz vouloyent ce jour estre yvres, il alloit qu'ilz eussent à boire*). In order to get some good wine Villon swiftly fills up a vat with water and makes his way to the winery, where he orders a vat of "very good white wine from Baigneux" (*ung tres-bon vin blanc de Baigneux*), inconspicuously placing it next to his vat of water. Then, starting an argument with the salesman, Villon ends up claiming that he doesn't want the wine from Baigneux (*par ma foy, point je n'en veulx*). Instead he orders a wine from Beaulne but, all while engaging the salesman in subtle conversation, he exchanges the vats, thus making off with two vats of wine.

Finally the time for the dinner has come. Villon has one more trick up his sleeve—after all, he still wants some roast chicken. Without much hesitation, he makes his way to a roastery, where he stages a fistfight. In the heat of battle, Villon grabs a chicken skewer right in front of the eyes of a shocked bellow operator (*celuy qui bailla le soufflet*), and, swinging it a weapon, he sets off to chase after his pretend opponent—taking home the entire spit of chicken.

Thus the story ends, the last line concluding that this is the way how, through their great exploits, the men had their bread, wine, meat, fish, and roast chicken.

39.   A *suroît* is a traditional Breton sailor's hat.

40.   The first of Corbière's poems selected by Colomer opens with three stanzas taken from Victor Hugo's *Oceano nox*. Notably, Hugo repeatedly points out the hierarchy aboard (*combien de marins, combien de capitaines* or *combien de patrons morts avec lers équipages*) and laments the fact that deceased sailors will be completely forgotten, not even to be remembered by a humble tombstone (*pas même l'humble pierre*). This stands as a great example for what Colomer points out later, namely Hugo's focus on the social aspects of the sailor's life and their pitiful fate. Corbière, however, opens his poem by quoting Hugo only to offer a fully contrasting description of the wild perils of the sea itself, while his sailors are proud and detached from social fates, detached even from their potential death at sea. In his verses, the sailors were already dead when they embarked on their journey (*sont morts—absolument comme ils étaient partis*) or they aren't dead at all, because death itself is a mainland concept (*la Camarde a pas le pied marin*). This image is further developed in stanza four when Corbière writes that for the struggling sailor, death itself changes face: it becomes the sea (*La Mort change de face: La Mer!*). Thereby, it is the very thing he faces for a living. Similarly, dead sailors don't drown, since on Corbière's account

drowning is a freshwater concept. Instead they sink, drinking the salt water with the same high spirits they had while drinking their Boujaron, their ration of alcohol. Then, instead of going six feet under to be eating by rats, Corbière's sailors go to the sharks while their souls breathe on instead of oozing underneath in your potatoes (stanza 7). They are visible in every wave, which Corbière compares to the butterflies of love raging in the stomach of a loving, slightly drunken girl (*On dirait le ventre amoureux / D'une fille de joie en rut, a moitié saoúle*). Finally, they roll on in the infinite seas, naked and with no restraints, no coffins (*sans clous et sans sapin, sans couvercle, sans cierges*)—while Corbière appeals to the trespassing earthlings (presumably Hugo) to let them roll on in peace.

41.    Théodore Botrel (1868–1925) was a French chansonnier who, like Corbière, grew up in Britanny before moving to Paris. If Colomer reflects negatively on him here, it may, besides Colomer's apparent dislike for his lyrics, also be because Botrel was engaged in catholic conservative movements and was an activist for a patriotic "cleansing" of culture.

42.    The second poem selected here plays on similar motives as the first. In the opening few lines of the poem, Corbière critiques the popular perception of sailors, who are presented in the opera wearing their stereotypical light blue suits and wildly swearing about (*vous marins de quinquets à l'Opéra . . . comique*). This is then contrasted to the misery of sailors fates as it is presented on the boulevards and in the press, with its horror stories of wrecks at sea. All to conclude that sailors are perceived as a different breed in every range of society, or rather, as a different breed altogether, completely separated from life on the mainland (*race à part*). This separation has some truth to it of course, for Corbière notes that no sailor is ever fully comfortable on the mainland (*a terre—oiseaux palmés—ils sont ternes et veules*), nor do they know those who Corbière describes as "the ones who can't tie proper knots" (*ces gens à rudes noeuds*). But on the mainland, sailors are simply dumbed down in plays or dramatized for the capital's reading public that reduces the sailors to their potentially tragic ends. From here Corbière goes on to vividly express the true reality of life at sea to his readership, but, through all the tortures, the struggles, the dangers, and the adventures (*à travers les tortures, les luttes, les dangers, les larges aventures*) a sense of superiority remains, in which the earthlings (*terriens*) are represented as docile in comparison to the proud and independent seamen (*gens au coeur sur la main . . . capables de tout*). Poignantly, these "brutes" have their own sense of beauty too, and even their own poetry, lived throught the chants of the sea—leading Corbière to praise them, their togetherness, as being "one living poem" (—*Ils ne s'en doutent pas, eux, poème vivant*) And after all, sailors know their true master: it is a block of wood (*d'un seul bloc de bois*) that separates them from the dangers of the sea below.

43.    Jesus Christ is sailor's slang for a policeman. —A. C.

44.    Having established Corbière's ancestry and authenticity as a sailor poet from Brittany, Colomer follows the flow of the poets biography to get to his move to Paris, a city he never fully felt at home in. This poem is proof of that. Comparing Paris to a crowded anthill and taking the reader through impressions of life in the city that clearly overwhelm the author, it serves as great contrast to Corbière's descriptions of life at sea, that, despite the hardships he expresses, seem to fascinate the author much more than the rather lifeless sentiment he faces in Paris. All the while Corbière's description of Paris

is also a reflection on poetry itself and his changing approach to his craft. In the poem, Corbière seems to reject spontaneous, more sincere poetry in favor of a more complex image-laden or artificial poetry—because following the somewhat oppressive trends and the state of poetry in his epoch, he feels that his poetry needs to be convoluted and nearly incomprehensible if one wants to be able to express any sincerity at all. Convoluted and incomprehensible, just as the city of Paris is to the small town sea poet from Brittany. These metapoetic reflections read as if Corbière applies the famous figure of the cursed poet (*poète maudit*) to poetry itself—making of him a cursed poet writing in an era in which poetry is cursed, too. In Paris, Corbière writes of his virgin muse (*muse pucelle*) standing on the pavement selling nothing, while "not hearing the silence, and watching the wind blow by" (*n'etendant pas soner le vide / et regardant passer le vent*). As such, he lives his bohemian life, unhappily with both his city and his craft, while his youth fades away (*la jeunesse . . . eh, c'est bon un jour!*). In this, he now solely lives for brief moments of happiness, which he calls "*quart d'heures d'immortalité*," fifteen minutes of immortality, while an uneasy sense of misery remains.

45.  This short fragment describes a heartbreak felt by the poet who, sitting on the pavement watching the people go by, waits for a girl he loves. When she finally comes by, after many hours, she looks down upon him smiling, and stretching out her hand—but only to give him some change, as if he was a beggar, not seeming to know or recognize him.

46.  In another heartbreaking and highly symbolist poem Corbière describes his relationship to a lover, and, ultimately, why their liaison would not work out. Despite true love being between them and him loving her "like a lizard loves the rays of the sun that follows after its sleep" (*je t'aimais comme . . . un lézard . . . aime le rayon qui suit son sommeil*), the poet's past prohibits him from a life with his love. Comparing himself to a broken trinket, he notes that a trinket can be glued together from its shards, while he, once broken, was rendered worthless (*mais un bibelot cassé se recolle; / rt lui, décollé, ne vaudra plus rien!*). In fact, in what is likely a reference to the famous anecdote of Alexander the Great standing in the way of Diogenes's sunlight, love itself becomes an obstacle that stands between Corbière and the rays of sun, symbolizing the woman he loves. Thus he considers that the pair would be wise not to be lovers, as that would destroy the human relationship, or the caring friendship that they do have. In the final stanza Corbière nonetheless hopes that the end to their relationship would be a beautiful one. Instead of cursing one another, he writes, he has hope that if they were to die, it would be of laughter—since he always loved her laugh (*moi qui l'aimais tant ton rire si frais!*).

47.  In this impressive piece, Corbière contrasts himself to the "free men" who, with shackles around their necks (*carcan au cou*), live in republics and their domestic homes. He, the pariah, the skinny, lonely one, may be always alone, but he is always free (*toujours seul, toujours libre*). His fatherland, he declares in the last stanza, is the world, and since the planet is round, he isn't scared to ever see the end of it. And thereby, his fatherland is always under his feet, whenever he stands upright (*ma patrie . . . elle est sous la plante de mes pieds—quand je suis debout*).

48.  This is a reference to the syndicalist and journalist Édouard Sené (1887–1932), who is ironically referred to as "citizen."

49. André Lorulot (1885-1963) was an anarchist writer who mostly focused on anticlericalism. He was the longtime leader of the Fédération Nationale de la Libre Pensée, the National Federation for Free Thought.

50. This can be read as a reference to Nietzsche's famous image of the child in *Thus Spoke Zarathustra*.

51. Note that Colomer wrote this in 1913, nearly ten years before Wittgenstein's *Tractatus*. This passage is likely a reaction to early analytical thought, something that Colomer criticizes elsewhere.

52. In the diverse landscape of publications in early nineteenth-century Paris, the *bonne presse* were the publications that were closest to the establishment, on neither the radical right nor the left.

53. See "At the Sources of Heroic Individualism 2: The Christian Soul" herein.

54. *Le temps* was a paper from the so-called *bonne presse*, and *L'humanité* was one of the premier communist organs.

55. The Fédération Communiste Anarchiste was the oldest and most influential anarchist organization of the time. Founded in 1910, it was dismantled when World War I broke out in 1914.

56. Mauricius was the pen name of Maurice Vandamme, a then famous writer for *L'anarchie*. The UP, short for "Université Populaire," was a cooperative initiative by many left-leaning organizations that allowed anyone to attend free public classes in order to improve the political understanding of the working classes.

# PART III

# Postwar Realism (1919–1923)

AND *L'ACTION D'ART* IS BORN AGAIN . .

*L'ACTION D'ART* (NEW SERIES) 1 (OCTOBER 1919)

—They crow of national heroism.

—They say: "Here are my medals—and long live the war!" or: "Here are my medals—and down with the war!"

—They think they have the right to talk because they have been there.

—They have fought it and now denigrate it. They have loved it and now spit on it.

—All of them—they only count themselves, and they only count in relation to IT. They are the Federation of Mobilized Artists, the Association of Combatant Writers, the International of Old Combatants, etc. They have established this spiritual Poilutism of which Henri Barbusse is the captain and Romain Rolland the marshal.[1]

—They only consider themselves safe when they are in bunches, in groups, in crowds—in the trenches of peacetime just like in the ones of the war. They conglomerate. They reassure each other in troops, just like they had alarmed themselves—also in troops . . .

—And here am I—who?— ME.

—I was not a hero on the battlefield—and I flatter myself for that.

—I have no medals and no decorations—and I am honored by that.

—I did not go—and I am proud of that.

—I have not killed a single "Boche"—and I am glorified by that.[2]

—I return from 1914 with clean hands and my soul lifted high. And that is my only title of glory.

—I belong to no party. I am alone, and I am not afraid of that.

—Meanwhile, I am far from "superhuman." For me, like for everybody, these terrible times happened. If I didn't want them, if I did not participate in them, that's still just too bad for me. This war happened. And, with it, *against* it, I have struggled.

—I return from it with scars.

—I am not an apparent cripple. I do not carry a "glorious wound"—but meanwhile:

—I left my sanity to it—and that is still the least of what bothers me.

—I have lost, on the fields of this cursed fatherland, all the friends of my childhood. Paul Favre, Jean de La Ville de Mirmont, Gabriel-Tristan-Franconi, Olivier-Hourcade, Raymond Guasco, and my companion of the action of the arts, Georges Audibert.

—And then the cruelest of the injuries to my heart opened up: at the dawn of *their* peace, which is as sinister as their war, their peace of famine after their war of mass graves—then the little fairy that illuminated these last five dark years of struggle has extinguished. My soft and clear Tristane—my daughter just passed away.

—I have my injuries and my hate. I have my pride. I have my love. I have my nobility. Here I am, still upright, and meanwhile, back on my route—in my sun. It's up to the both of us now, society!

All of that is what I would have written as an epigraph of a journal that I would have founded in my solitude—with this title: I.

However, I have found a companion: Marcel Say. Over a route that was different from mine, he has also crossed, in solitary pride, that horrible crossroads of death and stupidity: the war.

—He wanted to found his journal, *Le pal*, to express his revolt

against the universally triumphant mediocrity, in business, in politics, in literature; against the outrageous self-regulation of this republican era of decadent democracies, during which the bankers, deputies and "dear teachers" have manifested themselves to be pusillanimous, prudish and cowardly; against this scum of high and low bourgeoisie that speculates the stock markets during their little weeks, governs according to their little will, and stylizes their little shakeups; against this tread marking, this trampling in the swamps where this "gentilhommerie" of blushes and rubbish obstinate, where it is conveniently blinded to the golden or masterful, to aims that ray impure, to luxurious ideas and the earthiness of words; against this plebs that is so slow, heavy, vile, lackluster, a troop of vulgar, unconscious and unorganized that undergoes violence, flattery, promises, encouragements and lies with unchanging receptivity and a philistine incapability to discern the true from the false, to be reared in the face of the unjust.

—And, more specifically, more precisely, his revolt against the cults, the clans, the cliques, the literary chapels, against all these consortiums that bring together invertebrates of agreement or of failure, who have organized themselves, my dear!; to save what is left of them, in the practice of reciprocal belief, chiding instead of revenge, and mutual panegyrics."

And, in this revolt, Marcel Say estimated that "to cut down the cad, a fine blade is good, but the rapier is also good."

And that is how this preface ends:

Light, reckless, and passionate, it is with joy that we will slash open the scoundrels.

From critiques to outrages, via irony, invectives, and sarcasm; from the epigram to the funeral oration, via satire and pamphlets, the entire arsenal will serve us; and we will try to be arduous gladiators, proud, battle drunk of fights to the end, and, above everything, in love with the shocks and the sparkles of the swords in brilliant passages between "stark adversaries."

It is war that is "developing," through a logical grid, from contemplation and reflection. O happiness of my ideas; aren't they swords? O love of my wisdom, you, *philosophy*: you are sublime of wisdom, because you contain, powerfully, a struggle. Philosophy by the Gladius! What a way to live and to die.

Here we are, together. I have waited five years before meeting a French writer who spoke my language.

On this road on which we found each other, I give my hand to Marcel Say: For a long time, Hauteclaire already walks with me. And now we are joined by Mars Villers, Henri Strente, Marise, Gaston Delavière ... Tewfik Fahmy will come back, too! There is light in that group. Good luck, companions. Let's go. Heroic individualism glorifies us. The marvelous soul of Georges Audibert lends us its wings.

And here we are, again, *companions of the action of the arts.*

## INDIVIDUALIST HEROISM AND THE WAR: PRELIMINARY WARNING

### *L' ACTION D'ART* (NEW SERIES) 1 (OCTOBER 1919)

*I wrote this series as an individualist who was born and raised in France. The conditions that this geographical situation of my youth has imposed upon my life have led me to only talk for the French, to whom I owe my truths. I would wish that an individualist that was born and raised in Germany could, in his right, tell his truths to the German nationals. To each their language, according to the social contingencies that most immediately imprison them.*

*This declaration should suffice to shut the evil tongues that could reproach a degree of Germanophilia to the author of this series. I only love myself and I sell myself to nobody.*

—A. C.

## INDIVIDUALIST HEROISM AND THE WAR: WHEN THE WAR CAME . . .

When the war broke out in August 1914, I welcomed it without any surprise and without any fear. For a long time, my being had already desolidarized from society. It had found, for its thought and its will, a rhythm of life—outside of every collective action. It flared only for its joy and its beauty. Its actions could only be harmonious gifts from the fruits of its art, or a heroic struggle to preserve its harvest from the communal hands that only know how to sell—or muddy—or destroy.

By writing "At the Sources of Individualist Heroism" one year before the war broke out, I wanted to show how, in all circumstances, be it even during peacetime and in a socialist regime, a man who wants to live with soul is forced, to stay truly strong and beautiful, to break with his social environment. He is forced to make his life and his work as an individualist—by taking his distance from the troubles that are born out of the lowly struggles of economic life; as an anarchist—by refusing to submit himself to the law of a society, whatever it may be, because he cannot find motives for his action outside of himself—and the law of *his* happiness.

I had denied my participation in any battle as a part of a collectivity. I had made of this refusal a condition of my being. Any events could thus arise—whatever they may be. The troubles could be born out of the struggle between two classes or two races—what would I care! I knew myself to be outside of any class as much as outside of any race.

Wars or revolutions could break out. Neither one nor the other could count me in the ranks of its soldiers. Neither one nor the other could have my heroic blood in its ranks.

It ended up being war. And I lived it like I had anticipated.

The war unleashed as an overwhelming burst of mediocre brutalities. It was like a war of pestilence that dragged everything with it in its whirls of filth, ransacking the gardens of its fruits, uprooting the highest forests, toppling the bodies of young men, throwing them around and rotting them out as premature carcasses. It was before anything else the deafening triumph of social stupidity, to the sound of large dosages of "Marseillaises," in deafening parades for the sheep outside, while in the interior of the barracks, a few who considered themselves less stupid, reserved themselves, quietly, to the sound of the Louis and the pounds sterling, true victory.[3]

That was the war, the worthy sister of peace, because they both are, war and peace, children of gold. One, more violent, uses machine guns and bombs, the other, more hypocritical, serves itself of hunger, prisons, and the popular guillotine. But one and the other are providers of death, loyal guardians of the good of the race, ruthless preachers who sacrifice the individual soul on the altars of the god, society.

War! Peace! They are neither my war nor my peace. I hope for one not more than for the other. I expected nothing of either.

War or peace, then, why would I care? I do not depend on history. I carry my history within me, and I make it every day following my temperament, with my consciousness, and with all my strength.

## INDIVIDUALIST HEROISM AND THE WAR: A BUSINESS WAR

*L'ACTION D'ART* (NEW SERIES) 2 (NOVEMBER 1919)

Friends have told me, when speaking of the war: "It is a wind of madness that has blown over humanity! ... "

The war would thus be, for those charming utopists, just a bad moment to get past, a nightmare passing between two beneficial nights of rest, or between two enchanted evenings.

I am both more optimistic and more pessimistic than those dreamers. If the war is madness, peace is just as incoherent. But, conversely, if peace is reason, I do not see why war would be any less sufficiently so.

Internationally, war and peace are equally incurable and dangerous lunacies to the mind of the individual who only knows how to find motives for action within himself. But are they not products of one identical reasoning in the eyes of the social man who only sees external pretext for his movements?

And, to be precise, there never was, in the entire history of mankind, a war that was less mad than this one here.

For our contemporaries, men of societal progress and economical interest, it can, without a doubt, seem mad to fight for a cross, or for a crescent; for a Helena, or for a prince. But to pour the blood of others as well as one's own to consolidate the placements of French capital in Russia and to save the honor of the English merchants that was compromised by the scandalous concurrence of their German colleagues—that does not upset the indignation of the practical brain cells of a son of the twentieth century.

Far from being a lunacy, the war of today is a "business," and ... business is business. It is up to everybody to know, before he mingles in it, whether he truly belongs in the world of business, if he has a taste and the interest for this kind of occupation, and if he can find in it the law of his happiness. But the serious problem is not the monopoly of war. In times of peace it is equally posed against the free consciousness of the individual.

War and peace obey laws of the same reasoning. They are necessary movements in the rhythm of all national life like constitution and revolution are to all political life.

Every being who submits to social logic and makes peace with the men of the race or the class that the coincidence of birth has made them appear in, obeys the same logic by engaging in the war or the revolution that are necessary to the functioning of the collective organism to which he surrendered! This being no longer owns itself. The submission has killed the individual man. It made of him the cell of an organism, a cog in a mechanism.

## INDIVIDUALIST HEROISM AND THE WAR: ITS WRITERS

Writers are no exception to this law of social mechanics. Every thought that is thought in the service of a cause that is exterior to it does not own itself anymore. It has to be modified, no longer to its own harmony and for its intrinsic unity but as a function of the role that is assigned to it, for the maintenance and the prosperity of the cause to which it is a servant.

Let's apply this principle to the fact of war, and we can no longer be upset, nor even be surprised by the unanimous voice of the societal writers who boast, sing, and glorify the war of their fatherland. Peace, as I have said, is the sister of war; is it then not natural that the pacifist writers are good brethren to the warmongering writers? . . . The ones live through the others. They condition each other. They have different roles, but they are interchangeable, they are of the same world. They play in the same match, and their games are composed of cards that they share. The pacifist, in wartime, concedes the war, absolutely like the warrior knows to accept the state of peace during peacetime.

No idea of erstwhile or of later—be it the most seductive one—could have the force to rip Mr. France from his dear public in the hour when the fatherland has no longer any soul but to run to the divine massacres—just as Mr. Barrès, in peacetime, when he judged France to be putrefied under the spell of parliamentarianism, could not resist to also be one of its representatives in the Parliament.

One on its left and one on its right side, France and Barrès accompanied the same herd. They are the megaphones of the French crowd.

Meanwhile, when the herd of people has the leisure to roam here and there in the hours of sundown, over the countryside of spinelessness and its daily grazing—it splits up, in groups that each believe they have their own soul. And then, the voice of France seems to differ from the one of Barrès. But when a wolf howls in the distance or when a cloud menacingly stares over the horizon—and they all retighten, pack together, gang up. The herd reforms; it is now but a massive beast, blocking the roads with its fear and unanimously outing a single stupid bleating. Then the voice of Barrès no longer differs from the one of France.

## INDIVIDUALIST HEROISM AND THE WAR: ITS ANARCHISTS

It also no longer differs from the one of Jean Grave. The naive could have been surprised to see this "anarchist" surprising even himself with his little chant of war. As for me, I was not more touched than by Jules Guesde's patriotic homilies or the hymns of victory from the citizen Hervé.

Sometime before the war, on the occasion of the Anarchist Congress of 1913, I saw the work of Jean Grave and his companions of revolutionary communism. In *L'action d'art* I then stigmatized the social authoritarianism of these men, their taste for discipline, and for the brutal manifestations of their collective force. And I concluded by denying those demagogues the title of "Anarchist," that had been prostituted for too long by the seductive brand of their political party.

I do know very well that there was also the voice of Kropotkin. I remember that he had had until then a nearly perfect life, that he had, as Oscar Wilde said, "the soul of the beautiful white Christ." If his words of today stain this whiteness with red, should I be surprised? By speaking of this war, I propose to show where charity and pity lead, and of which crimes they are the abundant sources. Let it be enough to say here that Kropotkin, like every revolutionary, is a transformer of the social. His being only thinks, lives, acts in function of the collective mass of which he hopes to see it realizing equilibrium.

For him, even more than for anyone else, the individual can only be a condition for the unity of a social ensemble. A war, a revolution are but accidents of the history of humanity in genesis. Of what importance is blood spilled for a good cause! It is the seed from which the crop of a marvelous tomorrow will grow. For every sociologist, whether he be an evolutionist like Mr. Leroy-Beaulieu, or a revolutionary like Kropotkin, the individual is not at the center of things; he is no end in himself. All of his reason for being is drawn from societal life. He can thus die for the fatherland or for humanity. He will be, by doing so, one of the heroic sculptors of a future paradise.

The "White Christ" stained in red thus does not surprise me. He does not outrage me anymore. I do not condemn him more than Chares Peguy, the sons of Cassagnac, Raymond Guasco, or Charles Maurras. These men are sincere. They put their acts in accord with their thought. Some among them even pushed until their deaths for their firm ideas. I understand them, and I respect them. But faced off against their ideas that menace the harmony of my being, I raise all the force of my will to feel, to think, to act individually, and their worshiped phantoms will never penetrate me.

Evidently though, there also is the world of facts. I found myself in a country in a state of war. Bloody barbarisms were perpetrated. In the ferocious scramble, the socials soared to their weapons. The fatherland that claims me as its own called for me, too, in its defense.

What was I to do?

## INDIVIDUALIST HEROISM AND THE WAR: AS AN INDIVIDUALIST

As an individualist, I planned to remove myself entirely—mind, heart and body, idea and act, from the scramble of nationalist assassins.

I wanted to be neither a voluntary victim nor an involuntary murderer in the ranks of a social troop in arms for the fatherland. During the war, I wanted to stay, as I did in the cruel years of peace, a heroic defender of my individual integrity.

As an anarchist of the action of the arts, I further planned to refuse the shady promiscuities that are necessary means to ruse. I did not want to lie, nor did I want to beg—because it is more beautiful to speak one's soul the way that it is and to affirm one's life the way that one wants it. André Colomer could be in hiding as little as he could be a combatant. There was thus only one side left for me: insubordination. I took it without hesitation. For an idealist refractionary of my kind there was no attitude worthy of an individualist who pretended to be heroic but the one of an utter refusal of any military service.

In the hour during which so many young men stupidly sacrificed their most beautiful ideas to the material requirements of their societal destiny, it pleased me to feel myself ready to break anything that could have been left to tie me to a house, a family, a city, a country, a language, so happy to renounce all of these past objectivities and to make nothing of my future as a French writer, because I knew I sacrificed all of that to save the treasures that I took with me, that I kept within me, the inalienable treasures of my mind and my heart. I quit France the better to stay myself. By deserting I have abandoned nothing because an individualist carries everything within himself. If he leaves a country it is only because everything in that country had already left him! The individualist who has found his own cause does not cry over any memory. A past that could hinder him in his becoming is no longer his past. He will deny it without any regrets. The landscapes themselves could not retain him in a land that is hostile to his blossoming. The individualist is a visionary who appropriates all of the objects that his senses perceive without his needing them, or being born among those things, or to bind him to it until his death, or to make them "his property."

By deserting I did not renounce the action. I refused myself from societal actions that were destructive to my beauty, in order to stay able to the action of the arts. I affirmed my individual beauty and my will to save my harmony. By ripping myself from the national embrace, I gave myself to the embrace of my soul. I went to a land that still permitted me to put my acts in accordance with my idea, to stay the artist of my life, walking on whatever route, but always "under the only light of my conscience" in the music of my dream, and still letting my acts bloom in their tones and in harmony with my soul.

By deserting I did not run from the fight. I sought it.

I refused to deliver myself, with a hanging head, feet and fists tied together, to my only enemy: the social. To stay in the scramble would have been for me, in any scenario, an act of cowardice. Complicity and martyrdom are both a capitulation for the individualist. In order to truly be oneself it is necessary to break the chains of hypocritical solidarity. It is as pointless to aspire to live for humanity as it is to die for it. It is necessary to differentiate oneself from the collective with a strong candor that breaks all bridges, and not only the ones that permit me to go from me to it but just as much the ones that could permit it to come to me, albeit with songs and smiles. When it comes to free souls, there is no need to tie any bridges between us to join each other.

By becoming a deserter I broke yet another bridge between myself and the social. By denying every part of me to the fatherland I irrevocably distanced myself from collective life. I undid the possibility of any reconciliation and all mending of fences. I declared war on my state. *I positioned myself not only outside of but also against their scramble.* I fought my combat. I engaged in my struggle. I was an individual who was strong in his internal harmony, confronting all hostilities and the cunningness of social organization with his will as his only weapon—the individual ready to defend himself, in a bitter fight, if necessary until death, a life that managed to stay his own and that would never be anything but his own—an individual affirming his irreducible unity and ready to do anything to defend it.

Outside of the scramble of humans colliding in their troops of unconsciousness, I stood up. Against the monstrous scramble and its gusts of bloody mud, I rose up.

In the hour where the famous acts of old patriotic heroism trumpeted, I felt the sources of a young individualist heroism dance within me. And I was shuddering with love by thinking that here and there all over this world of old horrors and gregarious ugliness, a few virgin energies bloomed up when their hearts were drenched in the pure waters of its sources. Without flags or fanfares, without parades and without laurels, without orders and without support, with only the approval of their consciousness and only the stimulant of their ardent joy of life, young people with enlightened eyes have had the rare courage of affirming themselves in their own solitary beauty and affronting the social in a ruthless struggle until death. What is a soldier in the scramble of a battle? What is a lieutenant launching an assault of his section against an enemy company? They are heroes, surely—if they fight with sincerity. But their heroism, exalted by an old collective drunkenness, framed in military discipline, supported by authority, driven by glory, and acclaimed by the crowds, appears to us to be pale and vulgar when we think about the individualist heroism that stands up on its own, with its glowing consciousness and its eyes of iron willingness, creating a man whom all the armies in the world could not coerce into denying his soul.

## INDIVIDUALIST HEROISM AND THE WAR: WHERE MY HISTORIES INTERMIX WITH HISTORY

*L'ACTION D'ART* (NEW SERIES) 3 (DECEMBER 1919)

Only the "non-me" is hateful, and of all negations to the individual soul, politics is the most heinous. As such, I owe an apology to myself and to my readers if I happen to mix some acts of my own history with the events of history in these following lines. I am not at all ashamed to resort to the acts of my life in order to better illustrate in this recital the ideas that I support. But I strongly loathe for my individualism to play a role in the facts of national life. Meanwhile there is a way to touch them without being stained. It is to be at the same time aggressive and silly, it is a bit brutal, often even crude and offensive, but I have unsuccessfully looked for other options to permit myself to stay sincere and clean when the conditions of my struggle make me write on such a subject.

At the moment of the declaration of war, I was still "free of any military obligations." Five years before, I had already rejected the hypocrisy of obedience to the laws of a peacetime militarization.[4] Ignoring the reiterated requests from police officials, I had rebelled, and without any further preoccupations with the matters of the law, I had continued my literary activity as was my habit, publishing in journals, founding magazines, joining in artistic reunions, without the shadow of a *bicorne* ever troubling my poem.[5] I had only changed my address. The intelligence of the military authorities took two years to discover my new residence. I had nicely installed myself, with my brother, in a small hotel near the Closerie de Lilas. There I was arrested on a gently sunny May morning in the spring of Montparnasse by a smiling, bearded gendarme with a large cartridge belt who thought he was extremely bright to have managed this brilliant arrest. The poor man would not even gain his twenty-five francs, because in the meantime, I have come to suspect that he had an accomplice for this difficult operation in the person of a "poet" among my friends. Because gendarmes and men of letters do not scorn to sometimes align themselves in spicy cooperation.

I underwent a stay of a week in the "Cherche-Midi," a moist stay between the decaying walls of the old prison of which the chief guard, absolutely aghast at administering my socially not acceptable mane, showed himself liberal with respect to me in that he did not subject me to the disciplinary rule of the shaved head. A few friends with "important relations" worked with hands and feet to drag me out of these sinks by "reforming" me. It was peacetime after all, and it was spring. I preferred to sing my welcome to the young wooden isolation of the woods in Verrières rather than to rot away in peripatetic reflections about the narrowness of a prison yard. . . . I thus let the friendship of my dear Zaki Scandar be and successfully passed an opportune review panel.[6] I was reformed.

In August 1914 I was thus exempt from all service to the French nation. For some months then, I worked as a proofreader assembling the journal *Le bonnet rouge* in the Simard publishing house. That was an excellent post to observe the events that developed in the chambers of French politics from May to September 1914. In these five months of working, sitting with my ass on a chair and my eyes fixed on my tasks, among the nibbling of the linotypes and the snoring of the printing press gears, I learned more about human cowardice than in twelve years of painful peregrination through Paris.

## INDIVIDUALIST HEROISM AND THE WAR: GOLD, BLOOD, AND SHIT

*Le bonnet rouge*, an evening paper published each day, was born amid the Caillaux affair.[7] On its headline, in enormous letters, fat like spats in the face of sincerity, the name of Miguel Almereyda, the chief editor, was laid out.[8]

The history of this man would make the conscience of the last of the donkeys of the police shudder of appalled decency. The outgrowths of the cistern that serves Mr. Briand for a soul seem like nothing more than pleasant smells of moral sanity when one approaches the boreholes of shit that flow out of the brain of Almereyda.

Because once he was Miguel, dear Miguel of the "comrades," the providential flame that illuminated lives which were laced in doubts with a new belief.

He arrived in the circles of the revolted who had already crossed over, literary whims, curious aestheticists, opportunist politicians, all the vipers who are today showered in glory by the state after they ripened their treason in the good trusting warmth of the hearts of anarchists, who were often cheated, often hurt, but always rebloomed in a dawn of believing, in the joy of loving.

He was twenty years old, with feverish eyes, arduous movements, and an eloquent voice that was at the same time provoking, seducing, and harsh. Of course he had no style. But what tone and what allure! He could whip up the most careful skeptics. All were conquered and firmly believed in this young apostle.

But an acute observer like Stendhal was not fooled. He could recognize in his eyes the quality of their fever: a thirst for gold, an attraction to the low pleasures, the irresistible desire to roll around in all the luxuries of social manure. With his actions he could have unwrapped the farce of his valor and enthusiasm early on to display the dry movement of an opportunist machinery.

And when it came to his voice, he felt one by one nothing but the seductions of the whore who caresses for profit, the brutality of the pimp striking her for the profit, and the creepy spinelessness of the suitor who skims the profits.

He cut his hair to show us his skull free of any bumps, flat like all terrestrial platitudes.[9] And in his smiling chimpanzee face he had extinguished the misleading lights of the stage that are turned on only during the spectacle in order to let the little strike of the deviously imperturbable dagger within his merchant gaze glimmer in the tomblike shadows of his sockets.

And to finalize the revelation, the ruthless analyst described the entire life of the man by way of his jaws. They are not large, but he knows how to use them. They resemble those of rats and the type of small women who are apparently inoffensive, but whose entire nibbling friendliness would be capable over time of destroying a mountain. An important detail: despite his dark and plentiful hair, his moustache is of a rare, red fur.

Once Almereyda paid his dues to the anarchist scenes by agreeing to dress in a simplicity that was his in the place of taste; but as soon as he could, he did not hesitate to put his costume in accord with his temperament. Completely in light gray, with a pale, purple tie on a blue dress shirt with pink flowers, his shoes in a bursting yellow, and his coquette hands loaded with three massive rings with stupendous stones, M. Miguel Almereyda shows himself today in all of his true splendor, in all of his native force; he thus marvelously illustrates the worthy hero of the French democracy of tomorrow. He is the sanctified and triumphant *rastaquouère*,[10] the rastaquouère blessed by the laws and accessing to power in order to avenge France for having suffered the affront of having been the country of a Paul Verlaine and a Stéphane Mallarmé.

If the public opinions of Almereyda miss this coherence that forms the unity of his mind, then his acts would always be loyal to his conscience. From his rebellious childhood to his official maturity, the movements of his life are marked by a rare unity. Charles Baudelaire, speaking of Théophile Gautier, has told us that a taste for the beautiful was a fatum for him and that the unity of his life can be found in a sort of a fixed idea: an obsession over beauty. Miguel Almereyda instead has an obsession with excrement, and all of his acts were never anything but the logical materialization of this unmovable idea at the center of his being.

Be your own judge. At the age of sixteen, his first act that was authenticated and glorified by the French press during the famous trial of Métivier was an act of terrorism. He threw a bomb. But where? At the Elysée, in the Senate, on the path of a visiting tsar, or of a president in a procession? Please! These are the place of choice for a Vaillant or an Emile Henry. But an Almereyda, where did he launch this explosion of his heroic soul? In a pissoir on the boulevards. Not more, not less.

The life of this man had begun well. It only had to further unfold as a deduction of this superb initial act. Almereyda would meet Gustave Hervé.[11] The conjunctions of destinies are never fortuitous. It is our fixed idea that pushes us toward the ones who can facilitate its realization. The obsession with excrement could only conduct a young Miguel to a master like Gustave. That fat swine of Hervé had already rolled his gut through all the hallways of the university. But jaded from the taste of the mediocrely fat waters of the alma mater, his stomach was burning to plunge itself upon more substantially dirty pastures. He wanted to charm the most sensible organs of the crowd. That is why, during the Social War, he began to sing to it about the vicinity of his asshole.

For this task Almereyda was dedicated to Hervé as the most precious of his lieutenants. Miguel gave him with great enthusiasm a collaboration that permitted him to more than satisfy his fixed idea.

Thus, together, they planted the flag of their good fatherland very carefully and by choice in the smelliest of all manure.[12] They extended this taste as long as possible because these men are gourmets. But everything in this world has an end. When the tricolored flag was adequately planted in the divine national shit, Gustave and Miguel apologetically looked at each other. *Hélas*, it was all over. What to do now? For a while, they entertained themselves by collecting some clods of the valued matter and by decorating the loathed creases of their cursed idol. But that risked being too expensive. Some months in prison calmed these too refined perversions in them that have to keep a taste of fat in order to not upset the societal morals.

Thus Hervé had a genius idea. They were to accomplish the same work, but backward. After having planted it they would wrench it out again. After having dirtied they would purify. They did not have to leave the holy shit that enchanted their senses. Contrarily, they felt its presence even stronger, they who slowly, carefully, and with love went from then on to avow their tongues to the beatifying need to solemnly purify the French flag.[13]

## INDIVIDUALIST HEROISM AND THE WAR: A VISION OF THE MAN OF DEATH

*L'ACTION D'ART* (NEW SERIES) 4 (DECEMBER 1919)

During that time the ghastly Poincaré had just conquered the suffrages of mediocrity and ascended to power with the fixed idea of revenge. He immediately decreed a weekly retreat of the military on the evening of their pay, events of savage cacophony that had as the goal of unifying them with glassful alcoholics to make the hearts of the populace jump in epileptic convulsions of pure patriotism.

The glorious assaults of Choisy-le-Roi and Nogent-sur-Marne and the quadruple massacre of a morning of guillotining were not enough for this bleak executor to avenge France's double shame of having lost Alsace-Lorraine in 1870–71 and having trembled in fear, in 1912–13, under the heroic drive of a dozen anarchists. Only a war could save French honor and give its president one of those ineffable auras of human blood that lets the glory of those great men whom the fatherland recognizes in its history eternally shine.

A few days after the execution of the tragic bandits, I had the chance to meet the presidential procession in front of the Montparnasse train station. It was the first time that I saw Mr. Poincaré. The true face of this man was a revelation. I did not see this aura of good kid that is accorded to him by the pictures in the newspapers. His cheeks appeared to be flatter, his eyes a lot more immobile than on the pictures, his lips colorless and retreated. But mainly I was struck by his white laundry-like taint—a terrifying whiteness. I have never seen those rooms in the hospitals where those stricken by plague and ill with cholera see their staggering death tolls rise. But I am certain that they project an image of appalling whiteness onto the retinas of their dying patients, one that is analogous to the one I saw in the face of Mr. Poincaré. This figure is white like the one of a carcass is black. Some whites glare with life. This one was foreshadowing death. His appearance empties the senses of the one who contemplates it. This white hails from the decomposition of everything. It is an absence, a nothing. After one has looked at that white one sees only black.

With such a face I suspect that this man was predestined for the only crimes that truly scare me: those that are caused without acting in order to better enjoy them. He had already been the one who refused *a line with his plume*, that is to say a minimal movement of his hand, to save four blossoming lives. He would be the one who would pull this line with the plume, this ridiculous act of his fingers, to launch four million assassins into a massacre.

Oh! This pale face that I saw for only a second when the cars rolled by. I already saw it apply its sinister whiteness onto the flurry of mud and blood of this war, and I had a vision of horror of those men killing and dying in unconsciousness.

Symbolizing their crimes without a soul is the face of a Poincaré, the dismal white face of heinous pleasure, that seemed to me to be as ancient as the vision of charity that the martyrs in the arenas had while sacrificing their lives to the beasts of Rome to throw their souls as loving gifts in the face of Christ, the sublime white face of ruthless pain.

## INDIVIDUALIST HEROISM AND THE WAR: ALBION AND ITS SUPPORTERS

*L'ACTION D'ART* (NEW SERIES) 5 (JANUARY 1920)

Poincaré ascended to power to hit the big one, but it was two fun guys in pince-nez who had already worked in the shadows for a long time for him to prepare his great masterpiece of death. The hideous Delcassé and the grotesque Mille-rand, two very French guys, had put the entire genius of their people in play to advance this cause.

They proved to be, depending on the moment, braggadocious and cowardly, scheming and confused, cunning and blundering, villains and pawns, busy and inactive, smart and lacking any intelligence, animated by all bad intentions from hell and absolutely incapable of realizing them with any force. They were the purest fruits of the mediocrity that gave birth to them. Delcassé and Millerand are nothing but a new reincarnation of Bouvard and Pécuchet.[14]

During Fachoda, Delcassé had sufficiently reduced his dear fatherland to the state of a bug under the British boot so that England could count on the good services of French heroism from that moment on.[15] The events of Fachoda were the preliminary conditions for the *entente cordiale*, because the modest Albion could never give her heart to those of its lovers who possessed the exquisite delicacy to never ask anything else from her, but to know to give her everything that she knew very well not to look like she wanted.[16]

The imperialism of the French republic has consisted of forty years of colonial conquests, of sending its soldiers into massacres to reveal to the men of color the stunning beauty of this free administration that Europe sent them. Its imperialism was but the violent affirmation of its incomparable bureaucracy. England has always found an imperialism that consisted of letting the soldiers of other nations kill each other in order to impose the products of its economy upon the universe more profitably.

Meanwhile Germany engaged in a new type of imperialism, one that would not act like one or the other but that looked to combine the advantages of the two. It kept a large and well-organized army at home in order to support its voyaging salesmen, sent out around the world to compete with the British market by way of its menacing reputation. The Germans engaged in industry and commerce with the same meticulously analytic spirit that they employed in historical research, letters, and philosophy.[17]

But the methods of precision that do not always suit works of art or speculations of the soul are the only truly fruitful ones when it comes to practical science or material realizations. In commercial markets or chemical laboratories Germany quickly showed to be evidently superior to all its competitors. The English saw their traditional dominance fade a little bit with every passing day. What could they do? For a people who are truly in love with economical action and the game of competitions, only one open door was available: to look for the causes of this increasing force of the German market and to modify, to correct their own commercial activity according to the results brought about by a rigorous study of them. Thus, instead of screaming at "German rubbish," they would discover that in most German fabrications an apparently miraculous phenomenon was observable: a perfecting of the products that occurred simultaneously with a diminution of the price and an augmentation of the workers' salaries. And, instead of stupidly raging out against that and protesting against this violation of the traditional laws of economic policy, they knew that it would be more cautious to realize the intelligence of a people who managed to accord its acts with its new sociology, a sociology that all universities in France and Great Britain have taught for twenty years, without any of their practitioners ever using it to their advantage. Thus, the routineers and the speculators of London and Paris became aware that all the secrets of the industrial and commercial success of Berlin are in the right recognition of this social law that an organism that wants to produce good labor needs to function well, that is to say possess a unity of functioning between all of its parts.

They thus saw in the augmentation of the workers' salaries in Germany the *cause* of the falling of German prices and the perfecting of German goods, and they encouraged and provoked a strong organization of their proletariat in order to shore up social discipline; they gave them a more *golden* slavery in order to gain from that a better production that they could sell cheaper and in greater numbers.

But the English are not really interested in economic action and the game of concurrences. They have a greater taste for economic inaction and the game of money.

Business did not interest them for its own sake but for the benefits that could be drawn from it. Action for action's sake seems to them to be an illness that is as shameful as the one of "art for art's sake." Renouncing the support of the fight of their rigid moralism against the pure aestheticism of an Oscar Wilde, they preferred to get rid of it by throwing it to the labor camps. The English wanted to remove a "scandalous spectacle." They would not act differently with respect to Germany. Tired of the pitiful figure that their rigid mercantilism made in its struggle against the pure Germanic sense of business, they decided to remove a competitor who dared to be unloyal enough to not recognize their traditional superiority. But England always lacked the courage to execute its crimes alone and in plain daylight. It prefers to commit them in the shadows and to leave its realization to benevolent and imprudent accomplices. They needed subjects. France became one, and Russia another.

## INDIVIDUALIST HEROISM AND THE WAR:
## THE FRANCO-RUSSIAN ALLIANCE

*L'ACTION D'ART* (NEW SERIES) 8 (MAY 1920)

The Franco-Russian alliance already was the most colossal scam of modern times. The easel-like ways of the French statesmen and the drowsiness of their citizens fell, without any difficulties, into the greasy plan that the tricksters of Moscow had prepared for them. All that it took was an exhibition of Russian sailors of the boulevards, half a dozen fireworks over the Seine, and a thousand girandoles in yellow and the tricolor in the trees of the Champs-Elysées to prime the people of Paris. The visit of Nicolas and of the tsarina finished the job of wrapping them up. We found that "he did not have an evil face" and that "his daughter was very agreeable." That was enough to forget Siberia, the knout, and the massacres that do not cease to illustrate the charming tsarist regime, and it was enough to have the "refrain" of the Russian anthem be screamed out in every bistro in Belleville and Montparno.

The French public thus said, through the ironically hymnic mouth of Vincent Hyspa:

> Emperess, Emp'ror, the great duch'ess,
> Nicolas, Alexandra and the lil' Olga
> Their dog Lof'ki and their dry nurse
> Came here: I don't know why,
> But: Long live Russia!

Delcassé did not ignore this "why," and the French stock exchange would soon find out.

A caricature of the end of the reign of Felix Faure shows us this pallid little tsar in a corner of the salon of receptions, his crown resting on the edge of his skull in the way a gibus does at the end of a wedding,[18] looking quirky and clownish, discreetly pulling on the sleeve of this grand old Felix and whispering in his ear: "Hey, kindly lend me a hundred francs, will you?" And the old, cheap scavenger, still completely bloated from the impressive reception at Tsarskoye Selo,[19] lightening up in superhuman joy even at the idea of "obliging" an emperor, stretched out to the smiling croak of all Russians, with a royal motion taken from the repertoire of the cheesy movie characters that once had educated his proletarian childhood, a comfortable purse: the one of France.

When it comes to carrying out deep historical judgments on political events, nobody can surpass a chansonnier or a caricaturist. Their humorist spirit, when observing the "heroes" of these official adventures, strips them of their historical clothing and of their parade harnessing to show them to us in their grotesque attitudes of actors who continued to play the role of sumptuous monarchs without noticing that their wigs, pulled off by some malicious genius, no longer hid the strangely planted hairs of their mane, or that the falling of the purple coat revealed underwear that was little worthy of the bedroom scene in *Occupe-toi d'Amélie*.[20]

---

When Felix Faure succumbed to the Dreyfusesque embrace of Madame Steinheil and when this poor apprentice hairdresser of Casimir-Périer, who was used to more hygienic tools, was backed off into the Augean stables that the Elysées were now so awed by, there was but one single fellow in the entire French Masonry who was capable of fiddling, without heaving, with the queasy presidential politics: it was Father Loubet. Besides, he had sufficiently practiced, in his youth in the École Panamist, to be able to magisterially take the complex reigns of the Dreyfusian chariot into his hands and conduct it to triumph. Thus, he assured for himself the eternal recognition of the Jewish communities of the civilized world. But this sly little old man, cumbersome as he was, went to draw well many other surprises for the future of his country out of his legendary accordion gibus. From trip to trip, between Russia, England, and Italy, he would become, in small little steps, slowly and steadily, the smart and unnoticed peddler of the *bonne nouvelle maçonique* that would animate, ten years later, the Quadruple Entente. Emile was but the traveling salesman, Delcassé was the occult forge of power. But the big boss, the great master, the supreme point of triumph, and the arch of the initiating swords, the all-powerful key, was this former prowler of the nightclubs, this big baby with the luxury hookers, that had come to age on the cushions of the Parisian brothels and that, embittered by a fifty-year career as a failed monarch, was the prince of Wales who sought to avenge for the misguided maternal longevity of Victoria, when, finally, he managed to ascend on the throne by using the coffin of his mother as the indispensable stepping stone to uplift his clunky mass. During his principality, lacking a crown, Edouard has acquired a fantastic apron. The scandalous chronicles of his time teach us that, in a drunken night, a few malicious little hookers from Montmartre dragged him into a cab and, having found the luxurious masonic ornament in the pockets of his overcoat, they found it "funny" to further strip Edouard of all clothing and, naked as a pig, abandoned him in the vehicle after having, out of charity for the eyes of the driver, the touching care to wrap his adipose potbelly in the famous, symbolic apron. Once in power, Edouard surely remembered the anecdote, because he would never again leave this precious loincloth behind and used it on more than one occasion to seal much other disgustingness from the eyes of his contemporaries.

The *cochonnerie sanglante* was one of them. Édouard VII employed the high and low means of this cowardice assassinating force that is Freemasonry to surround Germany with the menacing coalition of all public opinions of the "civilized world." It was he who rendered the next European war inevitable.

But he would not have the joy of assisting in this spectacle of horror of which he was the able director. He died and left this heroic succession to his nephew Georges. Meanwhile France continued to empty its reserves of gold and silver into the tsarist coffers. For a moment we thought that the coming into power of the cow from Loupillon would compromise the success of this Russian scam. This poor Fallières was afflicted by such phenomenal obesity that it was much more than a governmental affair to him to just move his elephantine body. Thus the travels to Russia became less frequent. The perfidious nationalist tongues took this powerlessness for bad will and would not hesitate to call him an antipatriot, an anarchist, a nihilist.... The poor man! He avoided violent emotions, that was all, and it was also the only reason for his unpopular abstention during capital executions. And to say that France, outraged in its love for moralizing spectacles, became unanimous in its pursuit of this inoffensive hippopotamus with the name of assassin, though he was soft like a milk sheep.

## *MISE AU POINT*: THE ANARCHISTS IN THE FACE OF THE REVOLUTION

*Le libertaire* 148 (November 1921)

They tell us: "Cease your critiques of the Russian Revolution, because you thereby serve the cause of the reactionary enemies."

We ask ourselves: "Would you be with the communist on the morning after the revolution?"

THE REVOLUTION . . .

What a great, empty word! What a phantom! What a myth!

This word entailed all and nothing, like the word "ideal," like the word "God."

And, as realists, we respond to the preceding questions:

"Why would you want us to act differently with respect to the Russian revolution than we act toward ourselves? The bolshevist government does not treat anarchists better than the reactionaries do. It executes them and imprisons them. Why would you want us to sacrifice our critical mind and our temperament to serve the propaganda of a social state that promises us, for tomorrow, the jail cell?"

Members of the Communist Party have responded to us:

"In revolutionary times, before the communist state is solidly constituted, the dictatorship is indispensable. Please understand that and ally yourselves to our politics. Admit our centralist functionalism, our justice, our banks, our prisons, our police and our army. It is all for the common good."

The radical socialists did not speak differently. Neither did the republicans. Nor the royalists. Nor the imperialists.

It is in the same way that the *fraredemptori* of the Very Holy Inquisition once spoke when they embraced the poor "lost souls" whom they ushered to torture "for their eternal health." It is in the same way that all supporters of authority speak, all worshippers of spiritual or temporal laws, whether they are Catholics, democrats, or Marxists; all those who see in the individual but a matter to serve the collective form and who do not fear to use all means, trickeries, or violence to fold up personalities to the rigid laws of a fixed type.

The anarchists recognize no dogma whatsoever. They adore nothing. They love life. And they will not search for this life in an ideal paradise. They sense life within them, in the ephemeral reality that they want to harmoniously create with their own thoughts.

To ask the anarchists to deny their consciences, to make an abstraction of their judgments, of their critical minds, and of their will to personal creation, in order to submit themselves to the tyrannical laws of one or multiple dictators whose eloquence can describe the marvelous tomorrow of humanity's future . . .

Don't even think about it, Mr. Cachin! Is this truly not a pitch of the same caliber as those of the time of the Grrreat War when you, Mr. Communist Deputy, roamed through France and Italy to recruit cannon-fodder meat for the machine guns, demanding the *temporary* self-sacrifice of the *proletariat* by promising them a general disarmament, divine peace, and the reign of happiness . . . for the morning after the carnage?

From 1914 to 1919, in great numbers, the anarchists did not march in the ranks of the "Army of Justice and Civilization." They also do not count on enlarging the ranks of the Red Army.

—Then, how would you ever do a revolution?

—What revolution?

—*Eh bien*, yours . . .

We respond: our revolution is a fight to the death against all forms of authority. We are against capitalist exploitation because it is one of the expressions of "arche" that we combat. But if we slaughter industrial capitalism it won't be to constitute and defend state capitalism. Collectivism of the kind currently being realized in Russia is nothing but the centralization of all capital of a country in the coffers of the state, a centralization in the hands of a few dictators, a centralization of all powers of exploitation.

By revolting against the bolshevist state the anarchists are logically consistent with anarchist thought.

—And your revolution? . . .

—It will be the work of the workers themselves.

The producing individuals, grouped in ateliers, factories, etc. . . . need to methodically organize the seizing of their means of productions and workplaces. They will be armed with the workplaces themselves. They will not become soldiers; they will be armed workers, which is very different. And when the workers will be the masters, on the anarchist account, they will only be the *masters* of the inanimate matter that they activate with their efforts. To liberate themselves, organize themselves and defend themselves, the producing individuals have no need for politicians or generals or commissioners of the people.

Let them eliminate the state, its functionaries, its mechanisms, its laws, all of the old carcasses of oppression and collectivist obligation—and you will see, with only the interplay of interest and affection, the people produce, and individuals group up and avidly live the search for clarity and harmony.

## ANARCHISM IS NOT A SECT

*Le libertaire* 157 (JANUARY 1922)

On all sides there are misunderstandings about the meaning of anarchy. Among our adversaries as among our friends.

In some syndicalist environments there are figures who attempt to play the same game politicians play—and there are comrades who let themselves be abused under the pretense of impartiality. And they both fill our ears with this eternal formula: "Syndicalism must be influenced as little by philosophical sects as it may not be influenced by political parties. The workers' movement needs to be as weary of the anarchist groups as of communist or socialist parties."

Some libertarian comrades are mistaken in the opposite sense, but are just as misguided, when they complain about the lack of economic theories among the anarchists, of the defects in their self-organization, of their "lacking sociological doctrine," and when they preach the necessity to establish a sort of general plan of practical realizations for the libertarian future, some absurd type of anarchist politics that is beyond me.

Both the ones and the others are not aware of the nonsense they utter by combining two contradicting ideas, two conflicting words: Dogma and Anarchy.

Anarchy is the affirmation of the individual critique and the individual becoming. It is the negation of the state—that is to say of every fixated system, of every stop in the forms of life, of every authority that was established to obstruct the élan of intuitive expansion, of the free searching of human individuals. Anarchy is the opportunity for every being to take its part in the enjoyment of the common goods and to bring forward its contribution of creating efforts. It is a free field for initiative and desire. It is also the effort of each one to realize the harmony of all. It is like a vast musical consciousness of humanity. Anarchy is the art of the arts: it is art applied to the life of mankind. It is the expression of the beauty of living without constraints, without frames, without laws, without guardians. It is the flowering of hearts and minds.

Anarchy being the defense and the position of the individual in the face of every obstacle to its natural fulfillment, anarchy being the revolt against all oppression, all chains, all moral or physical hindrance, is really nothing else than the attitude that the scientist has before the facts of nature, the artist before the sensations and sentiments of the soul, or the syndicalist before the events of economic life.

All those who endeavored for mankind to no longer be subjected to the tyranny of the physical elements were anarchists without knowing it. Through their discoveries, with their inventions, they destroyed parts of the authority of the natural force over living beings bit by bit. They contributed to cutting down the power of God, to bringing the force of the rebellion of individual researchers deep into the mysterious core of the universal forces.

Anarchists were every poet, every painter, every musician who contributed to liberating, with their original visions and their synthetic creations, the human hearts and minds of the insidious authority of the passions and the dreams and the mysterious desires that haunted them.

Savants like artists create anarchist works by both revolting against routine and even tradition, in accomplishing the work of creators—by eliminating all that compromises the scientific or aesthetic ends of their research from the field of their experience or their study—by braving public opinion to be initiators—by living, most of the time, poor and persecuted by the powerful of the hour—by dying often as martyrs of their consciousness. Examples of this are innumerable.

The same is true for syndicalism. Whether one wants or not it is anarchist, and come the day where it is not anymore, it will consequently cease to be truly syndicalistic. Because syndicalism is nothing but a work of anarchism, its creation, the most practical means that it has found to express itself, manifest itself, expand itself and to prosper in the reign of economics.

Anarchy is no more of a sect than it is a party attempting to take a hold of the syndicalist movement to impose external ends on it and to fold it to rules imposed by a communal reason or a collective authority. It doesn't use moral policing any more than it uses the Red Army. Anarchy is the laborer becoming conscious of his needs toward well-being and of his love for freedom. Anarchy affirms the revolt of the individual against all those who exploit it and all that oppresses it.

Now, what is syndicalism? The only practical means to affirm anarchy on the economical terrain. Well before there were any trade unionists there were anarchists. Epictetus was an anarchist and before him there were men who refused the abdication of the individual consciousness before brutal forces of hypocritical oppression. Every individual who looked for the light of the mind and the warmth of the heart was a denier of dogmata and politics. This anarchy looked for weapons to defend the individual, means of free expression and of free organization among individuals.

Syndicalism is but one of its weapons, one of its means.

When the syndicates were but professional groupings, they were, like the corporations of the ancien régime, instruments of authority and tradition. They were like little professional nations. They had their privileges and their laws, and they were firmly closed to the ordinary crowd and the noninitiated. It was like a Freemasonry of the workplace.

Then syndicates were the prey of politicians. They were means of democratic action. As municipal advisors, influential voters guided them to incorporate the little professional nations into the republican nation.

Syndicalism only began to be born on the day it was revolutionarily animated by an anarchist life sap. Now, syndicalists had nothing to do with corporations. They ceased to define societal privileges. They no longer imposed themselves as superior collectivist entities over the individual producer. They united, in the Federation of Bourses,[21] to represent the revolt of the exploited. From that day on there were no longer syndicates but the workers' syndicalism, the weapon of individual liberation, the affirmation of the producer as the only master of his faith, the negation of all forms of exploitation and dictate, the will to create a new world following this beautiful maxim: "Well-being and Freedom."

On the header of their journal the libertarians inscribed this: "The anarchists want to implement a social environment that assures to every individual a maximum of well-being and of liberty that is adequate to every era."

The same mottos. That is why we, here, are not preoccupied to modify the principles of syndicalism. They are ours. They are only the affirmation of the libertarian ideal on the battlefield of practical life.

Syndicalism only adapts the current hopes of anarchism to the current necessities.

—"But anarchism is not limited to its economic activity. It has other ends, psychological ones, philosophical ones . . ."

Certainly. But I am persuaded, and I will show you why in a forthcoming article, that anarchy (which is neither a sect nor a party) and the anarchist spirit can, by penetrating, by impregnating, and by *fertilizing* syndicalism, can lead it and its realizations a lot further than the self-imposed limits of the revolutionary syndicalists of today.

## THE BELLY AND THE MIND

*LE LIBERTAIRE* 163 (MARCH 1922)

In this journal, among anarchists, we do not fight to be the smartest or the most knowledgeable. Controversies have their utility, but they should not degenerate into tournaments where, to empower one's own weapons, one accords to one's opponents the chimerical, worm-eaten lance of Don Quixote.

It would be easy for me to disregard the very "literate" jests of the correspondent who sent Fabrice his fancy commentaries on our conceptions of anarchism.[22] Everyone is allowed to amuse himself, be it at the expense of his comrades and even, if it is necessary for that, by misrepresenting the thoughts and activities of a fellow militant. It is permitted to sow confusion and doubt in the mind of those who read us without yet holding this knowledge of the ideas and the facts that affirm convictions. Everything is permitted, obviously . . . and I should be permitted not to take that seriously.

Meanwhile, out of camaraderie for the readers of *Le libertaire*, I will use the opportunity to clarify some ideas regarding the "Belly," the "Soul," and the "Anarchy."

I do not want to go in depth on the subject. That would not fit the scope of *Le libertaire*. I will instead soon publish a study that I completed five years ago, entitled *Matter, Mind and Me*. In it, I show idealism and realism, materialism and spiritualism to be theoretical systems onto which I superimpose the life of the individual justifying the ideal and the real at the same time, while simultaneously using matter and mind.

I do not ignore my physical needs and I do not despise them. I also do not ignore my spiritual needs, and I do not despise them either. Both are the means of my personality, and I struggle to assure all these means, because I know good and well that I cannot forgo one or the other to truly be myself.

But do not claim that "the life of the mind depends upon the life of the body"—that would be as absurd as to claim, "The life of the body depends on the life of the mind." The truth is that the individual needs his body as well as his mind and that he needs to hold account of both his material and spiritual necessities to live.

When I have not eaten enough to still my hunger, I am neither a poet nor a thinker; I am just a hungry beast: I am entirely absorbed by my need to eat and nothing else can preoccupy me.

Inversely, when I am obsessed by an idea or tormented by a moral trepidation, a sentimental suffering, I am no longer a good animal; I no longer grow hungry. "I lose hunger and thirst," as the popular proverb holds it. As long as I do not satisfy my mind or my heart, I will lack appetite ... I will be entirely absorbed by my need to know.

Among men there are some who are enslaved to their physical needs, not only when they are in depravation but also and primarily based upon the satisfaction and the desire to go even further than regular enjoyment. These men barely even live the life of the mind anymore. Their psychological activity is reduced to a minimum. The ideas are, within them, but pale reflections of the realities. These beings live the cult of the belly. The stomach is for them like an idol of which they are the vulgar worshippers.

There are other men who are enslaved to their ideas, to images of their mind, to passions of their heart, to the qualms of their soul, to the scruples of their conscience, to doctrines, to systems, to ideologies.

These are mystics, fanatics, believers of all sorts, spiritualists of the religions, of philosophy, of the arts, or the sciences. These are the monks, the savants, and the poets who only live for their Gods, for their hypotheses or for their chimeras, cloistered in their laboratories or their work cabinets—and leaving, just like the fakirs, their bodies wither in the absences of their natural functioning.

The soul and the belly are two idols that are equally dangerous for the individual. The physical and spiritual needs must find harmonious satisfaction in all of us, in a way that neither one nor the other of these needs command in us, but that we can direct our life by guiding them according to our own temperament, and toward an ideal that lets us grow.

To those who are only satisfied by the joys of the soul and who resign themselves to the depravation of the body, one must show the unhealthy egoism of spiritual riches that is only edified upon physical suffering. To the Christians, to the Tolstoians, to the dilettantes, it is suitable to shame them for all that they support without resisting, not only within them but also around them.

To those who only struggle to live their life of material joys without being occupied with the forms of their acts and the psychological repercussions of their adventures, to those who see only the positive material aspects of their own life, to all of those who neglect their consciousness and its inalienable treasures, it is suitable to say: "You are bad egoists, you are fake individualists; you neglect a good part of yourselves!"

Only those who are deprived of all exterior peace, only the proletarians who don't even have what is necessary for the regular life of their bodies, have the right to put material revindications above everything else. It is the matter for these, exploited by capitalism, to appease their physical needs, precisely to better hear the voice of the heart and the intelligence that slumbers in each one of them.

By struggling for the conquest of bread the worker simultaneously fights for the conquest of the book, for the conquest of his thoughts, of his reflections, of his consciousness, for the conquest of his personality.

Let's leave to the laborers, as ignorant as some may be, the attention to accomplish their emancipation on the economic field. By liberating their bodies, they will, all at once, give higher and higher rise to their mind. With every effort they give for their well-being it will likewise be, on their part, an effort for freedom.

But it does not suit us, the militants of anarchy, to content ourselves with only that for ourselves. We surpass, in hope and in comprehension, the limits of economic life. We always want more liberty for the individual. We want to liberate it from all authorities, from all chains, as much from those that are elaborated for the mind as from those that are forged for the body.

We also need to sacrifice, in the very heart of the exploited masses struggling for material reasons, a bit of our physical joy for the torches of these ideas that accord us moral, compensatory joys to shine for us!

All beings who consider themselves to be anarchists need to be the experimenters of their own conceptions.

Experiences must be lived intelligently, with a general sense of life, without forgetting all the givens of the human problem. This way the individual will not fall into his particular adventures and will not throw himself, under the pretext of anarchism or individualism, headfirst into bronze walls.

But the anarchist owes it to himself, in certain moments, to accomplish his destiny with heroism. And this heroism consists for him only to accord his acts with his thoughts.

Doing as much, he will not only attain the summits of his individual life, but he will also contribute to the harmonious fusion of the human forces and ideas in the entire universe.

## MR. BERGSON, *MAÎTRE A PENSER* OF THE THIRD REPUBLIC

*LA REVUE ANARCHISTE* 3 (MARCH 1922)

Mr. Bergson was the *maître a penser* of the "young people of today."[23] His name will feature in the history of Mr. Poincaré like the one of Descartes does in the history of Louis XIV. Mr. Bergson was the Descartes of bourgeois nationalism. Like the author of the *Discourse on the Method*, he sold his thought to the social powers of his time; he renounced the pure joys of philosophy to taste the enjoyments of celebrity. He prostituted himself to the glory of his century.

Henri Bergson was in the possession of a unique treasure, a superhuman treasure. He cashed it out into current coinage to the effigy of a president of a republic. Mr. Bergson lost his soul. He is today left with popularity and honors, but that is trivial, and it is very little for the thinker behind *Time and Free Will*.

Far from the large river of collective reason where the men of practical activity come to drink, wash themselves, navigate, and go about their social business; far from the fruitful plains that it feeds with its canals and through modern systems of irrigation; far from the cities that the river births on its banks to organize all things in an appropriate manner; the young philosopher Henri Bergson left toward the solitary heights where the mountains create the sources of the river. For a long time he searched for the miraculous spring between folds in the rocks: the spring that, during its entire long course, never once called upon the servitude of the large river of reason.

Often, having thought to have discovered it, his bouncing steps followed, in frantic course, whatever torrent in which the reflections of the world seemed to dance most freely. His bloody feet and the gasping of his chest drove him from cause to cause, all along the slope of material necessity, but only toward some of the bleak creaks where everything flows toward death.

But one morning, *while he was not searching* and while roaming through the wind of the treetops, his soul floated harmoniously on all its senses over the clarities and perfumes and caresses of the mountains; and over such childhood dreams about the simple joy of sensing, a music awakened. The music that appeared in this moment was one that he couldn't place—a music that seemed to sing from within things, and that seemed to sing of the things within him—a music with no liaisons—a music with no end, a indecomposable music and, while being one, still so prestigiously multiform that it was impossible for Bergson to place it in any form or style—a music of freedom. And the philosopher strayed from mountain to mountain, from valley to valley and from morning to the evening, and then even through the night, but the music always sang. It taunted time and space. Thus, he understood that he carried the music within himself. And since *in this moment* he was not reasoning and his thoughts had not stuck to a plan or followed a sequence of finite ideas since the morning, the philosopher understood that it wasn't his intelligence that sung within his being. Hence he went to sleep. But the music sang until the morning in melodies that he wouldn't forget. And when Henri Bergson awoke by the sunlight, his eyes finally saw the source of the music that had enchanted him. He discovered, bursting out of his senses in quivering, symphonic rays, the free stream of intuition. This stream didn't go toward the plains. It didn't lose itself in the bleak creeks or the communal waters of human reason. It didn't even flow, it gushed. It didn't follow the accidentally of any riverbed. No, it soared toward the treetops without needing to obey causal laws to propel itself there. In fact, nothing propelled its current. It attracted itself toward its own ends. In desiring itself, it had created itself, and its harmony was the only law of its activity. Its waves of musical clarity freed sensation from the yoke of rationalism. They freed it from the suffocating grips of collective intelligence to lead to its blossoming, to the rhythm of personality. By plunging into the intuitive rays, subjective sensation stopped being a mediocre element of universal servitude to become the infinite generator of individual freedom!

Henri Bergson thus showed that sensation is not that identical atom which psychophysicists use to reconstruct, with meticulous, multiplicative formulas, the composition of different souls. No, in a simple sensation, subjectivism manifests itself with as much vague, synthetic richness as in the most complex of feelings. And in nothing but a fleeting sensation, the entire psychological life of a being radiates in all of its creative personalization, just as it does in but the most prolific moments of imagination. The spiritual individual is not a composition; it is an infinite composer. Within himself all activity has only a single end: the harmony of its wholeness, and so in the slightest instant of its life, it passes in its entirety. One could rightfully apply to this psychological individual the formula that the theologians attribute to God: He is entirely Himself, everywhere and nowhere, in all instants and all places of his creation. In every moment of his life He creates Himself.

It is through sensation that he creates himself with the least amount of restrictive struggles, in all of his loving purity, as a unique flower. Through experiencing sensation, individuals unfold themselves *in all of their liberty* and *fully alive.*

However, each sensation is hindered by distracting elements. It can reason with itself. It can contain within itself an idea. Or ideas can associate themselves with it. Then the many ideas hold on to each other like the successive links of a chain that tie the individual to the collective of humanity. These collectivist ideas hail in from the outside ready-made and enter into a conscience to violate its intimacy. But they are not satisfied to just group among themselves and link the intellectual life of an individual in a way that abides the laws of human reason. Ideas also have the objective tendency to seize his emotional life in order to align its manifestations in accordance with the preconceived notions of a collective ideal. What we call the *human heart* is nothing but the product of this enslavement of individual sentiments by the prejudices of the idealism of a social epoch. The emotional life of most beings is thus constituted by the negation of its free will because instead of erupting nakedly and vibrantly into intimate rays of its sensitivity, it compromises itself by traditional concepts in order to follow down in the flows of collectivist imagination. Deformed as such, the sentiments deserve but to be treated like they are by the psychologists of the New Sorbonne. They no longer manifest anything of the individual soul. They are nothing but enchained epidemic illnesses of social conscience.

But Bergson sang to us of a sentimental life by emancipating himself from the chains of practical intellect, forgetting everything that it *had taught* him—and rediscovering at the sources of intuition the ascending sap of his freedom. And the philosopher became a poet who revealed to us by what musical rhythm intuitive conscience would push from sensation to sentiment like a "symphony where an increasing number of instruments will make themselves be heard."

While earlier psychologies, with their rationalism, gave but an auxiliary role to emotional life, it having to submit itself to the needs of knowledge, so as to merely supply it with the tools for its enhancement, Bergson's psychology showed that true psychological creation is the work of emotional subjectivity. Intuitive sensibility is no longer the slave of rational intelligence. Intelligence is meanwhile only considered to be the sum of all the means which individuality can utilize to operate in the practical and on the objective sphere. And ideas are then only artificial translations that exist to temporarily fixate an instant of subjective infinity in external symbols. They are nothing but tools of communication between different personalities. Every one of the involved consciences owes them nothing. Ideas are external to the life of the soul. They compose as little of psychological reality as the signals of a telegraph compose the speech of a man. Instead of sensible individualities having to subjugate themselves to ideas, it is the ideas that can be nothing but modifiable and reformable instruments of a personality that desires to freely flourish in its intuitive life.

It is quite interesting to note that the reign of ideas, which imposed a submission to the practical forms of collective being upon the individual soul, could simultaneously conduct the being to renounce all active living. By making spiritual life into a chain of ideas tied to God, or human reason, or universal harmony or any other riverbed of communal thought the individual was not only denied the irreducible originality of their soul, but the importance of their actions could also be dismissed. The only thing left was the unabridged force of the saying "*Veritas in dicto, non in re consistit* [Truth is in what is said, not in the thing]." This could be the main tenet of all the philosophies that were built on the ruins of pure affectivity. All of them talked as if there were only the "verb" and the "thing: " *Dictum et res.*" Bergson was able to reply to them: "*Veritas non in dicto, neque in re, sed in senso consistit* [Truth lies not in what is said nor in the thing, but in what is perceived]."

However, all while despising, torturing, or violating sensation, the philosophies of idealism have all elevated and praised the state of Ataraxia. Be it by Stoic "abstinence," by Christian "resignation," by Rynerian "discretion," or by the delightful irony of Remy de Gourmont, Ataraxia is always the same contemplation of the flow of universal ideas on its passing through the soul of a thinker. It is also always the renunciation of living life according to oneself, under the same pretext that holds that "thoughts are created to be thought and not to be acted."

In the divine reign of thoughts the ideal of the sage is to suffer and to indifferently endure the individual affections of emotional life like accidents that are not more than reasons for disdain or ridicule, in order to fully commit oneself to the passionate, serene, and dilettante contemplation of the universal flow of ideas. And this sage, be it Jesus or Epictetus or Remy de Gourmont or Ryner, could, like Jesus, let himself be torn up by the soldiery and still charitably carry the cross of his martyrdom up to the place of his execution. Or he could, like Epictetus, be a slave and let a master beat his leg until it breaks. He could also, like Han Ryner, suffer a long, poor life of daily, hard labor all while shouldering the even worse agony of speaking into silence. Or, like Remy de Gourmont, he could submit himself to the degrading demands of life as a writer at the end of the nineteenth century. All of those pains are, however, not more important to Jesus than to Gourmont, to Epictetus than to Ryner. What matters for all of them, however they want to call it, is an identical "kingdom of the father" or an "eternal and universal" land of ideas. They sacrificed their particular lives to general thought. All of them became in their way, tragically, silently, or ironically, martyrs of the mind. They all chose the existence of being over the death of sensation, and over the negation of all the joys of life. All those great thinkers thus turned a simple expression into a serene or tragic, harmonious or subtle ideology: the "I think, therefore I am" that Descartes coined only to immediately distort it to suit the trends of his time.

Yet, the sincere lovers and the shrewd pimp are both equally enslaved to the same divine prostitute: *human* spirituality.[24] Be it that Descartes described "the honest man" to serve the interests of seventeenth-century France, or that Christ turned himself into a "man" for love of mankind. Or be it Epictetus proclaiming "the kinship that unites men among each other and with God," and teaching "general truths" that make "a man of good faith;" or Han Ryner describing with "the heart of men" the idea of love fed by way of their reason. Or, even yet, be it Remy de Gourmont teaching to mankind the art of experiencing spiritual drunkenness, all of them united in identical mental judgment, "fraternizing at many tables, without any social differences between them" and "having listened to whispers, replying with words." All of them lose the individual in the conception of the "human." They drown themselves in the collective. They sacrifice themselves to an *order*. For Descartes it was the order of the state; for Jesus the order of the father; for Epictetus the "order of the many necessities for the ones who do not close themselves off from reason." For Han Ryner, just like for Gourmont, it is the order of the everything, where everything lives eternally for the ones who do not close their hearts, according to Psychodore, and for the ones who manage to open up their intelligence, according to Diomedes.[25] All of them, just like Descartes, define themselves by their thoughts only to then say to the sovereign: "Let your will be put into action, and not mine." They recognized their existence by negating their own liberty. They attribute the reason for their particular being by way of a submission to the laws of the collective being. For them life is founded on the principles of equality and identity, and "no deed is superior or different, and all manifestations of vital activity, or specific human activity, seem truly equivalent."

In their universal reign of intelligence, the human being thus lives according to the dirty ideal of the Stoic who says: "If mud had the capacity to think, it would rejoice to be tread by the feet of passersby, because it would know that this is its destiny, and it would submit itself to it with eagerness."

In the individual reign of intuitive sensation, every being affirms its existence while recognizing that it lives in its joyful activities. It finds its freedom in realizing the beauty of its actions. In one harmonious act, it creates itself, sensing, living, and free.

With the "I think, therefore I am," Descartes affirmed, through a mental application, nothing but the abstract existence of a human. It was not Descartes being astonished by personal life but a philosopher finding a proof of human existence in the human function of thinking. Descartes thus gave life to the collective being by placing it on the *chain of ideas*.[26]

With his intuition, Bergson was able to proclaim: "I sense, therefore I am free." Because sensation, when freed from its practical deformations and grasped intuitively is, like the philosopher would say, "either beginning of liberty, or it isn't." While thought can be "*compromised* by many and many things, and is consequently susceptible to create collective *links*, sensation is truly *unique*." It is within sensation that the individual founds his freedom and his integrity,[27] his entire autonomy. Sensation does not repeat, does not offer itself up, and does not spread. Sensation is not susceptible to any measurement. It has no link with anything except the individual who senses it. It is irreducibly a subjective phenomenon. Only through it can a being distinguish itself. It is the only generator of an integral individualism. By saying: "I sense, thus I am," no savant establishes the conditions of human conscience upon human sensation. Instead, it is me, the individual, who senses that only I am sensing how I feel, thereby sensing that I am living my individual life. I sense myself living by living myself sensing. This is no written demonstration of the existence of man, it is an experience that only I am able to sense and which I only find in *my reality and in my freedom*.

By founding his notion of psychological life upon the one of intuitive sensation, Henri Bergson gave to the individual soul the possibility to bloom in full resistance against both the psychological sciences and all forms of religion. With intuition spiritual life is saved from the laws of the collective. It individualizes. Thus, every personality can create its own psychology, because only the individual can feel themselves, in an intuitive symphony of the undefinable rhythms sparked by its unique and incessant self-creation.

Bergsonian intuitionism was the only source of integral individualism. In a preceding study, I explored by what natural slope Bergson's intuitive psychology would then flow out into Bonnot's anarchist heroism. But meanwhile the "young people of today" have figured out how to go from the same source of intuition to an entirely different type of heroism: that of Mr. Poincaré. And not only did Mr. Bergson let them do this, no, he even joined them, to pretentiously orchestrate these bad disciples who forced the free stream of individual intuition to irrigate with its pure waters all of the nationalist fountains of France.

Agathon and his friends only attacked the experimental methods of the *New Sorbonne* with the political motive of hindering German influence.[28] They became admirers of Bergsonian philosophy for purely practical reasons. The young proponents of Mr. Poincaré visited the translucent waters of intuition only to fish in them for the old ghosts of authoritarian spirituality. With the notion of intuitive conscience they wanted to reanimate the obscure soul of theology.

Henri Bergson, besides being an original philosopher, is a seductive speaker. He has a voice that pleases women. Additionally, and despite the fact that they do not understand much of the internal symphony of the master, the ladies of Paris would never miss the chance of being diligent members of his audience. These beautiful perfumed ladies went to cradle themselves in the smooth pronunciations of the psychologist on a twice-monthly basis, to devote their time to the small illusion they have of his ideal. Mr. Bergson granted them that incense of mysticism, which perfectly suits the composition of their ethos. He replaced Père Olivier. Thanks to him, the Collège de France became fashionable.[29] To attend his lectures, people send their minions to save them seats, just as they do at Notre Dame on the day of an important preach, or at the Saint Augustine for the musical nights when Lucienne Bréval comes to sing.

In Bergson a philosopher doubled as a snob. In order to make the youth sing, the door-to-door salesman of the Great War managed to meticulously play his cords. It all worked according to Mr. Poincaré's desires. Mr. Bergson was enough of a pooch to let his pure genius be mounted on the stages of the small theaters where he was made to repeat the first scenes of the "Cochonnerie sanglante" in the leading roles. And that how the farce of the "conversion of Bergson" played out.

After a while, Mr. Bergson made of this maliciously ignorant one, the only of his interested disciples. The writers of the *Opinion*, simultaneously with those of the catholic *Revue hebdomadaire*, suddenly started to chant an enthusiastic hymn of glory upon the author of *Matter and Memory*. All of a sudden, they all assumed a united voice to proclaim the death of analytical intelligence and to salute the soul by way of intuition. From then on this became like a wave of admiration that was propagated in all ecclesiastic and nationalistic newspapers. In all the pious circles of the studious youth, the directors of conscience stopped recommending to their trustees the dangerous meditations that were always liable to be poisoned by critiques. Instead they let their sheeplike souls float along the stream that would take their confused minds toward divine intuition. These gentlemen pretended to be unaware of the essentials of the teachings of the master, and their Bergsonian indoctrinations were but misleading commentaries on his chant that finally assassinated the free intuition. Henri Bergson, instead of denouncing them to protect the soul of his soul, jumped at their aid and directed their coup. He accepted the kisses of many Judases on his face and generously returned those kisses, many times more often, onto their asses.

With his army of Iscariots, General Bergson turned intuition into the new strategy of social misinformation. Thus the privileged position of psychological life over intelligent reason was maintained only to remove all possibility of free examination from the conscience of the individuals. While his main works rejected the totalitarian domination of analytical thought, Bergson's new articles in the

*Opinion* and the *Études* mainly dismissed the ways in which intelligence could be an instrument for individual liberation.

Among the patriots and Jesuits, Bergson wanted to forget *Time and Free Will* and the fine precisions of the *intelligent* analysis that allowed him to liberate sensation from the artificial chains of physical objectivity in which it withered to serve practical, collective activity. And just like his new admirers, he also pretended to overlook that, in order to find an intuitive soul in the soul of a man, one must first, to make it bloom in all of its subjective purity, use the same analysis with the entirety of his individuality. This is necessary to liberate it from the old shackles of social objectivity that oppress it to the point of suffocation.

All of this because the philosopher of intuition knew what he owed to intelligence. While the intelligent ways of knowing are worth little more in their logical structures than they are in their attempts to dig into the undiscovered depths of subjective psychology, they are, on the contrary, of uncontestable use when applied to the facts of practical objectivity. And while science can create nothing in the intangible infinite of my personal spirituality, it still holds all the power to destroy in the collective domain of matter. If we can never attain the soul except through the soul itself—and if forceful arguments from external sources cannot constrain nor annihilate an individuality that feels perfectly free in its interior harmony, then in the same way one can never defend oneself against attacks of matter except when using objects of matter, too. One can destroy facts only by confronting them with facts. One can only salvage brutes when confronting them with their own methods. To escape from the grasp of the collective one needs to turn to the weapons that were employed against oneself. The resistant who deserted the armies in order not to follow orders to become a murderer does not fear, when he is tracked down by policemen who threaten the freedom of his being with their weapons, to reply in the face of their ordinances to surrender or die with the only argument that law enforcement officials can understand: the revolver. In the same way a soul who wants to live harmoniously outside of necessities from which it is estranged flees the collective classifications of human reason to find itself in the freedom of its intuition. But when the general concepts, the old policemen of reason, again establish their menacing authority around a young blossoming of sentiment, the soul also knows how to *utilize* the same weapon that is most convenient to it, and it is a destructive weapon: a little reason armed with an analysis aimed against the monsters of analytical rationalism.

Intelligence thus can never be my end, but it remains a valuable instrument that I need to use individually to have it ready when the circumstances call for it, to know how to use it when it is useful to my well-being, and to be able to repel it when it risks passing beyond the limits of serving me, to continue its work of analytic destruction beyond the objective domain it inhabits up to the harmony of the subjective synthesis that lives within me through intuition.

Intellectual reasoning is to the individual who seeks his free, beautiful soul in the depths of his life as it was conditioned by the brutal laws of heritage and society like the pickax is in the hands of the archaeologist. He knows that a work of art lies in the depths of the soil. It is necessary to remove the dirty grasps of earth from the lines that, on the surface of a statue, sing the song of a soul. The pickax is available. The archaeologist knows that this piece of iron is designed for destruction and that with a single strike of his arms, he may either smash the brutal rock or the animated marble. But the researcher also knows *what he wants*. He *hears* the moaning for light from the contours in which the love of the artist survived, and he knows that down there some creation struggles with the destructiveness of matter. And thus he does not hesitate. He takes the pickaxe and violently confronts the brutal force that presses its deadly weight upon the sensible life with an opposing, but equally brutal impulse. He beats the ground with methodical force, he digs, he rummages; the rock gushes apart into fragments, the rips in it broaden with every hasty hit into the hostile ground, all while he still hears, in the far distance, the cries of the buried harmony. But then, when the voice becomes clearer and when it already sounds like enchanting music nearing true clarity. . . . When the soil that covers the work of art is but a fine layer of decay . . . the researcher knows to abandon the pickaxe that risks, with a single unprecise hit, to permanently damage the buried statue. Then, crouched against the ground on knees that tremble with emotion, with hands led by delicate hesitation, with rhythmic movements that are like caresses, he endeavors to deliver the beauty from her muddy sarcophagus.

This is the free research on which Mr. Bergson turned his back on the day that be became the master of the young politicians of the *Opinion*. He lacked the courage to take up the pickax to free the buried statue. He denied the free, critical role that intelligence can play to the individual who wants to remove all the weight that, by way of social education, suffocates the harmonious life of his soul. He left intuition hidden deep underground in its sarcophagus of old mud. He sentenced it to the torture of deep obscurity.

And so when he let the rightly thinking young people of France hear the buried voice, it could only be a horrible lamentation, an accent deformed by thousands of years in prison, a voice that seemed like the one of the poor tortured soul that the Inquisition made to speak during the terrors of the wheel of fire or of the tortures of the chairs, a voice of servitude hailing from the darkness.

By preaching the abandonment of all intellectual analytical function, he kept the individual from his only instrument of defense and rendered this anarchist critique impossible. It was the only tool that let the individual remove collective reason to give rise to intuitive creation. The social being who was deprived of intelligence is like the slave whose master snatched away the hammers with which he hoped to break his chains. He will never rediscover freedom.

To the young people of the French fatherland and to the Catholic Church, Mr. Bergson translated his philosophy as such:

In me is my intuition—vague and fluid movements of my internal life. From it, I receive my *sense* of life. I think, therefore I am. But this intuition is, in the first place, but a shapeless sense that does not suffice to create the internal harmony. Let us thus listen to the *human* voice that sings within us. Let us listen to the advice of this ancient one. It exerts itself since the beginnings, like an echo of creation. Let us listen to this human voice, this general intuition that symphonizes within itself all of the intuitive symphonies. It indicates what the sense is, the bigger sense—it is the *Good Sense*. Then say: I sense it well, thus I am a slave.

And he added:

Meanwhile, if you have a certain impetus that desires to surpass the common sense of humanity, if further inside of you a voice sings that is not in accord with the Good sense, then don't be too arrogant, my children, and don't let that allow you to consider yourselves outside of the universal. This higher-up voice, in fact, belongs even less to you than the chant from below does. Because this sense that makes you surpass the Good sense is not your individual clarity. It does not represent your individual powers of creation. It is, quite on the contrary, a universal clarity within you, a bedazzlement of God, it is the

Divine sense. With intuition, each one of you carries a little fragment of God within yourself. But these are just infinitesimally small rays that have no power upon the harmony of the Great Creator. Because God, who is a little bit in the intuitions, is only omnipotent and all-willing in his perfect totality. He is the great intuition, the only free one. Each one of us is only free in participating in his freedom. To know God in each of you, search in your soul for the voice of God's gift. Because you are a creature of God. And say: "I believe in God, thus I am free."

And thus Bergson played the role of Descartes. The rationalist of the *Discourse on Method* pronounced "I think, therefore I am," then, without any further discourse, drowned it in the Holy Spirit. The father of intuition was not any more loving toward his offspring. In an inspired tune, he sang "I feel, therefore I am," and then, in a few hymns while kneeling before the flag and the altar, he prostituted the "sense" to the "Good sense" and let his soul be drowned in the baptismal font of the Good God.

And one more time France was saved. It became the sweet daughter of the church once again. Bergson only found the individual key to the internal world to then sell it to Saint-Peter-Good-Sense. He added his gilded one to the traditional keychain holding the uncountable keys to the old paradise. Thanks to Mr. Bergson France possessed a soul: a single, submitted, and loyal soul. It was ripe for the master to pluck: Mr. Poincaré could arrive.

This happened in 1912.

Ten years have passed. The war has broken the world. Mr. Bergson continues to philosophize.

"Primum vivere . . ." a million deaths cry up to him. Yes, to live first, and to philosophize only to live better.

## ANARCHIST ACTION

*Le libertaire* 169 (April 1922)

For the individual who is mindful of affirming his independence, there are no more superior and transcendent laws in the mind than there are in matter.

Everything happens within him, the individual: everything comes from him, everything goes toward him—for his well-being and his freedom.

Matter is for an anarchist but the ensemble of facts that he experiences by adapting them to the needs of his body. It is the order that he externally realizes in order to find physiological satisfaction.

The mind is for him but the sum of ideas that he uses by appropriating them, by passing them through the sieve of his analysis, by submitting them to the incessant examinations of his personality, by drawing them from the past, decomposed and unformed, to push them toward the future in an entirely new shape, resembling the one who recreates them by thinking them.

This way, the individual will have no more respect for matter than he has for the mind. One and the other are but his means to live, his instruments of expression.

Often it will suit him, to forgo all sorts of servitude, to exercise caution of the predominance of this or that instrument. He will need to confront his ideas with his facts, his thoughts with his acts, and realize within him the harmony of them all.

With such a general conception of his activity, the anarchist can avoid many traps—whether they hail from philosophy or from revolutions—and he can follow the drives of his heart without fear of death because there is nothing that makes us fear death as much as the idea of falling into the service of a cause that is not ours!

<hr />

Among the ideas that I have endured, that have made me suffer, that have provoked the imbalance between my corporal and spiritual life that I call pain, there has been the idea of God, the idea of the family, the idea of race, the idea of the fatherland and the idea of the class. But dominating them all, like a Moloch with a hundred terrorizing faces, there is the idea of authority.

Among the facts that I have undergone, that I have judged and that have made me think, there are facts that put my corporal organism into such a situation that they parallelly provoked shame and trouble in my spiritual activity. They are the cause of a total restriction of my personality, of a diminishment of all my possibilities to expand. They are the negation of my free initiative and my creating powers. They impede me in my walk and paralyze me in my intelligence. They are capitalism, the state, centralism, corporatism. . . . But one fact summarizes them all: the exploitation and governance of men over other men.

———◆———

The individual, rich in this double awareness, is evidently brought to gaining his philosophy and to want a revolution.

His philosophy will not be a dogma. It could not even be a doctrine, because he could only edify it upon himself and for himself. It will also not be a teaching, because one does not teach others the thoughts that they should have and the way that they should order their thoughts. The conscience is inviolable in its individuality, and one learns to be one's own master only by forgoing masters.

But the philosophy of each one is a good piece of information for all. And the philosophy of all, be they the humblest, the most ignorant, is a useful piece of information for each one who is themselves looking for their own light within them—be it the most knowledgeable philosopher or the most profound thinker of all.

Anarchist philosophy does not doze around in libraries. It is not elaborated in the interminable pandering of metaphysicians or of sociologists, avid to realize their masterpieces for eternity. It is born out of the desire of every man to clearly see within him, to protect himself from the old ideologies of which other men suffered before us, and to generously cultivate all that grows in our mind of ideas that is ready to blossom and deliver us, tomorrow, its ardent flourishing of freedom and beauty.

This philosophy can never be separated from life. It does not fly away into the clouds. It never risks attaining God in any form whatsoever. It never forgets the only justifying center of all constructions, of all systems, of all theories: the human individual, feeling, suffering, thinking, judging.

The same goes for the revolution. It results out of the will of the individual to put the facts in harmony with his needs and with his ideas. The revolution is the individual liberating himself from the matter and the organization in function of his possibilities of production and consumption.

That is why the only revolution that can satisfy the individual is the one that finds its basis in the syndicates.

The one who refuses himself in the domain of ideas to all concepts of authority as harmful to the very life of his consciousness; the one who repels in the domain of the facts capitalism and the state as generators of exploitation, of misery, and of brutality; the one who judges it to be as degrading and as unhealthy to command as to obey; that one, a producing individual put into the impossibility to produce according to his original ideas and to consume according to his primordial needs—in the face of his work being exploited, of his solidarity with other individuals, who, producing with him, are exploited like he is—finds in syndicalism not a doctrine, but the recognition of a fact that is his, the recognition of a fact that he establishes to realize his own well-being.

I do not belong to a syndicate: it is the syndicate that belongs to me. I modify its form following my interests as a producer. I animate it by my own ideas I let it live off my suffering, of my hate, of my hopes, of my love. A syndicate is not a state (*status*) of which I am constrained to follow the laws before even being acquiesced to it. It is not a nation into which one is born and to which one has to participate voluntarily or by force. If I adhere to a syndicate I can, from that day on, transform its status. The syndicate only lives off the solidarity of the workers and of their efforts to appropriate the means of production and the products of their work for themselves.

Through syndicalist organization I put a method into the activity that I have to expend in order to assure my full material life.

By affirming the syndicate, by letting it live, by rendering it the master of production, I give a body to the revolution.

When I say that anarchy is the soul of this revolution, I simply want to affirm that the syndicalist organization is not a revolutionary force unless it can guarantee the libertarian activity of every worker.

It is not by philosophizing that one learns to live; it is by living that everyone will learn to philosophize.

It is not by chanting "Revolution" over all the rooftops that one will implement a more harmonious society. It is by participating in the organization of work and the struggles of syndicalism that everyone will take his part of freedom and well-being.

That way the individual will remain an anarchist in philosophy and in revolution, because he will never put a break to his own activity, not to find peace in an ideological system or by going to war in the name of a state.

The anarchist is a philosopher, but only in the measure that an ideal will not hinder him to act with his body. A revolutionary he will stay, but only as long as the "revolution" does not hinder him to think with his own mind.

And, by doing that, the anarchist will always be the *avant-garde* of every philosophy and of every revolution. He will surpass them both.

## FOR THE INDIVIDUAL, WITH THE PROLETARIAT

*LE LIBERTAIRE* 173 (MAY 1922)

"In the revolution the syndicates are the body and anarchy is the soul."

Some comrades have loved this formula. Others have been worried by it.

Some subtle and categorical minds have wanted to attribute an absolute meaning to it. And they have looked, in ways that are beyond me, for a metaphysical or even borderline religious message in a phrase that had no other ambition but to allow, by way of an image, the rapport between anarchism and syndicalism to be understood more vividly.

By the way, I could as easily have said: "There can only be actions and social transformations that are profitable to the individual in the reality of syndical organization, and with the animating force of the individual himself."

I thought I had sufficiently explained myself on the sense that I accord to the words "revolution" and "anarchy" for no confusion to be possible in this subject matter.

As much as anyone else I am challenged by the pernicious magic of words that can easily rally up the beings that they hypnotize to follow them toward collective destinies. As a supporter of free examining, I renounce faith in all of its forms. Let's leave it to Monmousseau to "make space for the new dogma, after having abolished the old dogma." In that, the French theoretician of the dictatorship of the proletariat meets, while *passing over* Auguste Comte (whom even one of the most bitter despisers of syndicalism recommended here a while ago), Mr. Léon de Montesquieu, the defender of the principles of social conservation, in according to the theories of the Action Française.[30]

We do not fear, when proclaiming the sovereignty of every individual reason, to "prevent the uniform establishment of an ordinary system of general ideas, without which there is no society." And we are opposed with all our forces against "the disposition of spontaneously belief, without prior demonstration, in the dogmata proclaimed by a competent authority." Because we know that all of that leads to what Monmousseau calls "the greatest unity of thought, the greatest unity of power," that is to say the suffocation of every initiative, to the death of all individual variety, to the castration of all originality, to dictatorship, *to monarchy*.

I understand by "revolution" all societal upheavals that procure to the individual new means to affirm himself in the face of the general principle of authority and of the forms of state that ensured from it, to affirm *his* capacities of production and his needs of consumption, that is to say find the power to live life with all his particularities—as an individual and not as a "piece of meat of society."

By anarchy, I understand nothing but the eternal revindication of the individual, the perpetual struggle of the individual, this living theory in which the individual is considered as the only motor, the only judge, the only spectator, the only witness with proof, and the only end in the world.

Anarchy means the negation of spiritual power and the negation of temporal power. Anarchy breaks all the ties that want to shackle me, shatters all the frames that pretend to enclose me, splits all the duties and all the rights that are imposed upon me and accorded to me.

Anarchy lets me find the force to enjoy life spiritually and temporally within me. I feel like a hotbed of ideas, a creator of actions. How will I use my power?

———◆———

Facts and ideas, these are the modes of my activity. What I call happiness resides in the harmony found by my being in the best possible knowledge of the facts and the ideas that I need, in the most complete assimilation of these facts and these ideas, and in their rapport to the ensemble of my life. If there is an authority that does not make me repugnant, it is the one of the individual itself on the realities of life and on the conceptions of the mind. This is the only mastery that does not imply slavery. It is the only power that is permitted in anarchy. By according the governance of oneself onto everyone, be it the least perfect person, we are opposed to every general system of governance, be it the most perfect, and thus we permit to everyone to exercise this type of individual authority of which the consequences could be in no case more perilous, more criminal, or crueler than the ones committed by the most perfect of the collectivist authorities. The most cynical bandit is less harmful to his contemporaries than the best-intentioned politician. Because the illegal does not try to generalize his case: he does not place his act under the aegis of a system. He does not build a constitution on his crime.

He is neither Napoleon, nor Mr. Thiers, nor Poincaré, nor a dictator of the proletariat.

Nonetheless, banditism is not sufficient. For one, this is because, in fact, many would not truly live as a bandit. And second, because it seems to me to be a misleading conception for individualism to limit the individual to a single conquest of his present goods. It pleases me to not only muse about immediate enjoyment, but to extend my desire to the fruits that I could pluck from the shrubs of which the cultivation is already a pleasure to me today. It pleases me to work on the realization of a tomorrow that will be for the children whom I cherish, for the young comrades whom I love, for a tomorrow that I carry in me with my ideas, my imaginations. . . . And not only do I not cease to be an individualist and a *creator* by working toward a revolution that could permit my "illusions" to become truths in the future—but even further, I believe that it would be a lack of respect on my part toward the best individual who I can be if I sacrificed these marvelous and uncertain possibilities to the petty and evident prey that tempts my senses in the present.

Thus confidence to the individual and its will to realize itself fully in the exercise of all its functions, materially and spiritually, with the maximum of intensity and daily security, and also with the greatest drive of its current toward the future.

Confidence in the individual who I am, and who I feel in all its creative activity, and, by analogy, confidence in all individuality. Hatred for all authority that wants to impose on mankind one single form of thinking and acting. Love for multiple sensibilities, reasons, and individual realizations. And it is in this way that we will search ourselves, by destroying all collective discipline, by annihilating all governance, by organizing the *free play of individualities* in life.

How to reach that point? Initially, by never forgetting the individual, by incessantly remembering it as the cause and end of all our searching, by repeating that no system may sacrifice it, because nothing is worth the effort of uplifting oneself except to assure oneself more well-being and liberty.

After having freed the individual from all social idealism, of all *collective illusionism*, of all *lies*; to give it the full surge of *its* particular idealism, the freedom of its creating idealism, the possibility of its emancipation by its subjective will of mastering the objects and the ideas of its consciousness—let's place it in its objective reality, in its sociological conditions.

In fact, whatever his consciousness may be, a dilemma will be presented to every man who wants to eat: *to be an exploiter or to be exploited*. He has to choose: one or the other side of the barricades.

No subterfuge can make us avoid this choice, which is uncomfortable for every anarchist who has the same prima facie disgust for obeying as he has for commanding. If you have an annuity, you participate in authority and exploitation; you are an accomplice of all the crimes of the justice system, of the police and of the weapons that protect your capital, as modest as it may be. If you steal, if you burglarize, or if you commit fraud successfully, you are an exploiter. If you are a miserable bandit who is being tracked you are amid the exploited. It is a dilemma that is without a solution in the current social state: you have to choose—exploiter or exploited.

"But the choice is entirely made by the circumstance of our birth," they will tell me. "There is thus no choice."

*Hélas!* Social heredity does guide the choice of most of mankind. Born into a capitalist family, this one will submit to his destiny as an exploiter, like that one, born into a proletarian family, will make a virtue out of a necessity and will curve his spine in resignation to his destiny as one exploited.

But there are nonetheless individuals who find the force to choose. Those who profit from their intelligence and their ruse to leave the proletariat and join the side of the exploiters are more numerous. The war has seen a rapid multiplication of these *champignons de charnier* who would be called the new rich.[31] However, I also know a few who could have joined the privileges of the possessing class and who have chosen the lot of the exploited.

The choice is thus possible, especially for the anarchist.

Will he, a born enemy of the authority, put himself under the protection of the constituted authorities? Will he take his part of the responsibility for the capitalist exploitation? Will he, by exploiting, undergo not only the hate of those who suffer under his orders but also, with the friendly association with those who maintain the reign of oppression, a proper disgust of his own conscience?

If he accepts this destiny of the exploiter, he can no longer call himself an anarchist. Carried on by the weight of his belly, he will no longer be, whatever he might think and whatever his good intentions may be, anything but a bourgeois, riveted to the chain of his slaves.

As a lover of human personality and a defender of individuality, the anarchist chooses the lot of the exploited.

There is a multitude of reasons to justify this choice. It is first that the exploited carry the destructive virus for this entire system of exploitation within them: the revolt, the daughter of suffering. Next, because the exploited are workers. They are the power of life, the force of creation. They seem like slaves, but they are the veritable masters, they who have the power to grow the goods of the earth, to transform matter, to model it to the image of our needs, to organize nature scientifically and aesthetically for the greatest possible pleasure of the human body and mind.

With the exploited, with the producers, the anarchist is on the side of life. In his instincts, he feels all the greatness of his role, by accepting the destiny of the proletariat. It will suit him to be there, disintegrating this exploited *mass*, generating and blowing onto the cinders of revolt, onto millions and millions of individuals to wake up to the full consciousness of their being, to the harmonious joy of life and to the free organization of their constructive capacities.

And thus we will see that for us anarchists the syndicates are neither "a way to resolve the conflicts among classes" nor a way to establish the authority of a class, but the best possible way to fight for the individual.

## TOWARD INDIVIDUAL SYNDICALIZATION

*Le libertaire* 175 (June 1922)

For my own liberation I accept the division of labor that permits me to have more confidence in my own effort, all while also according confidence to the efforts of others. This human collaboration gives me a certain security: it guarantees me a relative continuity for the work that I engage in.

Instead of being an animalistic man before the multiplicity of heterogeneous tasks that the material and intellectual needs of my being necessitate, forced to wait for coincidences (that is to say for disorder in the unforeseeable) to give me coarse satisfactions, I am effectively guaranteed that some men take care of a number of works that I do no longer have to worry about, and thus I can orient my activity in the sense of my personal capacities and my original dispositions.

But this liberating principle of the division of labor has been denatured by the exploiters and the governments that have made of it the most horrendous instrument of their domination.

By dividing labor, they have divided the workers.

By mechanizing labor they have mechanized the producers. To every laborer his mechanical movements, always the same. "Occupy yourself with your straightforward task. Don't look to the left, don't look to the right. I'll take care of that. Await your pay; I will arrange it according to the needs of the industry—I will judge your needs. Work in your nation and let me handle the rest."

Thus speaks the boss, socializing following the old formula: "Everyone for themselves and God for all."

That is not exactly the division of labor—not the one we intend, at least. Not only does our account not imply the division of workers, no, it cannot even be fully and intelligently realized without the conscious unity of the workers.

It is the division of labor by the laborers themselves. It does not recognize the organizational omnipotence of the supreme authority wielded by a management or a state, dictating the laws of production: it rather affirms the commodity of the producer; it vindicates the mastery of the one who acts on the means of his activity. It illuminates the force and the progress of humans with its consciousness.

Behold the current situation of a laborer. In a factory, in a bureau, in a printing office, he accomplishes a need of which *he cannot* take responsibility. He commits an act of which he ignores all the reasons and the ends. He executes tasks that can go against not only his taste but also his interests. He may be working against his life. The authoritarian division of labor justifies everything with the unawareness about the goals of their own activity in which it leaves the workers

Whatever be the act that I accomplish in a professional environment, it suits me to be able to place it societally and to recognize all of its value in relation to myself, materially and morally.

That is what permits the libertarian division of labor, that is to say, individualized syndicalization.

---

For the authoritarian division of labor, every one of us is coupled with a straight and unconscious task, in one's factory or in one's office. This metallurgist laborer works on a part over which he executes to the best of his abilities without knowing of which whole he is a collaborator. This printer executes the drawing of a book or of a journal of which he does not know the text. They are lost in the sense of production. They no longer have a notion of their activity. Without thinking, they produce any given thing in order to have access to a salary at the end of the week. It is a deplorable attitude that was encouraged by the old syndicalism, which was only concerned with immediate material advantages and was too inclined, with its workerism, to overlook of the intellectual factors of production.

Libertarian syndicalism grants all due value to the act of the worker. It does not see in it a succession of movements that are executed in individual unawareness for the best functioning of the societal machine. Quite on the contrary, it shows that the use of natural and social forces in a solidaristic community of efforts toward well-being is the greatest liberty of the individual.

It says to every worker: "Do not be content in doing your job well. Look beside you, at the atelier, at the factory, at all of society. Be interested in the economic history of the material that you are transforming. Where does it come from? Through which hands did it go before reaching you here? What technique has necessitated its industrial utilization? Toward which ends is it intended to serve? What will they make out of it? What workers will work on it after you? Where will it go? To what will the final product serve? And, as a last inquiry, do you find your individual account in this affair? Will the object that will leave your hands serve the enjoyment of your body, the joy of your heart or the nobility of your mind?"

Permitting the worker to respond to these questions. Permitting him not to be mistaken in his answers. Giving him the means to eliminate all that does not respond to the beneficial necessities of his being from his activity. Permitting him to harmoniously organize the modalities of his labor in order to be able to render all dictatorship over the workers inoperative. Raising the interest of the producer to the economic life of a factory, of a community, of a region, of the entire world, by sensitizing him to the effects of his acts on the entire human community, by making him realize the exact task that he could accomplish and the capacities that he will need to rely on others in order to render his own effort more fruitful. Proletarian solidarity taking possession of all the means of production and of all the consumable goods so that the individual can live without a government. The worker's control replacing the laws of the state. That is all that individualized syndicalization means.

It is anarchism in action. It is also the recognition of the forces of life and the scientific determination of the environment that is best able to play their game in the most intensely productive way. It is, for the individual good, the triumph of economics over politics. It is the actual fact of my happiness against all preconceived jurisdiction. It is for everyone the possibility to create and to consume according to their faculties and according to their needs, in the total harmony of the individual faculties and needs.

Individualized syndicalization is the only order that we can permit in the world. The order that, as a result of the decadence of all authorities of rights that are superiorly exercised of humans, is established by the will of all in the very practice of their action.

Individualized syndicalization comes to prove once and for all that, against the allegations of our adversaries, anarchy, far from meaning disorder, waste, disorganization, it the very soul of the lividest organization. It is the most logical and the most conscientious of human efforts.

## REFLECTIONS ON NIETZSCHE AND ANARCHY

*La revue anarchiste* 1, no. 6 (June 1922)

So many young people read Nietzsche between 1890 and 1914—those who then went to die for the fatherland, those again who presided over these nationalistic massacres, and even those who still profit from the bloodshed!

Why did Nietzsche have so many bad disciples—so many disciples, so many Nietzscheans who recreated, in his name, all of the very things that Nietzsche himself had destroyed? Nietzschean patriots, Nietzschean bourgeois, Nietzschean usurers, Nietzschean moralists . . .

I am rereading Nietzsche. Of course, he is still far from my own thoughts, but he is hundreds of millions of miles closer to me than he is to all of those "disciples" that boast about him.

But why?

*Eh!* Well it's exactly like it is with Han Ryner, but on the other side of the spectrum.

Nietzsche, like Han Ryner, spoke an old language—and thus he still seemed to speak for the people of his time. As much as Ryner didn't, Nietzsche didn't create his own language, either. Thus, both expressed themselves in the terms of a collective humanity—yet meanwhile, I believe that both were truly unique and incomparable personalities.

However, Nietzsche expressed himself in the terms of a collective force, like Han Ryner did in terms of collective rights.

Thus to sing of his "will" and his "power," Nietzsche played the cords of the old "will" and of the ancient "power"—the ones of our species—just like Ryner, while singing of his "spirit" and of his "idealist harmony," could not avoid the organs of the holy "spirit," and the ancient, plain chant of humanist "idealism," the voice of God.

But despite that, the warrior Nietzsche has nothing in common with the nationalist warriors, just as the pacifist Ryner cannot be confounded with the international pacifists of peacetime. However, these and those can still claim the paternity of him and the former—because both Nietzsche and Ryner have spoken to the ones and the others using words that did not renounce them, using music that could still involve them.

Nietzsche and Han Ryner reach further than their thought has materialized—but they need someone to push them to this "further," someone who cuts the old cords with which they tied themselves to their havens—their havens of reference. And then, in their company, what travels become possible—O Psychodore, O Zarathustra!

Nietzsche is a precursor of Individualism; he is no individualist; he isn't even a Dionysian: he is a Bacchanalian. And thus can be explained, even more clearly than by way of Nietzsche's oversights, the misunderstandings of the Nietzscheans.

Here is the essence of what the Nietzschean does not understand: A possession *is* only by virtue of the condition that it is *my* possession, the way I want it and when I sense it to be, in unison with my own. If I, myself, conquer a good for myself, it is my good. But the good that I conquer as a soldier for my fatherland is not only no longer my good, or even a possession. No, instead, it even renders me into more of a slave, because this good makes me, the person who conquered it, experience my submission even more, as I let myself get skinned of it by the fatherland.

And the same goes for the love of danger and the pleasure of battle. . . . These are Bacchanalian joys—drunken spells, unless I experience them solely for the integrity of my being, as a necessary stimulant to the free working of all my human faculties. If I do not overcome them as such, to make them serve my constructive senses of life, these drunken spells drag me out of my individual harmony. They are then bearers of my destruction.

The sentiment of power, as envisaged by Nietzsche, fatally collapses back toward a sentiment of powerlessness. By dominating, Nietzsche makes the domination into an end: he aspires to a reign. He intends to be the sovereign over subjects. He puts himself to the mercy of the reign. He must thus be counted among the subjects.

If, however, I exercise my domination—me, who pretends to neither know nor exert any power except my own—it is to attain possession of myself, to master myself. I only dominate in order to create myself. My end is to overcome my hunger. My end is the song of my joy, and I rejoice only to live in accordance with all of my possibilities: ideas and actions, sensations and imaginations, perceptions about the present and hypotheses about my future . . .

My harmony is the criterion for my power. Nobody can deprive me of it. What I look to dominate is all that attempts to escape my art, all that does not harmonize to my music, all that does not respond to outbursts of my love. I dominate to make mine. While dominating I take and hold against my heart. Whatever offers itself to me, I take in its entirety while respecting it. What rejects itself from me, I shatter. I hold the world against me so hard that I might crush it, I embrace it! I dominate to dominate *myself*.

The Nietzschean, on the contrary, dominates in order to dominate. There is a theory of "art for art's sake" that does not conceive of artistic creation as an individual pleasure of the artist, as a flower of a life, as a gift of the individual to himself, but only as one of the many anonymous expressions of aesthetic function: "Art is an end in itself." To Nietzsche, in a similar fashion, power becomes the ultimate end. His theory is one of "power for power's sake." The type of domination, or the consequences of the domination, thus lose all importance, both to the dominator and the dominated. Before anything else it is about dominating. The domination ends up becoming the Nietzschean's ideal, his religion, his obsession. He commits himself to it, he sacrifices himself to it, he loses himself in it, and he destroys himself by way of it. He dominates himself *for the sake of* domination: and in this the Nietzschean looks no more individualist than the believer who submits himself for the sake of submission, following the Christian ideal of universal submission.

———————•◄►•———————

Dominating to dominate does not make you more of a master over your life than making art for art can make you the creator of your art. Here you "make art," you don't create. There you don't dominate, you command.

My individualism—and that is to say my harmonious egoism—conforms no better with commanding than it does with obeying. If I don't want to command, it is out of love for myself, in the same way that I don't want to obey. It seems to me just as disagreeable, just as repugnant to *see obey* than to obey in my own right. This is why I do not command: in order not to provoke my eyes with a spectacle that disgusts me.

I experience my sentiment of power in the most fulfilling way, in the most intense way, in the most harmonious way, when I am in the state of *anarchy*: that is to say without commanding or obeying.

To command means to give orders. The one who commands (even be it to command to a single person) establishes a social order. By commanding he erects the fundaments of a government.

As I do not want any social authority, I will hold myself, first and foremost, from demanding of anyone to recognize an order. In order not to suffer the commands of anyone, I will begin by not imposing any commands myself. Because exercising authority justifies in the commanded subject the desire to command his master, it triggers his will to be a master and ends up, one day or the other, by finally making the subject a master over others. In order not to risk such justifiable obedience, I thus refuse for myself all commandments.

When I need something and it is denied from me, I tell nobody to execute my will; instead, I will execute it myself—for example, I can kill—I execute, but I do not order to execute. By executing I do not enact a rule; I do not impose a law: I accomplish an act—my act. By executing I remain an anarchist.

By killing I do not command to die, and nobody commands me to kill. It can happen that, one day, I will have to kill in order to remain an *anarchist*. What I kill is what participates in the *archy* that attempts to destroy me. I kill to save myself. I kill that which stands in the way of my life, what hides the sun from me. I do not kill for the joy of killing but for the joy of living.

***

By giving (and imposing) a law to other humans, I bind myself, I immobilize myself, I negate my mobile individuality—just like by accepting (and undergoing) the law of anyone else.

The master must count on the submission of his subjects, like the slave needs to count on the authority of his master. The master is at the mercy of *his* slave like the slave is at the mercy of *his* master. They are bound to one another. All the while the slave can still renounce his master, as he did not choose the law that he undergoes; but the master, the creator of the law that rules over the slaves, cannot renounce his slave.

The master thus undergoes the *society* of the slaves. The master lives in slavery much more than the slave himself.

As an anarchist I revolt against the society of the slaves and against the society of the masters. As an individualist I am an anarchist. As an anarchist again I am a revolutionary. Nietzsche, who saw individuals only as "advancers of intellectual colonization and of the formation of new links between the state and society," kept well away from predicting the overthrowing of the principle of authority and the abolition of the reign of exploitation. The success of a revolution might have convinced him, but, as he was interested in those who command, he was too scared to come across as a weak soul.

Being hypnotized only by the genius of power, Nietzsche, who was read and loved by so many anarchists, had no glimpse of the creative force of the anarchist idea. And was he not well closer to the dictators of the proletariat then we are, libertarians, he who wrote the following lines: "We count ourselves among conquerors; we think about the necessity for new orders, also for a new slavery—for every strengthening and enhancement of the human type also involves a new kind of enslavement."

Today a Nietzschean named Kibalchich is serving the government in Moscow. . . . There is your Nietzschean "moral in action."[32]

## THE SOURCES OF THE MODERN NOVEL IN FRANCE:
## STENDHAL, BALZAC, FLAUBERT

*LA REVUE ANARCHISTE* 1, NO. 10 (SEPTEMBER 1922)

The history of the French novel these last forty years delivers a most stunning spectacle in the eyes of a conscientious observer: an immense chaos and a whirlwind of multifaceted works that bring the most diverse images to every genre and make them dance to their rhythm.

To know and discern these works with justice it is useful to conjure up the vivid sources of this flood of recitals.

Let's look for these sources.

They appear to be uncountable. Maybe that is just an appearance. Maybe we take a couple of banal fountains, in which the waters spurt merely out of an artificial rock, to be sources. Rare are the writers who can find sources themselves. I do not think that the authors of novels, from 1870 to this day, all had enough powers of genius to be able to do without forefathers. Let us thus venture beyond the era that made them write, to look for the great creators whose push of life sap extended and was maintained in literary posterity.

Before 1870, three men created major oeuvres: Stendhal (between 1831 and 1839); Balzac (from 1840 to 1845); Flaubert (from 1857 to 1870). These were the sources. Let's examine them to see what our contemporaries owe them.

Stendhal and Balzac are more or less from the same era—an admirable era, a unique moment that had its drives, its struggles and the poetic blossoming of a Vigny and a Hugo, a Musset and a Lamartine. Stendhal and Balzac are from the romantic era.

It is interesting to note the reciprocal influences between poets and prose writers of a same time. More frequently the poetic soul uplifts and imposes its rhythm on the brain of the storyteller. There have been exceptions, however. But that was in the eras when prose was the lesser creator of imaginations, the less rich in innovations; it was in the eras of critique and satire, of discussion and pamphlet; like the French eighteenth century, during which we had to wait for Rousseau, the prose poet Jean-Jacques, this precursor of romanticism, to finally rediscover other things than spiritual games, precise attacks, or material philosophy in our literature.

In the centuries of idealism, it is always the poet who enthuses the prose writer. Think about the seventeenth century. See how much Bossuet or Labruyère, or La Rochefoucauld, whose temperaments and geniuses were so different from one another, appear to us nonetheless as classics of which the literary ideal seems to be the younger brother of the one in Corneille, Racine, and Molière.

It is also remarkable that precisely these eras of great poetic idealism see the most strongly and delicately differentiated personalities arise. Like the soul of Corneille, which differs a good amount from the one of Racine and the one of Molière, and like the qualities of mind of a La Rochefoucauld are so out of touch with the ones of a Bossuet!

Romanticism was one of those flare-ups of high idealism that permitted the great geniuses to recognize each other and to reunite in order to enjoy each other's distinct and irreducible beauties.

It was natural that Stendhal and Balzac would participate in that—each in their way, at the measure of their temperament.

If we only consider the exaggerations and the defects of romanticism—if we only call the parts of it romantic that appear to us to be the least supportable—then it is evident that Stendhal, in this sense, is not even slightly romantic.

He has a horrific verbalism. He finds an overt abundant use of details to be abhorrent; he is not worried about the picturesque. He prefers dryness to abundance. He is sober in his expression. He does not recite, and he does not weep. But it seems to me that Vigny does not either. In his novels, Stendhal does not stage himself to express confidence in his hopes and despairs. But it seems to me that, in his poems, Vigny was not more confident of his little sentimental miseries. Stendhal is a thinker who ruthlessly analyzes. And what was the poet of the *Mort du loup*?

Romanticism does not entirely fit the monologue of *Hernani* or in the *Nuits* by Musset. It is thus not only sparkle and lamentation—it can also be thought: it shows us that in Vigny and Stendhal.

In what, then, was the author of *Le rouge et le noir* worthy of the romantic era?

Heroism is, so I think, the absolute condition of the great literary eras. The classics were great tragedies because they created heroes in the theater: heroes of duty, with Corneille, heroes of passion, with Racine. The romantics were great poets because they managed to once again make heroic a literature that a century of materialist critique's had lowered down to the grade of the flattest journalism. Social heroism with Hugo, passionate heroism with Musset, metaphysical heroism with Lamartine, but also heroism of thought, heroism of a struggle for life with Vigny.

I do not know if you understand me well when I speak of heroism. Elsewhere I have extensively developed this subject. I call a hero the one who knows how to give himself entirely to his ideal—the one who does not fear of pushing his life until the point of extreme circumstances for what he loves—be it even to death—and what he loves might be anything, a virtue, a woman, life the way it is, or life the way he dreams it to be—or life as he wants to make it.

Stendhal relates to the romantics through the conception of heroism, which is so singularly strong in his novels that one of his heroes—Julian Sorel in *Le rouge et le noir*—had for numerous souls, for numerous generations up until today, an influence as large as the one any master could have had on them. A persuasive, contagious, hypnotic influence unlike the one wielded by any apostle his century has had.

Stendhal was, as he said it himself, an "observer of the human heart," but he did not lose his time and his art in the observation of mediocre types. He used a method of analysis, that is true, but that method was, in his case, not an instrument of destruction. He had created in his mind beings that were sufficiently strongly alive so that he could scrutinize them without any danger. The heroes of his novels were rich enough in their judgments and their will that he could demand from them to be reasonable in their acts. Julien Sorel creates himself, affirms himself, opposes himself, and rises more with every question that the author confronts him with. Julien Sorel exists, even more vividly than Stendhal does. He can thus withstand the tough challenges of analysis.

Our so-called "psychological" novelists have not understood these conditions for the analytic method in the Stendhalian oeuvre. Barrès, Bourget, Marcel Prévost, Abel Hermant pretend to be disciples of the master Stendhal, they are but vile counterfeiters of his. Of Stendhal they remembered only the method, but they forgot the soul. Stendhal had a heroic soul. These men have a mind. Stendhal put his analysis *at the service* of the free blossoming of his "heroes of energy." These men put the characters of their books *to the service* of their own analytical mania.

Stendhal wrote sixty-six years ago and his hero, Julien Sorel, lives on in the minds—he is an immortal force. What will remain, in only forty years, of the sickly puppets of Mr. Barrès, of the elegant maniacs of Mr. Bourget, of the small scatterbrains of Mr. Marcel Prévost, and the sleazy "purposes of a race" of Mr. Abel Hermant? Nothing except the memories of the literary scene.

Balzac is another source of the modern novel—but a source that immediately gushes into a wild torrent that floods everything, drags everything along with it, and imposes itself with unique power. I think it is barely necessary to demonstrate in depth all that romanticism can be within him. Everything is romantic with Balzac, everything affirms itself with the enthusiasm and the idealistic faith of the author—but what affirms itself in this way turns out to be the entire life of men, all their hopes, all their miseries, all their efforts of pain and of joy, all aspects of their activity in the daily struggle, all the human reality as Balzac had seen it, had imagined it, had recreated it in his visionary brains to compile it for us as a teeming spectacle. This way he managed to be the creator of an entire world—a world that would be a thousand times more alive than the real world, a world of intense life where all the virtues and all the vices, all the defects and all the greatness of men could be found immortally heroized. And meanwhile this fabulous world is far more real than the world of fragmentary realities.

Have you ever known beings who were more moving in their moral ugliness than père Grandet or père Séchard? Have you ever met beings as purely adorable as Eugénie Grandet, as Eve and David Séchard? Have you, in your youth, found an activity as feverishly surging as the one of Lucien de Rubempré? Oscar Wilde was complex enough that we could listen to him. His tears are not cheap outpourings of the kind that are everyday girly tears featured in feuilleton novels. However, I think that Balzac achieved this miracle of affecting both Oscar Wilde's and the girly tears to unite in the same simplicity of tears the most sophisticated scholar and the most naive and ignorant lectors, and that is but one of the hundred and one miracles of the Balzacian oeuvre.

Everything is possible in the world of a creator who is so formidably the genius Balzac was. The fact is that the life which he used was not a model to him, but a material that he powerfully kneaded with his resolute hands, in order to let, out of the embrace of his divine fingers, an entire new world arise, one that followed his own creation.[33] Take a month's time to read the *Comédie humaine* and you will be impassioned by it to the point that you will forget real life; you will no longer remember, in the morning, to learn the new events that are brought to you by the newspapers; you will no longer want to know anything about your history; all of contemporary life will appear to you to be of no interest, the beings who you know will appear to be shadows or puppets. Life, the real life, you will find it, intense, tormented, feverish, multiformly active in the stories of the novelist. You will pantingly follow his tragic course. You will live all the pain and all the hope of the heart of men though his heroes, in their hate and in their love. You will live all the conquests and all the chimeras and all the disillusions, and you will suffer the anguishes and trances of the struggle with death. And when you will have lived all the heroic Balzacian imaginations as such—you, who during this time will not even have thought about paying attention to the mediocre course of the life surrounding you—you will return to the combat of this life, not with lassitude and disgust for this hard and dull reality, but with a newly kindled flame and a young courage that you will have acquired in the company of certain heroes of the storyteller. You will see the world both uglier and more beautiful than it had seemed to you beforehand, and you will want to act, and you will have the force to engage in that activity—as if you did nothing else but pursuing, in your real life, the intense action of the novels that you had just read.

If Balzac is such a magnificent creator of illusions, if he is this fast-paced romantic who we just described, how could then contemporary realism claim him to be its father?

There is a bit of everything in Balzac's oeuvre, because it is everybody. There are souls of elites and of extraordinary monsters, as we have seen. But we find in it, as a contrast and to serve as a foundation of taints and grayness, also the crowd of mediocre beings with bleak, vegetating existences.

However, in a Balzacian novel none of those banal and vulgar lives become a principal subject. They always stay a mere detail that serves to better understand the development of the hero, the circumstances of his action. Balzac would also never get caught up in descriptions of the exterior world, whether the nature of the countryside or the city, if it was only to describe where something happened. If he does describe us a nation, a city, a house, an atelier, a factory, the reason is that that place is one about which the hero becomes impassioned either positively or negatively, out of which he pulls suffering or joy, or out of which he takes the opportunity to bring out his being until triumph, or until martyrdom. The objective world is for Balzac but a condition of his subject—and his subject can enrich himself in the details of the real because it was an idealist spirit that found this subject and chose these details.

When reading the naturalists, we can see how some of those writers, contrarily to Balzac, and all while considering themselves to be inheritors of Balzacian realism, were bleak slaves of a flat reality. And we can see that among them, the naturalists who deserve our admiration are exactly those of whom the intuitive creating spirit has overflooded, in powerful imaginations or in feverish sensitivities, the systematic barriers of narrow realism.

But the other great writer in which we see the third source of modern novels will already help us to discern the first problems of this literary prejudice. The case of Gustave Flaubert is the most complex one there is. To discern his personality, let's place it in his time and look for connections. Stendhal and Balzac were contemporaries of poetic romanticism and we have seen how they were worthy of it. It is not less important to know that the novelist Flaubert was the contemporary of the poet Leconte de Lisle. The ideal of Flaubert and the one of the author of the *Poèmes barbares* are brethren. Both were pupils in the school of the poet Théophile Gautier—the school of art for art's sake—both have drawn from it the worry about the perfection of the form, the love for the scrupulous and savant techniques. Both have looked toward erudition for the subjects of their works. Flaubert wanted to objectify the novel like Leconte de Lisle aimed at objectifying lyricism. The one and the other have wanted to eliminate themselves from their oeuvre in order to impassively reproduce the paintings of life.

Here the parallelism between the evolution of poetry and the one of the novel is affirmed. The contemporaneity and the similarity of ideas between Flaubert and Leconte de Lisle are striking, but we attach even more importance to them if we remember that they both were also contemporaries of Ernest Renan.

With Renan's work between 1848 and 1868 the methodological research of truth affirms itself with seduction and a clear sense of logic. Scientific rationalism finds in this writer an able defender. From that moment on everything will have to pass through the sieve of Renanian analysis: everything will be reduced to an experimental determinism. By the way, Renan only vulgarized, with distinctions, and introduced into the world of the letter those principles and methods that had already been affirmed for a while and were in full maturity with the philosophers of the nineteenth century.

After the positivism of Auguste Comte and the experimental psychologists of England, after Stuart Mill, Bain, and Spencer, it was the German psychophysiologies that were in fashion.

And all of that came, by the way, only as a result of great scientific discoveries in mechanics and chemistry, and of their physiological implications. Men were blinded by these discoveries and thought that everything had to be subjected to the methods of the sciences that had been experienced, that is to say that the same bodily sciences had to explain all and everything, even their innermost life, and by consequence their art and their literature. They did not take into account that the free play of their fantasy or their sensibility or their passionate imagination could contribute much more toward constituting the necessary documentation for the foundations of psychology. The naturalists wanted to accentuate this worry of exactness and objectivity in the arts, but that was not enough, luckily, to muffle the creative genius of some of them.

Stendhal, Balzac, Flaubert, those are the three powerful French sources of the modern novel. But there also were some abroad.

We have already explored some coming from England and Germany, but those were sources that were poisoned by the fatal microbe of experimental analysis.

There also were fruitful ones. There was, first, the gorgeous storyteller Dickens, who was a source of delicate emotionality, of tenderness and of poetic vision. Dickens, who taught our Alphonse Daudet to know himself, and to then tell stories in his own right.

There also were the Russians: Turgenev and Dostoyevsky, but most of all Tolstoy, and finally Gorky, of which the illuminating souls were lighthouses of love to a great number of French writers, leading them toward a new ideal. There was the altering song of solitude of the great and bitter Nietzsche, of which the ruthless individualism guided some of our novelists into less popular avenues. There also was Oscar Wilde, of which the aesthetic imagination gilded the end of the century with a beam of unforgettable legend.

Those are, good and bad, the primary intellectual or moral sources of the modern novel. But the brain or the heart do not guide the feathers of the writers by themselves. Social life is also to be considered—and the same goes for political life. Surely though, they are not the purest of sources, but sometimes they are the most powerful ones, those who develop into torrents and create rivers, rivers that drag a multitude of production with them—the works imposed by the moment, that the crowds acclaim and that steal the glory from the great works of beauty— until the day of posterity when they are annihilated together with the societies and the mores that engendered them.

## THE NOVEL OF THE "TRAGIC BANDITS"

*La revue anarchiste* 1, no. 12 (December 1922)

Now that the hour has come in which we talk about the "Bandits" once more, whether, as Lorulot does in *Chez les loups*, to disfigure them by making them ugly, or, like Armand in *L'en dehors*, to offer exact and measured memories, it seemed interesting to me to dig into an old unpublished manuscript, although I wrote it almost eight years ago now. These pages might perhaps strike some as wrong because they are more imaginative than documentarian. In any case, though, they have, in my eyes, the merit of not having disfigured the men who were courageous enough to try to attain the synthesis of their aspirations.

The only blemish of my pages would be that they no longer exactly reflect the synthesis of my own aspirations as I hold them today.[34]

They were written at the beginning of 1916.

They had found themselves on a hill—the highest of the ones overlooking Paris, on Montmartre and Rue du Chevalier-de-la-Barre. They had come there on some cold winter evenings to warm up their hearts to the words of an old savant. They had been harassed by the hard labor of the day. They left the factory crumpled, a million of mechanic jaws that, the entirety of their day, hadn't stopped to bite their young flesh to the rhythm of their brutal working order. But Libertad spoke. He was a strange cynic. Nobody knew where he came from, on his naked feet in his sandals, and on his poor shattered legs that he threw forward in a superb impetus of his poor man's crutches. He wore a long, black blouse with large sleeves, and, at the very top of that miserable body, his head flared proudly. He was always bareheaded, with a brow like Socrates and a bald head that was dented and battered of wisdom around which a few long hairs hung wayward like thorns. But his eyes ferociously burned of revolt, and his mouth distorted itself in bitter sarcasms.

Libertad spoke. His harsh and singsong voice counted, one by one—his inflections precipitating like an overflowing heart—the joy of life by the rhythm of the free sensations in the simplicity of acts without morals, the horror of agonizing under the mechanism of servile tasks and the complex monotony of conventional movements, the foolishness of politics, the complicity of masters and slaves, the authoritarianism of all collectivist forces, the cowardice of men who only know how to act in herds, the enjoyment of discovering oneself and of creating oneself and of sensing oneself in all one's sap, like a rod aiming straight and supply toward the sun, and of affirming oneself as living and free in its light. Libertad sang of anarchy as a liberatory force that everyone carried within themselves. And while he spoke, the eyes of these young people shone of interior light. By the rhythm of this voice they heard the soul of their youth awaken within them.

Sometimes, they also accompanied their "father" through town. Libertad went to the bars and restaurants where the people come to eat and drink. He stopped and stood between tables that were smeared with grease and wine and said to the laborers:

Slaves, who lull your dirty suffering under the word "Freedom," like the monks in their cold cells that fall asleep in hymnical paradises, learn to be free every day.

Do not eat the impure aliments of flesh that once was alive. The grease that nourishes you is for your muscles like oil is for the engine wheels of the machines. It facilitates their good functioning so that their usages can serve longer to ends that are a stranger to them. By eating an animal's flesh, you render yourself into accomplices of innumerable murders of which you do not profit. You are victims who let themselves be nourished of the blood of other victims.

Do not drink alcohol, do not smoke tobacco. Kill all these hereditary acts that were created within you, despite you, a need against you. Alcohol does not only kill: that would not be much in comparison. Like tobacco, it *lets you forget*, and it is bad to forget, you should not forget anything about you, of all that one has suffered and of all that one has enjoyed, of all that one has sensed, thought, wanted in one's entire life—in order to be able to, holding oneself entirely under the light of one's consciousness, say to be a truly free being—*an individual.*

Among the men who, now that the evening had arrived, were eating and drinking and smoking, who had been thrown together in enjoyment as they had been, during the day, at their work among human beasts crouched over their worktables, Libertad, standing on his crutches, his head held high, threw his words, proudly, like grain into a furrow.

First he surprised them. These slaves felt an instant of respect before the fire in his eyes. They felt power gush out of him. With gaping mouths, they sat and acted as if they were listening to him. Then, when his words turned toward them and their reality and when they understood the sacrilege of this iconoclast, all their love for what they heard blasphemed here rose up to their many uniformed mugs as a fat grin of mockery that horribly rumbled along.

Libertad, still standing upright, was not fazed by this ascending tide of popular filth. By his side, his "companions," shaking with intense disgust, tightened up a bit closer toward him.

Meanwhile, above this fecal sheepishness of stupidity, sometimes a young head arose with the uncertain, slightly dazed clarity of eyes that finally saw a great day after so many nights.... And Libertad told them: "Come, comrade, leave these brutes behind, come with us, live your life outside of the herd." And in an impetus of the entire soul, a new companion would heroically detach himself from the army of slaves to join the small gang of refractories.

But where he taught his children the most beautiful lesson of heroism was when he affronted the people in the worst area of their drunkenness: the one of politics.

As Pythagoras once went onto the agora to say to the Crotonians who had assembled to elect a tyrant, Libertad, during the electoral meetups, joined the discourses of the socialists to make them follow his explication of this idea which is deeply obscure both to the mind of savant and the mind of the illiterates: "A bean is bad for the one who gives it, and bad for the one who receives it." And while the eyes of the proletarian citizen became round in their utter incomprehension, he entered a moment of vigor, and insisted:

> You who pretends to be free, why do you vote? ... Listen ... Nobody can represent anyone but themselves. By voting, you are the worst of slaves. Because the one who has chosen himself a master belongs to himself even less so than the one whose master has imposed himself forcefully. The latter can disavow his master as a brutality that he does not recognize. The former could never revolt against his chains, he gave them to himself. Don't be this voluntary slave. Be your own liberator. Flee from this pest-ridden room where they intoxicate these poor brutes with greasy eloquence until they acclaim their own subservience. Do not listen to any of the promises of a paradise for tomorrow. They are all lying. It is today that you have to live. It is in your individual truth that your happiness lies. Outside, the sun of May shines onto the gardens of the earth. Go outside and, across the fields, under the lights, let your own march create your route.

Thereupon these human beasts ragingly unleashed in cowardly violence. They had understood. This monster violated the sovereign authority of the people. He shattered the idols of the temple to democracy. He denied the social ideal. The crowd growled up with clenched fists. A roar picked up and, wave by wave, insults and threats rolled up to Libertad. His young disciples already courageously pushed back the first assaults of the collective beast. But suddenly it was like a rout of drunken pigs, and the savant had a thousand savages in his face whose breath stank like shit to the point as to lose breath from that alone.

He received a kick to the stomach. Falling back, he kept up by leaning against a wall, still standing straight through a divine effort of his poor exhausted legs. He held himself on one crutch and, taking the other in his fist by its base, threateningly swung it around like a sledgehammer. Ah! If a savage had to die today it would not be like Pythagoras, who was pursued and stopped at the edge of a field to offer up his chest for the fists of the crowd. It had lasted long enough, through many centuries, that the societal men repeated, with great pleasure, the stories of how philosophers let themselves be killed in resignation. For once he would make an exception to the rule—this philosopher—and let them figure out what it cost to assassinate Libertad!

His naked head against the stone, his forehead up high in all his clarity, his eyes seeming to throw lightning, and, at the end of his black sleeve, floating around in rhythmic movements, in his iron fist, danced the old wooden crutch. It turned, turned without ceasing and returned back in a single movement like a windmill of death. It struck to the right, left, in front of it—all over the growling beast that surrounded its master. It shattered a clenched fist, it burst and hollowed out a hateful eye, it let teeth fly that were ready to bite, it flattened a stomach, cut off legs, beat, bumped, knocked, jumped, rebounded, created some space around the fist that maneuvered it, as if it were the wheel of the infinite, animated by the arm of an eternal destiny!

And when Libertad died, it still turned.

To the rhythm of this crutch, by this death of a savant, he taught his sons, unforgettably, the double lesson of heroic wisdom! At the same time he gave them the indomitable force to stay oneself by rejecting all crutches on the inside—and the art of playing the crutch on the outside. This invalid cripple, in this supreme minute, became immortally, for these beautiful young men full of force, both a master of thoughts and a master of dance.[35] He showed them, in a single act, how one could unite philosophy and sports in harmonious power. Heroically, he erected in their adolescent eyes a vivid sculpture of the individual soul playing in freedom of the weakness of its body among material necessities. Thus he taught them that sports are just a game. They have no outside utility. Their only end lies in the free joy of the being who engages in them. He also told them, in this last, demonstrative lesson, that the action of the individualist never ceases to be a sport. It is his great game—the most beautiful and most intense of all, the one in which he not only searches for, like in the small games through which he experienced his childhood, a few partial and fickle pleasures, but the entire pleasure of his being in all its harmonious unity. The action of the individualist is the perfect sport: the divine game where he finds his entire being in his joy of living to the rhythm of his free intuition.

These were the teachings of the death of the savant. It went on to carry its fruits superbly in those who we would go on to call the "tragic bandits."

---

After the assassination of Libertad, his young companions left the city and the millions of mechanized servitudes in which the young forces were atrophied. They went to the countryside, to practice sports according to the anarchist method.

Near Romainville they had a little house and a lot of land surrounding it. There were trees and a field. They went there to live and play.

By purifying themselves of any societal prejudices, they had simplified the needs of their bodies. They thus needed few things to maintain themselves. They did not eat the meat of animals, they did not drink any alcohol, not even wine, and they did not smoke. Some vegetables, fruits, and clear water, along with some bread, that was all they wanted for their subsistence. They happily cultivated their grounds. That was the first of their sports. None of them had ever been a peasant. These children of the pavement only knew fields from having crossed them in joyous little groups, long ago on their Sunday ballads. They all remembered having seen, in the crushing afternoons of the end of summer, curved spines under the burning sun, engaging in a servile mechanical movement that seemed to them to be quite the same as the one of the laborer among the gears of the factory. And each one of them carried an equal sense of disgust for both these forms of dehumanization within them. They approached earth not to exploit it, nor to be exploited by it. They were neither agrarian workers nor farmers or colonists. Each one of these boys and girls simply sought to play the spade, the shovel, and the rake in his fashion, and just sufficiently to help the harmonious contact of his act with the matter of the natural eclosion of what was necessary for his body to be nourished. But they did not intend for this action to cease to be one of pleasure. From the moment when it would become a constraint for them, they would have repelled it. These individualists had the same ideas on agriculture as they had on childcare. They fecundated the earth like they understood the fecundation of "flesh" among anarchists. In making love they wanted to stay free: they were not to be slaves of the laws of childbearing, but artists of love. They had learned to apply the ideas of old Malthus to their individualist anarchism.[36] *Eh bien!* They did not want to be the pack horses of the agrarian earth any more than they wanted to be the pack horses of the reproduction of their race. Following no other law than the rhythm of their pure pleasures, they stayed, in all their acts, harmoniously playful.

They also did not specialize their physical activity. Having not fixed any exterior ends, they could vary its forms in discretion of their own delight. When the dread of monotony threatened to transform the free pleasure of cultivating plants into a chore, they went to lie below the branches of the trees to rest their young limbs under the alternating caresses of light and shadow. Their nudity returned joyously in incredible purity after almost nineteen hundred years of Christianity had buried it under the black sheets of a costume. To the soft cooking of the sun, their bodies lost the tinned-meat decoloration of which civilized beauty, the way she is glorified in the same tones by the imbecile Paul Bourget and the very intelligent Rémy de Gourmont, is proud as if it were a mark of nobility. And their enlivened carnations and play of muscles sang, among the blues and the greens of the grass and the leaves, the magnificent symphonies of leather, of gold and of bronze.

They rediscovered the sport of the old Hellenics. They engaged in races, in wrestling. From branch to branch they threw themselves in supple leaps; they developed around their torsos a robust agility in their young limbs. They threw the discus that projects our own effort far away from us, through space, which our eyes love following through the air while it performs in its trajectory of light. They juggled an iron ball from one hand to the other, then let it fall back onto their chest—all along the slowly moving muscles like the banks of a river—and it danced from one shoulder to the other, then it bounced off the sun, and then along the back, as the body animated to receive it; and the ball either restarted its dance or rhythmically alternated, continuously in one single music, the efforts of the mass, the one of the atmosphere, and the one of the human body—to the single joy of the being that combined them in their free play.

They also engaged in typography in Romainville, and that, just like their agri-culture and their athleticism, would never cease to be a sport. They played with the "characters" absolutely like they did the ball, the pickax, and the discus. The "composition," the arrangement and the printing all were done with such youth-ful enthusiasm, with such a drive of freedom that their printing office was as har-moniously enjoyable as their vegetable garden or the lawn under the big trees. Nowhere had they wanted to cease their acts of being big playful children in the pursuit of their pleasure.

By the way, their printing atelier did not supply any societal work. This ate-lier made of simple planks, under its bright, lightful glazing, was well and only theirs. There they had transported, after Libertad's death, the "cases" and the "sinkers" and the little machine with which they had already, in the Rue Chevalier-de-la-Barre, worked in "free camaraderie" in printing *L'anarchie*.[37] The young individualists had learned from the savant to never lend their hands any more than their tongues to the reproductions of ideas that they did not love. They did not "work" for the "external." The printing press of Romainville was only an instrument of their own thought. It permitted them everything by playing, by fabricating their little journal which they sent around the world of minds like they threw the discus in the air of their prairie, and, if they followed the discus with a lovingly curious eye only to enjoy with their sights the transformation of their muscular energy into a trajectory of clarity, they cared similarly little about the consequences of their publications and playfully pursued their unforeseen cre-ating radiances only throughout the infinity of psychic atmospheres that their voyaging minds crossed without an itinerary for the lands of conscience.

They knew how to play sports without their physical activity ever impeding their intellectual activity. They also knew how to train their thoughts without that intellectual activity harming, denying, or disciplining their activities as a physical being.

Thus neither their thoughts nor their sports ever dragged them to renounce their individual harmony of sensation. Each one of them knew how to always stay oneself by playing their sport as well as their thoughts. They never forgot them-selves in the drunkenness of action or in the one of intelligence. They never let themselves be forced off course, and into collectivist reasons of being, by either of these two factors. They could keep their enlivened unity—in a sort of miraculously harmonious integrity—because in them their individuality had managed to equally dominate thought and action in order to make them both its game. They were intelligent like they were sporty, through the same joy of playing their lives without any constraints, in all of its joys. To the interlaced rhythm of its two games, the individual soul was free.

———◆◆———

Not one of the objective contingencies can attain a free personality. It is inviolable. So it doesn't matter, psychologically, what might happen, in the future, to the "friends" of *L'anarchie*. They carried a soul with them that could attempt all possible acts which yet could never be able to tarnish its glowing purity. For the public they would become the "tragic bandits" but, among themselves, they remained the anarchists from Romainville who let their vivid young individualities blossom by purely existing in acts and ideas of which they knew to stay the masters.

The epic of the "bandits" occurred entirely in their souls. What the newspapers of their time have reported must be truly little in comparison to what they had to feel themselves in the hours of their tragedy.

It is necessary to have loved them to be able to imagine and attempt to explain to the men who return from the war how the "friends" came to the point of leaving their little garden in Romainville to deliver themselves to much more perilous sports along the roads and the highways of the national domain.

The spectacle of free beauty is for our society of ugliness and of slavery an unacceptable affront. As soon as a being harmoniously flourishes, he denies the collectivist laws, he places himself outside of the frame, he shuns the public opinion. Thus, inevitably, the stupidity of the societal men embitters over the creator until they have annihilated all of his external works. In all eras, societies have assassinated the great philosophers and the purest artists; they have burned the books of the genius, chased down the author, and thrown all beings whose originality endeavored to enrich human nature in prisons or in mental hospitals.

The "individualists" of Romainville, once their time came, underwent this same law of social life. Upon their blossoming of youth, the hits of the monster struck down without mercy. It began with the ones of their neighborhood. In the small town of Romainville and in all of its surroundings there was, from as early as the first days of the "friends," a scandalous rumor. Young, half-naked people permitted themselves to live with their companions under the trees without doing anything else other than playing all day under the rays of the sun. They knew it was anarchists who did not eat meat like the rest of the people and permitted themselves not to drink wine! No butcher or any bistro of Romainville had ever received the slightest order from these monsters. Finally, worst of all, it was "good-for-nothings" who permitted themselves to edit and print and spread an appalling little journal that was called *L'anarchie*, and where one could read abominations of this kind, "Begging is safer than stealing, but stealing is more beautiful than begging," under the signature of a certain Wilde, who could only be a German spy. And all of that could occur on a plot in the peaceful municipality of Romainville. It was a shame for the entire district and a national danger. "It is necessary that the major take an energetic decision and that we free ourselves of these poor Romainvillois that are such social gangrene!"

That is what was said in the entire surroundings of the "garden of *L'anarchie*." It was a unanimous growling: never-ending complaints dripped out of the greedy mouths of the peasants who died of hate for these "lazy parasites who wasted with their frolicking a good piece of land that could amount to some profit." It swarmed of guttural and vulgar jokes of Caf' Conç'[38] under the tongue of every little suburbanite who took, every morning at 6:46, "his train" and disembarked every evening, at 8:32, in the station of Romainville in one of the streams of servile population that Paris vomits out for the night into its many sewers that are the banlieues. And to take revenge against the "friends" for being never present in any of these departures nor any of these arrivals, this peloton of servitude twisted themselves an entire train of fables by narrating, with cheap jokes, "their originalities" of " the great outdoors." . . . Eventually, it was again this same growling that held forth in the conservative prayers of the little annuitant who was "jealous over his ears," in the categorical formulas of the little civil servant who was proud of the order that he represented, and in the socializing declamations of the laborer who was protective of his dirt as if it were a nobility. For them the individualists were simply "wrongdoers" or "fools"—"bad cattle" to slaughter or to lock away. And societally these imbeciles were right.

For a while public opinion in Romainville contented itself with demanding the eviction of a commune where originality was forbidden and on the lands of which the "nomads should not sojourn." This double wish of the honest population would not tarry to express itself in decisive acts.

A visit from the local police force was followed by a skillful search by the Parisian police. All that was in the "garden of anarchy" was thrown over, ravaged, ransacked. Under the pretext of frisking, these men of public safety uprooted all the plants in the vegetable and fruit gardens. They pillaged the printing office, toppling the "forms" off the plaques, emptying the letter cases, slashing the white paper, seizing journals, brochures, manuscripts. After their departure, it was a true ruin. For at least a month the journal could not come out. For the entire season the garden could not supply anything to eat. And the loan had to be paid off in fifteen days.

On one June evening in the garden of anarchy, on one of those summer nights when the countryside of the Île-de-France, shrouded in noble luminary vapors, seems to softly cradle the flaring choir of the stars, the "friends" sat and talked softly for a long, long time, under the great trees where so often their young movements had sung under the sun. They avidly spoke the entire night. It was a strange symphony, that of the young voices among the shadows: radiance of the coppers, the enthusiasm—vibrations of the violins, the ardor of life—deep sobs of the cellos, the courage enduring the suffering—and the singing of the flutes, their beautiful hope without any expectations. But mostly, dominating over everything, up to the summits of the great trees and even higher—and much, much higher—the unique sound of the Choir, the one of the great Rolland, the prophetic son of the high-pitched horn throwing once more between the stars, and in the voices of these young men, its eternal appeal: their heroism.

They spoke the entire night like this, and, when the sun reddened the crowns of the great trees—there were no friends left in the garden of anarchy, but "individualist bandits" marching incessantly over the streets of the socialized world.

*Tant pis!* If the land was wanted from them that badly, they would change places, but nothing could ever compel them to change souls. As freely as they were under the branches of Romainville, they went, across the world, to pursue their individual joy of life to the rhythm of the same games. In their heroic period, they would not cease to be, like during the times of their pastoral life, free musicians of their "I" playing their incessant harmony on these two cords: sports and thoughts. Today, the cords were merely tenser—and the music was thus more intensely vibrant than yesterday.

They were chased from their "garden" only to be rejected in the social life. They thus reentered that life without compromising their beautiful pride. They penetrated it as if it were their domain—a new land to playfully cultivate. *Ah!* It was much larger than that of Romainville, the soil was much harder and the vegetables less plentiful. *Eh!* Of what importance could these matters be to them: they only looked within themselves, *because it was within them that everything occurred.* Instead of the beaker and the shovel to stir the tender loam of the garden, their hands handled the hook to break open locks, the crowbar to smash open safes, and the steering wheel as if to fly away the car—but in acts of indifferent suppleness and of gracious force that *lost nothing of their soul.* They played themselves. It was a sport. Also, just like they once did not assimilate with the peasants in their agricultural works, in their "illegalism" they never took up the flaws of the *apaches.*[39] They despised all professional activities. They stayed artists. Instead of the shears to prune hostile branches and the hoe to pluck out bad herbs, they would now have the revolver and even the shotgun, and by using these new tools they would not take any more lives than with their former ones. Because they felt themselves alive in all of their reality, they lived in their individual consciousness; they blossomed entirely in a unique life: their own. Each one of them lived for themselves—for their entire being, for their harmonious wholeness—for their liberty. These beings that had denied all servitude—and that had refused themselves to human activity, these individualists who had learned from a savant to walk without crutches now wanted to accept none. These anarchists who were free from all social laws and all collective moralities and who felt their joy of life irresistibly bounce within them had nothing left in common with the people who adhered to the societal pact by their obeisance as much as by their authority.[40] Slaves of their urges or masters of gold: the "bandits" felt both to be hostile matters around their exceptional blossoming—a "mass" of resistance against which they had no choice but to violently collide, to break it, and to go through it to keep living.

They danced in the sun to the rhythm of the bounces of their car—across the streets, across the highways—rue Ordener, in Chantilly, in Melun and in Poissy and in Nogent and in Choisy, and everywhere where they struggled, where they hit, where they fell, everywhere these former gardeners of Romainville, these courageous players of their life went joyously, as beautiful bandits![41]

And in parallel they did not fail to stay, until the very end, even in the most tragic days of their struggle, eternal players of their thoughts; with the same freedom they once had during sweet hours of chatting under the branches of Romainville. Nothing could trouble the serene course of ideas within them, of which they loved to delight their soul as much as with the frantic course of their actions. Nothing, not even death.

Muse about it. While the entire world, trembling in fear, extraordinarily fevering, only had thoughts for their exploits, and while the press printed their journals only to narrate all of their details, they themselves, the bandits, barely cared about their own actions and only dedicated to them the necessary time to decide upon them and to execute them, all while thinking about a myriad of other things. In the moment of action, of course they committed to it with their entire ardor and all their force as the good sportsmen they were. But once the game was over they barely obstructed themselves with memorizing the souvenir of what had happened. They had played well with all their body had to offer and, in the fatigue of their flesh, they went with their entire mind, with the same drive, into games of intelligence.

While the social men indulged in their daily lectures, in the meticulous details of the "crimes" that were expertly reconstructed by the macabre analysis of their reporters, Raymond Callemin left the study table where his powerful abstracting brain played so often in the discovery of its truth through the glimmering hypotheses of Darwin or Le Dantec—and he went to the Concerts Touche to silently dream with his friends, the souls of Beethoven and Schumann. The day when Mr. Jouin, to his misfortune, discovered Bonnot at Gauzy's store, the chased-down man was thinking in the company of Max Stirner and Mr. Anatole France. In that slum with closed shutters, in the light of a candle, with a revolver to mark the pages, the bandit was reading *Crainquebille* and the *Rôtisserie de la reine pédauque* and the *Unique and His Own*. René Vallet, in the historical villa of Nogent-sur-Marne, taught his friend Garnier and their companions the immense deepness of Baudelaire and Poe.

In the heat of the battle, they kept a complete mastery of themselves. Acting in full acts, sensing in full senses, they did not forget to meditate, to read, to write, to think with their full brains. They integrally lived their life. Above the fighting—of course, they did it infinitely, to the point where they even put themselves above their own battle.

As such, they knew how to die immortally. Their death was their last day on earth—the most sublime, in an impetus toward the eternal: the masterpiece of their great art.

Bonnot went first, assaulted by an entire armed gang and never ceasing, even riddled in bullets, even while dying, to touch lovingly, as a last accord of his being, the two cords of his lyre. And as such his willing hands threw, one by one and in the midst of opposing fire, his act among matter: and with strokes of the feather, he threw his thoughts toward memory with these last notes of his. This until, after further bullets hit him, with two shattered arms, he let himself die.

Garnier and Vallet went under the assault of machine guns, holding up a day and an entire night in their corner of greenery and of dreamery and of love for which society contested them—and they died there, standing upright, fraternally side by side, without a sneer of horror to trouble the purity of their faces for even an instant. As gods of youth they died in full beauty, under an immense onslaught of those who had to be, just a few months later, the soldiers of righteousness, of justice, and of civilization.

Finally there would be three guillotines. How could I even tell you about them? They surpassed everything. They were larger than Christ on the cross—because they did not await to be welcomed by the Father. And they went to their death, each one on their own, they who only believed in their life. But they also knew that it would be only them to walk up that path, and in themselves each one of them felt a serene soul.

Symentoff saw his mountains and their singing sources of clear water and he dreamed of his "petite"—the tender beauty that was so purely loyal to him and of which the sixteen-year-olds were to follow him by a mere few months in death. And, in one single drive, without seeing anyone, he threw himself onto the *bascule* like one would jump into the sea.[42]

Callemin was thinking. Lucidly, his strong genius enjoyed its last minutes of consciousness, in all superiority. He observed everything, to make it his good, everything until the guillotine itself. After the decapitation of Symentoff, it was his time. He knew it and, because Soudy, in his typical enthusiasm, generously stood up first, Raymond stopped him with a brief motion: "No, let me go first." And he went, his head held high. He saw the crowds and threw them, like an alm, a contemptuous smile and this brief critique: "Ah! It's beautiful to see a man die." Then, shrugging his shoulders, he directed himself decidedly toward death.

Finally Soudy, the youngest of the three, appeared in his charming pallor. He was white like a girl and his black eyes still glowed in some fabulous sense of hope.

And when the blade sank to slaughter for the third time, it did not break any blood: it had only cut off a lily.

That is the story of the "bandits," as I like to imagine it, during the winter of 1916, while the people savagely killed each other, "gloriously," by millions—in the field of honor—and for the love of humanity . . .

## ANARCHISM IN PRACTICE

*Le libertaire* 281 (December 1922)

The new does not frighten me.[43] Even when it upsets everything that I could think and desire until then, I will rejoice to welcome it in me without fear of confronting the dazzling rays of the unforeseen.

But I do not think that revolutionary opportunism and the use of money are very new questions, and if I was outraged in Saint-Imier it was precisely because I was seeing anarchists (and not the least important ones) obstruct themselves with such old prejudices.

Malatesta said: "We want to start a revolution as soon as possible."

It appears to us to be both wiser and more useful to say: "We want to start anarchism as soon as possible."

All while not neglecting the anarchist propaganda of ideas that permit us to reveal individualities, to generate will, to uplift militants out of the masses, we are not "educationists" who think that they can turn the world anarchist by moral action alone. Direct action seems indispensable to overthrow the practical powers of authority. It is for that reason that we are revolutionaries. But we do not consider ourselves "*revolutionarists*" any more than educationists. That is to say, we do not want to sacrifice this only living truth that is important to us to the "Revolution" any more than to "Education": the anarchist individual. Education and revolution need to serve this truth. I will not renounce the struggle and resign to endure blows for the pretext of educating all men on earth: my educative zeal will not push me as far as to content myself with enunciating truths in the face of the oppressors who martyr me. Why should I then, under the pretext of holding a revolution, sacrifice my holiest ideals and settle for processes and means that shock my heart and my reason?

Thus, if we want to start a revolution, we want to start it as anarchists. That is to say, we won't consider movements as revolutionary if they are susceptible to push those who engage them it to the goal of establishing an authoritarian regime of any kind, be it a federalist republican, socialist, or communist one.

"But then," Malatesta tells us, "a revolution will not be possible, because as an anarchy cannot be established by force or by the violent imposition of some, it is clear that past revolutions *and those of a near future* have not been and could not be anarchist revolutions."

What a great encouragement for anarchists. But luckily, such an affirmation is as cheap as it is pessimistic. Contrarily to Malatesta, we think that anarchy can be manifested by force and that it was at the origin of all revolutions. Politicians could contain the insurrections in 1793 or in 1917, they could grasp the sources of the libertarian revolution to aliment new societies of which they were the legislators, but it is nonetheless not less true that all revolutionary *force* starts by being an anarchist force. It is only on the day when ceasing to be a spontaneous movement of individuals in revolt to become an affair of "specialists" in "societal organization," the revolution stops with new masters and new laws. It is only on the day when insurrectional violence makes way for public force that the revolution ceases to be anarchist. But from that day on the revolution is dying.

Anarchy is thus the very manifestation of the libertarian force of individuals. For us anarchy is not an ideal, a utopia, a dream, or a quintessential abstraction. It is, for us, not a way to replace the republican formula of *"Liberté, egalité, fraternité"* with *"Liberté, justice, amour"*—and to then engage in education or a revolution: no matter what revolution, no matter with which means, even money! For us, anarchy derives from the individual realizing himself in ideas and acts: it emanates from the producing consumer transforming matter and ideas, creating for his needs and his art, with his pain and for his greatest joy, animating life itself, defeating all forms of authority with his liberating force.

"We cannot establish anarchy," declares Malatesta. Evidently, because anarchy is not a state. It is an incessant march forward. But we can as individualist anarchists, with our ideas and our actions, prevent the end of this revolution while it is happening and render it impossible, after the destruction of a political regime, to establish a new public power, to create a new justice system. It is perfectly possible for a few people using their violence, perhaps when organized into armed *bandes* as Makhno did,[44] to permit other individuals to attain their anarchy without them noticing it, to produce, in one word, in the revolutionary environment such an impression that an entire anarchy could be animated—under the condition, of course, that these few know to stay anarchists themselves, to stay *illegal*; that means that they do not regularize their power, that they do not create their right, that they *establish* nothing above the free interplay of individual forces of thought and action.

"No population is anarchist," says Malatesta. Without a doubt, not under the regime of authority. But let's destroy a bit of authority and we will see then what the respect of authority will become for the individuals of this same population!

In every living being there is a slumbering anarchist. Let's be more confident in the individual than in the ideal. By instinct the child boldly searches for its well-being and its freedom. It has the will to grow, the will to push back against anything constraining it. Only an authoritarian education teaches it to respect laws. If, like Malatesta, "we do not believe that an ideal of freedom, of justice, of love can be realized by way of governmental violence," we are nonetheless persuaded that the reality of individuals can liberate itself from authority by way of direct violence and of direct organization of individual among themselves.

Do not impose anything over individuals, so you permit them to act and to think without authority—nothing: no God, no master, no government, no representative, no dictator, no preacher, no prophet, no apostle. No religion, no law, no ideal.

Let the individuals *practice* their anarchism. Anarchist militants, let's help them in this practice by practicing it ourselves. Let's descend from the dangerous clouds of the ideal into the sane experiences of daily life. Here are men at work. Here are the producers. In the workshops, in the factories, they struggle against the owners. Like them all, we endure the infernal struggle of classes. There, we can do our practical anarchism, an anarchism that will not only have the goal to "demolish or weaken a government," but to assure the producing and consuming facts of the individual on the ruins of every form of state, of all sorts of "right." And thus *we will preoccupy ourselves with what will happen* because what is important are the realizations and not the intentions, the actions and not the principles. We struggle to live our anarchist life and not to assure the triumph of an ideal. We do not want to be those utopians whom we admire so much by despising or persecuting them. We do not work only for posterity but also for ourselves. Our struggle cannot be resigned to being only a violent form of opposition to a government. It is at the same time higher and more practical. It is not spent so stingily on the political domain. It intensifies and expands over the entire work life.

If violence served us only to repel violence, if we did not need to assign positive goals to it, we as anarchists might as well abandon all participation in social movements, we might as well surrender ourselves to our educational needs or rally to the authoritarian principles of a transitory period. But I do not confuse anarchist violence with public force. Anarchist violence is not justified by a right: it is not created by laws; it is not juridically condemned; it has no regular representatives; it is neither exercised by agents nor by commissioners, even be they from the people; it does not demand to be respected in schools nor tribunals; it is not established, it unchains; it does not stop a revolution, it lets it go on without refrain; it does not defend society against attacks from an individual; it is an act of the individual affirming its will to live in well-being and in liberty.

The occupation of factories and fields, the seizing of means of production, is that not a positive goal—and is it not with the exercise of violence that the workers can achieve it? Malatesta is well constrained to recognize this when he enumerates the modes of anarchist action in a revolution. But to be at peace with one's ideal and to conserve the good right on one's side, he wants to distinguish between defensive and offensive violence, a violence that capitulates before morality and an immoral violence. It is because of such prejudices that the anarchists always end up losing societal battles. Morality, justice, what *needs* to be done, what should not be done, the allowed, the forbidden, all of that was only created by the authorities themselves to justify their oppressive force and to put a break on the violence of individuals. "You will not steal; you will not kill, because you don't have the right to." But it would suffice for society to grant the right for the fact of assassinating and pillaging to become noble and heroic. The right is but the recognition of an authoritarian power of a fact judged by this very power to be useful to the enduring of its principle of authority.

The anarchists do not recognize rights for themselves any more than they accord them to others. They do not judge the facts that they accomplish, just as they don't judge the ones that they see being accomplished around them, but they freely examine them in the glow of their own conscience. The anarchists do not measure the societal life of individuals with fixed laws. They want to leave the joy to live without moral constraints to the individuals, with the care to let them determine the conditions of their production and consumption themselves. But like the anarchists will not stay in the clouds; they will not confine themselves in laboratories of sociology. The anarchists live their life as individuals. They participate in the struggle for life; they endeavor not only to "defend and assure the liberty of development" but also to be the realizers, the *actors* of this development. And thus without doubt they will have to employ violence for positive goals, for goals that are the most positive possible, the ones that every human finds within themselves: the need to produce and the need to consume, the need to create and the need to destroy. The anarchist, with this, affirms only one type of violence: the one of human individuality against all forms of authority, the one of life against all forces of death.

❧

The question of money remains. With the risk to pass for "simplicists," we barely hinder ourselves with such subjects. Because the matter to us is to look for means to live in anarchy, and not to attach ourselves to old processes that permit to uphold suffering under a regime of authority. The matter, for us, is also a revolution that we want to realize ourselves, as anarchists. If it were different, we would critique neither the bolshevists for their transitory period nor the reformist socialists for their republican evolutionism, and we would try in effect to accommodate an *ideally* anarchist sauce with old ingredients of government—including money.

Money is, according to Malatesta, the only imaginable means of human intelligence to *automatically regulate* production and distribution we have found until now. That is possible, but it is also certain that an anarchist cannot want to *automatically regulate* production and distribution—because to automatically regulate a regulatory authority is needed: a government. In anarchy it is the individual who determines the production and the consumption relative to his needs and his capacities. As anarchists we precisely blame automatic regulation as a source of all injustices and all misery: it is this automatic regulation that we want to destroy and remove. "To replace it with what?" asks Malatesta. *Hélas!* It hurts us to see the same question on the lips of the old anarchist militant who we see in the muzzle of the bourgeois, the authoritarian communists, and politicians of all kinds.

With what will we replace the reign of finance? With the organization of workers on the very fields of production; with the workers at work.

Money creates a right: the right to consume, be it even without producing: the right to conserve what we do not consume; the right to monopolize merchandise that one does not use; the right to immobilize products. Money permits its owner to declare: "This is my property, and you are not allowed to touch it." The owner, often, does not touch it himself. He is just a pathetic owner. But he has reserved himself the right—thanks to the "automatic regulation" of money.

To the right of the owner that money represents, guaranteed through social authority, we as anarchists oppose the fact of production and the fact of consumption. The individuals who produce organize their production between themselves, and distribute between themselves, for their consumption, these products of their daily efforts. The process of taking parts from the whole,[45] envisioned under the day of a liberalized syndicalization, is no longer a utopia but the best imaginable means of anarchist intelligence we have found until now that permits for production and distribution to be carried out according to the capacities and the needs of every individual.

But "if certain categories of laborers, the farmers, for instance, refuse to deliver articles that they hold and the services that they contribute for free, without receiving the money like they are used to consider as real riches, what would we do?"

First, permit us to doubt the relentlessness of the farmers to want a currency that will no longer be guaranteed by a power, of a value that would no longer have an exchange rate. When they realize that they can procure clothes, shoes, and tools and enjoy the goods of the city without using money, they will scoff at your money.

But let's admit this wild stubbornness for some people. What would we do?

We won't behave differently in regard to these farmer "capitalists" from those of the city. The peasant who tenaciously defends his capital and who, refusing to take his part in the free life that we chose, deprives us of certain goods that are indispensable to this life, is a reactionary force in the eyes of the revolutionary anarchist, a power of authority that is absolutely identical to the one of a politician, of an owner of industry, of a cop or a foreman who is loyal to an exploitative government.

We would have to, in this circumstance like in the others, use violence without scruples—without saying goodbye to anarchism for that reason. Quite on the contrary, it will be our antiauthoritarian will that will affirm itself as one fact, without generalization. We will remain in the field of the economical struggle, and it will be just an incident of the fight for a libertarian life for all individuals, an act of revolution.

Money, born out of authority, will create authority. Money is a legal system. He who uses money needs to guarantee and preserve the value of the money that he uses. By giving you the money that you want from me, capitalist peasant, I, revolutionary who made himself master over the banks to seize all money and to circulate it, would only reinforce in you the confidence in money and would only make myself the slave of your idol to flatter your follies. I would become a guard of money, a preacher of money. I would have constituted a government. I would no longer be an anarchist.

To the usage of money that maintains the right of property, we prefer the usage of violence that assures in fact the possession of indispensable objects of life.

In order to give no space to false interpretations, I want to specify that I speak here for a revolutionary period in which anarchists would have the initiative and the directive of the societal movement. In every other case, be it like it is today in France or in Italy in a prerevolutionary period or be it in Russia in a "revolution" dominated by a political party, it is well understood that to live we are good and well constrained, even as anarchists, to use money or any other mean that is imposed upon us by the authorities to automatically regulate the production and redistribution. We do not have the responsibility for such means right now. We are not their organizers. And with all our efforts, we work to ruin, corrode, and explode the regime that lives from such processes.

We would thus be ill advised even to think, come our turn, of using the same legal artifices, of restoring the same systems of exploitation of which the individuals in the present society suffer. Not after having taken all opportunities that could present themselves to start a revolution, not after having immersed ourselves and others in the torments, the turmoil, and the ordeals of a revolutionary upheaval.

If we did we would resemble the preachers of those religions who make their followers renounce the goods of this world only then, after death, to cast them into a rigorous hell or a stupid purgatory, the sky always having been reserved for the preachers alone.

## SPORTS FOR THE FATHERLAND

*LA REVUE ANARCHISTE* 15 (JULY 1923)

This is another extract of a book I wrote during the war which, I hope, will soon see the light of day. I remind readers that Agathon, the author of the "Young People of Today," was from 1912 to 1914, with Mr. Colrat, at the head of a neonationalist movement that provoked the entry to power of Mr. Poincaré and the explosion of the "War of the Right, of Justice and of Civilization."

———— ◆ ————

Young France was in a pitiful state. Agathon and his friends knew it as well as me. During their scholarly years, they never failed to prove their hearts were up too high to commit the same high school stupidities, whether in Paris or the provinces. I am certain that they also kept away in repugnance from the vile brutalities of the rugby fields and the sleazy exhilarations of the dormitories. Agathon and his friends must have had, in their childhood, enough delicacy of soul to not sully it in such communal disgustingness. But they grew up. Their idealism had become practical. They wanted to live off their literature and to write for their country. They engaged in politics. They no longer owned themselves. Their intimate tastes became secondary. The national interest predominated everything.

Indeed, the superior interests of the country of Mr. Poincaré commanded an irresistible renaissance of national energy. For that a young, admirable population was necessary, a heroic crowd of "young people of today" worthy of the ones who were massacred between 1789 and 1815 for the glory of Napoleon. The morning of the twentieth century would be even more stunning than the one of the nineteenth. That is why Agathon and his friends took on a patriotic task: that of galvanizing this heap of stinking human flesh with the national illusion in order to throw all those little cretins of the sporty and mundane France into the tricolored sky, to the sounds of a stylized "Marseillaise." These men of the *Opinion* would thus give a style to the youth of France, and they were quite capable men of letters, who knew how to embroider a couple of rhetorical flowers onto the jerseys of the vile brutes of the rugby. And their sophism never cluttered to find aesthetics and idealism even in these weekly sessions of pederasty that occurred in the dormitories of their adolescences by the same ignominious jerks and asses who are today always ready, as young substitutes or judges, to pitilessly demand the lightning bolts of article 330, in defense of their aggrieved morals, against a lowly couple of lovers who were caught *in flagrante* living out their natural expansions in the depths of springtime woods . . .

Agathon and his friends wanted to preach the moralistic virtues of rugby in the most Athenian of republics. But before that, it was well suited to teach the young corps of France a unique new method—a seducing method that managed to ally originality with uniformity, bluff, and tradition; a disciplined new game, something sensational and completely relaxing, something impressive and reassuring, in short, something very Parisian! An invention tailored to the taste of the day and of Mr. Poincaré, something that upset neither the Jews nor the Catholics nor the protestants nor the freemasons nor the free thinkers nor the Rue de Valois—a machine in the style of the one that Mr. Bergson obligatorily had perfected for the needs of the spiritual life of the "young people of today," yes, all of that, but of the sporting type.[46] They needed the physical element to the reviewed and corrected intuition.

It was the athletic method of the famous lieutenant Hébert.[47]

In the service of the fatherland, everything is coroneted and sanctified. Colonel Henry,[48] who turned into a phony to save France, is a national hero. Lieutenant Hébert, who committed a monstrous act of plagiarism in order to stop the softening of the young forces of the republic, is an important national genius.

Malevolent critiques have gone so far as to hold that the lieutenant had made it his garrison's hobby to work through the main treatises of the German *Fisikenkultur*. But even that would have been too much work for a French officer. Mr. Hébert did not need to commit such an effort to find the content of his larceny. He only had to skim through a few of the little propaganda leaflets that individualist anarchists threw around everywhere like grains of which they knew that thousands would dry out on rocks before a single one would find a little spot of young earth. Lieutenant Hébert's mind was neither a rock nor fertile earth but a sort of compost smoldered by good national shit, a very French terrain. The grains fell into it, the poor things, and they germinated to create monstrous vegetation.

Vegetarianism, teetotalism, natural activity, so many ideas that hardy prophets of anarchy had not stopped to profess in their integral purity as essential physical factors of individual liberty. They had said: "Be a free being." Start by liberating yourself from the false needs that enchain you. Renounce eating meat, which is as cruel for you as it is for the animals that it kills. Repel the alcohol and tobacco that weaken you and render you more stupid. Go into the fields naked, and don't be worried about exposing your young bodies to the wind and the sun. Be strong and beautiful out of love for yourself. Love your freedom and the hygiene of your body and it will be a marvelous current driving you to the free play of your spiritual faculties. Be vigorous in order to keep a taste for life—in order to intensify the joy of life within you—and in your body, freed from all barriers, your "free soul" can flourish in harmony.

Lieutenant Hébert, as you might imagine, took the practical givens of these teachings and hastened to change their tonality. On his account, he said: "Be a good soldier. Prepare your young energy for the national struggle. Train to survive without all that the state cannot give you in as much abundance as it can in peacetime. Take up the habit to eat less meat, which won't hurt you, by the way: most illnesses are transmitted by its consumption. Leave alcohol and tobacco behind, they kill your discipline and make you forget your orders. The next war will not demand the drunkenness of epic heroes but the cold-blooded calculations of practical heroes. You cannot lose your compass on its battlefields. Don't drink, don't smoke. Also, leave your scarf and your linen knitwear, flank yourself naked in frost and wind. You need to strengthen your skin, because it will get rough in a few months and only the "hairy" can withstand the trenches. We are no longer in the era of wars in lacy uniforms.

"Be a tough guy" out of love for the fatherland.

"Love good hygiene because it keeps you healthy. It is no longer fit for the times, Mr. le Vicomte, to pose as a *'petit crevé.'*[49] Your body does not belong to you anymore. It is the property of the fatherland that needs its children in good shape, and agile for the play of its rifles, its machine guns, and its cannons."

"Become vigorous in order to be able to kill well and to die a good death in battle. Become strong in order to intensify the joy of killing within you, and the joy of dying for the fatherland—and your fleshy, muscular, agile, and solid body will be exalting itself in the sacrifice of the soul of a national hero."

Thus spoke Lieutenant Hébert. But he also acted. His practical exercises were not more originally plagiarized than the principles of his method. They were a commercial parody of the first games in which the adventurous souls of the "bandits" were delighted. The importation of the "Made in England" "Boy Scouts" already existed, and their warlike expeditions—carrying wooden spikes resembling shouldered guns, buglers playing warlike fanfares and flags floating in the wind—patriotically and cacophonously caricatured the "young anarchist friends" and their playful ballads, between valleys and hills and woods and plains, through landscapes of which they, fully sensing, only demanded freshness for the soul and the rhythm of their shadows dancing in the light in order to accord harmonious and effervescent ideas that they felt hatching within themselves. And the "Boy Scouts," these appalling lads playing war, violated the countryside with their disciplined assaults as military apprentices who were taught to "utilize the terrain" against the enemy of the nation. For these little soulless brutes, a bush of blossoming roses was but a dangerous firing line. A hillside full of genets became a terrain to hold an assault.[50] These prepubescent idiots taught themselves to number the hillsides that they saw, according to the indications of the new map of the military staff. Across the Île-de-France, the "Boy Scouts" exercised with the moves of armies that raid woods, riddle fields with mines, ravage gardens, and ruin farms in order to spread, with great strikes of bayonets and machine guns, death, death, death . . . The young "Boy Scouts" of France are the little helpers of the old grim reaper.

I remember a very strange vision. It was Sunday night, near the Bastille. Ten years ago. A troop of "Boy Scouts" passed by the boulevard during sunset. They were young guys, about thirteen years of age, with pink cheeks and vivid eyes. They returned from an exhibition and marched in rows of two down the middle of the gravel road. All of a sudden they heard the rumbling of hooves on the pavement. Their captain turned around and saw a cavalry squadron. It was cuirassiers who heavily trotted toward Tivoli-Vaux-Hall, where some demonstration against the war was to take place. Thus, in one single hurried movement, the youngsters aligned themselves in a military formation on the edge of the sidewalk, feet together, and presented their spikes as if they were guns, in the position of an armed salute. The soldiers—the real ones—grudgingly moved to meet them, as if they went to their chores. They were pulling their faces into the grimaces of really bothered poor buggers. While passing by they saw, from the heights of their mounted animals, between two bumps, these kids who mimicked them in their misery. And then something completely unusual took place on the mugs of the cuirassiers—something that looked like laughter and like pity. Thus I looked, too, at the Boy Scouts and what I saw was neither comical nor pitiful. At the end of these immobile bodies that were militarily aligned in a neat row along the sidewalk, I discerned, instead of the rosy cheeks and the bursting eyes, an orderly arrangement of identical skulls, death heads . . . already ten years ago.

The college of national athletes was not less sinister and not less grotesque a spectacle. But apart from a macabre farce, it was also excellent business. Mr. Hébert was not a patriot for peanuts!

Like the "friends from Romainville," the "athletes" of the lieutenant lived in the open air. They also fought each other nearly naked in the sun and in the wind of the countryside, in order to give vigor to their limbs and agility to their young branches. But instead of the "Garden of Anarchy" it was the "Parc of the Collège."[51] Don't misunderstand there that, thanks to the complicity of a few capitalists, Mr. Hébert could supply his disciples with space that was hundreds of times vaster than the piece of land where the genuine adolescence of the "bandits" took place. It was a park: in it, only luxurious plants were grown; not a single vegetable plant broke the elegance of the place. The lawns were well kept, and the accidents that had to bring about the illusion of a natural life were ingeniously managed according to a progressive method.

The "garden of the friends" was not a public space and nonetheless, anyone who thought freely was welcomed in it without any suspicions. Their shanty had a table that was always ready to serve a vagabond or friend.

In the park of athletes entry was public but came with a fee. There was an establishment that offered all modern comforts: a restaurant and a casino. An orchestra of very French ladies played only national music. One could live there by subscription or by buying tickets.

The "clients" of Lieutenant Hébert were manifold and diverse. The "young people of today" were not the only ones to frequent the college of athletes. Some young people of yesterday and even of the day before that visited the park to nurse their baldness and obesity under the pretext of patriotism.

In the morning, after breakfast, a discrete electronic alarm reminded the athletes that the time had come to go sweat for France. The gentlemen stripped nude. There were people of all sorts. Small law students were pampered in their pimple-filled complexion with buttocks that were red like the cheeks of children at their first communion. The Sorbonnards shriveled around in their living, gauntly narrowness that seemed to ask grace for all the miserable bulges in their boney joints. The slightly plump hospital interns strutted down the park with the jovial obscenity of "all these ladies in the salons." The "handsome young men" of the world prided themselves coquettishly with little, cheeky shuddering movements of their muscles like the *oeillades* of great actresses. These were the nude forms of the young people of today.

As to those of the young people of yesterday and the days before that, they weren't any less diversely picturesque.

To begin, there were the convinced—a half-dozen old cookies who had, since 1870, never stopped to chew over the remnants of the endless chewing gum of *La revanche* in their skulls. They wanted to regenerate their bodies so that they were able to put them, in a day of glory, to the service of the army. A sad present for the fatherland! Under the brutal July sun, their gritty, white-haired skin was a disgusting spectacle.

Then there were the hobbyists—the true clients, the most numerous group here. They took it as a cure resort. They came to Hébert like they would have gone to the Doctor Doyen or the Institute in the Rue de Londres. They spent a month or two years in the college of athletes between a season in Vittel and a stay in Cauterets. They treated their infirmities—and they paid well.

One of them, elephant-like, amassed, in his crushing nudity, chunks of lard before which the most heroic phalanxes of American masseurs had been exhausted. Lieutenant Hébert was his last hope . . . Long live France!

This other one, drooping like the last quarter of brie in the window dressing of a dairyman, had come to the college of athletes like others would go to Lourdes. For him, Lieutenant Hébert was a Notre Dame of treatments. He asked a miracle of him: the return of his virility that forty years of a very French wedding had ignominiously devoured, and that none of the hundred thousand quick-fix, certain, and ingrained methods had managed to resurrect from in between the stones of its tomb. France needed children. For the fatherland, Lieutenant Hébert, under the resounding sound of the "Marseillaise," let the old walker . . . walk once more.

This one, congested to the point of nearly sweating out all of his blood through his pores, had come to "uplift his temperament." That one, torn up by nervous tics, had come to find peace of nerve. There were giants who hope to shrink and dwarfs who wanted to grow, hunchbacks and lames and knock-knees and goitrous and scrofulous and people heavily marked by smallpox.

And all of that, horrifyingly naked, amid the verdure under the sun.

They were the athletes of the new France, the champions of the victory in the war of tomorrow. Mr. Hébert catered to them.

With one blow on his whistle he launched them across a field, in gymnastic pace. A buffoonish insult to the light of day. Leading them, sticking out his chest like a peacock opening its tail, doing wheels with all his muscles, the "handsome boy" *knows himself* to be first. Then came the "lankies" of the Sorbonne in a quirky disproportional crawl, like epileptic spiders. Behold next, mannered like the little pensioners in the sea baths, the pupils of the school of law—very preoccupied with the awareness of rounding out their movements in the "antique form," of not stinging their feet on the stones too much, and most of all of not losing their glasses in the race. Next came the moribund students,[52] heckling their fleshy contractions to the blundering rhythm of their paws and making their buttocks jump up and down like the rump of a horse.

Now, behold the hobbyists. The old giant wobbled his cumbersome *guiboles* this way, that way, like false, cardboard columns on which he increasingly fell apart with every reply of the terrain.[53] The dwarf rolled breathtakingly along between all the legs with his arms always in the air like an appeal to height. The hunchback wedged all his body weight onto his bump—as if he carried the motor of his force in it and ran mechanically with well-learned mannerisms. The goitrous comfortably carried his head on his goiter like on a welcomed rest to help him breathe. And here is the old walker, more dead than alive, the eyes turned back, and running with only one arm, pressing the other desperately onto his kidneys. The "nervous tic" could not help himself to "tick on," and illustrated the movements of the gymnastic pace as a frenzy of ambulatory triggers. Twisting his neck, scratching his nose, convulsing his arms and legs, he still did not cease running and seemed, in his tortured nudity, like a random escapee out of the flames of Dante's inferno. The congested nearly burst of blood. His eyes were deorbited as two red balls ready to explode. Neck, face, and skull were but a deep purple mass out of which a breath like a fire bellow escaped.

Finally, behind all of them, as the very last, the fat man shook his way down the field. He looked like some mountain, mutated as a farce of Olympus and turned into a monstrous block of grease blessed with the movement skills of a snail. He obstructed the view of the horizon and cautiously moved, part by part, kilogram by kilogram, detailing every movement—in an infamous hurrying of sluggish and whitish things, leaving an immense trace of its slimy and laborious activity on the grass behind it. He sweated like a drooling slug, but with the abundance of the Nile during the season of the great floods. It was appalling in its disgustingness. In his passing, the trees of the park must have felt a cold wind of death blow by under the July sun.

This went on until noon. After the race, a massage, hydrotherapy, another massage, and then a rocking chair cradling to very French music while awaiting a luncheon of succulent national cuisine. After midday: a digestive rocking chair, a coffee, and the old three-star cognac of Monis. New patriotic accords and dring-dring-dring! General alert, everybody stand up on the field for a second session. The buffoonery repeated itself in even more grotesque fashion than it had displayed in the morning. The handsome man still swaggered his thorax around, not with his enthusiasm of the morning but only by a sense of duty. The "Sorbonnards" followed but without any quirks. They seemed to no longer have their bones, and their poorly articulated skeletons just did a macabre race in the park. The law babies lamentably danced on eggshells. The carbines slumped along, and their acts of this second race were the ones of the ladies when they executed their fourth "miche" on an evening of a festive Sunday.

The old giant has renounced the usage of his *guiboles*. They are now nothing but unending rubber pipes that let themselves be slung here or there following the will of the winds. They were carried by his trunk, his belly on the floor propelling himself with his arms turning like a windmill, moving like an immense legless cripple.

The dwarf was only a gutless balloon against which the other runners bounced their legs every now and again. The hunchback and the goitrous snoringly slept all while racing, one on his bump, the other on his goiter, and did not wake up except when they fell into a ditch and crashed onto each other, bump on goiter, screeching like cats when they are about to be slaughtered. The "old walker" seemed to have just left the refrigeration unit of a morgue. Broken in two, he only ran with his legs. With his arms behind his back, he embraced his kidneys with his two stiff hands. The "ticker" no longer ran horizontally, but vertically. His eyes, his nose, his mouth, his tongue, his chin, his arms, his legs, and his stomach— his entire body was in a storm of nerves, and he fiercely jumped, twitched, and startled with fury, as if he wanted to attempt an ascension to the sun all by himself, this unfortunate soul who only managed to incessantly trample on the same bare corner of the field, with the ignoble grimaces of a chimpanzee in a cage. The congested fell victim to an attack, on his entire body, his round eyes stretched out to the sky. And finally, far back at the horizon, moved, with the same precautious precision, even a bit slimier, a bit paler, kilogram by kilogram, the leaden fat man, the mound of grease that was still melting into enormous floods of sweat, still huge, still slow . . .

This went on until the evening. And when the old sun who has seen all colors and all forms since the beginning of men on earth, when this old jaded sun of eternal contemplations finally saw the moment of his bedtime on the point of the crust when all brazenly swarms under the joy of his beautiful rays, when he had let out his last sob of red rays onto the western skies like a last sigh of relief, the athletes went to take a shower, get a massage, get force-fed, get cradled, and went to bed. And all of that under the high command of a lieutenant, for France, and for the republic! Ah! The fatherland might be in danger . . . But it would have athletes to defend itself. Mr. Poincaré could take power. He would have proud wrestlers for his *Revanche*. With Frenchmen like that, Germany could only tremble and return Alsace-Lorraine.

## EXECUTIONERS OF CONSCIENCE: FROM ARISTOTLE TO MR. POINCARÉ

*LA REVUE ANARCHISTE* 18 (MARCH 1923)

Before the war, naive people could still be amazed at the considerable influence that "reactionary" writers have had over the democratic daughter of the Revolution. I hope that the phenomenon of the "Sacred Union" has demonstrated once and for all that in France, beyond the visible but transient differences between the parties, a vague, collectivist ideal of a social order exists, one that knows how to let the nation profit in all disciplines and all eloquences, whatever form they might have.

The most important thing in this country is that the writer, just like the orator, does not forget to talk for his audience. Misfortune to the one who writes only to express his own thought and talks only to defend the actions of his own being! This dangerous individual who does not understand that human speech only exists to translate universal ideas into a personal code, this criminal who withholds himself from employing his talent to the service of a collective, will be put into the dilemma of submitting himself or dismissing himself, to capitulate or to die. But from the moment on where a savant only has the goal to educate the group of humans to which he belongs and to let this group profit from the vast mass of all the resources that his intelligence has to offer, when he bequeaths them with one of those big, bloated words that can serve them as a principle so that they have it easier to move as one big block or movement, then this benefactor, who can relieve his contemporaries from the suffering of having to think for themselves, is a genius who deserves to be remembered.

The meaning of a word does then no longer matter, as long as it is spoken with a dogmatism that fits the right formal principle to impose itself onto many brains in one single vibration. All speech is good to the masses, as long as they can make a flag out of it. The most important thing for the men of a social movement is to unite and to become disciplined . . . why? And what for? For the masses, Ideas only follow, dictated by the coincidences of ensuing events. But what is shaping them is the experience of being there, flocking together in a reckless mob ready to propel itself at the orders of a chef—God, king, or law; behind a symbol of servitude— cross or crest—white flag, or tricolored, or red; egged on by a fanfare of copper or of words—into all of the collective graves of life or of death, of peace or of war, a pile of uniformity. This is how it is possible that one single epoch underwent, with the same good will, the heavy gesticulations of exaggerated socialization with Jaurès, the dry assertions of a Barrès, the garglings of common sense with Faguet, the clerical discipline of Brunetière and the humanist campaigns of the members of the league for human rights. It is because all of these people shared a common concept when it came to their method of uniformization. All in their way, they followed the same ideal: the establishment of a social order upon which the men of France were to found themselves. With scissors of different proportions, all of these movements cut out the same model template in accordance to which all personalities were to be neutered. They thought, wrote, and spoke only to this end: the complete and utter reduction of individuality to an ideal form of everything.

Thus the efforts of each one of them—whatever those efforts were—necessarily were to serve all of them. By teaching young men to discipline themselves to the rules of a socialist party that didn't forget to also be French, Jean Jaurès did the same labor that Ferdinand Brunetière did by teaching them hard lessons of obedience to the hierarchy of the church, or that Maurice Barrès did by inciting them to the moral gymnastics of becoming good patriots. When push comes to shove, the apparent motives are forgotten, the specters of ideas and principles disappear, but what will always stay and is identical to all movements is the habit of discipline, the mechanic movement of ganging up and organizing for a collective action. Then each one forgets their individual conscience but remembers the movements that make them march in unison to obey the law.

Jean Jaurès did not fault the nation that assassinated him. The tribune of French socialism was an underrated patriot. It is a certainty that if the nationalist politicians were both more worried about the true well-being of their country and more aware of the psychology of socialism, they would not have had Jaurès assassinated. And if their egos had then still have hindered them from adopting his policies, they would have at least understood that the simple existence of a war between France and Germany would have had him perform his "duty for France."[54] Because Jean Jaurès was as much of a Frenchman as Mr. Barrès or Mr. Bunau-Varilla. His political enemies committed a senseless crime.

Jean Jaurès was French like the southerners are; that means he terribly over-rated the small differences between himself and the rest of his country. He was eloquent. He was an admirable public speaker, because he thought only to talk to his public. Despite the appearances, the socialist tribune was a part of the same formalist school of thought that also includes Brunetière and Victor Cousin. But he was much more contemporary than those backward thinkers. Additionally, his coarse temperament was always carrying him more toward the successes of the squares rather than to those of public office. That's how he managed to go with his time and to adapt the forms of the past to the ideas of the day. Jean Jaurès makes me think of Bossuet. The Bear of Carmaux talked to the good citizens of our republic with the same superbly eloquent enthusiasm, with the same preaching phrases that the Eagle of Meaux employed to touch the "honest people" of his century. It is the same formal magnificence to serve the public domains. At the time of Jaurès, these public domains no longer were in the skies or in Versailles. They had descended to the height of the stomach and onto the electoral process. The public domains have been democratized, but they are still shaped as eloquently in the mouths of the orators and the writers who elevate them with their style.

And thus today we speak and write for the civilized people and good citizens like we did in the seventeenth century for the gentlemen of the world, in the sixteenth for the courts, and in the Middle Ages for the clergy. It is always the same formalism, one that lets us preoccupy ourselves with talking "as one should" and not as one wants, to respect the opinion of one's public and not one's own thought, to model one's expression after the general sentiments of a social moment in time and not on the intimate sentiments of an individual soul.

This is a humanist formalism in these times of an increasing international mercantilism, a national formalism in the times when social interest crystallized itself into patriotic ideologies, a socialite formalism in the centuries where one caste had the sad privilege to represent public opinion, a seigneurial formalism in the days of feudal powers, a Catholic formalism in the Middle Ages where only the clergy could read and think; but also an Aristotelian formalism in every epoch since Aristotle. Because, in all of these types of formalisms, whether they call themselves Catholic or socialite or nationalist or socialist, the same essences can be found, albeit in different applications. These are the old logical systems, falsely classified as eternal scholastic truths, which boil down to a fanatical belief in an ideal type that is to be uniformly lived by all people. There I always hear the same atrocious groans of suffering of a free spirit who is imprisoned behind the bars of universal rules. In all ideologies the ideal dismisses itself every time it wants to affirm itself into laws to conduct groups of people, because it can live collectively only if it dies in the soul of every individual who has to submit itself to it.

Meanwhile, to the ones who prefer to renounce the noble life of [individual] conscience to the benefit of the active unawareness of the social world, these ideologies have their use. They are the motors of the machine that push the force and regular function into its every gear. Their necessity is most obvious in those situations where the social mechanism needs its energy and precision the most of all times, and I mean by that the historical hours in which it only exists for the sake of murder.

In France wars or political revolutions have never lacked ideologies to stir up their eloquence.

As we have seen, "The Great War" kept igniting the most dilettante of our bureaucrats, until they became appalling devils, jumping and singing around a little fire of joy until it took the proportions of a blazing inferno from hell. We had the Lavedans, the Capus, the Bourgets, the de Flers, the Maurice Donnays, and the Marcel Prévosts of this world drop the plume with which they tickled their genitals to clutch the coal shovel to nourish the flames. We had the war of 1870, which carried these two stars of the Third Republic on its naked body: Thiers and Gambetta. These stars lit up the path of all schoolkids of France to walk over the poorly kept fields of public culture, so many good-for-nothings disguised as little sage kings promised since the times of social congratulations. They walked to the bar association, that Bethlehem of republican politicking, in order to find, in its cradle of lies and surrounded by golden beams, the divine electoral mandate.

With the Third Republic only the lawyers kept thriving. Mr. Poincaré is the result of sixty years of poisonous outgrowths. Since 1789 the lawyers have served France like the rats in its cheese. Now France and the lawyers are inseparable. Nothing could ever tear the two apart. France is the geographical expression of the lawyer, and the lawyer is the human expression of France. They form, in their strange symbolic relationship, all of what Charles Maurras, despite all of his intelligence and his daring, could never change. To separate France from the lawyer seems more impossible than ripping Germany away from the Kaiser.

The lawyer who currently rules France holds the reins of his chariot with too much authoritarian mastery, making it impossible to compare him to the many inoffensive Trouillots who populate the swamps of radical-socialist politicking. He is not one of those many good buggers of lawyers who make free chatter out of parliamentarianism, something far from the strict homologues of the courts. The man with the pale face does not laugh. He does not wildly gesticulate either, Poincaré is not the son of Gambetta but the disciple of Royer-Collard. He is a *doctrinaire*.

I know very well that the master of "doctrinarism" was a legitimist and that Mr. Poincaré is the president of the republic. But there is no contradiction here: the contemporary events have shown us well enough that a head of state can, if he knows to want it, exert his authority upon the nation as nonnegotiably in a republican system as in the most sovereign tsarism.

This way Royer-Collard married the rights of the sovereign to those of the parliaments. In a severe and dull, precise and cold, passionless and fantasy-less style, this lawyer turned professor of philosophy at the Sorbonne excelled in the art of accommodating the amenities of the bourgeoisie into political doctrines. Under the name of "new spirituality" this liberal economist found a way to make himself popular with the Catholics. His rhetorical philosophy reassured them about the intentions of the century. The Church smiled upon this man of good sense who finally understood the necessity of reattaching the material progress to the spiritual progress, economical faith to catholic faith, and the administration of the "good public" to the respect of divine authority! The frosty deputy of the Marne was the true intellectual father of the senator from the Meuse. Royer-Collar taught Poincaré the best recipe for all political glory: the art of being mediocre with radiance.

Another master of this old Sorbonne, who was so dear to the young Agathon, also contributed to the moral education of the mane with the pale face as much by his legend as by his writings. I want to talk about Mr. Guizot, who was not a funny guy either. The ideal of this grumpy dogmatic, who had the honesty of calling "reason" only a freely chosen ensemble of ideas that best fit his goal, was to transform France into an association of rich bourgeois of which he was the template and the chief. For this icy monster, nothing counted but the business of his country and every person was, in his eyes, but a small piece of the big capitalist machine. It was also natural that his political system had as a first priority to energetically oppress the individualities. When it came to practical applications of this, he didn't miss. Having instead of a soul one of those quadrangles of stone that the judges and prosecutors call their conscience, he loved nobody, not even the lawyers. But he knew to respect them for budgetary reasons. He also knew, to perfection, to want the best for his country. Mr. Guizot thus was an excellent statesman.

In the same way he showed himself to be a writer of the old order: despising individual manifestations of life, and being interested only in ideas that were general enough to not serve an individual to trouble the orders of the classes. Mr. Guizot treated history as he treated politics, authoritatively and dogmatically, submitting the events of the past to "moral laws" like he wanted to submit, through his actions, the men of his time.

As such, and through the force of his demonstrative logics, by getting the brains of his compatriots used to conceiving of history as a neat order of necessary events that suited his doctrine, the writer prepared the citizens to accept a submission to the laws of their government. In Guizot, the historian was but an auxiliary to the statesman. Guizot the writer was for Guizot the politician what in 1912 Agathon was for Poincaré: a link in the golden chain that paved the way for his ministry.

The "great" revolution had, if nothing else, one merit: to not let its politicians pick up the necessary hobbies to become men of letters. As they had no time to write, they contented themselves with talking. Thus, the results were only half as bad: instead of writing as one talks, they contented themselves with talking as one writes. They had the honesty of being only orators and to not also claim the title of writers. But sadly, there always are some characters with bad enough taste to permit themselves the vile factitiousness of uniting the notes of the orators in posthumous publications, which is why we now have the disadvantage of being able to judge the written works of all those tyrannical chatterboxes who only stopped wiggling their doughy tongues when it was time to butcher. The guillotine was always despicable, but I'd almost be tempted to consider its ugliness to be less monstrous when I muse about the times where it knew to recognize its own. Not even our "great war" possesses such a mitigation of its horrors. Because not only won't the ones who wanted it stop talking about it or stop writing about it in lovely tones, in prose and in verse, and in all improper places. No, sadly, the ones who sing about it are also not the ones being killed by it.

Similarly to the "great war" of our times, the "great revolution" germinated in the decomposition of all individual thoughts and arts, the worst mushrooms of social eloquence: snoring phraseology, apologies of the fixed type, general paralysis of imagination and sensitivity, flattening of all personality before the triumphing blunder in abstract phrases and posturing sentimentalities.[55] The words, for which the French *citoyens* murdered each other 125 years ago, singing the "Carmagnole," are the same in the name of which, in August 1914, the proletarians of Europe left for the fields of battle in order to slaughter each other while singing the "Internationale."

"Right," "Freedom," "Reason," "Justice," "Humanity," "Civilization," these were formerly the identical terms of eloquence used by Mirabeau and Verginaud, Danton and Marat and Robespierre, each in their turn to enflame their masses toward the drunkenness of murder and to justify their reciprocal guillotining. They are again the bombastic phrases used equally in the discourses of Guillaume II and Mr. Poincaré, the tsar and the king of Italy, François-Joseph and Georges of England, Mr. Briand and Bethmann-Hollweg; or by Lord Asquith when he aims to anesthetize his deplorable herds of armed humans whose reciprocal throat-slicings are supposed to further them in their obscure materialist competitions.

In any case, most of the leaders of the revolution did not only decree the guillotine, they also had to ascend it in their time. Of course, I don't find them any more worthy by virtue of being its victims as opposed to the guillotine's executioner, but at least they had to run some risk and did nothing to escape it. Up to the moment in which I write these lines, nothing lets me foreshadow that Mr. Poincaré or his colleague Guillaume could die from the war. France and Germany both need their decorative eloquence too much for one or the other to ever consent to see them assume the tunic of poilus in the trenches. Their lives belong to the state and . . . they are the state!

That is the same way of thinking that, in the era of the revolution, distinguished one of its rare leaders who had the talent and the ability not to die. Mirabeau did not experience the delicacy of the guillotine. It is entirely true that this revolutionary had all the fabric of a statesman. He was a politician to the core of his being. He knew how to mesmerize the crowds with enthusiastic speeches that he had never written down or memorized. He mobilized cohorts of youths, fed them with rhetorical masterpieces, and made them the workmen of his genius enterprise of popular eloquence. He possessed the art of using his capacities, in short,

Mirabeau was a modern man. Briand resembles him in the way that a hyena resembles a tiger.

Now, those two beasts have the same looseness of conscience to serve the same force of cruelty. Mirabeau, like Briand, had only material appetites. He had no more of a soul than Aristide. No part of him was independent of his cold, calculated intelligence that served only his ambition. From his childhood to his old age, this being aspired to enjoy the spoils and the goods of public office. He also didn't mind the means to reach that end. To be successful he would never hesitate to sell his conscience. Just like Briand, it would never bother him to sell out his associates. All the difference between the two crooks is that Mirabeau reserved treason for the crowning of his career, while Briand made it the dusk of his. At his zenith, he is the cause of this war. That promises for his dawn.

But the "patriots" of the revolution, just like the ones of the Great War, didn't mind such details. It was enough for them if Mirabeau or Danton or Marat or Robespierre had enough eloquence to persuade them of the righteous greatness of the crime that they were made to commit, and enough authority to represent, in their eyes, republican idealism.

The revolutionary orators stood in the tradition of French formalism. They are the distant relatives of Agathon and those traveling salesmen-academics of English law and Latin civilization who we saw travel the world and tour conferences from 1914 to 1916. All of them employ a phraseology of which all gimmicks only served one end: to impose on the minds of their masses the uniformity of a social type. The leaders of the revolution spoke of the "good citizen-patriot" like the leaders of the war today fill their speeches with calls for the famous "men of justice and civilization." But those are nothing but empty formulas. Behind these masks of idealist cardboard, painted in the colors of the day, there is always the same face of rotten old stuff. Ah! Their idealism is always the same farce. The puppets can change, and with them, the gimmicks. But the anarchist is not mistaken by them. He sees through the scene after the curtain has fallen, and he discovers the hideous social reality, always the same.

Today the "man of justice and civilization" hides his businessman snout with generous abstractions—miming to be harsh toward gains in all their forms. The "hero of the humanitarian ideal," the "warrior of righteousness," the "defender of the disenfranchised" all masks that which the human beast of the early twentieth century hides behind—that beast, organized and socialized according to all of the progress of practical science. The "great war" is nothing but a street of geographically assembled stomachs. Those are the human rights.

The French Revolution of 1789 was an affair of the same kind. Back then the standard type wasn't the stomach—it was the head, but that was hardly worth more—because the cerebral functioning of the social man is in nothing superior to his digestive tract. A man who does not possess himself individually thinks in the same way that he digests—with the same uniform unconsciousness, submitted to the same collective mechanism. However, while our stomachmen of today don't concern themselves with the matter they eradicate, the headmen of yesterday pretended to grant it some worth. They also decapitated each other for questions of "precedence" rather than disembowel each other, like our contemporaries do, for questions of "profit." Thus they had the mask of "good citizen" instead of the one of "good civilized" and the great revolution seemed to only pour so much blood in order to grant each citizen the equality of political rights. That seemed to be such a big fat material cause for such little moral effort. Come on then! Let's lift the mask of the "good citizen" and let's discover the face of the good bourgeois who assassinated thousands of young men in order to transfer, to his profit, material "goods" from the nobility and the church. Those are the republican rights.[56]

The revolution had affirmed a new social type. Through blood and fire, it had imposed upon men the form into which they had to mold themselves—the ones demanded by the interests of an ascending collectivity. The republican rights were nothing but the crowning of a bourgeois order to succeed the nobilities' order. It founded itself upon the ruins of the royal rights, but without failing to use the scattered part for its construction. The French Revolution was nothing but progress realizing itself abruptly. The terms interchanged, but the equation stayed identical. Under a new form the social order kept living "ideally" on the death of all individual harmony. Whenever the decadence of a "good subject" risked to miraculously resurrect an individual in any man, the "good citizen" emerged just in time to take, from the hands of the masters, the poor souls who the moronic phalanges of the old type would give up voluntarily. With a few swings of the guillotine, 1790 regularized the situation, and what the two terrors couldn't do, the twenty-five years of massacres in the wars of the revolution and the empire would largely accomplish. After 1815 France was ripe for republican rights. The restoration was nothing but a phase—something like a recovery after an operation, a kind of uprising of segments that permitted it to take some powers on the dreams of the past before recommitting itself to the vigorous regime of progress.

But these "good subjects" also had their golden days of adolescence. There was once a time where it existed in the smiles of the youth and masterpieces of thought.

During that time it hadn't yet become this regrettable senile title that was scared like hell of chants of the "scoundrels." It boldened its chest full of pride under the "strawberries" of the doublet and male shanks under the plies of its "Jabot."[57] It stood out in the mind and at war. It was the triumphator of the alleyways and the camps. It was in the courts, it was in the towns, and, when it crossed the fields, everything bowed before its power. It was the social type—back then they called it *fashionable*, but that is all the same—the model toward which all of the "good people" turned their attention. To realize it all endeavored tirelessly: the machine of the state only functioned for its well-being and the letters, always respectful of it, wouldn't stop illustrating it. It had its philosophy like it had its politics or its credence. But back then, in those days of flowering, it didn't call itself the "good subject." It enjoyed itself rather by decorating itself with the most noble title of "honest man."

In the seventeenth century we said "honest man" absolutely in the same way we said "good citizen" in the nineteenth and in the way the twentieth century says "free man." Human rights succeeded republican rights, which succeeded royal rights, but all of that is but a question of forms. At the bottom of things, nothing changes in the social sphere: "civilized man," "good citizen," "honest man," these are all but synonyms of a single term: *"man as required,"* that is to say the man according to the laws, rules and conventions of society of its time, the man according to the type—the type materialized as a man—the human being as it needs to be if it doesn't want to die of shame, of the guillotine or of hunger—the man tamed according to the needs of the social environment of which he needs to be a part if he doesn't have the courage to undertake a fight to the death with that stuff, a fight that is, however, the only condition to the life of his soul.

Extract from a long, unpublished manuscript, written in 1915–1916 during the war, which is still looking for its publisher.

## INDIVIDUAL AND AUTHORITY IN THE FIFTEENTH CENTURY

*La revue anarchiste* 2, no. 22 (December 1923)

In one of his adventures, Han Ryner takes Psychodore into a land that is completely unremarkable, a country that entirely resembles ours, but in which the inhabitants differ from us in that their past takes the place of their future and that, as they age, they progress toward the grave by way of childhood instead of by meeting their end in living through old age. This tale of the "Retrogrades" is not a symbol, it is a living reality that illustrates the fantastic history of French thought. When we start with Agathon and we move toward Cousin, Mirabeau, Boileau and Malherbe, I truly ask myself whether we move up through the ages or whether we go through them backward. Where are the living? Where are the dead? Where Is the youth of this tradition? Where is ageing? Aren't the elders the "young people of today,"[58] and aren't the children the old people of previous times? The old medieval monk who affirmed the virtue of its theology with the force of all combined faith, is he not more worthy of the prime of his life than the young opportunist who uses all of his talent to impose a form of civilization, in which he himself barely believes, upon his fellow men? And even if we consider him of equal sincerity, how could we ever say that Agathon is the younger of the two?

By going from a human to a republican, to a royal and then to a theological right, I see only different travesties of one same monster: the collective, authoritative mind that creates itself, consolidates itself, and organizes the death of the individual souls.

The civilized man of the twentieth century is not the son of the "citizen of 1790." He himself is not emerging out of the honest man of 1660, and he again did not grow out of the guts of the "humanist," a person who in his turn cannot be the fruit of the works of the Church. Instead they all are but one same phantom that incessantly refreshes its appearances in order to better exercise its powers over human brains. It is the abstract concept of a societal archetype that pretends to impose its uniform definitions to the manifold and mobile, infinite subjective. It's a collective power that affirms its past of brutal conquests and idealizes the name of justice, in the hope of dragging out, through the magic of that word on the resignations of its conquered, the profit of a single instance of power.

During the French Middle Ages, until 1420, the type on which this societal ideal was fixated was the "theological clerk."

Almost the entire fifteenth century was an admirable era, unique in its fertile grounds for individual blossoming.

In a time in which everything that was dependent on the principles that were in force in the old society dissolves, without any running communal ideas that can push the people toward a new form of organization, the individual can find, in this social chaos, the elements of his harmony. The soul is, in its essence, anarchistic. It can only benefit from the full drive of its sap to glow in the rhythm of its harmony when it disregards the external laws. In a society that is solidly disciplined, the soul can only live by concealing itself while waiting for better days, because its blossoming could only be a suicide. Meanwhile, in its desire for light, it will not cease to push against these shadowy walls with the force of its destructive will. And in what outbursts of enthusiasm will it throw itself around, the divine madwoman, in these rare hours of history when all of the social edifices seem to crack! Even if she knows that it will only be for a day and if, not being disillusioned over human wisdom, she foresees that tomorrow they will see the walls be erected anew and even more somberly by the same men who tore them down, using the same material used for its demolition, at least it will live on that one day to the best and most unique of its dream!

In the fifteenth century social chaos lasted for years, just long enough to permit François Villon to live his heroic life of the poet-bandit up to the point of perfect blossoming. In different eras these very same actions of his would not have permitted him enough time to write even a single one of his *Testaments*. In 1912 we have seen what would happen to individualists cut from the same cloth. The era of the tragic bandits, a time of glory, of true glory, one of the kind that history does not write, but that often are found by poets to sing about, was only a one-year-long flash in the pan; and if Bonnot had left his *Testament*, it would consist only of some sheets of paper stained in his blood and written during the battle while he, with only one other friend, the pure Dubois, enclosed within four brick walls that were pierced with machine-gun fire, resisted the assault of an entire army. Just ten or so pages ripped out of the hands of death in order to throw a bit of himself into the thoughts of his friends, with the same feverishly willing hand that would not cease to return lead bullets to the human carrions that sliced through his body until he died.

Villon could last ten times longer than Bonnot, but he always had to meet a brutal end. He was a true illegalist, and as such, like the anarchist bandits, he had to beat precisely and strongly into the coffers of the most powerful. In our day the banks keep the gold; in the Middle Ages it was the monasteries. The Collège de Navarre was, in 1450, the equivalent of what the Société Générale is today,[59] but in the fifteenth century the emerging royal authority competed enough with the old ecclesiastical powers that a bandit could still hope for the grace of the sovereign when fighting it. In our century the sovereign state is the representative of only capital. It is responsible for the power of the national bankers. It could thus never lose such face by feeling any indulgence for the evil jokesters who so directly challenge the very fundaments of its authority!

But if the power of the clerks of the fifteenth century generally declined in the political landscape of France, it did so only by consolidating in certain positions in which royal authority could not dislodge it. The Sorbonne was such an unsackable fortress, thanks to which the Church could hold on within the state for many more years. In that way, the clergy conserved the power of official moral action of France. It remained an educator, a founder of consciences, a master over the minds, while the king was but the possessor of bodies.

It was thanks to this divergence of authorities, of which the laws and edicts thwarted each other incessantly, that in the fifteenth century the bachelor-bandit Villon, an assassin of preachers, a robber of monks, a devalorizer of religious colleges, and a poet with no respect for people of any robe or uniform could run from the gallows for so long. And it was for that same reason that the early sixteenth century was able to hear the bitter voice of the master of arts Ramus, who affronted anyone in his way in order to combat, with his enthusiastic fire, the old Aristotelian formalism, the scholastics, and the disciplinary routine of the theological university before he was assassinated by the law on the third day of the Saint-Barthélemy.

Ah! He was so different than the legendary priest of Saint-Martin of Meudon. He had too much soul in his body to be able to bend over backward to please a Cardinal Du Bellay or a Diane de Poitiers. If Ramus did not leave a great body of work behind, it is without a doubt because after the censorship of his first writings, this man of consciousness and of force refused to deny anything of his ideas just to publish. He would not lend himself, like that fat coward Rabelais, to the good advice of the officials. Instead of dissembling with his pen, he preferred to break it and to enter into the active struggle. Similarly to the extraordinary author of the *Cymbalum Mundi*, to Despériers of whom the quirky irony broke the dogmatic stupidities of theology into laughter, Ramus could die as a hero of his thought. The artist of the *Pantagruel*, however, preferred to be a buffoon in order to live of his gags, temporarily, in his century, and of his works, eternally, in the memory of mankind. He also knew to have the prudence to reprint his books by removing all incongruities from the perspective of the theologians. He would no longer speak of *sorbonagre* nor of *sorbonicoles*.[60] Meanwhile the words stayed, though—because in Rabelais the artist surpassed the thinker and he was entangled, despite himself, by the vigor of the expression, to go even further than his intentions. He touches further than he can see. His verve drags his mind, irresistibly, outside of the limits of what he knows. But Rabelais can correct himself.

He could take back the work that had been finished and even printed in order to neuter all his audacious follies. If the artist of the *Pantagruel* is a madman, a bulldozer of touches, the philosopher is reasonable enough to teach him to not trouble his optimistic peace with imprudent visions or unfortunate findings.

It matters not! The creations of the artist were so loaded with vital movements that the corrective will of the philosopher cannot manage to kill them. They were thrown into the psychic universe from mind to mind, irresistibly, as soon as they saw the light of day; and nothing could stop the words that expressed them to bounce from mouth to mouth, and, like snowballs do, with their movement, to carry the true cause of their massive size with themselves. Nothing could stop them, not even the destructive decisions of its author.

And that is how the words "Sorbonicoles" and "Sorbonagres," scratched out of his two books by Rabelais, were forever inscribed onto the pediment of the old Sorbonne.

What is a "Sorbonicole?" The incontestable professor of theology and logics. The tyrant of minds, according to the laws of God and Aristotle.

What is Aristotle? Intelligence in the service of authority. This ostensible philosopher is but the universe's police prefect. This "first cop" of the thoughts served himself of logics as his baton. As if they were carriages, he stopped ideas on their drive, took down their details, and collected them in an organized system of files. All of them had to be subdued to the rigorous rules of his immovable hierarchy. When Aristotle had constructed his infallible system, order ruled the spiritual world in the same way as it could one day, let's say, rule over Warsaw. There was no more room to stumble. Everything was fixated on the crushing of the individual soul and under the entirety of the force of file number 1 of his system, which carried the holy name of God.

The laws of Aristotle are nothing but the logics of God. They are the ones that Catholicism utilized side by side with the Christian legend as a foundation of its power. It even aggravated them with absurd affirmation, which it called mysteries and commandments on the practical conduct of men. Furthermore, it would not be content to simply place God above everything else. It also surrounded him with formidably obscure clouds, all while narrating the tiniest details of his complicated operations with admirable precision.

Thus the mind of the societal man, which is completed by mystery as much as it is by certitude under the condition that neither one nor the other troubles him in his peaceful good senses, was fully satisfied. With Catholicism there was enough mystery to not have the need to be tormented with what surpassed his current knowledge of things and enough certainty so that he could think of an explanation for everything.

Theology further settled all the questions of the child-men by giving them this soothing response also given by good parents: "You are small, God is great. God has created the world according to the laws of all wisdom. Obey the laws of God, and you will grow up to understand the law of God: you are nothing without God. If you want to be something, be with God. Follow His law, and you will be happy; be a good creature of God; it is the only way of being for you, because God is all-powerful. But if you do not follow the divine law, commit a sin and you will have to expiate. You will suffer for all eternity. You will be wretched."

Theology in the Middle Ages thus expressed the divine laws. It shaped the minds of men in order to turn them into "good creatures," ready to faithfully follow the ways of their God, and these ways were traced by the representative of this God on earth. Theology served as a very spiritual instrument for a very corporal domination. God was but the ghost of a societal authority that prepared, with the rules of its teachings, the laws of its government. The discipline of minds was but a condition to the one of bodies. The Aristotelian conviction of the immutability of the order of things oppressed thought, cut off the wings of hope, and burdened the beings with severed, resigned submission. In the name of the holy laws, the church taught obedience to men. After having followed the laws of its theology, they would, without any hesitation, give them their money or their blood; pay their tithes if they were serfs, or found masses or convents if they were lords or nobles. And the ones as much as the others, whether they were leaders or soldiers, left as a mass, grouped in ranks and disciplines under the same hateful cross, to go on the crusades to kill and die in the service of God.

If this story amuses you, let us repeat it. It is one of every time . . . especially of ours. Call civilization "God," call general culture "theology," the Church, the state, and you will have the same type of education and the same political reality. The individual still agonizes under the form of the collective type. The "general culture" that is preached by our Agathons is but a travesty of theology. In it, the soul of the individual is sacrificed to the formation of the "civilized man" according to the traditional Latin formula, so that it has no other function in its life but to adapt the acts of its body to the practical interests of the reigning societal reason. Absolutely in the same way as, in the Middle Ages, the theological educators crushed the nascent consciousness of the future servants of the church by fabricating them into "creatures of God" according to the Catholic formula, to make sure that they had no other ideas in life but the one of submission to God's laws.

## KNOW YOURSELF, YES, BUT KNOW THOSE WITH WHOM YOU MARCH

*LE LIBERTAIRE* 314 (JUNE 1924)

It is clear and obvious that the individual is at the center of the heart of anarchism. Not an individual to put over all men and to adore; not a superhuman swollen with pride and sonorous rhetoric; not a hypothetical God without material needs, but also no shabby and crude individual who can pretend to justify all his cowardice and his brutality by the simple fact that he is human.

The individual whom we vindicate to affirm our anarchism is, at the same time, this reality that everybody finds when they try to live, the reality of the needs that we sense, of the acts that we accomplish to satisfy them; and this idealism that pushes every one of us to conceive of a harmony between these needs, a liberty in these acts, an incessant growth of the physical and moral plans of our individuality.

Such is our individualism, which is very neatly differentiated from "individumania" and petty egoism. It is the philosophy that pushes us precisely to fight not only for the amelioration of our particular sort, but also for the perfectioning and embellishing of the life of all of mankind. We have a conception of the individual who lets a personality neither slither down a spiral staircase nor get lost above the clouds.

We love to see the individual live, enjoy, and think sanely; we want him to work and produce fruitfully. We also do not isolate it and we do not neuter it. The individual finds an extension of its own originality in sympathy and cooperation, as well as the increase of its well-being and a condition to its freedom. The individual needs others to act like it needs air to breathe.

In theory it would thus be superb to open the gates of the heart, of the mind and of the house, genuinely, to all those who want to take all they need with us and from us.

"We are all brethren—brethren in anarchy . . ."

And, going off this principle, the following is the practice of our environments with more than fifty years of experience.

Absolute confidence. To the first, come. Take my *tutoiement* and the intimacy of my life and the secret of our struggles.[61] "Come into my place, share my roof, my bed, examine my writing, you are my brother because you have told me so. It's been only a day or an hour that I have known you. That does not matter. You are a comrade."

Admirable naivety. The freshness of the anarchist soul. It is quite enjoyable to let one go down the current of this pure source. . . . *Hélas! Hélas!* On its way, the water grows poisonous and every being trying to drink it on its path will endure its bitterness and noxiousness.

We are living in times of horrible struggles and infernal violence. Egoisms are confined. The parties of authority organize themselves. They take up arms. They use trickery. Their ambushes are multiplying.

A "good comrade" of twenty-four hours can have the "nerve" to undermine in five minutes of slander the work of long months of efforts accomplished by the militants.

The "companion" whom you have welcomed in your home, with open arms, will leave your household in ruins and will bring letters that you haven't even read to the police prefecture.

And when you will have been scorned, insulted, and beaten by the politicians of the right or the left, by the hawkers of the king or by the bolshevists, by the people of Mr. Daudet or Mr. Treint, you will find yourself all but alone, or truly alone. So many good friends of such easygoing discussions will leave you in the dirt at the moment of solidary action.

But nonetheless, we need to defend ourselves. We need to hedge our bets. We need to get organized.

---

Know yourself. Yes. That is the first tenet of the good anarchist. It hasn't changed since Socrates.

But that is not enough. You also need to know the people with whom you associate, the ones with whom you march. You could be sure of yourself, most harmonious, very wise, and very strong. Of what use would that be to you if you were alone amid a gang of menacing adversaries or associated with traitors? To die good, to end heroically. It's something, but it is not much nonetheless. That cannot be all that we want. We prefer living well over dying well. And to live well it is necessary to fight. We must look for our own. We need to get organized.

———••———

To stay an anarchist, to affirm the anarchy, to let our anarchist ideal triumph in our life, we need to grow capable to destroy the menacing organism of authority. We need to start by being capable to "stand firm" against the forces of authority. We need to be able to defend our anarchist existence against the fascists of the right and the left.

For that, sociologically, the operation is the same as its physiological pendant is.

To know oneself, to truly be oneself, one needs to *choose* within oneself the ideas and the sentiments, the passions and the acts that are worthy of an individual who loves the harmonious life and the noble thoughts. All that affirms in us images and sensations, instincts and wills and concepts, is not good for our individuality. I need to execute a careful selection if I do not want to be the prey of or misled by forces that constrain my well-being and my freedom, if I want to remain an anarchist.

Accordingly, if I want to efficiently act within society, I need to know and observe the people with whom I march with the same carefulness. We cannot give ourselves to anyone, blindly confide ourselves to the first-come so-called friend. We need to choose.

It is the reasoned choice of the companions of a common fight that constitutes the organization of anarchists.

The first matter is to know what should be *practically* realized together. There needs to be an agreement of the means of the defensive and the offensive strategy against common enemies, and on this general plan of action that excludes no particular ideal, the true clusters of combat need to be organized.

What does mine or your concept, or his particular concept on this or the next problem of psychology or morals matter? It is our affair, all of us. It is necessary, before anything else, to know each other as living individuals, as men of action.

Let's mutually know what we are capable of. That is important. The knowledge of our active value, that is what will bring us confidence in ourselves. That is the only thing that will give our anarchist movement its irresistible force of impulsion.

But to attain these goals there is but one means: give clarity in our rapports and coordinate our efforts. Let's, among revolutionary anarchists, organize ourselves strongly.

### NOTES

1.  From *poilu*, "hairy," which was used as a slang word for French soldiers during the World War I.
2.  A derogatory slang term or slur directed at Germans, similar to the English pejorative term "Kraut."
3.  This refers to the famous golden Louis coin, here metaphorically used to signify the finances of the French state.
4.  Colomer in fact had deserted from military service in 1906.
5.  A *bicorne* is the traditional hat worn by the French metropolitan police force of the time.
6.  My dear Egyptian friend Zaki Scandar, who was assassinated in Egypt on the twentieth of December 1915 by a gunshot fired by one of those mysterious hands who are valued by the criminal hypocrisy of the English government. —A. C.
7.  The 1914 Caillaux affair began when the right-wing newspaper *Le Figaro* started running a violent press campaign against Joseph Caillaux, then the minister of finances of the left-leaning Parti Radical. Caillaux's recently married wife Henriette was a major target of this campaign, as she had been his mistress while Caillaux was still married to his first wife. When the director of *Figaro*, Gaston Calemette, finally published intimate letters between Henriette and Joseph, Henriette procured a gun and made to its head offices, where she shot and killed Calmette. A highly mediatized trial ensued in which Henriette Caillaux was charged with "voluntary and premeditated homicide." Her lawyer pleaded that this was a crime of passion and heavily played on gender stereotypes to try to convince the all-male jury. In what was a major surprise, judge and jury acquitted Henriette of all charges, and she left with a blank record. Of course, Joseph Caillaux's vast political relations were said to have played a major role in the trial, furthering the controversy surrounding the couple before the affair died down with the start of the war mere days after the trial's conclusion. See Florence Monteil, "Grand procès: L'affaire Caillaux—coups de feu au *Figaro*," *Notre temps*, January 6, 2022, https://www.notretemps.com/loisirs/histoire/grand-proces-affaire-henriette-caillaux -coups-de-feu-figaro-50697.
8.  The pages were written in 1915. When Almereyda was alive he was in fashion. He was even the man of the day, the great man of tomorrow. I regret that the events have not permitted me to publish then what I have not ceased to believe today. Because a man dies, he does not acquire some purification aura in my eyes. And, by the way, I am relatively sure that Miguel will resurrect. He has disciples who will rise him from his tomb. In the fourth Social Republic, Miguel Almereyda will be beatified. —A. C.
9.  This is another reference to the then popular pseudoscience of phrenology.

10. *Rastaquouère* is twentieth-century French slang for a badly dressed clown, eccentric person, and the like.

11. Gustave Hervé, who before the war was a renowned socialist, ran the Jeunes Gardes and was perhaps the most radical antimilitarist in France. By now he had turned his socialism into national socialism and had campaigned in favor of the war. Accordingly, his paper *La guerre sociale* was renamed *La victoire* in 1916. See Gilles Heuré, *Gustave Hervé: Itinéraire d'un provocateur* (Paris: L'Espace de l'Histoire La Découverte, 1997), 9–10.

12. This actually happened, albeit rhetorically: Hervé, in 1901, during his antimilitarist days, had written an article about the Battle of Wagram, in which the point was that to celebrate it the only reasonable act was to plant the tricolored flag in the regiment's manure heap. This caused a minor scandal, and Hervé became known as "the man of the flag in the manure," especially in the nationalist press. See Heuré, *Gustave Hervé*, 10.

13. This quite absurdist passage is Colomer's commentary on what happened next for Hervé and Almereyda. After having spent twenty months in prison for their antimilitarist publishing, Hervé was released in July 1912. This is when "the man of the flag in the manure" started slowly shifting toward his eventual position of fascism, which Colomer allegorically retells with the cleaning of the flag. Almereyda was then, still, a close companion of Hervé. See Paulo Emilio Salles Gomes, *Jean Vigo* (Berkeley: University of California Press, 1971), 17–18.

14. This is a reference to the unpublished satirical work by Gustave Flaubert. Bouvard and Pécuchet are two blundering copy clerks who come into some money and to pass time start working their way through just about every field of intellectual stimulation, only to eventually decide to become copy clerks again.

15. "Fachoda" refers to the Fashoda Incident, an event during the imperial territorial disputes between Britain and France in East Africa. A war scare, it was the height of the 1898 crisis between the two countries that is considered to have ended in a British diplomatic victory.

16. "Modest Albion" is a reference to the term "Perfidious Albion," which is a pejorative phrase used within the context of diplomacy to refer to dubious acts by British governments in their pursuit of self-interest. See H. D. Schmidt, "The Idea and Slogan of 'Perfidious Albion,'" *Journal of the History of Ideas* 14, no. 4 (1953): 604–16.

17. It is important to note that by saying "the Germans," "the French," "the English," I exclude from that all individualities who have managed to distance themselves strongly enough from their people to no longer adopt its qualities. Leibniz, Kant, Schopenhauer, and Nietzsche are philosophers, while Wundt, Weber, etc. are German philosophers. Analogously, Marcel Prévost and Lavedan are French writers. Han Ryner is a writer. —A. C.

18. A *gibus* is a collapsible hat, also called an opera hat.

19. The Catherine Palace, identified by its location at Tsarskoye Selo, twenty miles south of Saint Petersburg.

20. A 1908 play by Georges Feydeau. In the second act, furniture is secretly moved around by manipulation of thin strings, so that the countess is convinced that it is haunted by ghosts.

21. The Fédération des Bourses du Travail was one of the first syndicalist organizations in France, founded in 1892 and most closely connected to the influential activist Fernand Pelloutier.

22. In the early 1920s, *Le libertaire* featured a column entitled "Libre discussion," or "Free Discussion," in which readers were invited to chime in on relevant current debates within the anarchist scene. This article by Colomer is, as he points out here, a reply to one of these reader submissions. The submission in question, published anonymously, is an eloquent critique that opens up the metaphor of the belly and the mind to single out a number of perceived shortcomings, particularly when it comes to Colomer's idealism. The central complaint of the reader is that Colomer is all mind, with his beautiful ideas of the arts, but without enough of an understanding of the practical side of anarchism. For example, Colomer is criticized as being "high up above the vulgarities of ordinary existences, throning among the muses." See *Le libertaire* 162 (February 24, 1922), 3.

23. Another reference to the famous work of Agathon, published in 1913.

24. *Human* is to be read as in *humane* here. This implies a moralized notion of humanity or humanism.

25. Psychodore, the cynic philosopher, is the main character of the *Travels of Psychodore* (1903), one of Ryner's most famous books. A "Diomedes" is less obviously present in Ryner's written work. Perhaps Colomer instead meant to refer to Diogenes here, who features in two of Ryner's publications, both entitled *Father Diogenes*.

26. This is the same imagery used earlier in the article, the metaphor of the chain of ideas that can link itself to sensation, thereby ruining its purity.

27. Surely a reference to the concept wholeness/unity/ownness, as coined by Max Stirner in *The Ego and Its Own*.

28. Specifically, the influence of German psychology.

29. The identity of Père Olivier is not obviously decipherable. It is likely that Colomer refers to a preacher who was locally famous at the time and would have been known by the intended readership of this article. In *A Wanderer in Paris*, Edward Verrall Lucas describes a preacher by the name of "Père Olivier" praying in Notre Dame on Good Friday of 1871, when soldiers stormed the cathedral. Perhaps this Père Olivier is the same one referred to here. The Collège de France, meanwhile, is much more famous: It is the prestigious, free, and publicly open university in the heart of Paris.

30. The *Action française* being a far-right monarchist journal, Colomer here makes the link between workerist politician Gustave Monmousseau and the reactionary forces of the day when it comes to their philosophical modus operandi. Interestingly, he finds it necessary to go out of his way to remove the positivist Auguste Comte from this link.

31. *Charnier* is French for "potter's field" or "paupers' grave." A *champignon de charnier* is thus a mushroom growing on the mass grave. In connection to World War I, the symbolism of this allegory is clear: Colomer refers to people who profited from the war and made their fortune during, in, or because of it.

32. This does not refer to the revolutionary Nikolai Kibalchich (1853–1881), but to Victor Serge (1890–1947), who used Kibalchich as a pen name. It is interesting that Colomer criticizes Serge here. A fellow poet and anarchist, Serge joined the Bolsheviks after visiting Russia in 1919, a change of heart that was not unlike Colomer's development

about ten years later, late in his life. When Colomer wrote these lines in 1922, anarchists considered Serge a traitor.

33. In French, this passage could both read as Balzac's creating this new world and Balzac's creating himself by way of creating his fictional universe.

34. This passage hints at Colomer's gradual move from radical individualism to syndicalism.

35. Master of dance, *maître à danser*, is a play on words on master of thoughts, or *maître à penser*. This speaks to Colomer's philosophy of enjoying life and sensation (illustrated by the imagery of dancing or sports) as much as or even more than thinking.

36. This is a reference to the English economist Thomas Robert Malthus (1766–1834).

37. *L'anarchie* would grow to be perhaps the most important anarchist publication of its day, in which Colomer also published a couple of articles.

38. Slang for *café chantant*, a kind of popular bar or club of the time that had a reputation for being the home of and enabling low pleasures.

39. *Apaches*, as noted earlier, are Parisian gangsters.

40. For more on this view, holding that masters and slaves are really both slaves of each other's, see "Reflections on Nietzsche and Anarchy."

41. The "dancing" referred to here is a euphemistic description of the following eventful moments or places related to the Bonnot gang: the robbery of the Société Générale at Rue Ordener; the attack on an office of the same bank in Chantilly; the prison of Poissy where gang members Bélonie, Charles Bill, and de Fleury were held and/or executed; the violent carjacking in Melun; the siege of Nogent-sur-Marne; the shootout at Choisy-le-Roi.

42. The *bascule* is the headrest at the base of a guillotine.

43. This article was produced as a written statement arising from a heated exchange between Colomer and the Italian anarchist icon Errico Malatesta. Malatesta, one of the most famous activists of the era, spoke at an anarchist conference in Saint-Imier, when an angered Colomer interrupted him from the audience and questioned some of the expressed views on the nature of revolution and the use of money. Both were then invited to publish written accounts of their side of the debate, which were printed side by side in *Le libertaire* 281.

44. Colomer here refers to the famous peasant bands that the revolutionary Nestor Makhno organized during and after the Russian Revolution. For more on these so-called *Makhnovshchina*, which attempted to establish a free territory in Ukraine and fought both against the Red and the White armies, see Antony Beevor, *Russia: Revolution and Civil War, 1917–1921* (Viking, 2022).

45. *Prise de tas* is the process of assembling all available goods and letting individuals take what is needed for each of them. This is an informal way of redistribution that would in theory work without the use of money.

46. The Rue de Valoise is the home of the French Ministry of Culture.

47. Hébert's method, also called the natural method or Hébertism, is a method of physical training that carries some relevance even to this day. Providing exercises to school in physical, mental and ethical behavior, the method became very popular in interwar France. See Pierre Philippe-Meden, "Georges Hébert et l'esthétique de la nature," in *Le*

*collège d'athlètes de Reims: Institution pionnière et foyer de diffusion de la méthode naturelle en France et à l'étranger,* ed. T. Froissart and J. Saint-Martin (Reims: Éditions et Presses Universitaires de Reims, 2014), 261–79.

48.    A leading anti-Dreyfusian during the famous Dreyfus affair, Henry was shown to have forged evidence and to have lied in court. The anti-Dreyfusards hailed him as a hero.

49.    Mr. le Vicomte is an overly formal title used to address someone. A *petit crevé*, meanwhile, is a slang term describing a small, weak, and effeminate young man. The type of the *petit crevé* was fashionable in the nineteenth century.

50.    A *genet*, or broom, is a delicate flower common in the south of France.

51.    The Collège, founded in 1913 in Reims, served as the basis of Hébertism in France. While Colomer ridicules it here, the college would train some of the premier international athletes of its day. See Philippe-Meden, "Georges Hébert et l'esthétique de la nature."

52.    For "moribund" Colomer uses the word *morticoles,* which is almost certainly a joking reference to a novel of that name written by Leon Daudet, an important nationalist writer and personal enemy of Colomer.

53.    *Guiboles* is an archaic French word meaning something like "huge legs."

54.    In fact, the war started but months after Jaurès's assassination on July 31, 1914.

55.    In the language of French revolutionary movements, Colomer here refers to fake activism that only existed for purposes of virtue signaling.

56.    This, of course, is very close to the Marxist interpretation of the French Revolution. We can assume Colomer was familiar with it, especially given the context of this passage appearing after a critique of Jean Jaures. In France, Jaures's *Histoire socialiste* was one of the major works involved in developing and arguing for this reading of the revolution. See Geoffrey Ellis, "The 'Marxist Interpretation' of the French Revolution," *English Historical Review* 93, no. 367 (1978): 353–76.

57.    These are references to fancy, expensive, and extravagant clothing of the time.

58.    This refers again to Agathon's famous pamphlet "Les jeunes gens d'aujourd'hui" (The Young People of Today).

59.    This refers to the two most iconic crimes of Villon's and Bonnot's gangs, respectively.

60.    That is, removing pejorative slander about the moralizing entities of his era from his works.

61.    *Tutoiement* is the act of speaking in the French casual tone, using *tu* instead of the formal *vous* that is expected when communicating with strangers.

# PART IV

# *Metaphysics and Idealism (1925–1929)*

## WHAT *L'INSURGÉ* WANTS TO BE

*L'INSURGÉ* 1, NO. 1 (MAY 1925)

*L'insurgé* is published because we are persuaded that there is a space to be filled in the revolutionary press: its place, its very own.

*L'insurgé* thus does not aim to replace any other journal, no more *En dehors* than *Le libertaire*. It is fraternally placed side by side with these two in order to complete, with its personal accords, the anarchist harmony, which needs to remain a good harmony or become one.

We would want all to understand, as we do, that we can work side by side with each other without that meaning that we position ourselves against anyone.

*L'insurgé* will be distinguished from *Le libertaire* by the initial individualism of its philosophy.

Here we can, in the same way that the Action Française inscribes and emphasizes "All that is national is ours," proclaim: "All that is individual is ours."

Before anything else, to want to balance the individual; to look for the conditions of this balance, the moral conditions, the physiological and sociological conditions; to boldly push the studies and the experiences that should permit mankind, the way it is, to realize individualist culture, that is to say to become human personalities worthy of conquering life.

*L'insurgé* will be differentiated from *En dehors* by not being weary of expanding and intensifying its propaganda and its activity onto the terrain of economic life.

As such it will participate in the life of the workers struggling for syndicalism. As such it will partake in revolutionary action.

*L'insurgé* will be with all who stand up to emancipate themselves. It will also be with all who accomplish acts of liberation. Appearing in France, *L'insurgé* will keep track of the situation in France. It will consider it an insurrectional necessity to stand firm with all who are oppressed by the current form of the French state.

Also, *L'insurgé*, in its revolutionary anarchism, will not consider itself to be perpetually obliged, "a priori" and blindly, to stand against the French communists and all of their activities.

The very meticulousness of our philosophical individualism will permit us to precisely forgo the sectarianism that radiates our practical lives.

Most of all, *L'insurgé* will strive to avoid quarrels between personalities and petty controversies among revolutionaries.

Instead it will reserve its pamphletary virulence, its best venom and most acerbic vitriol for the supporters of the bourgeois state that currently oppresses the workers of this country.

In its struggle against fascism, *L'insurgé* professes to add, in this decisive hour, an element of proletarian unity, the possibility to finally form a cluster of all revolutionary forces—in the face of the cluster of brutalities and reactionary hypocrisy.

———◆———

To all who this program interests and who want to subscribe to it—take up the task of supporting *L'insurgé* and of permitting it to regularly live.

This journal appears under the "direction of one man" because experience has shown us that there is no oeuvre of thought that can attain to unity and continuity without a pilot at its rudder. *L'insurgé* knows its path. To those who want to travel alongside it on the route described here, who want to bring aliments to its new furnaces, it is to those whom we address this, to say:

We have no commanders. We have no subventions. Not being the official organ of any party or of any group, we count on our friends, on our readers.

First, subscribe to us. Send, without delay, your twelve francs for the year or your six francs for six months to André Colomer, 259, rue de Charenton, Paris, with the postal check 724-45. With this, you will regularly receive *L'insurgé*.

Finally, participate, to the best of your ability, in the subscription opened from today in our columns entitled: "For the life of *L'insurgé*."

———•———

We have published this first number for the first of May, so that it can reach the workers on this day of antifascist demonstrations, but it will carry the date of Thursday, May 7, 1925.

Our next number will thus come out on Thursday, May 14.

From then on, it will regularly be sold on the Thursday of each week in the kiosks and bookstores of Paris and the suburbs.

For the province, in order to avoid the expensive service of the house Hachette in our early days, we ask our militant comrades to contact our administrator, at 259, rue de Charenton, Paris (12th), in order to organize the sale in each center where *L'insurgé* needs to penetrate the workerist masses.[1]

To the oeuvre, comrades. Let's get to work! *L'insurgé* will live.

## OUR ROAD UNDER THE STARS

*L'INSURGÉ* 1, NO. 22 (OCTOBER 1925)

At *L'insurgé*, we know our way: we are guided by the stars in our idealist sky—and no obstacle of human malevolence could ever deter us from it.

We are confident in the individual, the cell of every creation, the base of every realization—we might very well come across a few individual ugly faces, but that does not inhibit us from staying individualists. The deformations of the individual will not throw us into the claws of the social: we know that beings are only hideous precisely because they lack personality, because they renounce the individual at the hands of the all-powerful collective. And disgust of the effects of the monster will not blindly surrender us to the monster itself.

Adversaries of governmental authority, sworn enemies of every state, nothing can dissolve our anarchism: it is but the logical consequence of our individualism—our reaction against everything that opposes itself to the harmonious blossoming of the human flower. Our anarchism is not a party; it is the expression of our vitality, the instrument of our will to affirm the individual.

Thus, what do we care about the judgments, the injustices, or the insults of the politicians who pretend to understand the ideas of anarchism and to discipline the anarchists? ... We do not care any more about them than we do the Christian chatter of the preachers of the Catholic Church, when they excommunicate or anathematize lovers in the name of the idea of love.... And it is us who will remain here, us anarchists, against these officials, these officers of so called anarchy.

As revolutionaries, we will recommend, appreciate, and reinforce every action—whatever it is—that might serve to disintegrate the power of our masters. We will stand side by side with the forces that are the most violently destructive against the current social state—whatever their intentions for the future might be.

And we will judge, for example, that the Communist Party, with its practical methods of proletarian struggle, is currently the largest common dissolvent of the French nation, the bourgeois state in France, and French capitalism.

So their insults against us matter little! It is not because that boisterous donkey of a Monmousseau haunts us with his hostile and incoherent "hee-hawing" that we will sulk against the actions of the CGTU and ignore the admirable campaigns of the committee of action against the war in Morocco.[2]

The CGTU is not only Monmousseau. It understands that thousands of workers are animated by a true revolutionary spirit. It is the most important faction of the workerist front of this country—the most muscular, the most capable of violence. And the Communist Party possesses extraordinary forces of youthful heroism in its core.

Further, we here at *L'insurgé* will always be ready to unconditionally support the movement of general strikes advocated for by the Committee of Action, no matter what might be done to put us off it.

---

Nothing will stop us on our parallel march: individualist culture and revolutionary action. Nothing—neither the grimaces of those who want to mimic the individual, nor the contortions of those who ridicule the revolution, neither the spits of the ones, nor the quips of the others.

And we will tirelessly pursue our road under the most beautiful of stars: the ones that each of us can light in the infinite sky of his conscience.

## MATTER, MIND, AND ME

*L'INSURGÉ* 1, NO. 10 (JULY 1925)

*Live like I feel.*
*Think like I live.*

What is the genesis of the individual through facts and ideas, these two means of its realization?

A.—First the people were hindered by objects (realities). They had not yet brought order to nature: and they were even scared of it. It was, for them, the unknown. They respected it and turned it into the divine. They considered nature a tyrant.

These were the natural religions: (1) "higher" objects, (2) holy animals, (3) forces of nature (sea, thunder, etc . . .), (4) personalized forces (Zeus, Neptune, etc . . .)

These are still today, through entire populations, the natural superstitions (broken mirrors, crossed knives, spilled salt, etc . . .)

Next people organized the realities to free themselves from them. They dominated nature by submitting it to laws. Thus science was constituted.

B.—Next the people were hindered by ideas (God, the Fatherland, Humanity, Law, Justice, etc . . .)

They still are at this stage. They are full and well under the domination of these ideas. The world of the mind is full of unknowns for them.

That they free themselves of ideas as they freed themselves of realities, that they force them into an order—and only then the individual will no longer shiver from any fear, from any adherence, or under any yoke. He who is free would be able to serve himself of the ideal like he does of the real—for the sake of his love, and the joy of being himself. And this way I, as well, within these ideas organized for my commodity (reason), could choose like I can among the order of facts (science)—for my individual enjoyment—what suits me.

---

At the origin of being is a sort of nebula that freely transects mind and matter. It is a slave of two liberties: the liberty of matter and the liberty of mind.

Then, it becomes aware of matter:

1.  It loves it, it deifies it.
2.  It criticizes it (that is to say, experiences it and touches it).
3.  It orders and organizes it.
4.  It knows it.

Only then the being begins to become, to figure out its mind. It believes in its "spiritual soul."

Finally it becomes aware of the mind. It becomes conscious of it through the same slow evolution that was once necessary to gain knowledge of the material world.

1.  It loves the mind and deifies it.
2.  It criticizes it (that is to say, it experiments).
3.  It orders and organizes it.
4.  It knows it.

Then it can serve itself of the mind like it can of matter. It freed itself from one like it did from the other. The being has externalized both of them. This is the hour in which it becomes aware of the "I."

The being is now personalized, particularized. Within it the individualist is liberated from the enslavement of the two ancient gods: mind and matter—Nature and Reason.

It seized its means. The "I" can exercise itself in all its power, in all its harmony.

The one who equally overcomes the ideas and the facts—and who, a victor, claims *his* loot from among the facts and the ideas—and who raises his "I" on this double conquest—that is the one whom I call the *individualist hero.*


## MATTER, MIND, AND ME 2

L'INSURGÉ 1, NO. 11 (JULY 1925)

---

*Live like I feel.*
*Think like I live.*

---

When it comes to the bodies (matter), most people of today, advanced in their knowledge of chemistry and of physics, find it completely *natural* to not ask any questions of *why* to their subjects, but a simple *how* when it comes to individual usage.

For example, I use disinfectant—but how? I do not drink it, because that is bad for me. I put it on a wound, because that is good for me.

When it comes to ideas—everything is different for most people. The cult of ideas is so powerful on the contemporary consciousness that even the ones among us who consider themselves most individualized catch themselves falling victim to it.

As such, even I, in "At the Sources of Heroic Individualism 2: Art, Anarchy, and the Christian Soul," have hesitated for a long time before refusing to accord an intrinsic value to certain ideas. I was back then an idealist to the detriment of my life: I gave freedom to the ideas instead of giving it to myself.

But today I broke all absolutes that apply to ideas. I no longer ask myself any metaphysical "*why*" about them that I do not ask myself about a metaphysical *why* when it comes to the body.

Take this example: The idea of the fatherland. I do not utilize it. It is bad for me. Why? Because I do not utilize it. And that's that. In the same way as wine or tobacco. They are bad for me because I do not consider it in my personal interest to utilize them.

The fatherland, God, the state, the society, human love, etc . . . are spiritual poison to me, as arsenic or strychnine are bodily poisons.

But, they will answer me, we are able to measure out certain dosages of arsenic or strychnine to turn them into remedies. . . . That's right! There may also be certain dosages of the fatherland, of God, of humanity, etc . . . of which I could, exceptionally, serve myself as I do with remedies, in some cases. But I am their only organizer, the only prescriber. I alone can judge the circumstances and the dosages that suit me.

For the idea of the fatherland, for instance, I can consider a certain idea of the place where I was born, where I grew up, etc . . . but I make this idea mine by having it. This idea ties me only to myself, and not at all to the idea itself or to other individuals who use, in *their way*, the same idea.

I am the master of my ideas. I am their tyrant.

When every individual positions himself as egoistically before the entirety of the facts and the entirety of the ideas, he will be the judge of the world; he will be his own judge. He will be a master, his master. He will be free.

EXAMPLE:

What is the king for me?

An idea which I do not utilize.

—But, they will say, there is an X . . . king of. . . . and he exists.

Yes, that is: *a man + an idea*. And, as I deny the idea, only a man remains.

—But this man serves himself of this idea . . .[3]

Then, if you prefer that, it is a man holding, within himself, an idea that I deny—it's a man who thinks he is a king. And I, who do not believe in kings, consider this man like I do any other fool who thinks he is Saturn or Neptune—and evidently, this man would be in a mental hospital instead of in the palace if he were the only one to believe that he was the king.

—But there are subjects who also believe that he is king.

Yet more than that, it is his subjects who make him king. So what? This has no more importance for me than if, in the courtyard of an asylum, a superb fool proclaims himself king and a dozen other fools around him fall to their knees and proclaim him king, too.

Instead of twelve, it is twelve million. Instead of the courtyard of an asylum, it is a nation. I am weary of these fools—and, if they assault me, I defend myself.

———❖———

There exists a societal ideality that corresponds to a societal reality like there is my individual ideality that corresponds to my individual reality.

And all that I can say about that is that—within me—I feel that my individual ideality lives in opposition and in contrast with this societal ideality, like my individual reality does with societal reality.

To affirm my individuality, I deny my societality. When everyone will let their individual ideality and their individual reality live within them, there will no longer be a societal reality or a societal ideality.

God and his different forms (fatherland, state, humanity)—the government and its different forms (prince, king, republic, socialism, communism) exist as long as there is a collectivity that believes in them. But when everyone will have killed them *within themselves* to let their personality (ideal and real) bloom, it would be impossible for there to be a God or a government.

Likewise, the crowd and faith are equivalences of one same ugliness for the individual—and against the individual.

The crowds are a realization of faith.

Faith is an idealization of the crowd.

All crowds are religious.

All faith is proselytizing (that is today, tending to create a crowd).

Kill faith and you will have killed the crowd.

## MATTER, MIND, AND ME 3

*L'Insurgé* 1, No. 12 (July 1925)

> *Live like I feel.*
> *Think like I live.*

—Ideas are chained together in the world of ideas.

—Yes, like things are in the world of things.

So what? That does not mean that I have to chain myself to the ideas any more than I have to chain myself to things.

I do not belong to them. I refuse to yield myself to them.

And yet, to be myself, I am the one who appropriates them, I am the one who uses their enchainment for my own sake, for my own creation—and this appropriation that I enact over the things and the ideas, this uniqueness according to which I particularize my possession of the goods of "this world" and of "the other world" that is *my Intuition*.

There are thus two conditional currents to my life.

1. A current of my sensible life: matter
2. A current of my intellectual life: mind

To put practical order into my life I accord laws to each of those two currents. But in both of them I take according to my individuality. This personal choice, this subjective appreciation of what pleases me, of what is according to my harmony, that is what I call *my Intuition*.

There are facts, and then there are ideas.

Both present themselves to me, externally, according to the laws of *universal determinism* (causality and associationism). As such they are nothing to me.

But both the ones and the others I can take up, I can enjoy, and I can make mine according to the rhythm of my *individual intuition*.

If I direct myself toward the source of one or the other of these external currents—toward the spiritual infinite or toward the material infinite—I stray further from my own source, and I deny me to myself.

To affirm myself I have to not give myself anymore to the current of mind than to the current of matter, but I need to instead give both of them to myself, in order to be at the center of myself—united in my particularity.

My unity is my life.

It is to liberate myself—me as a unique and without laws—that I free myself from the thing by exteriorizing them and by according them a world and a law. It is by generalizing and regularizing them that I particularize myself exclusively.

The same applies to the ideas. It is true for rational logics as well as for experimental sciences: I enact a practical order that I make a condition of my life in order to better recognize myself in my ownness, removing science from being my conditions.

As a matter of fact, if I utilize things as I do ideas, I am myself more than experience and more than reason. I am not general but special. I feel my ideas, like my things, in their relation to me—irreducible, exclusive—like nobody senses them. Things and ideas become mine. From the moment on where they are *my* facts, *my* ideas, I render them unique; I render them special by the way they affect me. They enter into *my* music, and *my* play has nothing in common with your play, nor with anyone else's.

This is what Stirner calls uniqueness and what Bergson called intuition.

———————————◆◆———————————

My sensation—(a piece of) practical information[4] + and affection.

Likewise:

My idea—practical information + an affection

We can integrate practical information into a science. But affection is unique. It is I, and only I, who can understand it. It is my art.

Thus physical science is not the science of the sensations—but the science of all information is entailed in the sensations.

Similarly, a science of ideas cannot be a science of my ideas.

Both can be useful to me—but they do not encompass me. I do not belong to them. They can provide for me. They are my property. It is I who encompass science. I make it depend on me.

Of all that is but a practical mean to me, I consent that it might be turned into a human science. As such, I free myself of it in order to triumph of it. The establishment and ordering of my "praxis" is a commodity for my "poiesis."

And as such, the ideas of my knowledge can find their science, just as the objects of my sensing experience can. That is to say, they will be susceptible of research methods to perfect these methods—to classifications and practical laws on their successions, as the facts of nature are. My intelligence is, like my nature, but a means of my being.

But my cause and my end: me, that is what only I can "know"—or rather resent, by living it.

And on me alone depend my *affectivity* and my *will*. That is unique. It is my criterion, my "poesis." There cannot be any scientific method there. It is my art.

## MATTER, MIND, AND ME 4

*L'INSURGÉ* 1, NO. 13 (AUGUST 1925)

> *Live like I feel.*
> *Think like I live.*

Everyone recognizes affectivity in the sensations, the sentiments, passions, etc . . . But very few recognize affectivity in the ideas—or they do only to condemn it.

This is because almost everybody wants ideas to be in the domain of reason, that they remain general, and that affectivity (a condition for the individual, for the particular) won't come to "trouble them." They want to deny the individual property of ideas.

Eh! Well, meanwhile the ideas are never *pure ideas*, except in the desiccated mind of the theologians and in philosophy. Ideas affect me—and it is this "affection" that makes them mine.

An idea that does not affect me is a stranger to me. It can dominate me. I do not possess it. On the contrary, if an idea affects me, I can take possession of it, give it a part in my music—and make it a condition of my harmony.

———•——

The physical sciences are nothing but a history of experiences of my sensitivity: a history of facts. It is all of which I have liberated myself from—all my sensorial past out of which I realized *my matter.*

Similarly, a psychic science cannot be anything but a history of the experiences of my intelligence: a history of my ideas—as they were conceived modified, up until me. It is all of which I have liberated myself from, all that is henceforth extended, convened, finished, fixed—all my spiritual past: *my memory.*

Now, how do you want me to be a part of what has left me—caused by what is caused by me? How would you want the individual to assimilate with a fact for a sociological science, the individual who contains all facts and all ideas within him and who only lets them be externalized for his own commodity—according to his order, when he has lived them?

———•——

An idea thus has no worth within itself. It only *is* in relation to my usage of it. It *is* in function of my needs. It is born, it lives, and it dies for me and through me.

It won't even be thought anymore if nobody would use it—when nobody would need it.

But isn't it the same with a body? Yes, exactly the same. A body *is* only in relation to my usage of it. It will no longer be perceived when nobody will use it anymore; when it won't be useful to anyone, when nobody would need it anymore, it would have no reason to be. It won't be anymore. Every man, by abandoning it, will have contributed to eradicating it.

These ideas and facts are for me in relations of relativity. They are only the diverse measures of my diverse needs—and it is I who is at the center of my needs, the mental like the physical, the material like the spiritual.

In the same way, when we discover new matter (electricity, radium, etc . . .) we lose expired and used-up matter.

There certainly are matters that have disappeared, because they no longer corresponded to the needs of the human body; they have disappeared from the range of our perception. Now, as only our perception can give us reality, we can say that they have disappeared. They no longer exist. We have eradicated them.

There are also matters that, without our being aware of it yet (because evolution is so slow), tend toward their disappearance. We are destroying them—within ourselves—because our needs for them extinguish a little more with every passing day. On the other hand, there are some that new needs will create. Our young needs will end up spawning new matters. We will say that we discovered them. It is better to say: we invented them, we created them—or we created them for us.

It would be interesting to write a *History of Matter* in order to see how the bodies, all bodies, are born and die—and how they are born, and how they die. This would only be possible by studying, in parallel, the needs of men—and then we would see . . .

The same, absolutely the same, is true for the ideas—their birth, their death. We create them and then eradicate them based on our needs. Let us write a *History of the Mind*, according to an analogue method as we used for the *History of Matter*: the findings would be curious and quite instructive.

## MATTER, MIND, AND ME 5

*L'INSURGÉ* 1, NO. 15 (AUGUST 1925)

---

> *Live like I feel.*
> *Think like I live.*

---

What is the order of the material world? How do we divide up the bodies of the external world?

The order of the material world is nothing else but the order of our sensations. We divide the bodies of the external world along the model of divisions of our own body.

The order of the world is a painting of our fixed needs. It is the sum of our physiological conventions. It is the entire past of our corporal life—all that I have once sensed.

The same is true for the order of the spiritual world: reason.

Reason is all the past of our spiritual life, all that has been thought before me, that is all that I have finished thinking about.

Because *I*, me, is all that is the present and all of the future. I am becoming.

———◆———

The people who are obedient to matter, like the ones who are obedient to the mind, are slaves of their past. They immobilize themselves in a part of what they once were.

The ones who submit themselves to the laws of matter and to the laws of the mind immobilize themselves in the totality of what they have been. They are like adults who continue to act and think like toddlers.

The individualist knows that matter and mind are only the past. He uses them, he experiments with them—but as he would with instruments that he uses at his own convenience, because he has created them.

He is the creator who does not want to surrender, in order to be able to continue his creation—because *he is only what he creates*, that is to say, he creates himself. He *is* in proportion to his autocreation.

———◆———

As is true for induction (in the physical world), it is not successive experiences that created physical laws, but it is the idea of the physical law in the researcher's mind that makes him invent experiments that should find evidence for the physical law. It is the same for intuition (in the psychological world), where it is not successive experiences (ideas) that create psychological laws (consciousness) but the idea of the psychological (individual illusion) that necessitates experiences that should realize a personality.

———◆———

So here is a double problem to resolve: What is the action of the intuitive "I":

1.  for the methods of experimental physics—for induction?
2.  for the methods of experimental spirituality—for the association of ideas?

And we manage to show, in one case like the other, that egoistic needs should be given priority, and so the need of a choice, an individual synthesis, and the aposteriority of the general analysis.

A. *For induction*:

1.  One fact, two facts—as many facts as we would want—won't tell me anything new to establish a law, if I do not have an idea of what to look for within me.
2.  This idea I have in me, because it corresponds to my current need—I *need* this law for my practical life.
3.  Thus I take this fact + this fact + this fact, etc . . . and I create a law with the facts of which I provoked the succession in order to serve and content me.[5]

B. *For the association of ideas and deduction*:

1. An idea has no true inherent value. It has not any existing reason to be more closely associated with an idea than with any other—and it carries no principle of opposition or accord to any other idea within itself. Ideas that are added or juxtaposed with one another do not lead to a sum. They are only idea A+ idea B+ idea C, etc . . . without there being a possibility to calculate a total.

But I am me, and the idea N pleases me. Immediately I want it, and I call up within me all the ideas that I want and that I already collected—in order to take the idea N up within me too, among all the ideas that are already there. I order *my* ideas to make idea N my own.

Thus, idea A+ idea B+ Idea C+ idea D+ etc . . . + idea N are counted up in me and, thanks to myself, they can form a sum that is equal to my own sum. Because the addition is then presented as such:

Idea A + me
Idea B + me
Idea C + me
etc . . .
+
Idea N + me

———

Me.

Thus I assimilated myself by way of the ideas. I made them all mine. And I made them all me. I ate them. And it is absolutely like how corporal alimentation also works:

Body A + me
Body B + me
Body C + me
etc . . .

———

Me.

On the contrary, let's consider that idea N does not please me. Then I call up all ideas within me to refute it. And if they refute it, it is because I do not like it—because it displeases me.

I am at the center of my law, the God of all my laws.

## MATTER, MIND, AND ME 6

*L'Insurgé* 1, NO. 16 (AUGUST 1925)

> *Live like I feel.*
> *Think like I live.*

When I say:

A = B
B = C
thus
C = A

Then, in reality, I have started off by *seizing* (*introducing*) a certain resemblance between A and C—and my deductive reasoning only came up a posteriori, in order to support my intuition.

I accorded myself some reasons. But it would have been impossible for me to pass from A to C, through whatever intermediary there might be, if I did not already compare A and C, if I did not already intuitively trace a path from A to C–or rather if I had not, *in a singular act*, united A and C.

Afterward I practically established, in technical terms, in conventional terms, *in terms of the past*, of reasonable experience, with fixed intermediary points, only a demonstrative itinerary.

I have written an indicator–but beforehand I already knew the land very well. I have demonstrated–because I needed to. I wanted to.

By making a deduction I created a weapon for myself–in order to defend my will, and to prove it. A demonstration has some hostility to it. It's an imposition, a taking of goods, weapon in hand.

---

My power = me (my force) + the realities.

My will = me (my force) + the ideas.

To be myself:

1. I harmonize my power by individualizing–*id est*–by taking possession of the realities, in function of my original affection (my unique).
2. I harmonize my will by individualizing–*id est*–by taking possession of the ideas, in function of my original affection (my unique).
3. I harmonize the harmony of my power with the harmony of my will, and vice versa, in order to enjoy my harmony–or rather I incessantly tend to this harmonization.

This way it's I who sometimes sacrifices my power to my will, sometimes my will to my power, in order to never sacrifice *myself*. That is my art, my music, and I am the only one to know its specific secret.

Meanwhile I can reveal you that I could not tell you exactly if I can what I want or if I want what I can. Sometimes one thing is true. Sometimes another is. I also endeavor to intensely expand the power and will within myself. Because the more I can and the more I want–that means that I can and want more. This is the eternal parallelism: the one of my functions.

---

In sum, the individualist can call himself all-powerful. Can he not do all that he wants—he who can be "*himself*" and who wants nothing but that?

Of all the ideas, he only seizes the ones that enrich his power. Of all real facts, he only takes the ones that enrich his will.

Both when it comes to events and thoughts he does not even think about stopping their universal courses or about modifying their hypothetical ends. He does not accord absolute value to them—not to the ones, nor to the others. He only considers them in relation to his *I*. They are, to him, but relative conditions, and subjective illusions.

Thus, what can he be by willing, and what does he want by being able to—except to enjoy both for the harmony of his individual affection, except for personalizing them, to individually illusion himself, and to create music with them? To create his music, his most intense and most symphonic and most original music of uniqueness.

The individualist is much more powerful than all the all-powerful mighty and all the religions. He did not create the world: he creates it for himself, in every instant of his life—that is today, an infinite number of times. He is the creator of the becoming and a unique creator without a cult, without a preacher and without infidels.

## MATTER, MIND, AND ME 7

*L'INSURGÉ* 1, NO. 17 (AUGUST 1925)

---

*Live like I feel.*
*Think like I live.*

---

What are the realities upon which I can rely? The ones that I appropriated—the ones that I took from the collective, from the general public—the ones that I individualized and particularized. It is by dispossessing the collective that I created myself as an owner.

*And the same is true for my ideas.*

When it comes to those that I left to the collective, I am only familiar with them in order to defend myself from them. But *I can* even with respects to them, because *I can* fight against them and my struggle against them is all that *I want* from them. By rejecting them, I am affirming myself; by destroying them, I am creating myself.

Among the examples that are given for an *adaptation to one's environment*—it is never the adaptation of an individual to an environment, but the adaptation of his body to his environment: that is today, to be more concise, the adaptation of his physiological environment to his physical environment. Because the body is, as well, one of the environments of my self.

Now in some cases I adapt my physiological environment (the body) to my physical environment (nature). In other cases, the opposite is true, and I work to adapt my physical environment (nature) to my physiological environment (the body)—and that according to my own needs, following the needs of my individual creation.

Thus, in any case, I always adapt the environment to me, because the environment, *every environment*, only exists in function of my usage of it. The environment is all of which I serve myself. And that is why my mind (reason, consciousness, psyche) is also a part of my environment—something that I am adapting for myself.

All the sensations that I reject through the intermediary that is my body are *kaka* (as in the Greek κακά, *bad* things) to me.

Everything that does not delight one of my senses: what I refuse to assimilate through my organs—what I do not devour, what does not enrich me, what I reject, what is but waste to my uptaking of good materials (be it in my digestive, respiratory, auditive, sexual, etc . . . activity)—what I refuse, all that is against my harmonious, sensible functioning—thus, against my harmony—all of that I call, simply, excrement: shit.

Eh! Well, I will end up showing that the same is true for our ideal functioning, for our spiritual life.

When it comes to me, I already *feel* it—oh! Yes, I *feel* it—there exists psychic shit.

These are the ideas that I repel, that I reject from my spirit, with my spirit! The ones that do not assimilate to my spiritual life, the ones that cannot bring their note to my symphony. Let them rot away outside the borders of my functioning, of my composition, of my music.

The social men—they—reject nothing. They swallow everything and assimilate everything. They nourish themselves with "kaka."

It is because they are assimilated to everything. They are themselves "kaka." Yes, please do not be dissatisfied by this, but they are, spiritually like materially, shit—traditional shit.

They are all that they are made to be.

And who are "they"?!

Thus, I am not surprised that their life is but a cacophony.


## MATTER, MIND, AND ME 8

L'INSURGÉ 1, NO. 21 (SEPTEMBER 1925)

---

*Live like I feel.*
*Think like I live.*

---

The *fantaisiste* is at the mercy of events.[6] He listens only to his senses, his instincts, his caprices.

The philosopher is at the mercy of ideas. He listens only to his reflections, his thoughts, his mind, and his wisdoms.

I am neither a fantaisiste nor a philosopher. I am an individualist; the ideas and the facts of nature are at my mercy.

---

The beings who only act for the satisfaction of a single joy ("high" or low, sensual or spiritual)—and whom you condemn with the term "egoist"—are not egoists, but quite the opposite: they are slaves.

The "I" entails an infinite amount of needs. I am an egoist when I satisfy them all and when I am harmonious. Then I am happy in my harmony.

The one who satisfies only his sexual needs, to the detriment of all other needs of his I—he is not an egoist, because he does not own himself: he is the slave of his sexuality.

The same goes for the one who only satisfies his need to think. The "intellectual" is a slave—a slave of his intelligence. Thus, he can be a slave of God, of reason, of love, of science, etc . . .

I juggle all my means to find my end, which is *me*—intensively me, totally and harmoniously. I am an egoist.

I am heroically myself—when I create harmony among my actions.

Given the parallelism of my means (matter and mind), and that there is a particular affection that corresponds to my every sensation like to my every idea—then, when the affection of the sensation is *in accord*, in harmony, with the affection of the corresponding idea in the parallelism—I feel my hero, and then I am heroically individualistic. On the contrary, when the affection of a sensation is in disaccord with that of the corresponding idea, there is a diminution of me, a depression, a degradation. And vice versa for an idea.

Take this example: I receive or I take, as a client, the services of a prostitute I meet. Her touches might provoke, with their sensations, a very agreeable affection, but sooner or later this affection will become unbearable and disgusting to me—because, in parallel, an idea awakes within me: the idea that this woman that caresses me is a stranger whom I do not love—and that in just a few moments she may be touching the body of a random old man or drunkard.[7]

So a disaccord is within me—a disharmony, an impression of decay.

On the contrary: I receive caresses from my loved one. The affection-sensation marries with the affection-idea that I am being caressed by the one I love, and who loves me, and with whom I'm tied through true ties of uniqueness. The affection-sensation is intensified by the affection-idea and vice versa.

So a perfect accord is created, a harmony. An impression of elevation, of heroism.

We can also field examples when talking about ideas: The idea of beauty, of anarchy—or, better yet, particular ideas.

The ideas that satisfy me are those of which my affection is in accord with the affection of a sensation or of a group of sensations that correspond in the parallelism.

It is the ideas that I consume—my ideas—the ones of which I serve myself.

---

*My every power is in my accord, in my individual harmony.*

When I feel myself one, I feel myself free. And I feel myself one when I feel myself entirely and in accord with myself.

My experiences and my meditations are, for me, like the tentative operations of a violinist who tunes the strings of his instrument.

Once I am in accord, I look for nothing further, I perceive nothing more, I know nothing more. I enjoy myself and I delight in my own accord: I am a free musician, a poet.

## MATTER, MIND, AND ME 9

L'INSURGÉ 1, NO. 22 (NOVEMBER 1925)

---

*Live like I feel.*
*Think like I live.*

---

*Yes, I Want to Be the Master*

The social who call themselves masters usurp this title. They do not know what it means to be a master. What do they do?

They own slaves, or servants, or soldiers, or laborers.

Do they possess these men? *No*: they merely possess machines—because they treat these men as if they weren't men. They possess them the way they possess their dogs, their horses, their houses, their fields, their vegetables, their fruit, their weapons, their machines, their gold.

They are not their masters, because they do not possess their sensibility, or their intelligence, or their will.

To be masters they would need to be able to know the sensibility, the intelligence, and the will of each one of those men, and they would have to enjoy those.

That is what I do—and hence, I am a master.

I do not conquer, and I do not possess a flower like I do a vegetable—or a dog like a flower, or a dog like a man. I differentiate my goods, and thus I can enjoy them, I can possess them—by being a master.

Only the men who present themselves before me as plants or as rocks, without will or sensibility, those I treat like stones or plants. But I do always look for sensibility and will in a man—and, if I find it, to get a hold of this man, to enjoy him, I keep this will and this sensitivity in mind.

I am the master of those whom I conquer—but that does not make them my slaves. I do not impose a law over them. I am not stupid enough to subdue them, because that would mean subduing myself. By making them my slaves, I would make myself their slave, too.

On the contrary, I tell you:

I strive to make you my goods—to enjoy your being, to be the master. Do the same: conquer me, explore my will and my sensitivity, and you could grab a hold of my being and enjoy it—and you will be a master like I am a master.

Yes, be masters as strongly as you can. And me, a master, I will enjoy that, too—because I hate leveling, equality, submission, laws: I love the struggle, competition, and I know that a rose does not have to fear another rose next to it. Both stay unique.

Yes, struggle for your life, for your personality. Intensively search for your mastery. I am not afraid of your ambition.

It is not your pride, my brother, that worries me—but your slavish humility.

Ah! A beautiful life would be a stay in the kingdom of slaveless masters!

## MATTER, MIND, AND ME 10

*L'INSURGÉ* 1, NO. 23 (NOVEMBER 1925)

> *Live like I feel.*
> *Think like I live.*

### Idealism and Realism

I do not belong to the ideal any more than I do to the real. I create for myself my ideal. I create for myself my reality. That is my own ideal: it belongs to me. This is my own real: it belongs to me. I create one and the other in order to consume them, day after day.

My real is my accomplished being, or my being in the process of being accomplished.

What was my ideal yesterday becomes my real today. My ideal is a powerful force forward. If I were to renounce my ideal, I would no longer have my real, but *a* real. What I would possess, I would not have wanted, I would not have *had* the idea for (that is to say, I would not have made the idea mine—I would not have been individually affected by its idea). That real would be imposed on me.

Would it be possible to settle on my being of this very moment, if it wants nothing more, if it tends to nothing anymore. . . . If I immobilized myself in the accomplished, then I am nothing but an accomplished thing, I am inert, I am unable to feel—because feeling is but satisfying a tendency. Sensation is nothing without a becoming.

But on the other hand, if I do not enjoy my real, how could I claim my ideal? If I do not satisfy myself by what I have managed to possess, what force could I have to continue to want and to struggle for the chance for new conquests? It is the enjoyment of my real that incites me to pursue my ideal.

Thus the individualist who wants to enjoy his being is not to deny facts nor ideas. By making a fact his fact—he eats it. By making an idea his idea, he excites his appetite. But what is of importance to him is to not starve to death of a lack of facts nor of a lack of ideas. He sacrifices himself neither to a reality nor to an ideality. His present life is his good—he takes it, but "he won't rest on his laurels." He goes, he becomes. He creates himself. He idealizes himself.

Meanwhile, when he muses about tomorrow, it is to push his act there, it is in order to enrich his enjoyment of today with all his wills, with all his desires, with his "dreams."

While the "idealists" live their dreams, he, the individualist, lives of his dream. He realizes his ideal—in the same way as he idealizes his reality. He does not paralyze himself in the hope of a paradise for tomorrow. With his act in the present, he creates his future.

He lives integrally. Yesterday, today, tomorrow converge in his individuality in order to aliment him. But he is the subject—no, the sovereign!—that harmonizes them in order to create his unique being out of them.

His unity—that is his end.

## THAT IS ANARCHY!

*L'INSURGÉ* 1, NO. 28 (NOVEMBER 1925)

All official forces are skillfully maneuvered to halt the march of truth.

The mechanism of the state is meticulously aligned so that all the cogs of deception function with great certainty.

Our poor little *Insurgé* has, because it tried to denounce the scheming of the police forces, found itself being systematically boycotted last week by an administration of posts that are penetrated and terrorized by political policing.

Three-quarters of our subscribers have not received this last edition of their journal, this edition that was so dangerous for the tranquility of these assassins who are the public officials. And who knows in what proportion, in what state and on what date our depositaries in the provinces will receive their packages of the journals!

Despite everything, whether good or bad, our heroic publication has touched its public. Our cry of light has nonetheless broken through the stinking mist. Thousands of men have been able to learn in what truly anarchist state of mind we have stood before the Court d'Assises, how we have denounced the police frame-ups there, why we have exposed the horrible face of that mustached Le Flaoutter in clear daylight.

It was not only about Philippe Daudet but about all the young people with audacious minds and restless hearts who are at risk, like him, of falling into the bloody ambushes of the political police.

It was not enough for us to unmask the librarian who doubled as a police informant; we wanted to go to the source of this provocation: up to the public officials who certainly had to have guided his sleazy operations for a long time, and who knew how to direct him like they knew how to supply him with revolvers.

Thus we reached the crux of this police crime. We were a threat to collapse the monument of treachery, of espionage, of deceptions, of political compromising and greed under which the revolutionary movements in France agonize.

Halt! They need now to cut off our hands, to shatter our kidneys.

All means will be employed to halt us: we know that, but we are READY FOR EVERYTHING.

But the public, it is now also warned. And not only the people who read *L'insurgé* but all those who have followed the debates around the case of Bajot-Daudet, transformed now into the case of the political police. Almost all papers have had to print our declarations in front of the Assises. And if we fall—whatever hand might deal the blow—everybody will know who the assassin was, namely, once more, the political police.

* * *

"Nothing new this week. The mystery thickens more and more."

Come on now! There are silences and inactivities that are worth more than the most astounding admissions.

The uniformly stuttering tone of all these policemen—of high or low stature—from the top dogs among the public officials to the dogs of the commissioners, it enlightens us about the value of their testimonies.

There exists, among all these entities who serve the hideous 'State Reasoning," something like a freemasonry of assassination. They will not risk to "sit at a table," like those poor zany *apaches* who are being cooked alive in the questioning rooms. Not only are they in liberty, but they are the ones who continue to utilize their means to fabricate official virtues and to traffic the crime of which they live. This scum thinks it is omnipotent. It keeps the preachers of the Republic on a leash. Ministers, deputies, big industrials, directors of journals, people of finance and bankers tremble under the threat of the police. The officer holds the financier, and he holds power. He does not need to "sit at the table": he is force-fed. His silence is golden.

* * *

Two men have dared this week to affront the anger of the police in order to talk according to their own conscience—and they are two politicians: Edmond du Mesnil, director of the *Rappel*, and Pierre Bertrant, chief editor of the *Quotidien*.

M. du Mesnil dared to say:

> Once again, I have read everything, with great attention, all that has been said for or against a suicide. I tell you my opinion as the one of an honest man: I do not believe it was a suicide.

M. Pierre Bertrand has courageously issued a précis:

> Imagine if we knew nothing of the death of Philippe Daudet, nothing, apart
> for that it happened on the day of his death, at four in the afternoon and in
> the residence of a man of dubious morals, then imagine that on the same eve-
> ning, this man had a vision and that the next morning we would have learned
> that, truly, the young Daudet had passed in the way presented by the halluci-
> nation, what would you think?
>
> I do not believe in hallucinations. The police in general do not believe in
> it, and neither do the judges.
>
> I accuse nobody by name, but I say and I repeat that, in any scenario, Le
> Flaoutter, by his plotting before—and his silence after the facts, is to be held
> responsible for the spilled blood of Phillipe Daudet.

While these two republicans with rare independent minds spoke their gen-
erous voices against the police assassination of the son of a royalist leader, my
anarchist heart beat harder than ever within me, and the next morning I read
in the *Action Française* these extraordinary lines to open an article by Léon
Daudet:

> There is no nobler emotion than to see men, writers of the daily political
> struggle, overcome their fight and embrace the cause of an adversary simply
> for the sake of justice and humanity.

This simple worry of justice and humanity that, for a sublime moment, O Léon
Daudet, O Pierre Bertrant, O Edmond de Mesnil—but for a single moment,
*Hélas!*—made us forge the struggles of politics, to pile you against the courts and
the police state, is what animates us incessantly to fight without fear against all
forms of societal authority that does not cease to, with its arbitrary rules and its
institutional rigidities, restrain, in the flesh and the mind of men, this justice and
this humanity.

And this worry that does not leave us, that torments our life, that complicates
our human relations, that turns us to poverty and into rebels, that puts us at odds
with the cops and the army, that familiarizes us with the face of Judas-Le-Flaoutter
and that lets us instead ascend, with a crown of thorns, into a role of martyrdom—
this worry that illuminates us, that is our anarchy!

## NOTES

1. Hachette was already a large and influential publishing group in 1925. Part of its conglomerate was the Messageries Hachette, which specialized in printing and distributing journals. Of course, using this state-of-the-art system would have been unaffordable for a radical startup journal like *L'insurgé*.

2. Gaston Monmousseau (1883–1960) was a prominent member of the French Communist Party who would go on to take prestigious office as deputy of the Seine in the 1930s.

3. By the way, this man does not only necessarily serve himself of this idea—he serves this idea. He is possessed by this idea. He is no longer himself. He is the king. —A. C.

4. It would be better yet to say "technical information" or information for my human technique. That is the minimum that I leave to the collective, or rather to my rapports with the collective. —A. C.

5. An example might look like this: take, for instance, ordering practical facts in order of their utility to the task of generating heat. If an individual needs fire to survive, he or she will look for burnable material and experiment to find the best material and the best setup for a fire, thereby creating a science and laws of fire. These would never have existed if not for the need for heat.

6. French for an artist or writer who only obeys his fantasy, the word *fantaisiste* is also applied derogatorily to people who do not follow any customs, or who cannot act "serious" in the wider sense of the word.

7. A stranger to my ideas, to my personality, to everything that gives me sense in life. —A. C.

# Two Eulogies

## LET'S SPEAK ABOUT ANDRÉ COLOMER

*LA REVUE ANARCHISTE* 17 (FEBRUARY 1932)

In this journal, where I desire to stay in the shadows as much as possible, I have never put my real name under an article.

But today I will act differently because it is necessary to take responsibility, and a big responsibility, because the moment calls to speak, in an *anarchist* journal—that is read and commented on by *anarchists*,[1] of which many are sectarians—and to speak in all sympathy of a *former anarchist* who rallied over to become a communist. To speak of André Colomer, who has just died, still a very young man, in Russia.

I will explain why I think I need to grant such a large space here to this former comrade.

It is partially for personal reasons: I was intimately tied to him, and I think I would fail to respect the most elementary "task" of friendship if I associated myself with those who are silent about him, by not helping you get to know this strange figure, this curious individuality, a bit better.

But it is mostly because Colomer was, during his era, one of the greatest heroes of the anarchist movement. I believe that he has sufficiently contributed to our ideas—be it in *La foire aux chimères*, in *L'action d'art*, in *Le libertaire*, or in *L'insurgé*—that his name should have its place in an anarchist publication.

Finally, let us not forget that Colomer was the chief editor of the *Revue anarchiste*, published in 1923-24, and that this title alone should suffice for those who care about the new editions of the *Revue anarchiste* to remember his memory for a long time.

The anarchists, most of them ashamed, stay quiet; the communists do so as well—now that he is of no further use to the party.

He belonged to those who always knew not to let those who had a "temperament" be stuck in the shadows.

Whether an anarchist or a communist, André Colomer was always, and before anything else, a *poet*, an *artist*, and it is as such that we see him here. These titles, together with his enthusiastic southern nature, will largely explain his abrupt changes in his positions: he went from the fiercest individualism (read *A nous deux, Patrie!*) to the most organized anarcho-communism (didn't he advocate the foundation of anarchist blocks during the anarchist congress of 1924?) by wandering through syndicalism . . . only to finally end up backing the purest Marxism, after having nonetheless been an unrelenting enemy of the bolshevists.

It is quite possible that he would have been, sooner rather than later, excommunicated from the Communist Party for the independence of his mind—intellectual anarchism is a blemish that is hard to get rid of. He would then have gone wherever his enthusiasm of the moment would have taken him!

I remember, in that regard, one of the last visits that I paid him—because I stayed on very good terms with him, even after his "conversion."

Back then I avoided addressing questions concerning our different conceptions so that—knowing our temperaments—we wouldn't get angry by derailing the discussion. Nonetheless, we ended up talking about the topic of sincerity. "Evidently," I told him, "I consider yourself very sincere at the moment; I think that you are a very sincere communist. Also, if tomorrow you would become a royalist, I would not consider you to be any less sincere a royalist."

Well inclined as he was that evening, he took the joke and laughed loudly, and it was his wife, the good Madeleine, who assaulted me with a cascade of reproaches—because she loved and defended him, her André.

I had the lucky opportunity to listen to him for an entire night—the first one after his return from Russia—where he confided in me the impressions of what he had "seen" there. Never seeing a glass half full nor empty, naturally everything was wonderful. That did not hinder him from indicating to me that one had to differentiate between the Russian and the French bolshevists.

I had nothing a priori against the USSR, but not being as enthusiastic as he was and the warmth of his recital not managing to overcome my skepticism, he proposed to organize all that was necessary for me to undertake a trip to Russia—which I refused, as I was only going to accept a trip to the USSR on certain conditions and if I could freely choose all my companions.

I have to add that, despite my efforts, it was impossible for me, the circumstances being unfavorable, to have him discuss privately with Voline, which would have been much preferable to those public and tumultuous encounters that have unchained the passions of the supporters.

I never approved of the comrades of *Le libertaire* who so violently attacked him in the moment of his adhesion to communism. I did not approve any more of the unjust and brutal responses that he had published in *L'humanité*. There had been exaggerations on both sides, and, in a special letter, I had addressed him my point of view in this matter.

Obviously I very well understand the great deception of the many young comrades that Colomer brought up to anarchism . . . and who no longer understand him! But let's not go as far as to talk of the "Moscow gold." It was as such that, in Savingny, they searched every corner for that Moscow gold—just as was done before in Juvisy or in the Rue de Charenton—just to find the necessary money to cook up some meals and to buy medicine. And, returning from having spoken in favor of communism, the former anarchist orator writhed in pain, haunted by his ailment.

Sincere, yes, I have always and fundamentally believed that he was sincere. He lived according to his formula, "the sincerity of the moment." That was also, by the way, the opinion of Sébastien Faure, who, being more comprehensive than many of his comrades, wrote in the *Trait d'union libertaire*:

Colomer is a poet, a sentimental, a lyricist, an imaginative, a romantic, a man of theater, an author, a dramatist. As such, he is easily impressionable.

Officially welcomed in Russia as a member of the French delegation to the ceremonious celebrations of the tenth anniversary of the Revolution of October 1917, it ended up being impossible for him to conclude a serious assessment of this immense country of which he did not speak the language. He could not assess the material and moral conditions of existence that are imposed by the bolshevist regime upon the Russian working class, even less so to the rural population. He only had the chance to see what they had an interest in showing him; he only heard what they wanted him to hear.

He was a witness to monstrous processions, to grandiose rejoicing in which populations of all countries on earth will participate with enthusiasm, to knowledgeably organized ceremonies, parades and galas, to meticulously prepared visits to factories, schools, and museums.

In short, they have—so to say—overwhelmed him with impressions. And what could have easily been predicted to happen: he let himself naively be grasped by this skillfully arranged and combined number of spectacles, of costumes, of decorations, of scenarios that were specifically made to take a hold of an artist's imagination like his.

I thus have no single serious reason to suspect his sincerity.

I know it is customary, when a man leaves a party, an organization, a group, or an opposed party, to instantly skin him of all his merits, of all his qualities, of all the talents that one would have praised in prodigality only a day before.

I cannot overcome myself to consider him—suddenly and without proof—as a sellout, a cretin, an idiot, and a hypocrite solely because he changed his affiliation. Not he who I have known for a rather long time, against whom I have fought, and of which, whenever we then fought together, I have had the chance to appreciate and love the selflessness, the intelligence, the culture, and the sincerity."

And many share this view.

There is a lot more to be said about André Colomer, the revolutionary poet. Let's leave it to our writer Ganz-Allein to conduct the careful analysis that is necessary.

The ones who have known, appreciated, and loved him know that his memory will stay alive with certain, among whom we are, a memory of Colomer who had his defects but who was open-minded as much as he was enthusiastic.

And too bad for those who were his enemies simply because they were green in envy of the poet, the orator, the artist; it was simple for him, albeit involuntarily, to render them jealous: he had talent!

Fernand Fortin

## ANDRÉ COLOMER: APOSTLE OF THE "ACTION OF THE ARTS," OR THE ILLUSION OF LYRICAL INDIVIDUALISM

*LA REVUE ANARCHISTE* 17 (FEBRUARY 1932)

A biography, a necrography, has didactic value only if it is approached like an experiment in a laboratory, in a *human* laboratory, where the scientist, the researcher, armed with his tools of analysis, examines the open and transparent destinies, dissects them, and looks for the laws of the science of the human and the cells of his happiness . . .

I will try to complete this work of moral anatomy over the case of the effusive life and thoughts of André Colomer, the Pyrenean poet roaming through social and political action.

One could not understand André Colomer, who has just died of a devouring cancer at forty-five years old, in Russia, one could understand neither his momentous drive nor his blazing contradictions, nor his passionate embodiments if one were to neglect the fact that while many content themselves with being poets on paper, he always was one, himself, *physically*, in his blood, in his life, in the blood of his life, in the skin of his life. And his destiny demonstrates that a lyrical life is compatible with our crushed society only if it is dreamed along in eremitic fashion, if it is bathed in solitude.

Gérard de Lacaze-Duthiers, who was his childhood friend, and Roger Dévigne, who was his comrade at the lycée Louis-le-Grand and who founded with him, in 1907, *La foire aux chimères*, have characterized him as a "visionary" poet.

How was Colomer visionary? How did this ideological and sentimental conception conform to and fill up his life?

He explained it himself. "Having vision," he wrote, "to be a visionary, is indubitably more than just seeing, it's seeing as one *wants to see*. The true artists are egoists, but their egoism superbly thrives in the things and the individuals. . . . Proudly, we proclaim ourselves to be fleshly. The flesh, matter of movement, unceasing manufacturer of all incidents of the world, the flesh, molded by prestigious fingers, by reality, and itself moving to create in its own right."

If you study this phrase, if you analyze it and discern it, it will provide you with the key to the thoughts of this man that I have known, that I have loved in all of his variations. These variations which were, in effect, only *visions* for him, that is to say certain single-minded states that, in the moments where they dominated his mental and sentimental life, abolished the preceding states by that very fact.

We can regret that with respect for the unity of his life; but it would be as unfair to rigorously hold him by that as it would be to reproach to certain plants that they won't grow in the Parisian climate. You'd have to put them in a greenhouse. André Colomer put himself in the warm greenhouse of his sensations and of his impulses.

Schopenhauer wrote one day that we are crammed into our conscience as we are in our skin. Colomer *apparently* managed to change his conscience as some beings manage to shed their skin. But he kept his vital, mental unity that was, quite exactly, his visionary lyricism, his need to live lyrically. It would be irrational to reproach the evolution of his ideological states to this visionary, if you never thought to reproach him his long black hair or his swarthy skin that were, just like his ideas, normal secretions of his being. He was not a dogmatist. He was impulsive. One cannot use, to catch him in contradictions, a logical system that did not interest this distraught sentimental in the slightest.

To put it precisely, André Colomer comported himself with respect to ideas like a lover who is tense with desires does before the warm and tender body of his coveted woman. He frantically desired them *in the moment*, he satisfied himself within them, he looked for himself through them, *he lived himself* through them.

When, at twenty-one years old, he published his first verses in *La foire aux chimères* or in the *Actes de poètes*, when he subsequently founded *L'action d'art*, adhered to syndicalism, collaborated in *Le libertaire*, created *L'insurgé*, wrote the *Cochonnerie sanglante* or the *Gueuseries héroïques*, and finally was attracted by the colossal Russian universe that he perceived not sociologically but lyrically, Colomer has always stayed a man of the "action of the arts," and by defining this conception of life you will define his destiny.

The action of the arts was for him to assimilate his daily destiny to a work of art, the fact of living life as if one were writing a poem.

"The truly realized word of art," he wrote "is the one that gives the people the richest sensations, the most gasping joy, the most irresistible desire to live and to create. To reply to this will of the people, the artist was to realize a double prodigy of enthusiastic sensibility and of creative will . . ."

"It only takes a single *drive of enthusiasm* and of love to break the old idols of the people."

"Man will want to feel the push of all good life saps with ardor (similar to the most beautiful tree of the world), drawing from the natural forces all the elements of his terrestrial happiness, infinitely hear the powerful roots that tie him to matter. Man will make his art out of his thought and the blazing flowers of his harmonious vegetation."

And, continuing what he thought was a doctrine but was actually but a confession, but a graphic reveal of his entire being, Colomer added:

"I have seen that beauty and truth *are only sentiments* where the people express their joy to collect in nature, in bouquets of memories, landscapes, phenomena and discoveries that, since their childhood, have nourished their will and illuminated their hearts, to give them the power of life.... We love life exactly because it changes, because it takes elusive forms, because it permits our mind to *indefinitely modify itself.*"

That is the aesthetic philosophy of Colomer. And this is what clears up his social attitudes and his doctrinal variations.

"We do not see the need of our ways of life having to be universally recognized for them to be true. We no longer want to establish perfect 'ethics' nor 'demonstrations of correct morals'; we want to make mankind happy. It suffices, to believe in the value of a revolution or of a social reorganization, that it will content the generations of our era. We are modern and utilitarian. We merely joke about whether our works crumble or collapse in a thousand years, as long as their construction has succeeded in making us happy, us and those whom we love."

I have said earlier that Colomer was incapable of these cold virtues that develop only in the solitude of the mind and the body. Listen to another of these revealing confessions:

"On one moonless evening in the mountains, I have experienced the horror of immense nothingness. The sun had plunged the mountaintops into deep red during long hours of sundown; I had seen the valleys be engulfed into deep chasms of silent shadows ... and I asked myself whether you had ever ascended to tops of faraway mountains where one quickly feels the inextricable, instinctive, bestial anguish of solitude invade and overwhelm you? ... "

Are the character of this man and his life now clearer, for those who understand the sense of these so suggestive citations?

Exaltation of pure sensation and of sentiments, exaltation of *emotional states*, that is to say of those states where reason is always subservient to the fantasy of the moment. "Beauty," that is to say the sensual aspect of the real and "Truth," that is to say its intellectual aspect, were, for Colomer, but sentiments, that is to say accidents of sensibility. They were "states of the soul," to quote the formulation of Amiel, or transient states, somewhat animalistic states perhaps, if we admit that our brethren the animals do not have, as we do, the gift to synthesize their emotional states into concepts.

In other terms, the work and the life of André Colomer, the casual and contradictory way in which he burned in the morning what he had loved in the evening, are explainable for this hopelessly sincere man, who splendidly managed to strip himself of everything, if we are ready to understand that he undertook any action as if he were writing a poem, that he lived in a "lyrical state" and that he took, in good faith, for doctrines what were just emotions dressed by his rich eloquence and animated by his faith in himself.

"I have too often nourished myself with cheap food," admitted a melancholic, aging Tartarin when looking from the tower of Beaucaire onto the bourgeois microcosm that he had to leave behind.

If it had been gifted to the poet, to the revolutionary André Colomer, to become an old man, he perhaps would have consented to whisper the same melancholic admission. And I think that the objective explanation that I give of his essentially emotional character can permit those who judge him with anger to rectify their judgment with serenity and to tell themselves that this great enthusiast has always acted in accordance with his nature, has always been sincere with himself.

Thus, with attentive and comprehensive sympathy, I bend myself over the mute shadow of the one for whom life was but a shining and sonorous podium. As on the "billiard table" of a clinic, I extended his mental body to look for the fibers, the ligaments, and the cells of his thought.[2]

André Colomer, to speak frankly, has never been an anarchist, a syndicalist, or a communist. He was, with effusive and lyrical plentitude, what he called "visionary," that is to say: *himself*, that is to say, "Colomer," that is to say, a lyrical individualist.

But from the philosophical standpoint there are two individuals here: his *psychological* individual, reasoning, philosophical (similar to the one of an Epictetus, of a Marcus Aurelius, of a Stirner, of a Nietzsche); and a *carnal* individual sensible, sentimental, a type of egoistic blossoming of all impulsions of a being, subjected to all variations and contradictions of sensibility, a physical individualism, like the one of the plants, the animals, or small children.

The work and the doctrine of Colomer, so narrowly conditioned by the impulsions of his blood and his nerves, have coated this sumptuously and passionately oratory character that the southern people voluntarily take for sincerity.

To nuance and circumscribe his life, it can be said that he lived by releasing the throbbing foliage off of his impulsions. He has always been sincere, because the sentimental nature of his volatile states excluded the control of cold logics that this vibrant and passionate being did not want or need. That is why those who have known him well loved him even when they condemned him. And that is also why those who believed his successive sincerities will maintain some bitterness toward him.

However, this loyal and good being never disappointed or cheated anyone but himself. And his veritable intellectual fatherland was always, in his heart, the one of anarchist individualism. I ask that those who have known him execute, on his life and his destiny, this examination of conscience that I have tried; without a doubt, he has never truly done them wrong either, because what interested him was not to know but to *feel*. And thus they will honor their old comrade with the duty of indulgence, which is the cold virtue of reasonable beings. They will repeat, with different elements, this study in which I committed myself to stay objective, as if I had just dissected, on the aperture of my microscope, the organs of a butterfly or of a firefly.

And you will understand then, unknown comrades, that I have loved Colomer, because I saw him as he was, while those among you who judge him with rigor see him only not as he was but as he occasionally imagined himself to be. And you will remember that he died poor, rich only in his illusion, his visions, and his songs.

Ganz-Allein

### NOTES

1. It is evident that I give this word the sense of *anarchizing*, because, personally, I do not think that "pure" anarchists exist and I am even mistrusting of those who label themselves as such. —Fernand Fortin

2. "Billiard table" is a slang term used to describe the large operating table used in hospitals.

## A Colomerian Dictionary

**Affirm**        Colomer often speaks of affirming one's personality, one's ideal, and so on. Effectively, this can mean to act in a way as to materialize or "live out" such rather abstract notions, but it can also mean to claim them or to live toward them in thoughts. It is a bit of a catchall word that Colomer uses to describe pursuing whatever idea or act is being discussed. When in doubt, I recommend reading it close to the English words "confirm" or "endorse."

**Artist**        In addition to the ordinary meaning of "artist," Colomer often uses the term to refer to someone with a certain outlook on life. Specifically, in Colomer's wider conception, an artist is any person with a creative force driving their own individuality. This can manifest in a myriad of ways, both physical and mental: Their life is their art as much as their work is. One could thus, on the Colomerian account of anarchist aesthetics and lyrical individualism, be an artist (of one's own life) without ever producing a "work of art": "I mean to say by 'artist' those who put the high and harmonious expression of their individuality above everything, the ones who prefer to create their oeuvre sincerely, according to their intuition, according to their ideal, and to affront the ridicule or the indifference of the public rather than prostituting themselves for glory!"[1]

**Bande**        I have chosen to not translate Colomer's notion of *bande* but to keep the French word in the English text. The literal translation for *bande* would yield something like "band" or "gang," both of which describe Colomer's conception of the word fairly well but also invite other implications. Colomer's *bande* can very well mean a criminal or illegal grouping, as it does when he refers to Bonnot's or Villon's *bande*, but it is also a core concept of his productive social philosophy. While rejecting any type of society or social grouping, Colomer does believe that humans need a community and cannot healthily exist or develop as hermits. The idea of the *bande* solves the ensuing problem of seeing the need for social ties but rejecting all existing societal systems. One could say that it is an attempt to solve a similar problem that Max Stirner sought to solve with his "Union of Egoists." However, while Stirner's unions are driven by practical matters and the need to organize them, Colomer's *bande* is driven by the individual sympathy between its members. In fact, Colomer himself describes the *bande* as "the community of intuitive sympathies." A *bande* is then a group of individuals that socially thrive on each other and enjoy each other's presence, and thus spend (some of) their lives together. It is important to note that for this, the members of the *bande* do not need to share the same opinions, lifestyles, or even (meta)ethical views. In fact, Colomer even seems to tend toward the opposite, suggesting that radically different personalities can enrich each other more, as long as they all are, in their own way, heroic.

**Beauty**    Like every aesthetician or poet of his era, Colomer has his own conception of beauty. He further believes that the concept of beauty is translucent, almost indefinable, and defies universal explanation. Thereby, he refutes the Baudelarian idea of beauty.[2] He instead allows that each person will have their own notions about what is beautiful, which form that individual's principle of action: "And precisely because the sentiment of beauty is the least fixated, the least rational, the least settled, the most variable of human sentiments I choose it as the basis of my philosophy, as the principle of my action."[3]

**Believing in oneself**

Far from a cliché phrase, believing in oneself is a core conception of Colomer's lyrical individualism. A person with this self-belief will see himself "not like society constrained him to stay, but like his consciousness, his individual ideal, make him dream to be."[4] The act of believing in oneself is thus a constant process of individual revolt against societal constraints of all kinds, in which the individual tenaciously clings to and pursues its very own ideal.

**Blossoming, hatching**

Colomer employs metaphors like "blossoming" or "hatching" to illustrate the evolution or completion of an individual who finds his or her uniqueness. A blossoming personality is thus a personality that is emerging from former social constructs that hindered it, finally shining in individual beauty, like a flower that blossoms after a long winter or a being hatching from the monotony of a bland egg.

**Desolidarizing**

To desolidarize from a social construct means for the individual to cut all ties with this construct, including potential mental restraints hailing from a social education. A desolidarized individual may live within a society, but as an individual who merely endures the society around oneself without feeling part of it. It can be seen as a key first step to the blossoming of a personality.

**Dream**

Colomer, in his articles, often speaks of dreams in phrases such as living one's dream, finding one's dream, and so on. It should be noted that he never refers to the actual dreams one might have at night, or even to fantastical and unrealistic (day)dreams about the future that one might engage in. Instead, a dream for Colomer is a vision of oneself, a reality to chase, somewhat of an individually beautiful goal that an individual should live toward and attempt to enact every day. It is also an internal reality, one that is to be felt and realized independently of the environment that an individual finds itself in. To then live one's dream is to live one's belief in oneself.[5]

| | |
|---|---|
| **Élan** | Throughout the collection I have decided to keep the word *élan* in French instead of going with a near-translation such as momentum, impetus, or force. This is because of the close connection that Colomer's usage of the word has to the Bergsonian notion of *élan vital*, commonly translated into English as "vital impetus," a term Bergson coined in his 1907 work *L'évolution créatrice* to describe a creative developmental tendency inherent in evolution and biological life processes, which is said to manifest itself as a will to form and differentiate. |
| **Egoists** | Egoism is a concept that Colomer borrows from the work of Max Stirner. Contrary to common conception, egoists are not "beings who only act for the satisfaction of a single joy." Instead they are individuals who have recognized that they cannot assume a good that is external of themselves and thus make their own good (or, their own blossoming, Colomer would say) the priority of their philosophy: "The 'I' entails an infinite amount of needs. I am an egoist when I satisfy them all and when I am harmonious. Then I am happy in my harmony."[6] |
| **Harmonious (Harmony)** | Colomer readily uses music as a metaphor for his account of how individuals function. In this metaphor a harmony is the goal to be reached. To be in harmony with oneself means to have all aspects of one's physical and mental being aligned in a way that is best for the individual. An individual psyche in harmony accepts itself while dreaming of its most beautiful self, balances all its natural intuitions and instincts as well as its thoughts and feeling, and lives in well-being, able to chase its personal ideal. |
| **Hero/heroism/ heroic individualist** | To Colomer a hero is not made by fighting on a battlefield or winning some award, but by finding one's individuality in one's harmony. The "hero" in question is the image one has of oneself, in this case, of the best version of oneself that one aims to live like, a personal idol. The idea can best be explained as such: If your life was a theater play of which you are the protagonist, how should the hero be if your |

goal was to create the most beautiful hero you could think of? "Given the parallelism of my means (matter and mind), and that there is a particular affection that corresponds to my every sensation like to my every idea—when the affection of the sensation is in accord, in harmony, with the affection of the corresponding idea in the parallelism—then I feel my hero, and then I am heroically individualistic."[7] "I call a hero: the one who knows how to give himself entirely to his ideal—the one who does not fear of pushing his life until the point of extreme circumstances for what he loves—be it even to death—and what he loves might be anything, a virtue, a woman, life the way it is, or life the way he dreams it to be—or the life that he wants to make it."[8]

**Idealism**   In the many articles he wrote Colomer comes to speak of different types of idealism, be it notions of idealism from the history of philosophy, common social ideals like the ones held by socialists or communists, or nationalistic ideals held by reactionaries. Of course, it is also the word he uses for the individualized ideal, one that he wishes everyone to pursue. For the most concise account of Colomer's idealism and differentiation of his idealism from different brands of idealism, see "At the Sources of Heroic Individualism 5: Social Illusions and Scientific Disillusion" and "At the Sources of Heroic Individualism 6: Individualized Illusion" in this volume.

**Intense**   "Intense" is one of Colomer's favorite adjectives to describe his notion of a blossoming individual. To intensely feel and sense means to be very aware of stimuli, both those that are internal and those that are external to the individual. Given the importance that Colomer accords to feeling and sensing, "intensely feeling" is a particularly meaningful superlative in his work. "Intense" is also used to describe personalities. In this context it is closer to the everyday meaning of the term and designates very outspoken or fiery personalities—something Colomer typically praises in a person.

**Intuition**       The notion of intuition is one in which Colomer was heavily inspired by Henri Bergson. Bergson's notion of intuition, which is well documented elsewhere, can be abbreviated as a personal, subjective way of knowing, which is nonetheless absolutely true to the individual.

**Libertarian**    In early twentieth-century French, *libertaire* had a meaning that was much closer to the current word "anarchist" than to the currently common conception of libertarianism. For instance, one of the mayor radical anarchist papers of the era was simply entitled *Le libertaire*. The reader who comes across the word "libertarian" in the pages of this collection is thus advised not to make the association with contemporary libertarianism.

**Music**           Colomer's articles are full of musical metaphors, some of which are further explained in this section. Apart from that, Colomer often uses constructions such as "to the sound of the Internationale/Marseillaise" when he describes communists or nationalists, respectively. In his usage of the musical allegory, it is safe to say that whenever a reader comes across these or similar constructions, they are not (only) to be read as descriptive statements. For example, it is clear that the people marching to the songs he names are, in their very person, embodiments of these songs and the ideologies they stand as metaphors for instead of being their individual personalities playing to the sound of their own tune.

**Oeuvre**          An individual's oeuvre, which I have kept in French or translated to "works" depending on the context, is the fruit of their labor. Colomer does not differentiate in his choice of words between artistic and manual "oeuvre"— of, say, an artist or of a mechanic or fisherman. Colomer thus uses the term both for practical accomplishments and for artistic accomplishments, but also for ways to live life, similar to his usage of "Artist."

**Refractory**      A refractory, in the widest sense of the word, is someone who resists any given thing. For Colomer this is the best attitude to take in life. The beauty of the word "refractionary" is that it does not imply nor presuppose a collectivity of any sort, which, for instance, "revolutionary" likely would.

**Science**
Colomer employs a very twentieth-century French usage of the word "science." Essentially, everything practical or objective could be united under *les sciences*, the sciences. This is all the truer because of the then-popular positivist movement of scientism, which attempted to explain everything by interpreting physical phenomena. This movement, which in anarchist spheres was closely associated to Kropotkin, found an adversary in Colomer. He wrote: "We are seriously mistaken to turn the sciences into an all-powerful divine force."[9] Further illustrating this broad usage of "Science," Colomer also "understands societal facts to be a part of [the scientific] domain as much as physical or chemical facts."[10] This established scientistic attitude was largely to the detriment of the subjective, which Colomer, again, was a big advocate for. Often "science" can thus also be read as a simple opposite to the psychological, to the spiritual, or to the realm of ideas.

**Soul**
"Soul" is mostly used synonymously with personality or ideal or as imagery to describe intuition. Colomer also uses phrases along the lines of "a person with soul" to compliment someone's character.

**Sport**
Occasionally Colomer uses the imagery of sport similarly to his allegorical use of the word "art." An individual's life, then, is its sport, its great game, a physical experience to be enjoyed. Occasionally the word "play" will be used in a similar capacity, for instance when Colomer speaks of the interplay of individualities. As will become clear in certain passages throughout his articles, the idea of physical health is also of some importance here, further suiting the metaphor of sport.

**State**
Unsurprisingly for the anarchist that he was for most of his life, Colomer was opposed to the state. However his conception of the state can be wider than what is generally understood by the word. While we see usually think about established governments or nations when confronted with the

word "state," Colomer intends the word to be closer to the Latin *status*. That includes "political states" but also, in Colomer's words, every "fixed system, every stop in the forms of life, every authority that was established to obstruct the élan of intuitive expansion, of the free searching of human individuals."

**Stomach/belly**    Colomer often uses the stomach or the belly as imagery for emotional intelligence or even for the more animalistic and instinctual drives of individuals. They are to be contrasted with the mind (or the head, or brain), which signifies rational intelligence. As opposed to most philosophers, Colomer values both of these entities equally and views both as necessary for personal harmony. See his article "The Belly and the Mind" herein for a good breakdown of this.

**Sympathy**    Sympathy is the core element in Colomer's notion of the *bande* (s.v.). It is the feeling that people who fit one another's temperament have toward each other, which does not mean that they are necessarily similar people. More than just liking each other, people with sympathy for one another look out for each other's blossoming with good-will and blossom themselves as they enjoy the presence of sympathetic individuals with matching ideals. Yet they can be in competition; they challenge each other, as true athletes in the sport of life.

**Symphony (symphonic)**    Staying with the musical metaphor, a symphony is a harmonious interplay of factors within an individual. A symphonic personality has reached the highest levels of harmony, in which the many instruments (which stand as symbols for the many elements that make up a person) blend perfectly and add to a whole that is more than the sum of its parts.

**Synthesis**    Synthesis is the process of aligning all aspects of one's personality, temperament, ideals, and so on to create a harmonious symphony. "Making a synthesis" is effectively a process of getting to know oneself, to understand one's intuition, to learn how to balance one's instincts and drives with one's thoughts and actions to create the individual well-being at which much of Colomer's metaphysics aims.

**Temperament**   In eighteenth- and nineteenth-century French *tempérament* resembles the current English terms "urge" or "impulse" and was mostly used to describe sexual drives or strong, hot-tempered personalities. Some of this conception survives in Colomer's later use of *tempérament*, which he uses to describe an individual's composure, general mood, or nature of social behavior. It is an unconscious attribute that an individual cannot influence. One has to understand one's temperament in order to align it with one's other characteristics to achieve a healthy wholeness.

## NOTES

1.   "Anarchist of the Action of the Art," 27.
2.   See "Libertarian Aesthetics on Célestin Manalt," 5.
3.   "At the Sources of Heroic Individualism 4: My Freedom Is My Beauty," 44.
4.   "At the Sources of Heroic Individualism 8: What Is Our Heroism?," 54.
5.   See "Refractory Poets 2," 68, for a description of this in Colomer's own words.
6.   See "Matter, Mind, and Me 8," 260.
7.   See "Matter, Mind, and Me 8," 260.
8.   See "The Sources of the Modern Novel in France," 183.
9.   See "Idealism and Anarchy," 102.
10.  See "At the Sources of Heroic Individualism 10: Heroic Individualism and Daily Actions," 59.

# Index

GPSR Authorized Representative: Easy Access System Europe, Mustamäe tee 50, 10621 Tallinn, Estonia, gpsr.requests@easproject.com


www.ingramcontent.com/pod-product-compliance
Lightning Source LLC
Chambersburg PA
CBHW022135020426
42334CB00015B/906